P. 53 Bull, No Ir[...] Righteousness of C[...]tian.

Thomas Barlow
William Beveridge
John Edwards
John Pearson
Thomas Tully

OXFORD THEOLOGICAL MONOGRAPHS

OXFORD THEOLOGICAL MONOGRAPHS

ORIGEN ON THE SONG OF SONGS AS THE SPIRIT OF SCRIPTURE
The Bridegroom's Perfect Marriage-Song
J. Christopher King (2004)

AN INTERPRETATION OF HANS URS VON BALTHASAR
Eschatology as Communion
Nicholas J. Healy (2005)

DURANDUS OF ST POURÇAIN
A Dominican Theologian in the Shadow of Aquinas
Isabel Iribarren (2005)

THE TROUBLES OF TEMPLELESS JUDAH
Jill Middlemas (2005)

TIME AND ETERNITY IN MID-THIRTEENTH-CENTURY THOUGHT
Rory Fox (2006)

THE SPECIFICATION OF HUMAN ACTIONS IN ST THOMAS AQUINAS
Joseph Pilsner (2006)

THE WORLDVIEW OF PERSONALISM
Origins and Early Development
Jan Olof Bengtsson (2006)

THE EUSEBIANS
The Polemic of Athanasius of Alexandria and the Construction of the 'Arian Controversy'
David M. Gwynn (2006)

CHRIST AS MEDIATOR
A Study of the Theologies of Eusebius of Caesarea, Marcellus of Ancyra, and Anthanasius of Alexandria
Jon M. Robertson (2007)

RIGHTEOUS JEHU AND HIS EVIL HEIRS
The Deuteronomist's Negative Perspective on Dynastic Succession
David T. Lamb (2007)

SEXUAL AND MARITAL METAPHORS IN *HOSEA, JEREMIAH, ISAIAH,* AND *EZEKIEL*
Sharon Moughtin-Mumby (2008)

THE SOTERIOLOGY OF LEO THE GREAT
Bernard Green (2008)

# Anti-Arminians

*The Anglican Reformed Tradition from Charles II to George I*

STEPHEN HAMPTON b 1972
M.A. DPhil

OXFORD
UNIVERSITY PRESS

**OXFORD**
**UNIVERSITY PRESS**

Great Clarendon Street, Oxford OX2 6DP

Oxford University Press is a department of the University of Oxford.
It furthers the University's objective of excellence in research, scholarship,
and education by publishing worldwide in

Oxford New York

Auckland Cape Town Dar es Salaam Hong Kong Karachi
Kuala Lumpur Madrid Melbourne Mexico City Nairobi
New Delhi Shanghai Taipei Toronto

With offices in

Argentina Austria Brazil Chile Czech Republic France Greece
Guatemala Hungary Italy Japan Poland Portugal Singapore
South Korea Switzerland Thailand Turkey Ukraine Vietnam

Oxford is a registered trade mark of Oxford University Press
in the UK and in certain other countries

Published in the United States
by Oxford University Press Inc., New York



Reprinted 2008



First published 2008



British Library Cataloguing in Publication Data
Data available

Library of congress Cataloging in Publication Data
Data available

Typeset by SPI Publisher Services, Pondicherry, India
Printed in Great Britain
on acid-free paper by
Biddles Ltd., King's Lynn, Norfolk

ISBN 978–0–19–953336–7

3 5 7 9 10 8 6 4 2

# *Preface and Acknowledgements*

This book grew out of a doctoral thesis on the thought of five post-Restoration divines: Thomas Barlow, William Beveridge, John Edwards, John Pearson, and Thomas Tully. That research opened my eyes to the strength of the conforming Reformed tradition within the later Stuart Church, a tradition which has, for various reasons, been overlooked by most of those who have written on the period. This book is intended as a corrective to that neglect.

I would never have completed this book without the assistance of my doctoral supervisor, Diarmaid MacCulloch, upon whose breadth of learning, patience, and astonishing attention to detail, I have constantly relied. I must also thank my doctoral examiner, Nicholas Tyacke, whose masterly writing on the seventeenth century has been a spur and an inspiration to my own research in this area.

I have been greatly assisted by the insights, encouragement, and criticism of Stephen Sykes, David Brown, David Hoyle, Anne Dyer, Alan Bartlett, Kenneth Padley, Philip Hobday, Michael McClenahan, and Robin Hopkins, and my thanks are due to all of them.

I am especially grateful to the staff of the British Library, the Bodleian Library, Durham Cathedral Library, Durham University Library, and the libraries of Exeter College and the Queen's College, Oxford, who have patiently brought me the books, pamphlets, and manuscripts upon which this study rests. I must also thank the Rector and Fellows of Exeter College, Oxford, and the Council of St John's College, Durham, who have afforded me the opportunity to pursue my research during the last eight years.

# *Contents*

# *Abbreviations*

| | |
|---|---|
| *CTJ* | *Calvin Theological Journal* |
| *HJ* | *Historical Journal* |
| *JEH* | *Journal of Ecclesiastical History* |
| *ODNB* | *Oxford Dictionary of National Biography* |
| *PRRD* | R.A. Muller, *Post-Reformation Reformed Dogmatics*, 4 vols (Grand Rapids, 2003) |
| *SCG* | Thomas Aquinas, tr. A.C. Pegis, *Summa Contra Gentiles, Book One: God* (New York, 1975) |
| *SCJ* | *Sixteenth Century Journal* |
| S.Th. | Thomas Aquinas, 'Summa Theologica,' in A.C. Pegis (ed.), *The Basic Writings of Saint Thomas Aquinas*, 2 vols (Indianapolis, 1997) |

Note: the spelling in all quotations of English sources has been modernized.

# 1

# The Anglican Reformed Tradition after the Restoration

## THE BISHOP OF CARLISLE'S SERMON

On Monday, 2 April, 1716, the Lord Mayor, Aldermen, and Sheriffs of the City of London processed in their scarlet robes to hear a sermon at St Bride's, Fleet Street. The Church building was, of course, strikingly new, its elegant neoclassical stonework still crisply detailed. For St Bride's was the most ambitious of the racily avant-garde churches which Sir Christopher Wren had designed after the Great Fire, and it had been crowned, just fifteen years before, by a spectacular baroque steeple. The preacher that spring Monday was William Nicolson, Bishop of Carlisle, and the occasion was one of the Spital Sermons, which were customarily preached to the Corporation of London every year during the Easter season.

In the early years of the Hanoverian regime, William Nicolson was definitely a man to be watched. A scholarly northern archdeacon, he had been made Bishop of Carlisle in 1702. Upon the accession of George I, his particular significance to the new government had been underlined by his appointment as Lord Almoner, a post which effectively made him the premier preacher at the royal court. Nicolson was also, importantly, close friends with William Wake, the man who had been confirmed as the new Archbishop of Canterbury barely three months previously. So Nicolson was, without any question, a front-rank representative of the Hanoverian Church of England.

The Bishop chose as his text that day, Ephesians 2:8–9: 'For by grace are ye saved through faith; and that not of yourselves: it is the gift of God: not of works, lest any man should boast.' And he used this text to explain the doctrine of justification, the doctrine which explains how it is that human beings, despite their sins, can stand sufficiently righteous in the eyes of God to enter heaven.

Opening with extended citations of the Thirty-Nine Articles, and the Book of Homilies, he took a brief but perennially crowd-pleasing swipe at the errors of Rome, before undertaking his own exposition of the matter. 'The text teaches us,' he says, 'that our salvation, the everlasting inheritance of life and glory, into which we hope to be admitted through the gate of a temporal death, is a gracious free gift.'[1]

The reason the gift of salvation is free is that, when we are justified, we are actually counted righteous in the sight of God because of the righteousness of Christ, a righteousness which God graciously reckons as if it were our own.[2] Our sins, in the meantime, are counted as if they were Christ's, who, accordingly, bears the punishment for them on our behalf. Nicolson underlines the wonder of this merciful transaction, 'What an amazing complication of benefits do I here see in the mystery of my redemption? Through the perfect obedience of Christ my redeemer, imputed to me, I find acceptance with God; and through the imputation of his agonies and death, my sins are pardoned.'[3]

Of course, God does expect something from us, before he will count Christ's righteousness as ours, and bestow on us the heavenly inheritance which that imputed righteousness has won for us. And, as Nicolson points out, 'Though the inheritance be the gift of God, and transferred to us by grace, yet there is still somewhat required on our part (as a means of conveying the benefit to us, and preparing us for the due reception thereof) and this is faith.'[4] In other words, we must put our trust in Christ, and rely upon him for our salvation, and God will then reckon Christ's righteousness to our account.[5] This faith, Nicolson underlines, must be a living faith. It must be a faith, in other words, that is fruitful in good works. But we should not, for all that, make the mistake of thinking that those good works are part of what will justify us in God's eyes. Because, he points out,

> our own works, be they never so seemingly good (never so righteous) in the esteem of ourselves and our fellow-Christians, are not (in their own nature) of any sort of efficacy towards the attainment of everlasting salvation; which never can be had otherwise that by grace; through faith. Salvation will ever be, as both justification and sanctification are, the gift of God.[6]

And because salvation is a gift, and in no way dependent on our own actions, our part in the new covenant is truly an easy yoke. He sums up the situation succinctly: 'The mild and generous spirit of Our Lord's gospel speaketh on this wise; believe only, and thou shalt be saved.'[7]

The view of justification which Nicolson is advancing here is a teaching that had been sounding from Protestant pulpits for the previous two centuries. This was the doctrine of Luther and of Calvin. This was the doctrine of Cranmer, of Jewel, and of Davenant. But this should surprise us: because

[1] W. Nicolson, *A sermon preached before the Right Honourable the Lord Mayor* (London, 1716), p10.

[2] Ibid., p11.

[3] Ibid., p12. [4] Ibid., p14. [5] Ibid., p16. [6] Ibid., p21. [7] Ibid., p27.

this is not what the historians have told us to expect from the lips of an Augustan prelate.

## ANGLICAN 'CALVINISM' AFTER THE RESTORATION

There is a venerable tradition of thought which argues that, by the end of the seventeenth century, the Church of England had effectively thrown off the shackles of her Reformed inheritance. In particular, according to this tradition, during the later Stuart period, the classic Reformed teaching that we are justified by faith alone without works, was all but eclipsed by a new doctrine, which made good works essential to the process of justification.[8]

Two distinct but related streams of historiography have encouraged this kind of thinking. The first is rooted in the assumption that, for there to have been an Evangelical 'revival' in the eighteenth century, there must have been a falling-away from the Evangelical (i.e. Reformed) teachings of the Protestant Reformation during the seventeenth. J.C. Ryle was an early exponent of this view, writing of eighteenth century preaching that:

> Natural theology, without a single distinctive doctrine of Christianity, cold morality, or barren orthodoxy, formed the staple teaching both in church and chapel. Sermons everywhere were little better than miserable moral essays, utterly devoid of anything likely to awaken, convert, or save souls.... And as for the weighty truths for which Hooper and Latimer had gone to the stake... they seemed clean forgotten and laid on the shelf.[9]

Ryle, of course, now seems an archaic figure as church historians go, but more recent historians of the Evangelical movement are certainly not immune to the allure of this picture. Bebbington, for example, writes that, within the eighteenth-century Church of England, 'the doctrine of justification by faith had well-nigh disappeared. Calvinism was at a discount after the Restoration.'[10]

The second stream of thought at play has been the search for a distinctly 'Anglican' theological identity, an identity distinct from continental Protestantism, and more particularly from the Reformed branch of continental Protestantism. Historians of this persuasion have argued for the steady coalescence, over the course of the seventeenth century, of the initially diverse

[8] C.F. Allison, *The Rise of Moralism—The Proclamation of the Gospel from Hooker to Baxter* (London, 1966), passim. J. Spurr, *The Restoration Church of England* (London, 1991), p303.

[9] J.C. Ryle, *The Christian Leaders of the Last Century* (London, 1885), p14. One of those forgotten truths was, of course, justification by faith alone, p27.

[10] D.W. Bebbington, *Evangelicalism in Modern Britain* (London, 1989), p36.

spectrum of belief within the Church of England, in which the Reformed tradition held a prominent place, into a unitary and definable 'Anglicanism', in which it did not.[11] According to this view, Anglican writers felt increasingly free, during the course of the seventeenth century, to depart from Reformed teaching and forge their own path, one aspect of which was a growing rejection of traditional Protestant solifidianism, in favour of a distinctly Anglican 'moralism', which made good works part of what God requires from the believer in the process of justification.[12]

The confluence of these two currents of thinking has meant that the true extent and significance of Reformed theological sympathy within the Church of England after the Restoration have been obscured. Indeed, in the hands of some historians, the Reformed tradition has been virtually excised from the picture. Cragg, for example, writes:

> The second half of the seventeenth century saw many changes in English religious thought, but none more striking than the overthrow of Calvinism.... At the beginning of the century, it had dominated the religious life of England; by the end its power had been completely overthrown.[13]

There were, he admits, a few Reformed figures active within the post-Restoration Church, but that is only because they were 'too old to refashion the framework of their theological system.... Their Calvinism was a survival from the past, and bore no real relation to the interests and ideas of the new day.'[14] And, sure enough, this moribund tradition shrivelled as the seventeenth century wore on.[15] As a result, in the view of Stromberg and others, the eccentric John Edwards of Cambridge (of whom we shall hear more later) was 'by 1700... about the only remaining example of a prominent Anglican Calvinist. High and Low Churchmen alike were Arminian'.[16]

More recent writers, such as Nicholas Tyacke and John Spurr, have painted a more nuanced picture than this, but the broad outlines of the canvass have remained the same. The Anglican Reformed tradition is still consistently held to have been of marginal significance to the development of the post-Restoration Church.

[11] P.E. More, 'The Spirit of Anglicanism,' in P.E. More and F.L. Cross (eds.), *Anglicanism* (London, 1935), ppxix, xx. H.R. McAdoo, *The Spirit of Anglicanism* (New York, 1965), p5.

[12] J.H. Newman, *Lectures on the Doctrine of Justification* (London, 1874), pp343–404. A.E. McGrath, *Iustitia Dei*, 2 vols (Cambridge, 1986), ii, pp109–10. McGrath, unlike Newman, notes that there were dissenting voices.

[13] G.R. Cragg, *From Puritanism to the Age of Reason* (Cambridge, 1950), p13.

[14] Ibid., p18.

[15] Cragg, *The Church and the Age of Reason, 1648–1749* (Bristol, 1962), p66.

[16] R.N. Stromberg, *Religious Liberalism in Eighteenth Century England* (Oxford, 1954), p111. R. Worck, *School of the Prophets* (Yale, 1973), pp99–100. The lonely state of John Edwards is reiterated by Rupp. G. Rupp, *Religion in England, 1688–1791* (Oxford, 1986), p326.

Tyacke, for example, has argued that there was a tenacious Calvinist rump within the University of Oxford until the end of the century. However, he concludes his study by writing:

> Calvinism might still survive in Oxford, but elsewhere Arminianism had emerged supreme. During the 1660s an aggressive brand of anti-Calvinism had rapidly become established at Cambridge University, and Archbishop Sheldon increasingly lent his authority to such views in the English Church more generally. Meanwhile the public affirmation of the English Calvinist heritage was left almost exclusively to dissenters. . . . The apotheosis of this long term development was achieved in the 1690s with the triumph of religious 'latitudinarianism' which was clearly Arminian in its theological emphases. In this context Bishop Gilbert Burnet's *Exposition of the Thirty-Nine Articles*, published in 1699, both outlined the rise and fall of English Calvinism and set the seal on the new Arminian dispensation.[17]

Spurr, for his part, although underlining that Reformed theology did persist within the Church of England after the Restoration,[18] has nevertheless argued that 'the renunciation of the old orthodoxy, associated with the younger generation of churchmen, was fast becoming the dominant school of the day'.[19] The old disputes between Calvinist and Arminian, he asserts, became gradually irrelevant to a generation nourished on this new way of thinking.[20] And such Reformed dinosaurs as did survive in this new theological world were increasingly reduced to a life of impotent marginal scribblings.[21]

All this, of course, makes William Nicolson's Spital Sermon rather difficult to explain. If the Anglican Reformed tradition had become such a marginal voice within the later Stuart Church, how is it that we hear Reformed doctrine from the mouth of someone who would still be a bishop in the 1720s? Before we can answer that question, we need to address an important point of terminology. As we have seen, most historians of the later Stuart period are content to use the word 'Calvinist' to describe those Anglican theologians who continued to work within the Reformed tradition. But this is not a label those theologians would have been happy to accept. George Morley, for example, whom both Cragg[22] and Spurr[23] identify as a Calvinist, is in fact very careful to distance himself from the eponymous Genevan reformer, and

[17] N. Tyacke, 'Religious Controversy,' in N. Tyacke (ed.), *The History of the University of Oxford IV: The Seventeenth Century Oxford* (Oxford, 1997), p617.

[18] J. Spurr, *Restoration Church of England*, pp314, 315.

[19] Spurr, ' "Latitudinarianism" and the Restoration Church,' *HJ*, 31, p82. See also Spurr, *Restoration Church of England*, p281.

[20] Ibid., p314.

[21] Ibid., p315.

[22] Cragg, *From Puritanism to the Age of Reason*, p18.

[23] Spurr in *ODNB* s.v. 'George Morley.'

to underline that the Reformed theological tradition is both broader and more ancient than its opponents care to grant. Morley writes, of John Calvin:

I call him the patriarch of the presbyterians, because he was the first that after 1500 years government of the Church by Bishops, invented and set up a government of the Church by a parity of presbyters without Bishops; and this and this only can properly be called Calvinism; whatever he holds besides, even the most rigid of his tenets, having been held by some of the schoolmen and some of the fathers also.[24]

John Edwards makes a similar point in the preface to his *Veritas Redux*, the opening work in his extended Reformed system, the *Theologia Reformata*. He writes:

I have taken care to satisfy every unprejudiced person, that that which we now call Calvinism, is to be found in the writings of the ancient fathers of the Church, and is the very doctrine which the first reformers of our own Church professed, and maintained, and which is contained in our Articles, Homilies and liturgy, and which our Archbishops and Bishops, and the whole body of our English Clergy have generally asserted and vindicated.[25]

Edwards underlines that the Reformed theological tradition had always encompassed a spectrum of views, in which Calvin was at the harsher end. Furthermore, although Calvin was a significant figure within that tradition, 'we are not to think that he had a monopoly of truth, or was infallible'.[26] Like Morley, Edwards points out in particular that 'our churchmen did not admire and esteem Calvin and Beza, and their followers, for their ecclesiastical government'.[27]

Morley and Edwards illustrate a point which has been repeatedly made by the contemporary American scholar, Richard Muller. Arguing against the tendency of some writers to compare all Reformed theology with Calvin, in order to judge of its quality and authenticity within the Reformed tradition, he writes:

To claim that later theologians lost the 'balance' of Calvin's theology, or that their systematic efforts 'misplaced' or forgot Calvin's doctrinal emphases, is to miss the point that Calvin was but one of several significant second generation codifiers of the Reformation and not at all the sole point of reference for later Reformed theological formulation. Indeed, the further one moves beyond the confines of the sixteenth century, the less useful comparisons between Calvin and the so-called Calvinists become.[28]

[24] G. Morley, *The Bishop of Winchester's Vindication* (London, 1683), p275.

[25] J. Edwards, *Veritas Redux: Evangelical Truths Restored* (London, 1707), pxix.

[26] Ibid., pxx.

[27] Ibid., p551.

[28] R.A. Muller, 'Calvin and the "Calvinists": Assessing Continuities and Discontinuities between the Reformation and Orthodoxy' *CTJ*, 31 (1996), p138.

As a result, Muller argues that using the term 'Calvinist' to describe theologians working within the Reformed tradition is profoundly unhelpful. For that tradition was both far more various, and far less dependent on Geneva, than the term 'Calvinist' implies.[29] Consequently, he argues, 'the better part of historical valor (namely discretion) requires rejection of the term "Calvinist" and "Calvinism" in favor of the more historically accurate term, "Reformed".'[30]

Using Muller's more refined approach, we shall be better able to get to grips with the Reformed theological tradition of the post-Restoration Church. For very few of the writers within that tradition were ordinarily prepared to resort to Calvin as a source of authority, and none would have endorsed Calvin's views on Church polity. The Reformed Anglicans of the later seventeenth century much preferred to point to the English writers of earlier generations. So John Edwards, underlining that 'our churchmen, from the beginning of the Reformation, and afterwards, have always upheld these doctrines,' points to the great galaxy of Elizabethan and Jacobean Reformed writers who had advanced positions similar to his own. Thomas Barlow, in his manuscript lectures on justification, repeatedly cites Jewel, Whittaker, Rainolds, White, Hooker,[31] and Davenant[32] as illustrations of the orthodoxy of his own views, as compared with those of his theological opponent, George Bull. Thomas Tully deploys a similar list to much the same effect against Richard Baxter.[33]

The Anglican Reformed after 1662 were certainly conscious of their links with the wider European Reformed tradition, but it was vital to their polemical task to show that they were the exponents of a home-grown and respectably Episcopalian branch of that tradition. 'Reformed' was, therefore, an appellation they would have happily embraced. 'Calvinist', with its seedy foreign overtones, and its hinterland of regicide and Presbyterianism, was not.

This change of terminology should be accompanied by a subtler grasp of what it means to identify a late seventeenth century Anglican as a Reformed theologian. Whatever their date or nationality, describing a given writer as Reformed is not meant to imply that they simply reproduce, in pristine manner, a monolithic theological system. As Richard Muller points out 'Reformed orthodoxy was a varied movement both intellectually and geographically.'[34] The Reformed tradition was a broad church, encompassing a

[29] Muller, *PRRD*, 4 vols (Grand Rapids, 2003), i p30.

[30] Ibid. This is timely, because even John Spurr has shown signs of becoming distracted by the established terminology. Spurr, *The Restoration Church of England*, p316.

[31] MS QCL 230, p151.

[32] Ibid., p155

[33] T. Tully, *A letter to Mr. Richard Baxter occasioned by several injurious reflexions of his upon a treatise entitled Iustificatio Paulina* (London, 1675), p26. It includes Jewel, Abbot, White, Field, Whittaker, Perkins, Andrewes, and Davenant.

[34] Muller, *PRRD*, i p 28.

wider range of views than it has often been given credit for. Consequently, identifying a given writer as Reformed is not meant to pinpoint their precise theological location, or to confine the individuality and originality of their thought within a rigid systematic cage, but rather to express their kinship with other thinkers, whose theology is similar at certain significant points, even if it is not necessarily identical in all respects.

Furthermore, the Reformed tradition was far from a static tradition. For, as Muller argues,

> When this orthodox or scholastic Protestantism is examined in some depth and viewed as a form of Protestant theology in its own right rather than merely a duplication or reflection of the theology of the Reformation, it is clearly both like and unlike that of the Reformation, standing in continuity with the great theological insights of the Reformers but developing in a systematic and scholastic fashion different from the patterns of the Reformation.[35]

In other words, identifying a writer as Reformed does not mean that they will hold all and only those theological views held by their predecessors within the tradition. The Reformed tradition adapted to new insights and circumstances, adopting and engaging with new patterns of thought as they emerged. As Muller underlines, the organic development of Reformed theology 'ought to be understood as one example of the way in which the Christian intellectual tradition maintains useful forms, methods and doctrinal ideas while at the same time incorporating the advances of exegetical and theological investigation'.[36]

It is particularly important to bear this in mind when analysing the development of Anglican theology after 1662. Conforming churchmen of the later Stuart period were officially committed to a range of liturgical practices and ecclesiological claims that appeared decidedly eccentric from the perspective of the wider European Reformed movement. For that reason alone, identifying any conforming Anglican as Reformed is never a straightforward matter. There are certain facets of the Reformed tradition which no conforming Anglican could easily exemplify. As a result, the Anglican expression of the Reformed tradition is inevitably a somewhat peculiar branch of the wider intellectual movement.

Furthermore, the Anglican Reformed were as subject as other writers to the intellectual developments of their environment, some of which were experienced by all the Reformed, and some of which bore particularly on those working in England. Anglican churchmen in this period were therefore forced to engage with, and adapt to, the widespread perception of moral decline in

[35] Muller, *PRRD*, i p28. [36] Ibid., p29.

post-Restoration England, the rise of the New Philosophy, the late seventeenth-century flowering of patristic study, and the robust anti-Calvinist theology being advanced by many of their contemporaries.

As a result, the Anglican Reformed of the late seventeenth century frequently hold their views in tension with emphases drawn from outside the Reformed tradition. So John Wilkins, for example, though he holds to a Reformed soteriology, advances a much more confident view of the scope and usefulness of natural theology than is common within the earlier Reformed tradition.[37] John Pearson, although holding to a Christology which (we shall argue) is broadly in line with that of other Reformed writers, is nonetheless influenced by the subordinationist tone of much Ante-Nicene (and contemporary) writing in this area.[38] And, on one occasion, Robert South, anxious to preclude any antinomian inferences from the doctrine of justification by faith alone, at least entertains a conception of faith as including good works in its essential definition, a conception (as we shall see) more akin to Arminian than to Reformed thought in this area.[39]

In the theology of these late seventeenth-and early eighteenth-century churchmen, therefore, the theological emphases of the Reformed tradition were inextricably intertwined with insights from other sources. The Anglican Reformed adapted their theology in the light of these insights, and, in so doing, qualified, re-expressed and developed Reformed thought in new ways, as we shall see in due course.

Identifying these men as part of the wider Reformed family is not meant to obscure this important observation. It does however imply that, amidst the changing religious environment of late Stuart England, and alongside the diverse theological insights which they adopted from other sources, these churchmen nonetheless held fast to a certain set of key theological motifs in their soteriology, Christology, and their doctrine of God, which they shared with the wider Reformed tradition, and which distinguish them from those of their contemporaries whose thought was no longer marked by these motifs. It is the striking persistence of these Reformed motifs which means that it makes sense to consider these writers as contributors to a generously understood Reformed tradition, rather than to locate them within an undifferentiated Anglicanism. These motifs will, therefore, be the doctrinal focus of this study.

If we take this more generous view of the Reformed theological tradition, then it becomes both possible for us to account for Nicolson's 1716 sermon,

[37] J. Wilkins, *Of the Principles and Duties of Natural Religion* (London, 1710), passim.

[38] J. Pearson, *Exposition of the Creed* (London, 1845), pp58–62.

[39] R. South, *Sermons* (Oxford, 1842) 5 vols, ii pp147–8. He entertains this view, but steps back from it almost immediately.

and necessary for us to qualify sharply the picture of the later Stuart Church which many historians have painted. Because, once the red herring of 'Calvinism,' and too narrow an understanding of Reformed theology are removed from the scene, the full depth and extent of the Reformed tradition within Anglicanism after the Restoration starts to become clear.

## THE REFORMED THEOLOGIANS OF THE LATER STUART CHURCH

William Nicolson will serve as an excellent entrée to this neglected circle, because, like many clever boys from the North, he was educated at the Queen's College in Oxford. In 1670, when he went up as a batteler there, the Queen's College was arguably the centre of English Reformed theology, for the college was then under the rule of Thomas Barlow (1608/9–1691). Barlow had been Provost since 1658, Lady Margaret Professor of Divinity since 1660, and Archdeacon of Oxford since 1664. He was, as a result, one of the most powerful men in the University, as well as one of its most celebrated divines. In 1676 he was duly consecrated (against the will of Archbishop Sheldon, who refused to take part in the ceremony), as Bishop of Lincoln, a post he occupied for the rest of his life.

Just across the road from Queen's lived Barlow's great friend and theological collaborator, Thomas Tully (1620–76), Principal of St Edmund Hall, an institution which was then under the governance of Queen's College. Tully was made Dean of Ripon in 1676, and it was planned that he should succeed Barlow as Lady Margaret Professor, but his premature death made that impossible.[40] Tully's rule at St Edmund Hall was of sufficient distinction that the eminent dissenting minister, Henry Newcome sent his sons there, rather than to Cambridge, where he had been himself.[41]

Barlow and Tully were both energetic in their encouragement of Reformed thinking amongst the students at the University. Barlow promoted it in his lectures in the Divinity School, and Tully in his published works. Barlow was also not beyond using coercion to support his views. Anthony Wood recounted him using his authority as Vice-Chancellor to haul the Chaplain of All Souls up for questioning after a University Sermon in 1673, 'because he insisted much on the Arminian points'.[42]

[40] *ODNB*, s.v. 'Thomas Tully.' [41] *ODNB*, s.v. 'Henry Newcome'.
[42] A. Wood, in P. Bliss (ed.), *Athenae Oxonienses*, 4 vols (London, 1813–20), i plxxi.

The dissenting historian Louis du Moulin, lamenting the spread of heterodox Socinian and Arminian opinion within the Universities after the Restoration, recalled a conversation with Barlow, in which the Provost of Queen's

> told me that had it not been for Doctor Tully and himself, those heresies would have infected the whole University of Oxford, but they had some private conversations with many of the best disposed youth, and gave them such wholesome instructions, as might be sufficient medicine to preserve them from the poison of those pestilential heresies.[43]

Clearly those medicines were still proving themselves effective for William Nicolson, some thirty-five years later.

Although their influence may have been significant, Barlow and Tully were not, by any means, the only Reformed figures active within Restoration Oxford. Barlow's successor as both Provost of Queen's and Archdeacon of Oxford, Timothy Halton's (bap.1633–1704), who also served as Vice-Chancellor from 1679–81 and again in 1685, clearly had Reformed theological leanings.[44] So did John Hall (1633–1710), the man elected as Lady Margaret Professor in Barlow's place.[45] Hall had been master of Pembroke since 1664 (having been elected in the face of yet more resistance from Archbishop Sheldon), and was made Bishop of Bristol in 1691. Indeed, William III seriously contemplated him as a successor to Tillotson in the see of Canterbury a couple of years after that, but the Latitudinarian Tenison was eventually chosen instead.[46]

As Lady Margaret Professor, Hall was a highly popular lecturer, and he was said by the dissenting writer, Edmund Calamy, to be able to expound the whole of the Westminster Confession out of the Church of England's Catechism.[47] Hall was certainly more sympathetic to dissenters than some felt became him.[48] Anthony Wood, when greeting the news that Hall was to preach the sermon to mark the coronation of King James II in 1685, commented, rather waspishly, that 'he takes all occasions (being a Presbyterian) to show himself loyal'.[49]

[43] L. du Moulin, *A Short and True Account of the Several Advances the Church of England hath made towards Rome* (London, 1680), p31.

[44] This can be seen in his manuscript sermons: MS QCL 497, passim.

[45] It should be remembered that the Lady Margaret Professor, unlike his senior colleague, was elected by his peers within the Divinity Faculty at Oxford. As Robert Beddard underlines, the succession of Hall to Barlow indicates the breadth of Reformed sympathy within Oxford after the Restoration. R.A. Beddard 'Restoration Oxford and the Remaking of the Protestant Establishment,' in Tyacke (ed.), *History of the University of Oxford IV: The Seventeenth Century* (Oxford, 1997), p834.

[46] *ODNB*, s.v. 'John Hall.'

[47] Ibid.

[48] A. Wood, *The Life and Times of Anthony Wood, antiquary of Oxford, 1632–1695, described by himself*, 4 vols (Oxford, 1891–1895).

[49] Ibid., p137.

Another head of house, Thomas Marshall (1621–85), a celebrated philologist, and Rector of Lincoln College from 1672, produced, for his part, a staunchly Reformed commentary on the Prayer Book Catechism in 1679, which was duly published at the University Press, bearing the Vice-Chancellor's Imprimatur.[50] In 1681, Marshall became Dean of Gloucester. Anthony Wood noted of Marshall that he had been so moved when hearing the Reformed divine James Ussher preach in Oxford in the early 1640s, 'that he was always resolved from thenceforth to make him the pattern of all the religious and learned actions of his life'.[51]

John Wallis (1616–1703) was another prominent Oxford academic with impeccably Reformed credentials. Having studied initially at Emmanuel College, Cambridge, Wallis had actually served as secretary of the Westminster Assembly in the 1640s, and had joined the University of Oxford as the Savilian Professor of Geometry in 1649. He remained in that post until his death, combining his mathematical research with cryptographic work for a succession of governments, as well as the occasional foray into the field of polemical theology.

Oxford's University Orator, since 1660, had been the celebrated Reformed preacher Robert South (1634–1716). He was also a Prebendary of Westminster (from 1663) and a Canon of Christ Church (from 1670), as well as holding the living of Islip, a few miles outside the city. South would be joined in the Chapter at Christ Church in 1678 by William Jane's (bap.1645–1707). Jane was appointed to the Regius Chair of Divinity in 1680, a post he clung on to until his death, despite further preferment as Dean of Gloucester (as Thomas Marshall's successor) and Precentor of Exeter (in 1704). Jane was also repeatedly elected as Prolocutor of the Lower House of Convocation, and was consistently a thorn in the side of the Latitudinarian Bishops in the Upper House. Of course, Jane's doctrinal sympathies meant that, from the date of his appointment to the Regius Chair until Hall's elevation to Bristol, both senior Divinity Professors in Oxford were Reformed theologians. Indeed, they worked together in framing the University's condemnation of disloyal and seditious books in 1683.[52]

That Jane and South also knew each other personally is clear, because they were both involved in the theological disputation which preserved Laurence Hyde, Earl of Rochester, from Roman Catholicism in the reign of James II. Hyde had originally nominated Jane and South together to enter the lists

50 T. Marshall, *The Catechism set forth in the Book of Common Prayer* (Oxford, 1679). The Vice-Chancellor in question was Timothy Halton's predecessor, John Nicholas, although the catechism was published in the year Halton took office.

51 A. Wood, in P. Bliss (ed.), *Athenae Oxonienses*, 4 vols (London, 1813–20), iv p171.

52 Ibid., iii p61.

against James's Roman Catholics; but such was South's reputation for hot-tempered polemic, that James refused to accept the nomination, forcing Rochester to appoint Simon Patrick instead.[53] South was, however, closely involved in the preparations for the debate, and as his biographer notes 'Dr Jane has often owned (though an excellent casuist himself) that the auxiliary arguments contributed by Dr South did more towards flinging their antagonists on their backs, than his or his colleague's.'[54]

A younger associate of Jane's in the world of Oxford politics during the reign of Queen Anne was William Delaune (1659–1728). He became president of St John's College in 1698, and served as Vice-Chancellor from 1702 to 1706. Delaune was involved with Jane in the face-saving proposal to give William Nicolson a DD by diploma, after a cabal of the younger dons had successfully interfered with the ordinary procedure, and embarassingly left him to be consecrated as Bishop of Carlisle whilst a mere MA.[55]

Given the strength of the Reformed tradition within the University after the Restoration, it is not surprising to find that it produced a significant number of Reformed theologians during this period. We have mentioned William Nicolson and William Delaune already. We should add Benjamin Jenks (bap. 1648–1724), an Anglican devotional writer, who had also studied at Queen's under Barlow from 1664 to 1668. Josiah Woodward (1657–1712), the celebrated moral reformer, studied at St Edmund Hall under Tully from 1673 to 1676.[56] Peter Newcome (1656–1738), son of the dissenting minister Henry Newcome whom we have mentioned, initially went up to St Edmund Hall under Tully, moved to Brasenose, and eventually decided to conform. He later produced a thoroughly Reformed set of catechetical sermons which he dedicated to his bishop, Henry Compton. Edward Welchman (1665–1739) matriculated at Magdalen Hall in 1679, and was one of the choristers at Magdalen, before becoming a probationer fellow at Merton in 1684.

The Reformed grandees of Oxford had, of course, many like-minded friends outside the University itself. Chief among them were two of the most formidable prelates of the later seventeenth century: George Morley (1598–1684), Bishop of Winchester from 1662, and Henry Compton (1631/2–1713), an old Queen's College man, who was made Bishop of Oxford in 1674, and then Bishop of London in 1675. Compton was also of particular significance to the religious life of the nation in that, as Dean of the Chapel's Royal from 1675, he interfered

[53] E. Curll, 'Memoirs of the life and writings of Dr Robert South,' in R. South (ed.), *Sermons Preached upon Several Occasions*, 5 vols (Oxford, 1842), i plxxviii.

[54] Ibid., i plxxix.

[55] Bennett G.V., 'The Era of Party Zeal 1702–1714,' in L.S. Sutherland and L.G. Mitchell (eds.), *The History of the University of Oxford V: The Eighteenth Century* (Oxford, 1986), p65.

[56] Woodward's Reformed sympathies are clear from his *Short Catechism* (1709).

successfully with the Duke of York's attempts to convert his daughters to Roman Catholicism. Morley's Reformed theological sympathies are well documented.[57] Compton's are less widely recognized. Indeed his biographer, Edward Carpenter, accuses him of 'an almost complete lack of interest in theological discussion for its own sake'.[58] Andrew Coleby, for his part, argues that the works published in his name 'seldom shed much light on his personal life, being largely of an official nature, with few clues as to his deeper motivations'.[59] That may be true up to a point, but, as we shall see, Compton's most substantial encyclical, *The Bishop of London's Tenth Conference with his Clergy* (1701), makes quite explicit his profound dislike of Arminianism.[60]

George Morley was a great friend, and lifelong correspondent of Thomas Barlow's. It was he, in fact, who presided at Barlow's consecration as Bishop of Lincoln, in place of the disgruntled Sheldon. Morley was also the dedicatee of Tully's defence of the Reformed understanding of justification, the *Iustificatio Paulina* (1674). Morley equally connects us with the Reformed writers of an earlier generation, since he was a close friend of Robert Sanderson (1587–1663), having known him since before the Civil War.[61] This was an acquaintance he shared with Thomas Barlow, who frequently consulted Sanderson in theological matters,[62] and arranged for Sanderson to be paid a salary when he fell on hard times after being deprived of the Regius Chair of Divinity in 1648. Sanderson was eventually compensated with the Bishopric of Lincoln, which he received in 1660, but he died three years later.

Morley certainly knew Henry Compton as well. He instituted him as Master of St Cross Hospital in Winchester after 1667, and then appointed him to the living of Witney in Oxfordshire, to alleviate Compton's perennially shaky financial situation. Morley was also one of the bishops who were present at Compton's consecration. It seems reasonable to assume that Thomas Barlow knew Compton too, since he had already been a fellow at Queen's for twenty years when Compton passed through there during the 1650s. Furthermore, both Compton and Barlow seem to have enjoyed the patronage of Sir Joseph Williamson (1633–1701); though, unlike Compton, Barlow does not appear to have owed Williamson any money.[63]

[57] *ODNB*, s.v. 'George Morley.'

[58] E. Carpenter, *The Protestant Bishop* (London, 1956), p58.

[59] *ODNB*, s.v. 'Henry Compton.'

[60] H. Compton, *The Bishop of London's Tenth Conference with his Clergy* (London, 1701) pp16–17.

[61] I. Walton, 'Life of Bishop Sanderson,' in R. Sanderson, *Works*, 6 vols (Oxford, 1854), vi p267.

[62] Ibid., p356.

[63] *ODNB*, s.v. 'Henry Compton.'

Williamson was an absentee fellow of Queen's who was de facto head of Charles II's secret service and served as Secretary of State from 1674 until 1679. He was a consistent supporter of the members of his College, securing preferment for Timothy Halton and William Nicolson, as well as Compton and Barlow. He also seems to have been sufficiently interested in Reformed theology to have been sent a copy of Tully's *Iustificatio Paulina*.[64] Williamson was equally a close friend, distant relative and active patron of yet another Reformed Queen's man, Lancelot Addison (1632–1703), who served as Dean of Lichfield from 1683 and Archdeacon of Coventry from 1684.[65]

Henry Compton was, like Morley, an active supporter of various Reformed clergymen, particularly William Jane (q.v.). He invited Jane to preach at his consecration as Bishop of Oxford, and then appointed him as his chaplain. When Compton moved to London, Jane was soon afterwards instituted as rector of Wennington (1678), before being made Prebendary of Chamberlainswood and Canon Treasurer in St Paul's Cathedral (1679) as well as Archdeacon of Middlesex (1679). Compton was also involved in securing Jane's election as Prolocutor of the Lower House of Convocation.[66]

Compton appointed another Reformed theologian, William Beveridge (1637–1708), to serve him as Archdeacon of Colchester in 1681. Beveridge was a learned orientalist and Patristic scholar, who had been educated at Cambridge, before being presented to the living of St Peter's Cornhill in London by the Lord Mayor and Aldermen in 1672. Beveridge was a prominent figure on the London scene, becoming Prebendary of Chiswick in St Paul's Cathedral in 1674, and President of Sion College in 1689, as well as being heavily involved in the Anglican voluntary religious societies which sprang up during the 1680s, and in the establishment of the Society for the Propagation of Christian Knowledge in 1698. He was eventually appointed as Bishop of St Asaph in 1704, having turned down, in 1691, the offer of Bath and Wells, out of loyalty to the deprived Thomas Ken. Beveridge acknowledged Compton's personal role in his preferment in the dedication of *A Sermon concerning the Excellency and Usefulness of the Common Prayer*, where he described the bishop as his 'patron'.[67]

[64] Tyacke, 'Religious Controversy,' in Tyacke (ed.), *History of the University of Oxford IV: The Seventeenth Century* p607.

[65] Addison's Reformed leanings can be seen in his commentary on the catechism. L. Addison, *The Christian's Manual in Three Parts* (London, 1691), passim.

[66] *ODNB*, s.v. 'Henry Compton.'

[67] W. Beveridge, *A Sermon concerning the Excellency and Usefulness of the Common Prayer* (London, 1682), Dedication.

Elsewhere in the diocese, Compton was personally involved in the appointment of William Burkitt (1650–1703) as vicar of Dedham, Essex, in 1692, as Burkitt gratefully recalled in the initial dedication of his popular *Expository Notes, with Practical Observations, on the New Testament* (1700). A close associate of Burkitt's was the equally Reformed Nathaniel Parkhurst (1643–1707), who preached at Burkitt's funeral. Parkhurst's own patron was Lady Elizabeth Brooke, a woman had family connections with the Reformed Bishop of Norwich, Edward Reynolds.[68]

Compton was equally a patron of William Stanley (1647–1731), the Prebendary of Codrington Major in St Paul's (from 1684), and William Beveridge's brother-in-law.[69] Compton secured for Stanley his appointment as Chaplain to Princess Mary in the Netherlands in 1685.[70] As we have mentioned, whilst Dean of the Chapels Royal, Compton had supervised the education and spiritual formation of Princess Mary, and was anxious to ensure her continued loyalty to the Church of England. So Stanley's appointment indicates the degree of trust in which Compton held him. Stanley did not disappoint him, and proved a reliable source of information from The Hague, as well as actively working to undermine the relationship between Princess Mary and the Latitudinarian divine, Gilbert Burnet.[71] When he returned to England after the Glorious Revolution, Stanley was duly rewarded in 1690 with the rectory of Much Hadham in Essex, and then the Archdeaconry of London (1692). Stanley also benefited later on from William Beveridge's patronage, becoming Dean of St Asaph in 1706, shortly after the latter's appointment as Bishop there.

Morley and Compton were probably the two most significant patrons of Reformed clergy, but they were not, by any means, the only Reformed men on the Bishops' bench. Several of the more moderate leaders of Commonwealth Oxford had been promoted upon King Charles's return. One such was John Wilkins (1614–72), who was Bishop of Chester from 1668. Wilkins was a famously broad-minded man, with friends from many different theological parties. Indeed, he left the posthumous publication of his manuscripts to John Tillotson, who had no time at all for Reformed theology. But Wilkins's own sympathies were demonstrably Reformed, as can be seen from two works which he published during his lifetime: the *Discourse Concerning the Gift of*

[68] N. Parkhurst, *The Faithful and Diligent Christian Described and Exemplified* (London, 1684), p74.

[69] Stanley's broadly Reformed sympathies are evident from his *Faith and Practice of a Church of England Man* (1688).

[70] Carpenter, *The Protestant Bishop*, p107.

[71] Ibid., pp107–11.

*Prayer* (1667)[72] and *Ecclesiastes: or, a Discourse Concerning the Gift of Preaching* (1669).[73]

As Warden of Wadham, Wilkins had been a prominent head of house in the Oxford of the 1650s. He gathered around himself a circle of conservatively inclined academics who did what they could to impede the progressive initiatives of the then Vice-Chancellor, John Owen.[74] This circle included John Wallis (q.v.) and Seth Ward (1617–89), who remained close friends throughout their lives.[75] Ward had been a student at Cambridge, where he was a protégé of Samuel Ward, a prominent Reformed theologian and Master of Sidney Sussex, whose works Seth Ward assembled, and published in 1658. Seth Ward was appointed as Savilian Professor of Astronomy in 1650, and invited by Wilkins to become a member of Wadham.[76] Wilkins and Ward also worked together on a defence of England's Universities from radical Protestant attack, the *Vindiciae Academiarum* (1654).

After the Restoration, Ward became Vicar of St Lawrence Jewry in London, but was soon promoted, first as Dean of Exeter (1661) and then Bishop there (1662). Robert South (q.v.) preached the sermon at his consecration.[77] Ward's excellent administration of the diocese of Exeter soon led to his translation to the wealthier see of Salisbury (1667), where he remained, despite being offered further preferment to the see of Durham in 1674.[78]

Whilst in Exeter, Ward had the opportunity to become acquainted with Ezekiel Hopkins (1634–90), another product of Interregnum Oxford, who was minister of St Mary Arches there. Anthony Wood recalled that Hopkins was 'much approved and applauded for his elegant and dextrous preaching by Seth, Bishop of [Exeter]'.[79] And indeed, Ward wrote a very favourable report

72 Where he writes, for example: 'In brief, when men become skilful and expert in any faculty, whether disputing, oratory, praying &c each of these does proceed from the Spirit of God, as the principal author of them, dividing to every man severally as he will. All other helps, whether from nature or industry; being but secondary, subordinate aids, which are by him made effectual for the accomplishing of those ends'. J. Wilkins, *Discourse Concerning the Gift of Prayer* (London, 1667), pp7–8. He is also quite explicit in offering a Reformed account of human nature, and its depravity after the fall—p80—a Reformed understanding of justification—p178—and a Reformed presentation of the nature of the New Covenant—p 207.

73 Where he describes polemical divinity as that writing 'relating to several controversies about discipline, episcopacy, presbytery, independency. Doctrine, with the Papists, Lutherans, Arminians, Anabaptists, Antinomians.' J. Wilkins, *Ecclesiastes: or, a Discourse Concerning the Gift of Preaching* (London, 1669), p86. His placing Arminianism in that list is, of course, a fair indication of where his theological loyalties lay.

74 B. Worden, 'Cromwellian Oxford' in Tyacke (ed.), *History of the University of Oxford IV: The Seventeenth Century* p738.

75 W. Pope, *The Life of the Right Reverend Father in God, Seth, Lord Bishop of Salisbury* (London, 1697), p32.

76 Ibid., p27.

77 R. South, *Sermons*, 5 vols (Oxford, 1842), iv p42 et seq.

78 *ODNB*, s.v. 'Seth Ward.'

79 A. Wood, *Athenae Oxonienses*, 4 vols (London, 1820), iv p287.

of him to Gilbert Sheldon, in an attempt to find him a more substantial appointment.[80] As it turned out, however, Hopkins had also caught the attention of John Roberts, Baron of Truro, who took him as his chaplain when he became Lord Lieutenant of Ireland in 1669. Once there, Hopkins enjoyed a highly successful career, becoming Bishop of Raphoe in 1670, and then Bishop of Derry in 1681 before being forced back to England by the rebellion supporting James II in 1688. He took refuge in Henry Compton's diocese of London, becoming preacher at St Mary Aldermanbury shortly before he died in 1690.

Also in Exeter, Ward would have enjoyed the services of the pugnacious Francis Fullwood (d.1693) as Archdeacon of Totnes, a man whom Ward collated to a prebend in the Cathedral there shortly after his own consecration in 1662. Fullwood had been educated at Emmanuel College, Cambridge, where William Dillingham (see below) was a fellow, and, despite his deeply Reformed theological leanings, he was a ruthless persecutor of dissent within his Archdeaconry. Fullwood was also, significantly, a protégé of George Morley (q.v.), as he acknowledged in the dedicatory epistle to his *Roma Ruit* (1679).[81]

As Oxford's leading mathematicians during the 1650s, Ward and Wallis were both involved in another circle that Wilkins fostered during the interregnum, a circle with overlapping personnel, but a rather different focus from the academic political party which he led. This was the group of natural philosophers from whom the Royal Society would eventually emerge. A key member of this group was, of course, Sir Robert Boyle (1627–91). His scientific endeavours are well known, but his theological leanings are less so. However, it is clear from his early theological work, *Some Motives and Incentives to the Love of God* (1659) that his own theological position was decidedly Reformed.[82] This may explain why he developed, during his time in Oxford, a particular and life-long rapport with Thomas Barlow, who became his casuistical adviser.[83] Boyle was also a great admirer of Robert Sanderson's. Indeed it was Boyle whom Barlow successfully prevailed upon, to provide Sanderson with an income in return for publishing his casuistic writings.[84] Boyle's sympathy to Reformed theology also explains his great admiration for

[80] MS BL Add D 105 f 175.

[81] Fullwood wrote to Morley: 'I rejoice in the acknowledgement, that I owe my public station, next under God and his Sacred Majesty, to your Lordship's assistance and sole interest.' F. Fullwood, *Roma Ruit: the Pillars of Rome Broken* (London, 1679), Epistle Dedicatory.

[82] He writes, towards the end of that work: 'Perhaps I need not mind you, Lindamar, that divers passages of the foregoing discourse, suppose the truth of their doctrine, who ascribe to God, in relation to every man, an eternal, unchangeable and inconditionate decree of election and reprobation.' R. Boyle, *Works*, 14 vols (London, 1999–2000), i p108.

[83] Ibid., pxxv.

[84] *ODNB*, s.v. 'Robert Sanderson'.

William Beveridge (q.v.), whom Boyle also knew, and apparently considered to be the living icon of true Christian leadership.[85]

Wilkins was not the only Interregnum moderate promoted after the Restoration. Perhaps the most notorious was the Bishop of Norwich, Edward Reynolds (1599–1676), one of handful of Presbyterian leaders offered a bishopric in 1660, though the only one who accepted. Reynolds had briefly been Vice-Chancellor of Oxford and Dean of Christ Church (from 1648 until 1650 and 1651 respectively), but lost both appointments when he refused to pledge his loyalty to the republican regime.

As Bishop of Norwich, Reynolds worked hard to reconcile dissenters with the established church. He had two notable successes, one was Samuel Crossman (1625–84), the author of a collection of Reformed-flavoured religious poems, the most celebrated of which is probably *My Song is Love Unknown*. Having been ejected in 1662, Crossman decided to conform in 1665 and was duly ordained deacon and priest by Reynolds. In 1667, he became Prebendary of Bristol, and in 1683 Dean of that place.

The other high profile convert was Reynolds' own son-in-law, John Conant (1608–94), whom Reynolds ordained priest in 1670. Conant had been a highly significant player in Interregnum Oxford. He was elected Rector of Exeter College in 1649, and made Regius Professor of Divinity in 1654. Richard Cromwell made him Vice-Chancellor in 1657. Since John Wilkins (q.v.) was by that stage Richard Cromwell's right-hand man within the University,[86] Conant's appointment must have met with his approval. Certainly, Wilkins, like Seth Ward (q.v.), was regularly part of Conant's congregation in All Saints, Oxford, where Conant was lecturer. In 1658, Conant managed to secure the election of John Wallis (q.v.) as University Archivist, apparently by keeping the polls open after dark, until enough of Wallis's friends had voted.[87] In 1659, Conant joined Wilkins and Ward when they went to London to oppose the granting of a university charter to Durham College.[88] So it would appear that Conant was also an integral part of the moderate party which dominated Oxford during the last few years of the Commonwealth.

Naturally, Conant's significance was eclipsed by his initial refusal to conform, but when he did, he was appointed vicar of All Saints', Northampton in 1671, and then, by his father-in-law, Archdeacon of Norwich in 1676. Sir Joseph Williamson and John Wallis (qq.v.), who had known Conant in Oxford, were active in seeking further preferment for him,[89] but were either unsuccessful, or secured nothing that Conant wished to accept.

[85] *ODNB*, s.v. 'William Beveridge.'

[86] Worden, 'Cromwellian Oxford'. p747.

[87] P. Beeley and C. Schriba (eds.), *The Correspondence of John Wallis*, 2 vols (Oxford, 2003–4), i pxxxiv.

[88] *ODNB*, s.v. 'John Conant'.

[89] *ODNB*, s.v. 'John Conant'.

Another Reformed divine who initially refused to conform, but later became reconciled to the Church of England was Thomas Horton (d.1673). He was a significant figure within Cromwellian Cambridge. Having been a fellow of Emmanuel from 1631, he was elected Professor of Divinity at Gresham College, London, in 1641. In 1647, he moved to Queens' College, Cambridge, where he had been elected President. He became Vice-Chancellor of that University in 1650. His refusal to conform was short-lived, and in 1666, he was admitted as Vicar of St Helen's Bishopsgate, in London. At Emmanuel, Horton had been one of John Wallis's tutors, and Wallis took upon himself the task of editing a large collection of Horton's sermons, which was published as the *One Hundred Select Sermons* in 1679.

Wallis was not the only person who thought that Horton's sermons were worthy of a wider audience. Another was William Dillingham (1617–89), who had produced a smaller selection of them as the *Forty Six Sermons* in 1674. Dillingham, like Wallis, had been a student at Emmanuel, where he also became a fellow in 1642. In 1653, he became Master, and in 1654 was appointed one of Cromwell's visitors to the University, eventually serving as Vice-Chancellor on the eve of the Restoration. Like Horton, he initially refused to conform, but when he did so, he became Rector of Woodhill (Odell) in Bedfordshire in 1672.

Dillingham was friendly with another Reformed grandee within the Restoration Church. This was John Hacket (1592–1670), with whom Dillingham shared a prolonged correspondence on theological matters during the 1650s.[90] Hacket was a vigorous Bishop of Lichfield and Coventry, where he had been appointed in 1661, and where he presided over the restoration work which saved Lichfield Cathedral, after the violence and neglect it had suffered during the Interregnum. Despite their common theological ground, Hacket could not stand John Wilkins, and was quite incensed when Wilkins joined by him on the Bishops' Bench in 1668.[91]

Hacket would presumably have been happier with Wilkins's successor at Chester, John Pearson (1613–86), since Hacket donated a very large sum of money to his old college in Cambridge, whilst Trinity was under Pearson's governance. Pearson was an old Etonian, who became a fellow of King's College, Cambridge in 1635. John Davenant, the scholarly Reformed Bishop of Salisbury, appointed him to the prebend of Netherhaven in Salisbury in 1639. In 1643, he had preached a controversial University sermon in defense of the established liturgy. His ministry was disrupted by the Civil War, but he was a lecturer in St Clement's Eastcheap in London by 1654.

After the Restoration, things quickly took a turn for the better, and after a veritable flood of other preferment, including the Archdeaconry of Surrey in

[90] MS BL Sloane 1710, ff 182–202. [91] *ODNB*, s.v. 'John Hacket.'

1660, Pearson became Lady Margaret Professor of Divinity in Cambridge in 1661 and Master of Trinity College there in 1662. As Lady Margaret Professor, he delivered a series of lectures on the divine attributes, in which he struck a decidedly Reformed tone, asserting, against the Arminians, both individual predestination to life and individual predestination to damnation.[92] In 1673, Pearson became Bishop of Chester, keeping the Archdeaconry of Surrey *in commendam*, presumably with the approval of George Morley (q.v.), who had been his diocesan bishop in that post for the previous eleven years. As Bishop, he retained his academic interests, and was in contact with William Beveridge (q.v.) on matters of Patristic scholarship.[93]

Pearson was a lifelong friend of Seth Ward's.[94] The diarist John Evelyn, recalls dining at Ward's grand new house in Knightsbridge on 25 March 1674 in their joint company.[95] It is no surprise, then, to find that Evelyn was also intimate with Thomas Barlow,[96] since Barlow, too, was close friends with Pearson. Pearson's nephew, John Thane, wrote a letter to Thomas Barlow upon his uncle's death, explaining what would happen to Pearson's literary remains, and noting 'the particular friendship, the singular respect and kindness towards each other' of the two bishops.[97]

Pearson was also familiar with one of the most productive Reformed authors of the post-Restoration Church. This was John Edwards (1637–1716), the second son of the celebrated Presbyterian controversialist, Thomas Edwards (1599–1648). Edwards had been at St John's College Cambridge with William Beveridge, where both of them enjoyed the favour of the Interregnum Master, Anthony Tuckney.[98] Like Beveridge, Edwards was ordained deacon and priest in unusually swift succession by Robert Sanderson (q.v.), though Edwards alone enjoyed the singular distinction of being invited by Bishop Sanderson to preach the sermon at his own priesting. In 1664, he became the minister of Holy Trinity, Cambridge. It was there that he was heard, and applauded, by John Pearson.[99]

Unfortunately, Edwards did not similarly impress all those he encountered. He had a very patchy career, eventually retiring from the active ministry in 1686

[92] J. Pearson, in Churton (ed.), *Minor Theological Works*, 2 vols (Oxford, 1844), i p260.

[93] MS BOD Tanner xl f 48. This is a letter from Beveridge to Sancroft, in which he refers to his collaboration with Pearson.

[94] Pope, *Life*, p11.

[95] John Evelyn, *Diary and Correspondance*, 4 vols (London, 1906), ii p299.

[96] He was shown round the Bodleian by Barlow in 1654. Evelyn, *Diary*, ii p55. He was also invited to Barlow's consecration feast. Evelyn, *Diary*, ii p310.

[97] MS BOD Tanner, xxx f 119. The letter is dated 21 September 1686, and Thane wrote it to inform Barlow about what was happening with Pearson's literary remains.

[98] *ODNB* s.vv. 'William Beveridge' and 'John Edwards.'

[99] *Biographia Britannia* (London, 1793), v p543.

so as to dedicate himself to writing, something he continued to do with great energy right up until his death. Like his father, he liked nothing better than to portray himself of the embattled defender of Reformed orthodoxy against prevailing error, which means, of course, that his claim that Arminianism was rampant within the Church of England may need to be taken with a pinch of salt. His writings are, nonetheless, distinctly more level-headed and systematic than Thomas Edwards's famous rant against heresy, the *Gangraena* (1646).

## THEIR CHARACTER AND ENGAGEMENT IN THE LIFE OF THE CHURCH

The sheer range and significance of the people we have touched on is sufficient, of itself, to demonstrate that the Reformed theological tradition remained a potent force within post-Restoration Anglicanism. Of the men we have mentioned, twelve were bishops and six were deans. Several of them held senior divinity chairs in Oxford or Cambridge, and so were in a position to influence the thinking of successive generations of Restoration clergy. The circle included several of the greatest scientific minds of the Restoration Church (in Boyle, Ward, and Wallis), one of her most celebrated preachers (in South), two of her most eminent Patristic scholars (in Pearson and Beveridge), and two of her most influential ecclesiastical courtiers (in Morley and Compton). These are men, in other words, without whom it is simply not possible to paint an accurate picture of the later Stuart Church.

Furthermore, there appears to have been a network of personal relationships between the great majority of these men sufficient to establish that they should be considered as a coherent group. They not only shared a common commitment to the Reformed theological tradition; in many cases they also knew each other, dedicated books and sermons to each other, sought advice from each other, and, where the opportunity presented itself, favoured people who thought as they did.

This is not, then, the moribund and marginal tradition which the historians have led us to expect. Nor was it peopled with inflexible thinkers, men who were clinging to unfashionable dogmas because their theological system was unable to engage with the changing intellectual environment. As we have already argued, the Reformed tradition was quite capable of adapting to new thinking and of absorbing new insights. The presence amongst their number of John Wilkins, perhaps the chief patron of the new learning in Interregnum England, as well as some of the most significant figures in the scientific awakening which took place in the later seventeenth century, is sufficient to demonstrate that. Consequently, whereas Spurr has shown that the most prominent Latitudinarians were not as closely linked with the scientific world as has sometimes been claimed,[100] it would appear that several of their Reformed contemporaries were.

Furthermore, in the field of theology, however strong their overarching commitment to Reformed system, this was also far from being a sterile or monochrome group. Many of them, for example, despite their Reformed credentials, are notable for their commitment to the neo-Laudian liturgical agenda of the later Stuart Church, something they exhibited both in their support for elaborate church architecture and furnishings, and by their unflinching loyalty to the rites of the established Church. In this, they were pushing the Reformed tradition in directions it had not much travelled before the Civil War.

Bishops Ward, Hopkins, and Hacket, for example, were famously active within their cathedrals. Ward spent significant sums on the beautification of his cathedral at Exeter and the installation of an organ there.[101] Hopkins was yet another Reformed supporter of organ music, installing an instrument in his cathedral at Derry shortly after he arrived, as well as donating to the cathedral a handsome set of communion plate. Hacket, for his part, not only dedicated £3,500 of his own money to the restoration work at Lichfield, but raised a further £15,000 for the organ, the choir stalls and the altar ornaments—just the sort of High Church stage props which would have found scant appreciation amongst the Reformed divines of an earlier generation. Theirs was, therefore, Reformed divinity, but with Restoration curlicues.

This unexpected alliance of Reformed theological system with High Church liturgical tastes is most striking in William Beveridge. Here was a man who was quite happy to preach both irresistible grace[102] and limited atonement.[103] Yet, in his religious bestseller, the *Sermon concerning the Excellency and Usefulness of the Common Prayer*, Beveridge could rhapsodize like no other upon the manifold excellencies of the Anglican liturgy.

He wrote: 'There is nothing necessary to be known or believed, but we are taught it; nothing necessary to be done but we are enjoined it; nothing necessary to be obtained, but we pray for it, in our public form of divine service.'[104] To his mind, every single aspect of the Book of Common Prayer is conducive to our edification: its language,[105] its order,[106] the various postures it prescribes,[107] its frequent repetition of the three historic creeds,[108] its

100 J. Spurr, ' "Latitudinarianism" and the Restoration Church,' *HJ*, 31 (1988), p75.
101 Pope, *Life*, p56.
102 W. Beveridge, *Works*, 12 vols (Oxford, 1842), x p589.
103 Ibid., p579.
104 Beveridge, *Excellency and Usefulness*, p14.
105 Ibid., p13.
106 Ibid., p19 et seq.
107 Ibid., p28.
108 Ibid., p15.

preference for brief and theologically precise collects, over the long-winded extemporary ramblings beloved of the dissenters.[109]

Of course, as Beveridge pointed out, for its full glory to be appreciated, the Prayer Book needs an appropriate liturgical setting. Indeed, at one point, the sermon begins to dwell as much on the excellency and usefulness of the chancel screen as it does upon the liturgy. Beveridge laments the many modish London parsons who were happy to dispense with this essential and theologically significant fitting when rebuilding their churches after the Great Fire.[110] He had, of course, famously irritated Christopher Wren, by insisting that his rebuilt parish church at St Peter's Cornhill be equipped with one.[111]

And just as the post-Restoration Reformed tradition could embrace a neo-Laudian attitude to the liturgy, so it could accept the high-flying claims that were increasingly being made about the role of bishops within the Church.[112] Beveridge, for example, was quite certain that bishops were essential to the being of the Church. Without divine assistance, neither word nor sacrament was effective.[113] However, that divine assistance was promised only to the apostles,[114] who transmitted their office, and the promise annexed to it, to their successors by the laying on of hands.[115] This apostolic succession, he argues, is 'the root of all Christian communion',[116] and he is quite happy to un-church those congregations which do not have it. He writes of the dissenters:

> In their private meetings, where their teachers have no Apostolical or Episcopal imposition of hands, they have no ground to pretend to succeed to the Apostles, nor, by consequence, any right to the Spirit which our Lord promiseth; without which, though they preach their hearts out, I do not see what spiritual advantage can accrue to their hearers by it.[117]

The Holy Spirit, for Beveridge, ordinarily worked only within the boundaries of the apostolic succession, and so the Holy Spirit could only be found in a church where there were bishops. This high doctrine of the episcopate accounts in part for Beveridge's refusal to accept the see of Bath and Wells, when he was offered it in place of Thomas Ken, who was deprived in 1691 for refusing to swear the oath of allegiance to William III and Mary II.

John Pearson's view of episcopacy was similar to that of Beveridge. He, too, was convinced that episcopal ordination is the root of all communion within the Church.[118] Only bishops, he believes, have the power to ordain, so only ministers ordained by a bishop are lawfully called.[119] He writes:

[109] Beveridge, *Excellency and Usefulness*, p17. [110] Ibid., p26.
[111] *ODNB*, s.v. 'William Beveridge.' [112] Spurr, *Restoration Church of England*, pp132–63.
[113] Beveridge, *Works*, i p11. [114] Ibid., p4. [115] Ibid., p10. [116] Ibid., p23.
[117] Ibid., p24. [118] Pearson, *Minor Theological Works*, ii p233. [119] Ibid., i p287.

That the order of the ministry is necessary to the continuation of the gospel according to the promises of Christ, as it was to the first implantation of it according to his institution, is a doctrine indubitable. That this ministry is derived by a succession and constant propagation, and that the unity and peace of the Church of Christ are to be conserved by a due and legitimate ordination, no man who considereth the practice of the Apostles and ecclesiastical history, can ever doubt.[120]

Bishops, Pearson argues, are the legitimate successors of the apostles, with sole power to ordain, to govern the clergy and to excommunicate.[121] Once again, it is a case of no bishops, no Holy Spirit.

In fact, unless we get to grips with the ways in which the Reformed tradition evolved after the Restoration, it is difficult to account for the strenuous resistance which several Reformed divines offered to the various royal attempts to relax the terms of Anglican conformity. William Beveridge repeatedly irritated John Tillotson with his intransigence in these debates, and William Jane was the ringleader of the High Church opposition to such plans during the reigns of William and Mary. Thomas Barlow, for his part, felt that any toleration of nonconformity was entirely unnatural,[122] and Henry Compton was a vigorous supporter of the Tory campaign during the reign of Queen Anne to roll back such toleration as had been granted by her predecessor. Indeed, the majority of the clergy we have mentioned were convincingly enthusiastic in their persecution of dissent.

But if the Reformed tradition was still developing after the Restoration, and so capable of expressing itself in some unexpected ways, it was also diverse. So, for example, some of the men we have mentioned were prominent supporters of some kind of rapprochement with the dissenters, and so found themselves opposed to the more High Church Reformed men we have just mentioned. John Wilkins was a key proponent of the comprehension scheme that was being discussed early on in the reign of Charles II. Edward Reynolds sought to adopt a Reformed model of episcopacy which would woo dissenters back into the fold. John Hall remained on the commission examining the options for comprehension in 1689, when William Jane and his allies had ostentatiously walked out.

Likewise, not all Reformed writers embraced the strongly Episcopalian views of Pearson and Beveridge. Barlow, for example, took a rather different position. He agreed with Pearson and Beveridge that bishops are of apostolic origin, and that their office involves and inherent superiority to presbyters in the matter of church government.[123] However, in Barlow's view, originally a

120 Ibid., ii p232. 121 Ibid., i p274.

122 R.A. Beddard, 'Tory Oxford,' in N. Tyacke (ed.), *The History of the University of Oxford IV: The Seventeenth Century Oxford* (Oxford, 1997), p884.

123 Barlow, MS QCL 340 p1.

bishop could not act apart from his presbyters. The true locus of spiritual power in the primitive church was the assembly of the bishop and his clergy, not the bishop alone. He writes:

> The bishop (before the division of the provinces into parishes) had such a number of presbyters in the city with him; he had not the sole power (no not in ordination) but he and they together made up that . . . Church Consistory (as fathers and councils anciently called it) in which the spiritual power and government of the Church originally resided, so that neither he without his presbytery, nor they without him could exercise acts of ordination, excommunication etc.[124]

Barlow argued that this situation became corrupted partly because of the pusillanimity of the lower clergy and partly through the growing pride of the bishops. Be that as it may, it would seem to follow from his remarks that the power to ordain is not necessarily the prerogative of a bishop. And indeed, in a letter discussing ordination, Barlow asserts that the spiritual power necessary to Christian ministry is conferred at the laying on of hands 'by any who has a just power to do it.'[125] So, although that letter discusses only ordination by bishops, the door is left open for valid ordination to take place within a non-Episcopal polity.

Furthermore, in his lectures on the nature of schism, whilst Barlow makes it clear that a breach of ecclesiastical discipline such as the renunciation of Episcopal authority would be a schismatic act,[126] he also asserts that a schism does not necessarily cut the schismatic off from the Church.[127] There can be schism within the Church as well as schism from the Church.[128]

John Edwards, similarly, does not limit the power to ordain to bishops. He writes that the ordination of a minister is accomplished 'by the pastors of the Church, who have power given them to set apart such by imposition of hands.'[129] Like Barlow, he is clear that bishops, as an order, are 'really distinct' from presbyters.[130] Again, like Barlow, he considers that the role of a bishop is to rule and govern the Church, but only 'with the assistance and concurrence of their presbyters.'[131] But he goes beyond Barlow in maintaining that there was a time when the Church had no bishops,[132] and expresses scepticism about the authenticity of the patristic sources used by Anglican writers to demonstrate the inherent superiority of bishops to presbyters.[133]

Given his attenuated view of the Episcopal order, Edwards does not have a problem with accepting that non-Episcopal congregations are still part of the

[124] Barlow, MS QCL 279 pp627–8. Edward Reynold apparently held similar views: Spurr, *Restoration Church of England*, p162.

[125] Barlow, MS QCL 279 p318. [126] Ibid. 236 57r–57v. [127] Ibid. 236 69v.

[128] Ibid. 236 76r. [129] Edwards, *Theologia Reformata*, i p531. [130] Ibid., p528.

[131] Ibid., p529. [132] Ibid., p523. [133] Ibid., p529.

true church. Indeed, he is not actually prepared to call the dissenters schismatic at all. He writes:

> As for those who dissent from our church, purely on the terms of conformity, it may be thought that they are not obnoxious to the charge of schism, because they separate not from the Catholic church, that is that church of Christ in the whole world professing the fundamental truths of the gospel and practising the essentials of Christian worship.[134]

The implication of this is that Edwards does not hold episcopacy to be necessary to the Church at all. It is merely one acceptable form of Church government amongst others. In Edwards, therefore, the Reformed tradition is decidedly less marked by the ecclesiological fashions of post-Restoration Anglicanism, than it is in Pearson or Beveridge. This may, of course, reflect the influence of Edwards's ferociously Presbyterian father.

Edwards also had no time for Beveridge's liturgical absolutism, or the musical enthusiasms of some of the Reformed bishops. Although fond of the Prayer Book,[135] he admitted that John Calvin had found many 'trifles and fopperies' in it.[136] He is also adamant that the clergy are entitled to indulge in extemporary prayer. Set forms, he insists, should not be imposed.[137] He is also convinced that musical instruments other than the human voice have no place in well-ordered Christian worship.[138] So in Edwards we can still hear the accents of the old Puritan tradition sounding from within the post-Restoration Church.

It is the very strength, breadth, and flexibility of the Anglican Reformed tradition that accounts for its continuing survival and significance after the Restoration. As John Spurr has made clear, Reformed divinity had many enemies. He has argued that the one thing which really united those clergy commonly known as Latitudinarians was their common dislike of Reformed thinking,[139] He speaks of Fowler, Glanvil, Tillotson, and others engaging in 'a hard-fought campaign against Puritan or Calvinist soteriology'.[140] Reformed divinity was characterized in this campaign as irrational and conducive to the spread of immorality.[141]

And it was not just the Latitudinarians who were prepared to level this charge. Nicholas Tyacke has pointed out the encouragement that Archbishop Gilbert Sheldon gave to George Bull's attacks on Reformed thinking, and the support he extended to Thomas Barlow's Arminian opposite number, the Regius Professor of Divinity in Oxford before Jane, Richard Allestree.[142] It is, therefore, no surprise to hear that Sheldon opposed the advancement of

134 Ibid., p753. 135 Ibid., p620. 136 Ibid., p621. 137 Ibid., p618.
138 Ibid., p657. 139 Spurr, 'Latitudinarianism,' p69. 140 Ibid., p76.
141 Ibid., p70. 142 Tyacke, 'Religious Controversy,' p606.

Reformed figures such as Hall, as Master of Pembroke, Wilkins, as Bishop of Chester, and Barlow, as Bishop of Lincoln. In certain quarters, Reformed theology evoked quite visceral hostility, and could be an obstacle to preferment. Anthony Wood writes, for example, of Thomas Tully that 'He was a person of severe morals, puritanically inclined and a strict Calvinist; which, as may be reasonably presumed was some stop to him in his way to preferment.'[143]

Yet, despite the powerful opposition it provoked; despite its associations with the execution of Charles I and the evils of the Commonwealth; despite the astounding popularity of Arminian works such as Allestree's *The Whole Duty of Man*;[144] the Reformed tradition retained a hold over the minds of many theologians long after the Restoration, and well into the reign of Queen Anne. It remained, in other words, a compelling way of understanding Anglicanism far longer than most historians have recognized. Indeed, some of the evidence which has been interpreted as pointing to a growing Arminian hegemony is capable of quite another reading.

As we have seen, Tyacke has singled out Gilbert Burnet's *Exposition of the Thirty-Nine Articles* (1699) as indicating the ultimate triumph of Arminianism over the Reformed tradition. But it is far from clear that Burnet's book should be interpreted in that way. First, Burnet explicitly states that his *Exposition* is not designed to establish the normative character of an Arminian reading of the Articles, but rather to show how both Reformed and Arminian readings are equally legitimate. He underlines, for example, that he sought to present both the Reformed and the Arminian approach to predestination as accurately as he was able. He confesses that he did indeed differ from the Reformed view on that matter.[145] But he writes:

> I weighed the Article with that impartial care that I thought became me; and have taken a method, which is, for aught I know, new, of stating the arguments of all sides with so much fairness, that those, who knew my own opinion in this point, have owned to me that they could not discover it by anything that I had written.[146]

His aim in this, was to promote understanding between both parties, so that the Church could avoid the damaging disagreements which affected it in the past, rather than to promote a rigid new orthodoxy to replace the old.[147]

Commenting upon the relations between Reformed and Arminian clergy within the English Church at the time he published the *Exposition*, Burnet wrote:

[143] Wood, *Athenaa Oxonienses*, iii p1058.

[144] Spurr, *Restoration Church*, pp281–96.

[145] G. Burnet, *Exposition of the Thirty-Nine Articles* (London, 1819) pxi.

[146] Ibid., pxi.

[147] Ibid., pxii.

> We of this church are very happy in this respect; we have all along been much divided, and once almost broken to pieces, while we disputed concerning these matters: but now we are much happier; for though we know one another's opinions, we live not only united in the same worship, but in great friendship and love with those of other persuasions. And the boldness of some among us, who have reflected in sermons, or otherwise, on those who hold Calvin's system, has been much blamed, and often censured by those who, though they hold the same opinions with them yet are more charitable in their thoughts and discreet in their expressions.[148]

Burnet saw his work, then, not as establishing the dominance of Arminian theology, but as a call for peaceful coexistence between Arminian and Reformed divines. That, of course, is only a call worth making when both parties still need to be taken seriously: that is to say, in a Church in which Reformed divinity still has a significant following. So, far from witnessing to the triumph of Arminianism, Burnet's book is actually good evidence of the tenacity of Reformed thought within the Church of England.

Secondly, it is important not to forget just how controversial Burnet's *Exposition* proved to be. He may have intended it as an irenic work, but his opponents did not choose to interpret it in that way. When Convocation was called in 1701, a committee of the Lower House, under the chairmanship of the Reformed theologian, William Jane, decided to investigate Burnet's work alongside the much more obviously heretical *Christianity Not Mysterious* of John Toland (1696). In June, the committee duly resolved to make a formal complaint about Burnet's *Exposition* to the Upper House. Their complaint was:

> That the said book tends to introduce such a latitude and diversity of opinions as the Articles were framed to avoid; that there are many passages in the exposition of several articles which appear to us to be contrary to the true meaning of them, and to other received doctrines of the Church; that there are some things in the said book which seem to be of dangerous consequence to the Church of England as by law established, and to derogate from the honour of the Reformation.[149]

The Upper House responded crossly to this attack on one of its members, and demanded that the committee produce a more precise account of its objections. The committee duly did so, but did not have time to present it to the Upper House before Convocation was prorogued. Martin Grieg has, however, unearthed that account, and it is instructive.

[148] Ibid., ppxii–xiii.

[149] H. Aldrich, *A Narrative of the LowerHouse of Convocation relating to Prorogations and Adjournments* (London, 1702), cited in M. Grieg, 'Heresy Hunt: Gilbert Burnet and the Convocation Controversy of 1701', *HJ*, 37 (1994), p584.

The committee complained that Burnet's argument that different interpretations of the Articles could be legitimate undermined their principal purpose, which was to promote unity by avoiding all obscurity and ambiguity.[150] If there was any doubt about what the Articles meant, then recourse could always be had to various established authorities, including, in particular, the (unambiguously Reformed) Book of Homilies.

The committee then went on to home in on Burnet's discussion of Articles IX–XVIII as being especially problematic. But these, of course, were the very Articles in which Burnet was presenting, side by side, the Reformed and Arminian approaches to questions such as Original Sin, Justification, and Predestination. The committee argued that in discussing these matters, Burnet had presented, and then failed to refute, many opinions which were either erroneous or heretical.[151] Furthermore, it argued that Burnet frequently contradicted the true meaning of the Articles, offering views which were clearly contrary to the received opinions of the Church of England.

Gilbert Burnet was, therefore, being attacked for introducing too much latitude in the interpretation of the Thirty-Nine Articles, especially in the matter of soteriology. But the latitude he was specifically attempting to introduce, and to which the Lower House of Convocation evidently objected, was a breadth which could encompass an Arminian reading of the Articles. And that objection was expressed through a committee led by one of England's foremost Reformed divines. So it is certainly plausible that sympathy for Reformed theology was a significant factor in the Lower House's hostility to Burnet's *Exposition*.

This interpretation of the situation is lent further credibility by an intriguing exchange which took place between the Oxford High Churchman, Henry Sacheverell, and Gilbert Burnet's chaplain, Richard West, very shortly after the Convocation Controversy. In his studiedly offensive pamphlet, *The Character of a Low-Church Man*, Henry Sacheverell had complained that a typical Low Churchman 'thinks the articles of the Church too stiff, formal and strait-laced a rule to confine his faith in, and complements them out of their rigour and severity'.[152] This, of course, was exactly the complaint that the Lower House had made about Burnet's *Exposition* a few months earlier. Richard West, responding to this specific accusation, wrote,

> I subscribe and give my unfeigned assent to the Articles of the Church, in such a sense only as the scriptures will justify me in; and if I think that the scriptures most favour

[150] Grieg, 'Heresy Hunt,' p585. [151] Ibid., p586.

[152] H. Sacheverell, 'The Character of a Low-Church Man,' cited in R. West, *The True Character of a Church Man* (London, 1702), p20.

the Arminian tenets, as they are called, I am sure I can't honestly assent to them in a Calvinistical sense.[153]

Sacheverell's complaint was, therefore, that Burnet's reading of the Articles was too loose, and West assumed that the looseness to which he was objecting was one which permitted an Arminian reading of the Articles.[154] In other words, to West's mind, the Reformed leanings of the Lower House were part of what had motivated them to persecute his Arminian bishop. This seems all the more likely when one considers the make-up of the 1701 Convocation. For, of its 135 members, no fewer than 96 were Oxford graduates,[155] and Oxford, as we have seen, remained the chief bastion of Reformed theology in England.

Consequently, both in the way it presents itself, and in the way it was received by the wider Church, Burnet's *Exposition* seems to offer evidence for the strength, not the weakness, of the Reformed tradition in the early years of the eighteenth century. In other words, rather than setting the seal on a new Arminian dispensation, it points forcefully to the fundamental doctrinal tension which still lay at the heart of the Church of England, a struggle for Anglican identity in which the dominant adversaries were the Arminians on one side, and the Reformed on the other.

## THEIR WRITINGS

It was the teaching, writing, and polemical engagement of the men we have mentioned, which ensured that Reformed divinity still had to be taken seriously at the dawn of the eighteenth century. In a catalogue of their works, almost every kind of theological literature is represented. In Samuel Crossman's *The Young Man's Calling* (1678), there was Reformed poetry. In Benjamin Jenks's *The Poor Man's Ready Companion* (1713), there was Reformed family piety. In William

153 R. West, *The True Character of a Church Man* (London, 1702), p21.

154 Nicholas Tyacke certainly favours this reading of the exchange: 'Arminianism and the Theology of the Restoration Church,' *Britain and the Netherlands*, 11 (1994), p80. Opposition to Burnet's Exposition was not, however, confined to the Reformed. As Burnet pointed out in his manuscript autobiography, Arminian theologians opposed him as well, an opposition he put down to their being prepared to strike at themselves, so long as they could damage him. H.C. Foxcroft (ed.), *A Supplement to Burnet's History of My Own Time derived from his original memoirs, his autobiography, his letters to Admiral Herbert, his private meditations, all hitherto unpublished* (Oxford, 1902), p508.

155 G.V. Bennett 'Against the Tide: Oxford under William III,' in L.S. Sutherland and L.G. Mitchell (eds.), *The History of the University of Oxford V: The Eighteenth Century* (Oxford, 1986), p57.

Burkitt's *Expository Notes* (1700), there was Reformed exegesis. In Robert Sanderson's *Cases of Conscience*, there was Reformed casuistry. In William Dillingham's *Latin Lives of James Ussher and Laurence Chaderton*, there was Reformed hagiography. In Henry Compton's eleven published letters to the clergy of his diocese, there was Reformed pastoralia. The very breadth of this publishing endeavour no doubt contributed to keeping Reformed opinions high on the Church of England's theological agenda.

Naturally enough, most of these men were energetic producers of the most popular form of ecclesiastical literature: sermons. Good quality preaching was, in the later seventeenth century, the surest way to acquire an appreciative public and impress potential patrons. Bringing those sermons to print only increased the impact they might have. As a result, almost all the Reformed published individual sermons from time to time, and several did so regularly throughout their lives. These, along with other sermons unpublished but still extant at their author's death, were often then lovingly assembled by admirers, and published posthumously. That is how the breathtakingly extensive collections of sermons by Sanderson, Hacket, Horton, Hopkins, Conant, and Beveridge all came to print. Robert South, for his part, was such a famous preacher, that he was able to sell numerous volumes of his sermons well before his death. At the end of the seventeenth century, the Reformed South was read with just as much enthusiasm as the Arminian Tillotson.

Those with a particular penchant for polemic were equally productive. Thomas Barlow, Francis Fullwood, and William Stanley all weighed in forcefully against the Church of Rome. As we shall see, Thomas Tully, John Wallis, and Robert South all set their sights on enemies rather closer to home. John Edwards argued with anything that moved: particularly if it did not do so in an acceptably Reformed way.

What is noticeable amidst all this publishing activity is that, after the Restoration, the Reformed did not publish a great deal by way of properly 'academic' literature, that is to say Latin lectures, disputations, or theological systems. This stands in marked contrast to the Reformed divines of an earlier generation, such as Davenant or Prideaux. Some of the post-Restoration figures certainly produced work of this kind: as professors within the two Universities, Barlow, Pearson, Hall, and Jane all lectured and resolved disputations throughout their university careers, and some of their efforts survive (in the cases of Barlow and Pearson). But neither they, nor their posthumous admirers, thought to publish what they had taught.[156] The only exceptions to

156 Only a couple of Barlow's disputation resolutions occur in his *Genuine Remains* (Oxford, 1693). The letter which John Thane sent to Barlow on the death of John Pearson was explicit that there were no plans to publish Pearson's lectures at that stage: MS BOD Tanner, xxx p119.

this rule were heavyweight works of Patristic theology such as Pearson's *Vindiciae Epistolarum S. Ignatii* (1672) and Beveridge's *Synodikon* (1672).

This relative lack of academic theology is further evidence of the evolution which the Reformed tradition underwent as the century drew on. Realizing that there was little public appetite for old-fashioned academic divinity, the Reformed adapted to the new taste, and sought to present their views in a more approachable way.

Pearson, for example, consciously adjusted his style for public consumption. He notes in the preface to his *Exposition of the Creed* (1659) that some readers can understand the original languages in which the Biblical authors and the Church fathers wrote, whereas others cannot. But he underlines that

> When I make this difference and distinction of readers, I do not intend thereby, that because one of these is learned, the other is ignorant; for he which have no skill of the learned languages, may notwithstanding be very knowing in the principles of Christian religion, and the reason and efficacy of them.[157]

For this reason, Pearson placed all materials in the original languages in the margin of his work, rather than in the main text. That way, he hoped, the unlearned reader would not be disturbed in his reading or his understanding. He also underlined that he had 'endeavoured to deliver the most material conceptions in the most plain and perspicacious manner; as desirous to comprise the whole strength of the work, as far as is possible, in the body of it.'[158] Beveridge followed Pearson's lead and similarly consigned learned languages to the footnotes in his *Ecclesia Anglicana Ecclesia Catholica.*

Edwards, too, consciously adapted his writing for a wider audience. As he pointed out in the general preface to the *Theologia Reformata*:

> I have not gone in a systematic way, lest I should be too dry and formal; but I have used a greater latitude, and have proceeded in a method which I have found to be most natural, easy and useful... for I have calculated my work for the benefit of the ordinary and unlearned reader, as well as of the intelligent and studious.[159]

So here, too, the Reformed were moving with the times, and altering their output in response to changes of taste in the reading public. The new fashion for clarity and simplicity of expression found their home as much within the Reformed fold as amongst the Latitudinarians.[160]

157 J. Pearson, *Exposition of the Creed* (London, 1845), p4.

158 Ibid.

159 Edwards, *Veritas Redux*, pv.

160 Gerard Reedy makes precisely this point in connection with the sermons of Robert South. G. Reedy, *Robert South (1634–1716): An Introduction to his Life and Sermons* (Cambridge, 1992), pp4–5.

This copious publishing endeavour did not fall on an unreceptive audience. Several of the Reformed writers were recognized as opinion-formers, even by contemporaries of a very different theological persuasion. The most celebrated of all the Reformed was, undoubtedly, John Pearson. In the later Stuart period, his reputation as a theologian was second to none. Recording Pearson's death in 1686, Gilbert Burnet, who was an avowedly Arminian theologian, nonetheless wrote that Pearson

> was in all respects the greatest divine of the age: a man of great learning, strong reason and of a clear judgement. He was a judicious and grave preacher, more instructive than affective; and a man of spotless life and of an excellent temper. His book on the creed is among the best that our church has produced.[161]

Burnet also singled out Pearson's *Exposition of the Creed* in the preface to his *Exposition of the Thirty-Nine Articles*, writing that: 'Bishop Pearson on the creed, as far as it goes, is the perfectest work we have. His learning was profound and exact, his method good, and his style clear: he was equally happy both in the force of his arguments, and in the plainness of his expressions.'[162]

Certainly, Pearson on the Creed was an immensely popular work. First published in 1659, it had already passed through ten editions before 1715, not counting the abridged version produced by Basil Kennett in 1705,[163] and it must rank as the most highly esteemed book of dogmatic theology produced during the later Stuart period. Divines who were normally reluctant to cite their contemporaries, were quite happy to pepper their works with references to Bishop Pearson. Kennett wrote that it was a work 'than which the Christian world has seen nothing more accomplished, since the divine truths of scripture have been guarded by the succours of human learning'.[164] The Classical scholar Richard Bentley wrote more generally, speaking of 'the most excellent Bishop Pearson, the very dust of whose writings is gold'.[165] Pearson was, in other words, one of the defining religious thinkers of the period.

William Beveridge was another highly influential writer. As we have seen, he was perhaps the most striking example of that unexpected alliance between Reformed divinity and High Church ecclesiology that several theologians forged after the Restoration. Beveridge was a very productive writer, though the larger part of his opus was published posthumously. His devotional works clearly caught the spiritual mood of the day: his *Excellency and Usefulness of*

[161] G. Burnet, *History of His Own Time*, 2 vols (London, 1724), i p694.

[162] Burnet, *Exposition*, pix.

[163] B. Kennett, '*A Brief Exposition of the Apostles' Creed according to Bishop Pearson in a New Method* (London, 1705).

[164] Ibid. ppi–ii.

[165] R. Bentley, *Dissertation on Phalaris* (1699), pp424–5.

*the Common Prayer*, which has already been mentioned, went through no fewer than fourteen editions between 1681 and 1700; his *Great Necessity and Advantage of Public Prayer and Frequent Communion* had gone through seven editions by 1721, and his *Private Thoughts upon Religion* through ten editions by 1728.

The crypto-Arian Daniel Whitby recognized that Beveridge was a widely read author, and was sufficiently worried about his influence, that he put together a pre-emptively critical pamphlet before Beveridge's commentary on the Thirty-Nine Articles had even been published. In his *A Short View of Dr Beveridge's Writings* (1711), he wrote

> Bishop Beveridge in his lifetime published in the way of divinity a catechism; and since his death we have had his *Thoughts* and *Resolutions*, and a great many volumes of sermons. These I have read over as far as ever my patience would let me; and shall venture to give my opinion of them; to stop, if possible, the mischief that they are doing, and that which the publication of his *Articles*, which is promised, may do.[166]

Despite Daniel Whitby's note of alarm, however, Beveridge's Reformed commentary on the Articles, unlike Gilbert Burnet's Latitudinarian work, was published without controversy.

Even the distinctly eccentric John Edwards appears to have enjoyed a significant degree of influence among his contemporaries. His extensive systematic, the *Theologia Reformata*, was written with the specific aim of promoting a Reformed approach to divinity within what Edwards saw as a predominantly Arminian Church.[167] Edwards lamented the fact that he could find very few subscribers to lend financial support to his project.[168] Nonetheless, a decade or so after its publication, the Arminian Thomas Stackhouse, in his *Complete Body of Divinity* (1729), mentioned that Edwards' *Theologia Reformata* was, when Stackhouse wrote, one of the best-known and most widely used works of systematic theology then in circulation.[169]

The Anglican Reformed after the Restoration were, therefore, a highly productive group. Responding to the steady growth in rates of literacy,[170] and the corresponding growth in the public appetite for accessible theological literature, these men published significant amounts of popular writing which promoted, defended, or simply assumed the Reformed tenets. They adapted the style of their writing to suit post-Restoration tastes, generally forsaking

166 D. Whitby, *A Short View of Dr Beveridge's Writings* (London, 1711), p3.

167 Edwards, *Veritas Redux*, pxxiii.

168 Edwards, *Theologia Reformata*, pxi.

169 T. Stackhouse, *A Complete Body of Divinity* (London, 1729), Introduction. He goes on to write that 'Dr Edwards was a very learned man, and his *Theologia Reformata* is a magazine of knowledge,' even if its principles were 'purely Calvinistical'.

170 T. Harris, *Restoration: Charles II and his Kingdoms* (London, 2005), pp17–18.

the academic emphases of an earlier generation of Reformed writers, in favour of a more approachable output designed for a wider readership. As a result, several of them were recognised by their contemporaries as amongst the key opinion-formers of the post-Restoration period.

## CONCLUSION

The Anglican Reformed tradition has been ill-served by the great majority of those who have studied the Church of England after the Restoration.[171] Both those historians who have sought to portray the post-Restoration Church as theologically fallow ground awaiting the seeds of the Evangelical revival, and those who have, instead, painted it as the nursery of a distinct 'Anglican' identity, which sat increasingly light to its roots in the Protestant Reformation, have downplayed the ongoing significance of Reformed theology in the life of the English Church. This is, at least in part, because historians have taken too narrow and inflexible view of what it might mean to be part of the Reformed theological family.

The Reformed tradition has generally been presented as a thoroughly marginal factor in the Church's history, the outmoded dogma of inflexible men, who were unable to engage with the new intellectual environment of the later seventeenth century, and whose influence on the Anglicans of their day was, consequently, in terminal decline.

As we have seen, however, this was far from the case. The Reformed theologians of the later Stuart Church were both numerous and powerful. Several of them, in fact, were so influential, that an accurate grasp of the post-Restoration Church simply cannot be had without them. Their number included amongst the foremost scientists, preachers, academics, and ecclesiastical politicians of their day; and their varied, plentiful, and evolving theological output ensured that the Reformed tradition was still a force to be reckoned with in the reign of Queen Anne.

This group of men was united by personal as well as theological links. Their chief redoubt was the University of Oxford, which harboured a vigorous Reformed presence throughout this period. Their key power-brokers, Bishops Morley, Barlow, and Compton, were as active in the promotion of Reformed theology and Reformed theologians, as they were in their attempts to restrain the spread of Arminianism.

[171] This point has also been made by John Walsh. J. Walsh, 'Origins of the evangelical Revival,' in G.V. Bennett and J.D. Walsh (eds.), *Essays in Modern English Church History in memory of Norman Sykes* (London, 1966) pp155–6.

Such indeed was the strength of the Reformed tradition, that the two key controversies in speculative theology which erupted within the Church of England after the Restoration, are best understood as a Reformed reaction to new Arminian ideas. In the first controversy, which blew up after the publication of George Bull's *Harmonia Apostolica* (1670), the doctrine in question was justification, and the specific issue was the role that good works could be said to play in that process. To the Reformed, George Bull's ideas threatened the Church of England's commitment to the doctrinal heritage of the Reformation, a heritage which she shared not only with the Reformed but also with the Lutheran churches of continental Europe. Two theologians in particular responded to the challenge: Thomas Barlow, in his University lectures at Oxford, and Thomas Tully, with his *Iustificatio Paulina* (1674). They both vigorously reaffirmed the Church of England's Protestant identity, and her historic and constitutional conviction that justification was by faith alone.

In the second controversy, which was provoked by the publication of William Sherlock's *A Vindication of the Doctrine of the Trinity* (1690), the doctrine in question was the orthodox expression of the Trinity, and the specific issue was the language that should be used to describe the central mystery of the Christian faith. Sherlock suggested that the traditional credal and academic language of 'nature' and 'person' etc. was unhelpful and made the Church vulnerable to attacks from anti-Trinitarian writers. So he proposed what he thought might be a sensible alternative. To the Reformed, however, to abandon such language would be to cut the Church of England off from her patristic and medieval roots, and to open the way for the very heresies which such language was intended to prevent. The two champions of the Reformed position on the Trinity in this debate were John Wallis and Robert South, though their approaches were rather different. Both, however, sought to underline the Church of England's historic commitment to the traditional language of Trinitarian orthodoxy which was embraced by Protestant and Catholic alike.

As we shall see, the key Reformed players in these two controversies were merely expressing, in a polemical context, views which were widely held within the post-Restoration Church. They are, in other words, the vociferous tip of a larger Reformed iceberg. As we shall also see, their opponents sparked the controversy in each case by promoting to an English audience views which reflected the theology of the leading European Remonstrant writers, Simon Episcopius, Etienne de Courcelles, and Jean Leclerc. The post-Restoration Church was, in theological terms, a deeply divided body, and that division was defined, to a significant extent, along Arminian and Reformed lines.

We shall examine the controversies on justification and on the Trinity in detail, with the aim of demonstrating that they are clearly instances of

Reformed–Armininian conflict within the post-Restoration Church. We shall also look behind these very public arguments, and show that there was a growing divide on the doctrine of God, a divide which was also defined along Reformed and Arminian lines. In doing so, we shall demonstrate both the consistency and resilience of the Reformed theological tradition within the Church of England into the Hanoverian age, and the ongoing significance of the Reformed–Arminian divide to the theological landscape of the later Stuart Church.

# 2

# A Timely Antidote

## THE *HARMONIA APOSTOLICA*

When George Bull published the *Harmonia Apostolica* in 1669, he was spoiling for a fight. Setting a pugnacious tone from the outset, he described the book, in its opening *Advertisement*, as:

> A timely antidote against this solifidianism, or rather libertinism, which some in these dregs of time teach openly and shamelessly, and which many, by incrusting it with empty distinctions in sermons and writings, have palmed upon their readers, and still do so.[1]

Since solifidianism, the teaching that the sinner is justified by faith alone rather than by good works, had been the near-unanimous teaching of English divines until the 1640s, was still the confessional stance embraced by the continental Reformed and Lutheran Churches, and was commonly understood to be the position endorsed by the Thirty-Nine Articles, Bull was being willfully, indeed outrageously, provocative.

But the *Harmonia* was more than just another barbed contribution to the spiky theological conversation of Restoration England: George Bull had the backing of a very powerful man. Bull had originally attempted to have the *Harmonia* published by the University of Oxford in the mid-1660s, but the Reformed Vice-Chancellor, Robert Saye, would have nothing to do with it.[2] Unwilling to accept this rebuff, Bull approached a higher authority, and his book was published with the imprimatur of the Archbishop of Canterbury, Gilbert Sheldon, whose hostility to Reformed thought has already been underlined. By giving his official backing to Bull's work, Sheldon was effectively sparking a confrontation between his proxy and the Reformed theological establishment, an establishment which included, at the time, most of the leading men of Oxford University—the proudest redoubt of Restoration Anglicanism.

[1] G. Bull, *Harmonia Apostolica* (Oxford, 1842), Advertisement.
[2] Tyacke, N., 'Religious Controversy,' pp606–7.

When the *Harmonia* duly provoked a furious response, Bull published a second book in its defence, the *Apologia pro Harmonia* (1676). Continuing in the provocative vein that had marked his first book, Bull explained that, although his adversaries' lack of intellectual sophistication had initially made him reluctant to respond to them, several pious and learned friends had pointed out to him that

> One ought to look to the credit and reputation of our most renowned theologians, and, further, of the much revered prelates of our church, since it requires no great wisdom to see that however unimportant a person I may be myself, they are wounded through my side.[3]

In other words, Bull was presenting himself, not as an individual writer, but as the champion of a significant party within the Church, a party with numerous allies on the Bishops' Bench.

Bull also made it clear that he knew exactly who his enemies were. He wrote of them, in the *Apologia*:

> In this controversy about justification, we are innovators, in the eyes of Dr. Tully and his friends, because we will not have thrust upon us those empty and inexplicable shifts and subtleties (to say no worse of them) with which they themselves have interpolated the eleventh article of our Church... we are innovators, because we prefer the consent of all antiquity to the single opinion of Calvin. We are innovators, because we do not give the same place and respect to the Synod of Dordt as we do to the decrees of general councils, received in the whole Christian world.... We are innovators because we are unwilling that that system of theology (which has been patched up by new teachers, and those foreigners too, who were by no means favourable to the doctrine or discipline of our church) should any longer have such a hold in our schools and universities, that one is not permitted even to hint or whisper any thing, against its definitions, theories or conclusions.[4]

Bull was, therefore, openly claiming to be waging a war against Reformed orthodoxy and his avowed aim in this match was to eliminate the theological stranglehold he felt it enjoyed over the Church of England.

It is significant that this second book, too, bore the Archbishop of Canterbury's imprimatur. Gilbert Sheldon was not only prepared to endorse Bull's controversial ideas on two separate occasions, but also content for Bull to present himself as the standard-bearer of all those who were opposed to Reformed theology, himself among them.

Bull's biographer, Robert Nelson, clearly recognized the wider implications of the controversy surrounding the *Harmonia*. This was not simply a speculative skirmish between ambitious theologians, it was a contest about the

[3] G. Bull, *Apologia pro Harmonia* (Oxford, 1843), p227.

[4] Ibid., p230.

shape that Anglicanism would take after the purging fires of Civil War and Commonwealth. In particular, it was an argument about the extent to which that shape would continue to reflect the priorities of Reformed theology. Sheldon and Bull were determined to end the Reformed intellectual hegemony that had been restored during the Commonwealth.[5] Tully and his allies were equally determined to preserve it.

As Nelson noted, those who took offence at what Bull had written, did so because they were 'zealously affected for the names of Luther and Calvin, whom they honoured as the two apostles of the Reformation.'[6] Nelson singled out George Morley, Bishop of Winchester,[7] Thomas Barlow, and Thomas Tully[8] as those who led the charge against Bull. Nelson also underlined that Tully was chosen to represent the Reformed party in print because he was himself a famously loyal churchman, an eminent head of house, and a chaplain to the King, and that 'all this could not but make it to look somewhat more like a battery from the side of the Church of England'.[9] Tully's book was, of course, dedicated to George Morley, who had encouraged him to publish it, and was printed in Oxford in 1674 with the permission of Tully's superiors within the University.[10] And, by 1674, it was arguably George Morley, not the Archbishop, who had more influence at Court.[11]

So it was not only Bull's work that was being lent semi-official status by powerful men within the Church. His opponent's work was as well, by a rather different, but no less influential party. As a result, the controversy surrounding the *Harmonia* must be seen, not as an argument stirred up by one maverick divine, but as an intellectual tournament between two theological parties who held conflicting conceptions of what Anglicanism was. And it is intriguing that the preferment which Barlow and Tully received, to the bishopric of Lincoln and the deanery of Ripon respectively, was both swifter and more exalted than Bull's.[12] But then, even Bull's biographer felt compelled to grant that Tully's work 'was learnedly writ, and with some spirit, and by many at first it was approved of, who concluded that he had the better of the Harmonist.'[13]

[5] Tyacke, *History of the University of Oxford IV: The Seventeenth Century* p597.

[6] R. Nelson, *The Life of George Bull* (London, 1714), pp97–8.

[7] Ibid., p101.

[8] Ibid., p102.

[9] Ibid., p214.

[10] Ibid., pp218–19.

[11] *ODNB* s.vv.'Gilbert Sheldon' and 'George Morley'.

[12] Bull was granted a prebend in Gloucester in 1678, partly because of his efforts during the justification controversy. *ODNB*, s.v. 'George Bull'.

[13] Nelson, *Life*, p224.

## THE CAUSALITY OF SALVATION

The modern interpretation of Bull's work has been decisively shaped by Charles Allison's study of seventeenth-century soteriology, *The Rise of Moralism*. Allison tells a story in which the originally Reformed teaching of the English Church was gradually eclipsed, as the century wore on, by a novel understanding of justification in which good works played an unhealthily significant part. He traces the origins of this new theological school, which he calls 'moralism,' to mid-century English writers such as Henry Hammond, Jeremy Taylor, and Herbert Thorndike, but he argues that George Bull represents the most advanced statement of the movement's thought. He writes: 'George Bull's theology represented a more extravagant departure from classical Anglicanism than that of any other member of the "holy living" school.'[14]

Allison also argued that Bull's writings are compelling evidence that, by the 1670s, the moralist position had effectively swept Reformed orthodoxy from the field. He writes

> The mere fact that Bull produced his works at all, and the absence of any respectable alternative discussion of theology, make it incontestably apparent that the trend during the seventeenth century away from the classical or orthodox Anglican position possessed a remarkable virulence and an implacable momentum.[15]

In other words, he portrays George Bull's work as setting the seal on the moralists' dominance of Anglican theological discourse.

There are, however, a number of flaws in Allison's work, flaws that make its discussion of George Bull less than trustworthy. The first, and most significant, is Allison's near-total neglect of the respectable alternative discussion which the Reformed Anglicans did indeed advance during the latter half of the century. He does not consider, for example, either Tully's answer to Bull's work, the *Iustificatio Paulina*, or the six years' worth of lectures that Barlow gave on the subject, let alone the substantial discussions of justification which appeared in the published works of many Reformed writers quite independently of Bull's provocative attack. As a result, Allison's picture of the Church of England's remorseless slide into moralism is deeply distorted. And while it is probably true that the moralist position was held by the majority of Anglicans at the turn of the eighteenth century,[16] the Reformed alternative remained an entirely respectable option, partly as a result of the counter-attack mounted

[14] Allison, *The Rise of Moralism*, p199. [15] Ibid., p194.

[16] J. Edwards, *The Doctrine of Faith and Justification set in a True Light* (London, 1707), pxii.

by the post-Restoration Reformed churchmen. The publication of the *Harmonia Apostolica*, therefore, did not so much signify the triumph of moralism as reinvigorate the debate in a new historical context.

The second flaw in Allison's study is that he considers the post-Restoration writers through the lenses of pre-Restoration theology. He sets out to identify which divines fell into the orthodox Anglican camp, and which ones fell instead into the moralist 'holy living' school. His substantive theological analysis is devoted to the earlier writers; and, of the later ones, his principal concern is to establish whether they 'must be placed with Taylor, Thorndike and Hammond'[17]—which he says of Bull, as also of Fowler, Allestree, and Baxter—or instead remained true to 'classical' Anglicanism—the happy fate of Barlow, Stillingfleet, Beveridge, and Barrow.

As a result, the post-Restoration authors suffer from being squeezed into the categories provided by earlier writers, rather than being studied individually to any depth, or being placed in the specific intellectual context of late seventeenth century theology. And this is problematic because the theological conversation of later Stuart Anglicanism was not simply a repetition of the earlier debate. It had moved on, not least because of the ways in which Bull and his contemporaries extended and focussed the discussion.

The third flaw of Allison's study is the imprecision in his analysis of a central area of the discussion. Allison finds the key to understanding the seventeenth century debates in a discussion of the causality of justification. The general drift of his argument, namely that the moralist writers saw good works as being necessary in some way to the process of justification, whereas the Reformed did not, is probably correct. However, his treatment of the technical language of the discussion is inaccurate and so, ultimately, misleading.

Before we examine the specifics of the terminology it is perhaps helpful to give a brief introduction to the metaphysical vocabulary which the seventeenth century writers used when discussing matters of causality. It was a vocabulary which was originally derived from Aristotle, and, although it had been somewhat refined during the medieval period, it is probably easiest to approach it in its original form.

Aristotle argued that there are four 'causes' which account for the existence of any given thing. They were: the material cause (the stuff out of which the thing was made); the efficient cause (the agent which made the thing); the final cause (the purpose for which the thing exists); and the formal cause (the specific characteristics which make it this particular thing, rather than something else).

17 Allison, *The Rise of Moralsim*, p137.

It might help to apply Aristotle's analysis to a concrete object to see how it worked in practice. So, imagine a china cereal bowl. Its material cause is the clay out of which it was made. Its efficient cause is the potter who made it. Its final cause is holding milk and cornflakes. And its formal cause is its specific size, shape, and colour; the things which make it this specific bowl, and distinguish it from the other bits of crockery on the shelf.

In the case of actions, rather than specific things, the same analysis can be applied, with a slight variation. Since actions per se are not obviously made out of anything, it might appear that they fall outside Aristotle's scheme, since they have no material cause. But the medieval writers argued that actions do indeed have a material cause in two respects. First, they have a material cause *in which* the act arises—the agent who initiates the act—and, secondly, they have a material cause *about which* the act arises—the object of the act.[18]

So, if we alter our example slightly, and consider the act whereby the potter makes the cereal bowl, as opposed to the bowl itself, we can once again apply Aristotle's analysis. The material cause *in which* the act arises, and also the efficient cause of the act, is the potter herself.[19] The material cause *about which* the act arises is the lump of clay she uses. The final cause of the act is the making of a cereal bowl. And the formal cause of the act is the decision to make this specific cereal bowl, rather than a milk jug, or indeed anything else.

Now to this structure we must add a further complication or two. Because, when something is made, its maker often chooses not to act upon it directly, but to use a tool to focus and facilitate her work. The tool she uses has no inherent causative power—it cannot act by itself—but, when wielded by the maker, it is part of the causal nexus which explains why the thing is what it is. This tool could, therefore, be described as the instrumental cause of the thing—the instrument through which the efficient cause acted upon it.

In relation to concrete objects, and acts which relate to them, the concept of an instrumental cause is fairly easy to grasp. In the case of the cereal bowl, for example, the instrumental cause might be the potter's wheel on which the potter shaped the bowl. In relation to acts without a material dimension, the situation is perhaps less clear. Though one example of such a purely moral instrument might be the elements of bread and wine in the Lord's Supper. To a Reformed Protestant, of course, the bread and the wine have no inherent spiritual power, yet God uses them to communicate, in a spiritual manner, the body and blood of Christ to the believer. They could, therefore, be described as the instrumental cause of his spiritual act.[20]

[18] See T. Barlow, MS QCL 233, pp72–3.

[19] I am grateful to Dr Richard Cross for his assistance with the technicalities of causation.

[20] Edwards uses this example. J. Edwards, *The Doctrine of Faith and Justification set in a True Light* (London, 1708), p320.

In the specific context of the seventeenth-century debate on justification, yet another cause was added to this list, namely the meritorious cause. This cause was understood to be a type of instrumental cause which contributes to the desired effect, by rendering the effect worthy to take place. The meritorious cause is, in other words, whatever it is that earns the effect. To many Roman Catholic writers, the good works that flowed from grace could be considered, to some degree, as a meritorious cause of justification; because those good works had some inherent merit. To Reformed writers, of course, they could not, because all human works are corrupted by sin. Indeed, the only possible source of merit in the Reformed system are the works of Christ himself: only his works are truly worthy, being both unalloyed by sin (since Christ alone was without sin), and infinite in value (because Christ was God).[21]

A final element of seventeenth-century analysis which must be mentioned is the idea of an indispensable condition, or condition sine qua non (which was sometimes, confusingly called the cause sine qua non). An indispensable condition of a thing or act is a circumstance without which that thing or act could not exist, but which is not actually a cause of the existence of that thing or act. To return to the cereal bowl, for a moment: a necessary precondition of its existence is the property of nature whereby clay, when heated to a certain temperature for a certain time, becomes solid. This property of nature does not, of itself, cause the cereal bowl to exist, but the cereal bowl could certainly not exist without it. So this property of nature can be called a condition sine qua non of the cereal bowl's existence.

A significant aspect of the seventeenth-century discussion of soteriology was the attempt to clarify exactly how this causal scheme applied to the process of justification. And it is here that Allison has gone astray.

Allison's core thesis is that 'The question of the formal cause of justification . . . is central to the understanding of seventeenth-century soteriology.'[22] He chooses some influential theologians of the pre-Civil War period, and from their writings constructs a picture of what he calls the 'classical' or 'orthodox' Anglican position on the matter. Prominent among these earlier theologians is John Davenant (1572–1641), Bishop of Salisbury, whose polemic against Cardinal Bellarmine over this issue, the *Disputatio de Iustitia Habituali et Actuali* is perhaps the most sophisticated English treatment of the doctrine to have appeared before the Restoration.

In his discussion of Davenant's position, Allison writes:

[21] R. Muller, *Dictionary of Latin and Greek Theological Terms* (Grand Rapids, 1998), p63, s.v. 'Causa Meritoria.'

[22] Allison, *The Rise of Moralism*, px.

> Formal cause was agreed upon by all sides as the central problem in a discussion of justification. The form—or formal cause—of a thing is 'that by which a thing is what it is'. There was agreement that Christ's satisfaction was the meritorious cause . . . and faith was the instrumental cause . . . of our justification. It was however, the formal cause . . . of justification that separated Roman Catholic from Reformed theologians.[23]

For Roman Catholic theologians, such as Cardinal Bellarmine, the formal cause of justification, that, in other words, which makes it justification rather than some other process, is the infusion of inherent righteousness into the sinner. In the Roman Catholic scheme, therefore, what justifies a sinner before God is actually the personal righteousness of the individual justified, albeit given him by grace. For Reformed theologians such as Davenant, by contrast, the distinguishing characteristic of justification is the imputation of Christ's righteousness to the sinner. Accordingly, in the Reformed scheme, the righteousness which justifies a sinner before God is the personal righteousness of Christ, which God has graciously accounted to the believer. Allison contends that almost all pre-Civil War theologians were in substantial agreement with Davenant's presentation of the matter, and considered the imputation of Christ's personal righteousness to the believer to be the formal cause, the defining characteristic, of justification.

Allison then argues that this broad consensus broke down as the century wore on. Later Anglican writers, such as Taylor, Thorndike, Hammond, and Bull, refused to accept that the imputation of Christ's righteousness was the formal cause of justification. They insisted that Christ's righteousness is not imputed to the believer in a personal sense—it is not credited to the believer's individual account. Instead, Christ's personal righteousness has won a more lenient covenant for all believers. Because whereas, under the Old Covenant, complete and perfect obedience to God's law was required for one to be just in the sight of God, under the New Covenant sincere, though imperfect, righteousness is acceptable instead. The role of Christ's own righteousness in this scheme is thus limited to winning these more generous terms of salvation. Even so, since it is only because of Christ's righteousness that the new terms can be enjoyed, it is proper to call that righteousness the meritorious cause of justification.[24] For it is only on account of the righteousness of Christ that God chooses to treat imperfect human righteousness as if it were truly righteous.

Allison contends that the consequence of this approach, is to make sincere Christian obedience a constitutive part of justification. Because the essence of justification in the moralist scheme, he argues, is God's acceptance of sincere, in place of perfect, obedience as sufficient to justify a sinner. As Allison puts it

[23] Allison, *The Rise of Moralism*, p6.

[24] Ibid., p132.

in his discussion of George Bull: 'On account of Christ's righteousness our works, faith and repentance are accepted as righteous, our sins forgiven, and thereby we are justified.'[25] This process, whereby God imputes to our imperfect faith and works a righteousness which is not inherently theirs, on account of the merits of Christ, Allison describes as the 'imputation of faith for righteousness'.[26] And he is convinced that, for Bull, as for the other divines he discusses, it is the formal cause of justification.[27]

It is clear that John Spurr, in his more recent study of Restoration Anglicanism, has accepted the main outlines of Allison's thesis. His conception of pre-Civil War orthodoxy is clearly dependent upon it. Spurr writes, for example, echoing Allison:

> In the scholastic terminology of the sixteenth-century theologians, justification has three causes: the formal cause, which is what makes something what it is, the meritorious cause, and the instrumental cause. The formal cause of our justification was the imputation of Christ's righteousness to us. The meritorious cause was Christ's sacrifice, and the instrumental cause was faith.[28]

Equally, Spurr is dependent on Allison when it comes to analysing the precise nature of the theological shift which took place in many post-Civil War writers. He gives a representative survey of their writings, and then asks: 'But what was the formal cause of justification in this scheme? Modern critics are surely correct in suggesting that it was the conditional covenant.'[29] The modern critic he footnotes at this point is, of course, Allison. As Spurr puts it, the moralist writers 'had shifted the formal cause of justification from the imputation of Christ's righteousness to the condition upon which one enters the covenant of grace,'[30] namely, the sincere, though imperfect, Christian obedience, which brings a believer justification under the more lenient Gospel dispensation.

There are two problems with Allison's (and so Spurr's) presentation of these questions. The first relates to the claim that the Reformed writers agreed with their opponents about the meritorious cause of justification, but disagreed about its formal cause. In fact, the split between the formal and meritorious causes of justification is something which Reformed theologians deliberately resisted.[31] As far as Davenant is concerned, these two causes cannot be separated. He writes:

> In truth, such a formal cause of justification must be laid down as, at the same time, can be meritorious too. For unless it have in itself that dignity, on account of which

25 Ibid., p132. 26 Ibid., p180. 27 Ibid., p179.

28 Spurr, *The Restoration Church of England*, p299.

29 Ibid., p301.

30 Ibid., p302.

31 Davenant, *Disputatio de Iustitia Habituali et Actuali*, tr. J. Allport (London, 1844), p160.

man is reputedly justified, it never will be the formal cause through which he stands justified in the sight of God.[32]

Equally, although Davenant does hold to the idea that the imputation of Christ's righteousness is the formal cause of justification, he is aware that this is a technical term of metaphysics, and needs further clarification. He writes, for example:

To dismiss however philosophical speculation concerning the nature of the formal cause; when we are seeking for the formal cause of our justification, we seek for that on account of which, the sinner is received into the favour of God, through which he stands immediately well pleasing to God and accepted to eternal life; by the benefit of which he escapes the condemning sentence of the law, and, in fine, on which he may and ought to depend, for obtaining the favour and approbation of the heavenly judge.[33]

In fact, the metaphysical subtleties surrounding the nature of formal causes meant that Reformed writers frequently used other terms which, to them, appeared clearer. For example, a continental contemporary of the Restoration writers, the implacably orthodox Francis Turretin, used the phrase 'impulsive and meritorious cause' to describe it;[34] and, as we shall see, Thomas Barlow used, with equal readiness, the terms 'motive,' 'reason,' 'meritorious cause,' 'formal cause', and 'impulsive cause' in describing his position.[35] So, to the Reformed, the key question was not so much the technical one about the identification of justification's formal cause, as the more practical one about what exactly motivates God to forgive a sinner.

In addition to this misreading of the Reformed emphasis in the debate, Allison has gone astray in his description of moralist theology, at least insofar as it applies to George Bull. As we have seen, Allison's contention is that the moralist theologians, and George Bull amongst them, made God's acceptance of sincere, though imperfect Christian obedience, the formal cause of justification.

However, when George Bull discusses the precise scholastic terminology which Allison has employed, that is not quite what he says. Indeed he is very anxious to deny that works or Christian obedience bear any causal relation to justification at all, and he certainly does not include them in his definition of the formal cause of justification.

[32] Davenant, *Disputatio de Iustitia Habituali et Actuali*, tr. J. Allport (London, 1844), pp160–1.

[33] Ibid., p162.

[34] Turretin, *Institutes*, Topic XVI q.2 & q.3. R.A. Muller also uses 'causa impulsiva' to describe the Reformed orthodox position in the article on 'iustificatio' in his *Dictionary of Latin and Greek Theological Terms* (Carlisle, 1985).

[35] See, for example: Barlow, MS QCL 234, passim, in which all of these terms are used.

Bull's most explicit presentation of the matter comes in his reply to Tully's *Iustificatio Paulina*, the *Apologia pro Harmonia*.[36] There, he is attempting to identify the precise point at issue between him and Tully. And, contrary to Allison's reading of the matter, Bull asserts that there is actually no disagreement between him and Tully about the formal cause of justification. Indeed, Bull writes that 'Reformers are agreed concerning its formal cause, namely, that it consists in the remission of sins and acceptation of a man to eternal life.'[37] He goes on to say further that: 'all the Reformed are agreed . . . about the primary meritorious cause of our justification, that it is only to be sought in the satisfaction of Christ our Lord'.[38]

For Bull, the nub of the debate is, therefore, not so much a matter of the formal cause of justification, but the necessary precondition (or condition sine qua non) for it. He writes:

> The whole controversy therefore is concerning the indispensable cause, or *sine qua non*, or condition on our part which is requisite for justification. In short, this is really the point to be decided; on this the question turns, 'Under what conditions the remission of sins and the right to eternal salvation are promised in the gospel covenant?' Dr. Tully says, under the condition of faith alone, as a single virtue; we . . . confidently assert that it is under the condition of faith and repentance. . . . In the gospel covenant, procured and ratified by the meritorious satisfaction of Christ our Saviour, remission of sins and a right to eternal salvation is obtained on our part by faith and repentance, and these privileges are preserved by the fruits of faith and repentance.[39]

In other words, for Bull, Christian obedience is not part of the formal cause of justification.[40] The formal cause of justification, the essential definition of that process, is simply the gracious divine decision to justify the sinner and admit her to eternal life. Good works, or Christian obedience, bear, in Bull's presentation of the matter, no causal relationship to that decision, though they are a necessary precondition for that decision to be made.

So, in Bull's view, Christian obedience is best described as the condition sine qua non of justification. It is something without which that divine act will not take place, but it is not accurately described as a cause of that decision. And this is significant, because it enables him to argue that the only true cause of justification, in his scheme, is the merit of Christ.

36 Bull, *Apologia pro Harmonia*, tr. Burton (Oxford, 1843), pp258–9.
37 Ibid., p258.
38 Ibid., p259.
39 Ibid., p260.
40 Allison actually cites this passage, but its does not appear to influence his reading of Bull to any significant degree. Allison, *The Rise of Moralism*, p132.

Early on in the *Harmonia Apostolica*, Bull is expounding James 2:24 'Ye see then, how that by works a man is justified and not by faith only.' And he writes of that verse:

> by the phrase 'by works' St. James does not mean that our works are the principal or meritorious cause of our justification, for that depends on the mere and gracious mercy of God the Father, whereas the cause thereof is to be placed solely in the death and merits of Christ, and by the Apostle is really so declared.[41]

Although, he points out, the particle 'by' occasionally does denote causality in scripture, he writes, it does not do so here. Instead, it is used in a lowered sense, 'signifying the means of obtaining any thing, or the preceding condition, which is generally called the indispensable cause',[42] that is to say, the condition sine qua non, which, Bull thinks, is not a cause in the strict sense. Bull argues that his interpretation of the word is in line with other examples of scriptural use, for example in the phrase 'justified by faith', since, as he says, 'no one can be said to be justified by faith itself as a principal cause, or even as a cause at all, unless inaccurately speaking'.[43] In fact, he assumes that Christian obedience occupies the same place in his scheme that faith does in the Reformed scheme.

To sum up: Allison's contention is that in Bull's theology, the formal cause of justification is God's acceptance of imperfect human obedience as sufficient for a sinner to be counted just under the new, more lenient, covenant. Allison's claim is, therefore, that Bull believes that human works are part of the causal nexus which explains justification.

In fact, Bull carefully limits the formal cause of justification to the gratuitous divine decision to forgive the sinner and accept her to eternal life. To his mind, this guarantees that the obedience required under the new covenant bears no causal relationship to the process of justification. He conceives of obedience as merely a necessary prerequisite, a condition sine qua non, without which that gratuitous decision will not be made.

Now Bull is certainly engaging in some deft, and quite possibly suspect theological footwork here. And, as we shall see, his opponents argued that his description of good works as a condition sine qua non was actually a smokescreen which concealed a darker reality. But, for Bull, it was a vitally important point. To grant (as Allison argues that Bull grants) that good works or Christian obedience were included in the formal cause of justification, would be to stray too close to the Roman Catholic position outlined above. And that, in post-Restoration England, would be theological suicide.

[41] Bull, *Harmonia Apostolica*, p10. [42] Ibid., p10. [43] Ibid., p11.

For these reasons, both Bull's work, and the responses it provoked require renewed attention. Allison's core contention that the formal cause of justification is the key to understanding the developments in seventeenth-century soteriology has led him to distort his treatment of the debate. Neither Bull, nor his Reformed adversaries were unduly preoccupied with identifying the formal cause of justification, precisely because that was potentially confusing technical matter. When pushed to use the term, Bull deliberately limits the formal cause of justification to the divine decision to remit sins, and refuses to extend it to the acceptance of human works. Human obedience is for him, the condition of justification, the means to justification, even the instrument of justification—but it is not the cause of justification.

## THE ARGUMENT OF THE HARMONIST

The *Harmonia Apostolica* is an attempt to show how the teaching of St James in James 2:24: 'Ye see then, how that by works a man is justified, and not by faith only', is consistent with the teaching of St Paul in Romans 3:28: 'Therefore we conclude that a man is justified by faith without the deeds of the law.' It is set out in the form of two dissertations.

In the first dissertation, Bull lays out his understanding of James's doctrine of justification. In the second, he shows how Paul should be interpreted, so as not to contradict with it. Even the overall plan of his work shows how revolutionary Bull was being, and explains how shocking his work was to traditionally minded Protestants, because in the *Harmonia*, it is the 'epistle of straw' which provides the interpretative lens for the entire Pauline corpus, not vice versa.

Later on in his work, Bull sets out in more detail the hermeneutic assumptions which are implicit in this approach to the question. He writes:

> this may be laid down as a foundation; that it is more agreeable to explain St. Paul by St. James than the contrary... the words of St. James are so very clear and evident, that he who hesitates about their sense may well be said to seek a knot in a bullrush.[44]

In Bull's eyes, the meaning of the epistle of James is quite clear. So, whatever difficulty there is in the matter has to be attributed to Paul's writings. He notes that even Peter found Paul's writings a little opaque at times,[45] and further

[44] Ibid., p57.

[45] He cites 2 Peter 3:16: 'As also in all his epistles, speaking in them of these things; in which are some things hard to be understood, which they that are unlearned and unstable wrest, as they do also the other scriptures, unto their own destruction.'

remarks that, since, according to tradition, James's epistle was written to counter some misunderstandings of Pauline theology, it makes sense to start from James if one wishes to avoid making the very mistakes he was intending to address.[46]

Bull opens his first dissertation with an attack on the overprecise arguments employed by Reformed theologians to explain how their teaching squares with the Bible. 'What minute distinctions,' he writes,

> ingenious devices and contrivances, have interpreters used to reconcile this conclusion of St. James with the epistles of St. Paul . . . they have involved the doctrine of justification itself, which before was sufficiently easy and plain, in so many distinctions and subtleties, that theology does not afford an article more hard to be understood.[47]

Bull promises to avoid all that confusing technical paraphernalia, and return to what he claims is a simpler, more ancient theology.

He begins by unfolding what James means by justification. Bull writes: 'First, the word "to justify," according to its Greek and Hebrew acceptation, is used by him in its most usual sense, that is, as a term of law, meaning "to acquit," or "pronounce guiltless." '[48] Justification does not mean, therefore, to free someone entirely from sin, nor does it mean to make someone righteous. It means, quite simply, to remit sins. Accordingly,

> the justification which is preached in the gospel of Christ, is nothing else than the gracious act of God, by which, for Christ's sake he acquits those who truly believe, namely, those endowed with a perfected faith, and frees them from the guilt and punishment of all sins.[49]

This definition of justification, of course, accounts for his restriction of the formal cause of justification to the divine decision to forgive. This gracious divine decision, he believes, is the real essence of justification. And any preparatory conditions for this decision are nonetheless quite distinct from it, and so from the formal cause, the essential definition, of justification.

As we have seen, Bull underlines that when James talks of justification by works, he does not mean that our works are, in any way, the cause of justification. Rather, they are the necessary condition of justification. The only cause of justification beyond Father's gracious decision to forgive the sinner, is the meritorious death of Christ.[50] Bull sums up what he sees as James's position in the following words:

[46] Bull cites various unnamed 'ancients,' and Augustine, who held this view of the purpose of James's epistle. Bull, *Harmonia Apostolica*, p57.

[47] Bull, *Harmonia Apostolica*, p2.

[48] Ibid., p6. [49] Ibid., p8. [50] Ibid., p10.

A man, therefore, is said 'to be justified by works', because good works are ordered and established by God in the gospel covenant as the necessary condition for a man's justification, that is, that he may receive the forgiveness of sins, obtained through Christ, and become accepted of God to salvation.[51]

And, as he insists later on, that the only link between good works and salvation is that the first are the condition for the second.

The only foundation of that connection which our works have with eternal life is this: that they are a condition required in the gospel covenant, to which condition, upon its performance, are most graciously promised, in the same covenant, eternal rewards.[52]

It should be underlined that Bull's definition of justification makes no reference to the imputation of Christ's righteousness to the individual believer. To be sure, the righteousness of Christ has won for humanity the more lenient gospel covenant. And, as we have seen, Bull is prepared to describe it as the meritorious cause of justification for that reason.[53] But there is no sense in which the righteousness of Christ takes the place of the believer's own righteousness. Indeed, Bull argues that to impute righteousness to the believer means no more than looking upon the believer as just.[54] There is, here, no mystical transfer of the merits of Christ to the believer—the personal imputation of Christ's righteousness has simply dropped from the picture. Rather, on account of the merits of Christ, God freely justifies all those who fulfill the condition of the gospel covenant by their sincere, albeit imperfect works of faith and obedience.

Bull is adamant that his description of faith and obedience as the condition sine qua non for justification makes far more sense than the Reformed idea that faith is the instrumental cause of the process. 'What they advance,' he writes, 'respecting the instrumentality of faith in the matter of justification, is a trifling piece of sophistry.'[55] Instruments properly so called, he argues, are secondary efficient causes, assisting the principal efficient cause in the production of an effect, and faith simply cannot fulfil this role in justification. He argues:

For, in the first place, since justification is the act of God alone, and produced entirely without being merited on our parts, how our faith or any action of ours can give any assistance in effecting our justification is inconceivable. And in the next place, every instrumental cause... operates according to its own particular nature, and the production of the effect may be properly attributed to it. Now since justification is entirely the gracious act of God, by which he pardons our sins, and grants us salvation, it is extremely absurd to say, that either our faith, or our works, or anything else of ours, forgives our sins or grants salvation to our persons.[56]

[51] Ibid., p11. [52] Ibid., p31. [53] Ibid., pp10, 11.
[54] Ibid., p8. [55] Ibid., p17. [56] Ibid.

In other words, since justification is purely a gratuitous act of God, no action of ours can be said to contribute to it. Consequently, it is inept to describe our faith as an instrumental cause of justification: God needs no tool to pardon a sinner.

Bull thinks that faith might possibly be called an instrument in the process of justification, but only in the very limited sense that it is

> commanded by God and performed by his grace. For a condition being performed, may in a certain sense be called the means or instrument by which we obtain what is promised upon that condition, and this is called by some, the moral instrument.[57]

But if this is what is meant, then, Bull thinks, it must be categorically denied that faith is the only such instrument.

He argues instead that wherever in scripture promises are made to those who have faith, the faith meant 'is not to be taken for one single virtue, but comprehends, in its complete sense . . . all the works of Christian piety'.[58] In other words, when the scriptures discuss the faith which justifies, they do not mean faith considered as a single virtue, but the whole complex of obedient Christian living. Indeed, Bull notes, where faith is considered as a single virtue isolated from the others, such as in 1 Corinthians 13, Paul ranks it below charity. The only sense in which Bull is prepared to allow some degree of primacy to faith, is that it is the root and source of the other virtues. But even here, he sets himself apart from Reformed orthodoxy, because what he means is not that true faith necessarily produces the other virtues (as the Reformed insisted), but simply that a person endowed with faith is rather more likely to produce good works than one who is not.

Furthermore, Bull argues that 'if faith be considered alone, and separated from every other virtue, there is no act of it which is saving, or which may not take place in a wicked and therefore unjustified man'.[59] He deploys the traditional Reformed division of faith into the three acts of knowledge, assent, and reliance, and argues that none of these are necessarily confined to justified people. He notes that knowledge of the contents of faith can exist in the worst people; that one can assent to its truth even when void of charity (and so, by Paul's own admission in 1 Corinthians 13, be unjustified); and, finally, that any reliance upon the promises given in the faith for salvation must be a conditional reliance, and therefore ineffective unless the condition (i.e. good works) stipulated in the promise is fulfilled. He concludes:

> since knowledge without practice, assent of the mind without love of the heart, confidence in the promises of the gospel without a sincere endeavour to fulfill its

[57] Bull, *Harmonia Apostolica*, p17.

[58] Ibid., p18. [59] Ibid., p22.

conditions, are of no avail with God, we must necessarily conclude that no one is justified in the sight of God by faith alone without the other virtues.[60]

To Bull's mind, if there is one virtue which should be singled out as having a singular importance for salvation, it is not faith but charity. Bull calls charity 'the form of justifying faith.'[61] Love for God and one's neighbour is that which makes justifying faith complete, because only works inspired by such love are acceptable to God. Good works receive their goodness from love, not from faith. Bull writes: 'it is true that every good work really arises from faith; but it is also true that faith is not of itself sufficient to perform any good work, nor to be accepted of God to salvation: for love must be added to it, by which a man comes to God.'[62]

The driving force behind Bull's understanding of the relative place of faith and good works in the process of justification is his understanding of the New Covenant, since that is the judicial context in which justification takes place. He argues that justification, like any forensic process, involves a judge, an accused, and a law. In justification, of course, the judge is God and the accused is the sinner who needs justification. But Bull argues that the law involved could only be one of two mentioned in the scriptures: either the Mosaic law of the Old Covenant, or what he calls the Law of Christ, the requirement of the New Covenant. To be justified, one must be acquitted under one of those laws. But, as Bull notes, 'no man can be justified or acquitted, unless he hath obeyed the law by which he is tried'.[63] Thus, in his scheme, obedience is equally essential under both Covenants. Acquittal, under either Covenant, comes only upon condition of the obedience which the Covenant in question enjoins. There is no such thing, therefore, as an unconditional covenant.

So Bull believes that the Reformed, like Martin Luther before them, have misunderstood the nature of the New Covenant. He writes: 'they taught that the gospel consisted of promises only; that Christ gave the world no law, but explained the law already given; and freed it from the faulty comments of the scribes and Pharisees.'[64] As Bull saw it, in the Reformed view obedience is not required under the New Covenant. Salvation is simply offered without any conditions. And this, he feared, would inevitably lead to libertinism, particularly amongst the uneducated. He writes: 'In one word, whoever of the common people shall receive this doctrine undisguisedly delivered . . . though you should afterward invent a thousand distinctions, you will never persuade him to perform any good works.'[65]

He continues:

[60] Ibid., p28. [61] Ibid., p26. [62] Ibid., p37.
[63] Ibid., p19. [64] Ibid., pp20–1. [65] Ibid., p34.

> to prevent this dreadful error it must ever be observed, as an undeniable truth, that Christ, in his Sermon [on the Mount], not only explained the moral law, but also laid it down as his own, and required its observance, assisted by the grace of the gospel, from all Christians, as a condition of the covenant indispensably necessary.[66]

The law of Christ is called the law of liberty, therefore, not because it frees us from the obligation to obedience. It is called the law of liberty because it is comparatively more liberal than the Mosaic law in three particular respects: first, because it frees us from the ceremonial law; secondly, because it offers us forgiveness, which was not available under the Mosaic law; and thirdly, because it promises us the assistance of the Holy Spirit, which the Mosaic law could not provide. These more lenient conditions have been won for us by the sacrifice of Christ. Nonetheless, Christ's new law remains a law, and so cannot be fulfilled without obedience. So Bull is quite clear that, even under the New Covenant, we shall be judged according to our works. He writes 'if according to our works we are declared just in the judgement by Christ, by our works we must be made just in this life by the law of Christ.'[67]

Bull also argues, in opposition to the Reformed view, that justification is not a once for all change of status, but an ongoing process. He writes, when considering a particular Reformed objection to his scheme:

> this objection is built on a false idea, that justification is, as they assert, an instantaneous act, entirely completed at once, in a single moment. This can by no means be admitted. For justification is a continued act, and only then perfectly finished, when a man hath entirely, and to the last, fulfilled the condition of that covenant, by which he is justified.[68]

In other words, we must continue to fulfill the precondition of justification by sincere obedience throughout our lives. And if we cease to fulfill that condition, if we cease to perform those good works, then we are no longer justified.

Of course, Bull underlines that the suspension of justification upon our good works must not be understood in a Roman Catholic manner. Our works are never inherently meritorious nor deserving of reward, they are merely the conditions to which the gracious terms of the gospel covenant attach rewards which far outweigh their real value.[69] Good works are therefore not merely the signs of a faith which justifies, they are the conditions of justification and so also of salvation, 'for when we are justified in this life, a right to eternal life is truly conferred upon us, according to the law of Christ, when we are judged.'[70]

[66] Bull, *Harmonia Apostolica*, pp21–2. [67] Ibid., p29.
[68] Ibid., p44. [69] Ibid., p31. [70] Ibid., p30.

Bull goes on to note two established Reformed assumptions which, he thinks, actually lend support to his own position. The first is the Reformed insistence that justifying faith must be productive of good works. 'Here then,' he exclaims,

> what is the difference? Whoever properly attends to this subject will assuredly allow, that the point on which the controversy turns is a metaphysical subtlety. Whether, forsooth, the faith *which is living*, or faith *in that it is living*, is required to justification? In short the matter comes at last, as some very learned divines have clearly shown, merely to the use of the particle, *quatenus*, as far as. . . . The mountains are in labour, and they have produced a mouse.[71]

Of course, what Bull calls 'this trifling and almost imperceptible point of distinction',[72] is, to the Reformed mind, the theological Rubicon between orthodoxy and heresy.

The second Reformed tenet Bull refers to is the assertion that good works are necessary to salvation, something, he notes, which is also universally acknowledged. He argues that, since justification confers a right to eternal life, there can be no distinction between the terms required for justification and those required for salvation. He writes: 'Whoever therefore allows that good works are a condition necessarily to be performed to the obtaining of eternal life, by the divine promise, he by this very act confesses, that a right to eternal life cannot be obtained without works.'[73]

So, in his first dissertation, Bull lays out his substantive doctrine of justification. His second is a sustained attempt to square this with the doctrine advanced in the Pauline epistles. He considers various proposed ways of reconciling Paul with James: that James was talking about justification before men, and Paul about justification before God; that James was speaking of a dead faith, and Paul of a living one;[74] and that Paul wrote of our first justification before good works, and James of our second justification, by good works.[75] But he rejects all of these in turn as inadequate.

Instead, Bull argues that if Paul and James are to be reconciled, the faith which Paul is talking about must include good works. So that when Paul says we are justified by faith, he intends to include the whole complex of Christian obedience as well. He writes: 'Faith, then, to which justification is attributed by St. Paul, is not to be understood as one single virtue, but denotes the whole condition of the gospel covenant, that is, comprehends in one word all the

[71] Ibid., pp33–4. [72] Ibid., p34. [73] Ibid., p39.

[74] Both of these are accepted Reformed positions which we shall re-encounter.

[75] This was a position advanced by some Roman Catholic theologians.

works of Christian piety.'[76] It therefore follows that the works which Paul excludes from justification are not the works of the moral law, or the law of Christ, but merely the works of the Mosaic law.[77]

Bull, of course, admits that the Mosaic law did include the moral law, alongside the prescriptions of the ritual law. So, prima facie, Paul must have excluded both of them from justification. But Bull answers this objection:

> The works of the moral law, are not excluded from justification by St Paul simply as such, but only so far as they are required in the Mosaic covenant, and are part of the condition annexed to that covenant; in a word, so far only as they may be considered separate from evangelical grace.[78]

It is therefore moral works that do not arise from grace, not moral works pure and simple, that Paul excludes from justification.

As we have seen, Bull considered the Mosaic law to be deficient in several respects. These were principally that the Mosaic law does not offer forgiveness of sins, and that it does not promise the assistance of the Holy Spirit. Indeed, Bull argues that the law contains no spiritual or heavenly promises at all, but only earthly and temporal ones: it made promises about the land, in other words, not about heaven. Bull writes: 'as the old law gave no full and sufficient pardon for past sins, so neither did it afford any assistance to prevent future ones.'[79] Indeed, Bull's opinion of the Mosaic law's effect on human behaviour is rather low. He writes: 'the Mosaic law, by containing only temporal promises and threatenings, was therefore inclined to produce in men a mean and sordid disposition, entirely foreign to true and genuine piety.'[80] And since the law was actually unable to produce this genuine piety, Paul excludes the works performed under its influence alone from the process of justification, because they were not really good.

In concluding the second dissertation, Bull writes:

> St. Paul rejects from justification the following descriptions of works: 1st ritual works prescribed by the ceremonial law. 2nd moral works performed by the natural powers of man, in a state either of the law, or mere nature, before and without the grace of the gospel. 3rd Jewish works, or that trifling righteousness inculcated by Jewish masters. 4th and lastly, all works separate from Christ the mediator, which would obtain salvation by their own power, or without reference to the covenant of grace established by the blood of Christ. . . . On the other hand, that the moral works arising from the grace of the gospel do, by the power of the gospel covenant, efficaciously conduce to the justification of man and his eternal salvation, and so are absolutely necessary,

[76] Bull, *Harmonia Apostolica*, p58. [77] Ibid., p75.
[78] Ibid., p78. [79] Ibid., p95. [80] Ibid., p119.

St. Paul not only does not deny, but is employed almost entirely in establishing. And this is the very point for which St. James contends.[81]

And so the apostles are reconciled.

## THE ENTRENCHMENT OF MORALISM

From what has been said so far, it should be clear that homing in on the formal cause of justification is not the most helpful way to approach George Bull's theology. Bull makes a series of innovative and interlocking doctrinal moves which together distance him from the Reformed position. We need to grasp the breadth and subtlety of his approach if we are to understand both why it commended itself to many of his contemporaries, and why it provoked such a furious reaction from his theological opponents. Because Bull's stance of justification was not an attack on just one aspect of Reformed teaching, but deliberately engaged with his opponents across a broad front.

It might, therefore, be helpful at this point, to give a summary outline of Bull's understanding of the doctrine of justification. The key points of his argument are:

1. The New Covenant, just like the Old, is conditional in nature.
2. The Old Covenant was defective because its promises were material rather than spiritual in nature; it offered neither forgiveness of sins nor the assistance of grace to those who fulfilled its terms. It also required from human beings perfect and comprehensive obedience to the commands of the law.
3. The New Covenant, by contrast, offers both forgiveness of sins and the assistance of grace to those who fulfill the condition it lays down. And that condition is not perfect obedience, but sincere obedience.
4. These lenient new terms are won for us by the righteousness of Christ, upon whose account our imperfect works are accepted as a sufficient condition for our justification, although they have no inherent merit.
5. The righteousness of Christ is, therefore, the sole impulsive or meritorious cause of justification.
6. The righteousness of Christ is not, however, imputed to the believer in a personal way.

[81] Ibid., p194.

7. Justification is defined as the purely gratuitous act of God, whereby He pardons a sinner and accepts her to eternal life.
8. Justification cannot be separated from salvation, and the conditions for both are therefore the same.
9. The obedience required as the precondition of justification bears no causal relationship to that act, but is rather the condition sine qua non for it.
10. It follows that when Paul states that we are justified by faith, he intends, by the word 'faith,' the whole complex of Christian obedience to the law of the New Covenant—a faith, in other words, accompanied by all the other virtues, and perfected by love.
11. And when Paul states that we are justified by faith alone without works, he means only to exclude the ceremonial works of the law, and such works as are performed without the help of grace.
12. The Reformed insistence that faith as a single virtue is the instrumental cause of justification is philosophically incoherent.
13. The Reformed teaching on justification is dangerously vulnerable to an antinomian inference.

As we have pointed out, the *Harmonia Apostolica*, though it became the lodestone of an intense theological debate, did not result in significant preferment for its author. His opponents came out of the controversy rather better. But we should not conclude from this that Bull's views were significantly discredited. Rather, as his biographer noted, they became increasingly fashionable.[82] Indeed, Nelson believed that Bull's opponents, by making the controversy so public, actually assisted with the spread of Bull's ideas. He commented that 'they of the English clergy, who were the least favourable to it, became the greatest promoters of it, while by their endeavours to suppress it, they made it effectually spread the more'.[83]

To see just how swiftly Bull's controversial views became an acceptable option within the Church of England, we need look no further than Gilbert Sheldon's successor but one as Archbishop of Canterbury, John Tillotson (1630–94). Tillotson's teaching on justification is virtually a facsimile of Bull's. Yet it provoked an overt protest only from that irascible Reformed polemicist, John Edwards. In other words, the controversial doctrine that Sheldon had supported from a distance, had become an acceptable teaching for the Primate to advance from the pulpit, and in the press. In order to make

[82] Nelson, *Life of Bull*, p257. [83] Ibid., p99.

clear the full extent of the overlap between Tillotson's position and Bull's, we shall follow the summary outline given above.

Like Bull, Tillotson is clear that the New Covenants, like the Old, is conditional in nature.[84] Again like Bull he believes that the New Covenant is superior to the Old, because its promises are spiritual in nature, whereas those of the Old were predominantly temporal. He writes of the New Covenant: 'It is a testament established upon better promises, the clear promises of eternal life, which were but darkly revealed in the Old Testament, that being established either solely or principally upon temporal promises.'[85]

Tillotson is clear, as Bull is, that the condition of justification under the New Covenant is not a perfect but a sincere, though imperfect, righteousness, and that these more lenient terms have been won for us by the merit of Christ. As he puts it, Christ became incarnate so that he could 'by the merit and satisfaction of his death and sufferings appease and reconcile God to man, and purchase for them the pardon of their sins upon the condition of faith and repentance and sincere obedience'.[86] And he points out that 'after the gospel was revealed, we were set free from the severe and harsh dispensations of the law'.[87] and the severe requirements of the Old Covenant were replaced with these 'easy and reasonable conditions'.[88]

Tillotson is again at one with Bull in arguing that the lenient terms of the New Covenant are won for us by Christ. He underlines that 'all our obedience is imperfect, and is so far from meriting that it stands in need of pardon.... Christ hath merited that our imperfect obedience should be accepted by God, notwithstanding its imperfection.'[89] And, for this reason, he too describes the righteousness of Christ as the 'procuring or meritorious cause' of justification.[90] And, falling discreetly silent just as Bull does, he makes no mention of a personal imputation of Christ's righteousness to the believer beyond this.

Echoing Bull, Tillotson confines his definition of justification to the gratuitous divine decision to forgive a sinner. He writes: 'Justification in scripture signifies no more than the pardon and remission of sins.'[91] Though, again like Bull, he does not instinctively reach for the technical term 'formal cause' to express his view.

Tillotson is clear that justification is inseparable from salvation, and so the conditions for both are the same. He notes: 'I think this is universally agreed by divines, that whatsoever puts a man into a state of justification and pardon: puts man into a state of salvation.'[92] And again:

[84] J. Tillotson, *Sermons* (London, 1696–1704), xii pp242, 273.
[85] Ibid., p2.
[86] Ibid., p214.
[87] Ibid., p247.
[88] Ibid., p256.
[89] Ibid., p288.
[90] Ibid., p239.
[91] Ibid., p230.
[92] Ibid., p272.

I put these, justification and salvation, together, partly because they are of the same consideration, as to the influence which faith hath upon them; and the latter follows upon the former, for if we are justified by faith, that is, have our sins pardoned, by the same act of faith we are saved from hell, and consequently made capable of eternal life.[93]

Tillotson describes the sincere obedience which is required for justification consistently as a condition, rather than as a cause. He calls it 'the whole and entire condition required upon our parts, upon the performance of which, God hath promised to pardon our sins and to save us'.[94] But he is adamant that these acts of obedience 'have nothing of virtue, or merit, of any natural or moral efficacy to deserve, or procure such a benefit as the pardon of our sins',[95] and for that reason, God's act of justification is properly described as gratuitous.

Justifying faith, in Tillotson's view, again as in Bull's, 'doth include in it obedience to the precepts of the gospel',[96] And when Paul excludes works from the process of justification, he meant only works performed outside the New Covenant. He writes:

St Paul doth plainly oppose faith to the law, and the righteousness of it to the works of the law; and it will clearly appear to anyone that will carefully read over these discourses of St Paul's that by faith is meant the dispensation of the gospel; and by the law the Mosaical administration: and the result of all these discourses is, that men are not justified by performing the works which the legal dispensation required, but by assenting and submitting to the revelation of the gospel.[97]

Just like Bull, Tillotson can make no sense at all of the Reformed description of faith as the instrumental cause of justification. He asserts that 'faith can in no propriety of language be said to be the instrument of our pardon'.[98] And he argues his case on similar grounds to the writer of the *Harmonia*, namely that the Reformed wrench the term well beyond its ordinary use. 'An instrument,' he writes, 'is something subordinate to the principal efficient cause, and made use of by it to produce the effect; and this, in natural and artificial causes may be understood, but what notion to have of a moral instrument, I confess I am at a loss.'[99]

Finally, he is quite as convinced as Bull is, that his understanding of the situation 'is a doctrine more according to godliness, [and] tends more to quicken men to obedience and a holy life';[100] and, for that very reason, his teaching should be preferred to the teaching of the Reformed. Because, he says, it is impossible to show the need for obedience if one can enjoy remission of sins without it. He concludes, of his opponent's theology, 'I never could see how antinomianism could solidly be confuted upon those principles.'[101]

[93] Tillotson, *Sermons* (London, 1696–1704), p228. [94] Ibid., p230.
[95] Ibid., p256. [96] Ibid., p219. [97] Ibid., p245. [98] Ibid., p230.
[99] Ibid., p239. [100] Ibid., p259. [101] Ibid., p260.

As can be seen, the extent of the overlap between Bull's position and Tillotson's is truly remarkable. And it is the more surprising because Bull and Tillotson have tended to be seen as exemplifying rather different groups within the later Stuart Church. Tillotson has been seen, almost universally, as a lynchpin of the Latitudinarian party,[102] whereas Bull has usually been identified as a prominent member of the High Church party.[103] But it would seem that, whatever their ecclesiological and political sympathies may have been, Bull and Tillotson embraced a virtually identical teaching on justification. And it may have been that which encouraged Tillotson to suggest Bull for the prebend that he received in 1678.[104]

But Tillotson is by no means alone in his similarity to Bull. Indeed, shortly after Bull's work was first published, there was a rash of publications advancing views akin to that of the *Harmonia*. Edward Fowler (1632–1714), for example, advanced very similar views, both in his defence of Latitudinarian churchmen, *The Principles and Practices of Certain Moderate Divines of the Church of England* (1670),[105] and in *The Design of Christianity* (1671).[106] So did William Sherlock (1641–1707) in his *A Discourse Concerning the Knowledge of Jesus Christ and our Union and Communion with Him* (1674).[107]

Indeed, in some respects, Fowler and, more particularly, Sherlock extended Bull's assault on the Reformed position by launching an overt attack on the Reformed teaching that Christ's righteousness is imputed to the believer in a personal way. Fowler is certainly more open than Bull about the way in which theologians of his ilk have reconceived the imputation of Christ's righteousness. He writes, of the Latitudinarian churchmen he defends:

> This, then, is their notion of Christ's imputed righteousness: that those which are sincerely righteous, and from an inward living principle allow themselves in no

[102] E.g. M.I.J. Griffin, *Latitudinarianism in the Seventeenth Century Church of England* (Leiden, 1992), p118; W.M. Spellman, *The Latitudinarians and the Church of England, 1660–1700* (London, 1995), p5.

[103] C.J. Abbey and J.H. Overton, *The English Church in the Eighteenth Century* (London, 1902), p40; H.R. McAdoo, *The Spirit of Anglicanism* (New York, 1965), p398.

[104] *ODNB*, s.v. 'George Bull'.

[105] E. Fowler, *The Principles and Practices of Certain Moderate Divines of the Church of Englandi* (London, 1671): for faith as including obedience, p114; for God's acceptance of imperfect righteousness for the sake of Christ, p126; for faith which includes obedience as the condition of justification under the new covenant, pp165–6.

[106] Fowler, *The Design of Christianity* (London, 1760): for obedience as well as faith as the condition of the New Covenant, pp76–7; for the defects of the Old Covenant, p134; for the tendency of the Reformed view to encourage antinomianism, p189.

[107] W. Sherlock, *A Discourse Concerning the Knowledge of Jesus Christ and our Union and Communion with Him* (London, 1678): for God's acceptance under the New Covenant of imperfect righteousness for the sake of Christ, pp33–4; for the weakness of the Mosaic law, p165; for Christ's death as improving the terms of the Covenant, pp184–5; for our imperfect righteousness as the condition of the New Covenant, p209.

known sin, nor in the neglect of any known duty, which is to be truly evangelically righteous, shall be dealt with and rewarded, in and through Christ, as if they were perfectly, and in a strict legal sense so.[108]

Bull, of course, understood the process similarly, but was not quite so explicit as Fowler that this was a point of conscious disagreement with the Reformed. Fowler takes his argument further by denying that there is any scriptural warrant for the Reformed understanding of imputation at all. He writes:

That Christ's righteousness is properly made ours, I am confident that there is no scripture that tells us so. All that we find asserted in the gospel, as to this matter, is this: that real benefits and advantages, which are likewise exceedingly great and excellent, do by the grace of Christ accrue to us.[109]

William Sherlock's *Discourse* occasioned a small controversy of its own. Sherlock's professed target was what he saw as the excesses of puritan piety. But, since he focused his attack on a doctrine right at the heart of Reformed belief, it was equally offensive to Reformed Anglicans as to their dissenting brethren. An Anglican layman, Edward Polhill, wrote a rejoinder to Sherlock's work in *An Answer to the Discourse of Mr. William Sherlock* (1675). And in his preface to his *Animadversions upon Dr Sherlock's Book entitled, A Vindication of the Holy and Ever Blessed Trinity* (1695), the implacable Anglican loyalist, Robert South, described Sherlock's work as 'a very heterodox book'[110] which 'utterly evacuates and overthrows the doctrine of free grace, and the redemption of mankind thereby; and indeed by consequence, the whole economy of the Christian religion'.[111]

Sherlock targeted

those who are very zealous to advance Christ's person, to the prejudice and reproach of his religion. Who, instead of those substantial duties of the love of God, and man, and universal holiness of life, have introduced a fanciful application of Christ to ourselves, and union to him.[112]

His opponents, he argues, have encouraged believers to rely upon a fictional union with Christ for salvation. But he is adamant that the only sort of reliance on Christ which is proper to the believer is 'expecting to be

[108] Fowler, *Principles and Practices*, p126. [109] Ibid., p129.

[110] R. South, *Animadversions upon Dr Sherlock's Book entitled, A Vindication of the Holy and Ever Blessed Trinity* (London, 1695), pii.

[111] Ibid., pix.

[112] Sherlock, *A Discourse Concerning the Knowledge of Jesus Christ and our Union and Communion with Him* (London, 1678), pp7–8.

saved according to the terms of the gospel covenant; that is by believing and obeying the gospel of Christ.'[113]

As we have noted, Sherlock's approach to justification is similar to Bull's in several significant respects. However, he goes beyond Bull in launching a fearsome assault on the Reformed teaching about the mystical union of the believer with Christ. Sherlock writes:

When scripture describes the profession of Christianity, a sincere belief and obedience to the gospel, by having Christ, and being in Christ, and coming to him, and receiving him; these men expound these phrases to... signify I know not what unintelligible union, and spiritual progress and closure of the soul with him, and union of persons, instead of an agreement in faith and manners.[114]

Of course, the language of puritan piety he criticises here, was based on the theological concepts of Reformed orthodoxy. The doctrine of union with Christ was, in other words, quite as important to Robert South as it was to the dissenting Reformed, since it underpinned the notion of imputed righteousness which was essential to the Reformed understanding of justification.[115] And Sherlock, for his part, was aware of who his adversaries were. He writes,

How dangerous it is to pre-possess our fancies with some arbitrary notions in religion, which naturally force men to pervert the scriptures to make them speak the orthodox language. To this we owe all those nice and subtle distinctions, which constitute the body of systematical divinity, which commonly have no other design than to evade the force of scripture, or to bribe it to speak on their side.[116]

Like Bull, in other words, he knew that he was taking on the champions of Reformed orthodoxy.

Sherlock argues that the scriptural metaphors describing the relationship between Christ and believers, metaphors so dear to Reformed piety, refer primarily to the whole Church and not to individual Christians.[117] He further notes that this relationship, this union

is not a natural union, but a political union, that is, such a union as is between a prince and his subjects: Christ is the spiritual king, and all Christians are his subjects, and our union with Christ consists in our belief in his revelations, obedience to his laws, and subjection to his authority.[118]

[113] Ibid., p15.
[114] Ibid., p67. Tillotson took a similarly dim view of the metaphorical language of Reformed piety. Tillotson, *Sermons*, xii pp231, 262, 265.
[115] Cf. Barlow, MS QCL 234, 135r and Tully, *Iustificatio Paulina*, p81.
[116] Sherlock, *Discourse*, p83. Cf. Bull, *Harmonia Apostolica*, p2.
[117] Sherlock, *Discourse*, p88.
[118] Ibid., p96.

The believer's union with Christ, therefore, is identical to the condition for justification under the New Covenant: namely, belief and obedience. We are united to Christ only in the sense that we become like him. Sherlock writes: 'Herein consists our union to Christ, that we have the same temper of mind which he had: for there can be no union of souls and spirits without this, that they are acted by the same principles, and love and choose the same things.'[119]

Union with Christ, for Sherlock, means, therefore, little more than agreement with him. And holiness of life, in his view, is not the effect of our union with Christ, but the condition of it:

> For the scripture places the formal nature of our union to Christ in a subjection to his authority, and an obedience to his laws . . . and therefore an holy life must not only follow our union to Christ as the effect of it, but must at least go before it, because by this we are united to Christ.[120]

Sherlock emphatically rejects a more organic or mystical understanding of this union, and refuses to see it as a particular source of grace. He writes: 'when Christ is called our life, the meaning is, that he hath published the word of life to us, which contains the most express promises of a blessed immortality, and the most plain and easy directions how to attain it.'[121] He is equally clear that this union cannot possibly be a source of righteousness for us. He writes,

> how vain and precarious this principle is, which too many make the foundation of their faith, that Christ as mediator fulfilled all righteousness in their stead, whose mediator he was. . . . There is no foundation in reason or scripture to fancy such a union between Christ and believers . . . as should entitle believers to the personal righteousness of Christ.[122]

Sherlock emphatically rejects the idea that righteousness can be transferred from one person to another. He writes:

> personal and inherent perfections cannot pass out of one person, nor be made over to any other, as money and lands are: and therefore whatever other privileges we may enjoy by our marriage to Christ, his personal excellencies cannot be ours, though his person were.[123]

Under the gospel covenant, a personal righteousness is required of us, and no external relation can supply our lack of it.[124] Christ is our mediator in that he improves the terms of the covenant, not in that he fulfills the terms for us.[125] As he makes clear:

> the righteousness of Christ is our righteousness, when we speak of the foundation of the covenant, but if we speak of the terms of the covenant, then we must have a

119 Sherlock, *Discourse*, p107. 120 Ibid., p217. 121 Ibid., p142.
122 Ibid., pp198–9. 123 Ibid., p174.
124 Ibid., p181. 125 Ibid., pp184–5.

righteousness of our own, for the righteousness of Christ will not serve the turn: Christ's righteousness and our own are both necessary to our salvation, the first as the foundation of the covenant, the second as the condition of it.[126]

Sherlock attacks the Reformed contention that Christ's active righteousness could be transferred to us. He maintains that Christ was bound to fulfill the law for himself, as all human beings are, and so he needed that righteousness for himself.[127] Sherlock also criticizes the Reformed for having too unforgiving an understanding of God. He writes, of the orthodox position:

The sum of this argument is, that there never was, nor ever can be, a covenant of grace, that God still exacts the rigorous perfection of the law from us, and that we must not appear before him without a compleat and perfect righteousness of our own, or of another.[128]

But this, he says, denigrates divine justice, 'For all mankind have accounted it an act of goodness (without the least suspicion of injustice in it) to remit injuries and offences without exacting any punishment.'[129]

So Sherlock extended Bull's attack on the Reformed understanding of justification by dismantling the orthodox understanding of the nature of Christ's union with believers. Bull had come up with a new understanding of justification, but it was Sherlock who led the charge against the idea of imputed righteousness. He was not the only one who did so,[130] but his attack was the most comprehensive, and the most notorious, and the Reformed who came after him were forced to defend the doctrine of imputed righteousness with renewed vigour.

## THE ROOTS OF MORALISM

A question naturally arises as to how Bull developed his new understanding of justification. Most recent studies have seen him as part of the 'holy living' school, a group of divines holding similar views on the matter, who emerged in England during the Civil War. Spurr,[131] McGrath,[132] and Allison[133] assume

126 Ibid., p209. 127 Ibid., p191. Cf. Barlow, MS QCL 233 p222.

128 Sherlock, *Discourse*, p195. 129 Ibid., p28.

130 Edwards cites Glanvill and Humfrey as doing the same. Edwards, *Doctrine*, pp300–1.

131 Spurr, *Restoration Church of England*, pp299, 304–5, 312.

132 A.E. McGrath, *Iustitia Dei: A History of the Christian Doctrine of Justification*, 2 vols (Cambridge, 1986), ii p108.

133 Allison, *The Rise of Moralism*, ppx, 192.

that this group was essentially home-grown, their theology representing a response to the pressures of the Commonwealth period.[134]

It is certainly the case that Bull read, and was influenced by, two of the most prominent mid-century Anglican theologians who departed from the Reformed understanding of justification: Jeremy Taylor (1613–67), Bishop of Down and Connor, and Henry Hammond (1605–60). Bull's biographer, Robert Nelson, counts these two men as amongst the most significant influences upon Bull's thought.[135] Intriguingly, though, Nelson also lists two continental Arminian, or Remonstrant, theologians as having played an equally important part in Bull's theological formation: Hugo Grotius and Simon Episcopius.[136] And this is significant, because Grotius, through his exegetical works, and Episcopius, through his systematics, were the leading articulators of the Arminian opposition to continental Reformed orthodoxy. They were the writers who gave to Arminianism a breadth and coherence which increasingly commended itself to rationally minded Protestants across Europe as the century drew on. So if Bull was learning from these men, he was receiving both an intellectually robust and battle-hardened critique of Reformed theology, and a fully fledged alternative system.

Bull's positive engagement with these Arminian authors might surprise us. Bull has been portrayed by some scholars as essentially hostile to their school of thought. Henry McAdoo, for example, has written of Bull:

> Nor was it accurate to call him an Arminian, for that admiration of Episcopius and Grotius which was shared by so convinced a Laudian as Hammond, so scholastic a writer as Bramhall as well as by the Latitudinarians, found no place in his writings. On the contrary, he regarded Episcopius and Grotius as undermining the authority and the necessary function of the Fathers.[137]

It is true, of course, that Bull did write one book entirely dedicated to the refutation of Episcopius, the *Judicium Ecclesiae Catholicae* (1694). But it is important to remember that Bull only intended, in this, to address Episcopius' contention that the divinity of Christ, although a true doctrine, was not an article of the Christian faith necessary for salvation. And, as we shall see, Bull's *Defence of the Nicene Creed* (1695) shows marked evidence of agreement with Episcopius. Indeed, in the preface to that work, Bull describes Episcopius as 'a most learned theologian,' though lamenting his lack of familiarity with

[134] Allison, *The Rise of Moralism*, pp194–5.

[135] Nelson, *Life of Bull*, p24.

[136] Ibid. Robert Cornwall rather unaccountably fails not mention the two Arminian writers in his account of Bull's theological formation, though Nelson mentions them in the same breath as Hammond and Taylor. *ODNB*, s.v. 'George Bull'.

[137] McAdoo, *Spirit of Anglicanism*, p398.

the patristic writers.[138] And if one turns to Episcopius's teaching on justification, the agreement between Bull and the foremost exponent of systematic Arminianism becomes clear.

Episcopius advanced his position on justification first in the *Disputationes Theologicae Tripartitae* (1646), and developed it further in his *Opera* (1650, 1678). The many similarities between Bull and the Dutch writer begin with his understanding of the two Covenants. Like Bull, Episcopius is clear that the New Covenant is every bit as conditional as the Old.[139] He also asserts that the promises made in the Old Covenant were purely carnal and temporal in nature, involving neither the forgiveness of sins nor the gift of the Holy Spirit.[140] Episcopius is even willing, just as Bull is, to make rather derogatory remarks about the requirements of the Old Covenant, writing at one point: 'the ceremonial commandments were many, varied and sordid.'[141] And like Bull, he concludes from that that Paul meant to exclude from the process of justification only the works of the Mosaic law, not all good works whatsoever.[142]

Episcopius' reading of the terms of the New Covenant is also exactly the same as Bull's: what is required from us is sincere, not perfect righteousness.[143] Like Bull, Episcopius is clear that the only thing that makes our sincere but imperfect works acceptable to God is the righteousness of Christ, though he denies that Christ's righteousness is credited to us in a personal sense. He writes, of the righteousness which is the sinner's as a result of justification:

> It is not, therefore, Christ's own righteousness, still less [his] active or passive [righteousness], but that which Christ merited by both, and which we attain by Christ Jesus alone. For Christ's own righteousness is not properly that which is imputed, but that on account of which righteousness is imputed to us, who believe in Him.[144]

Like Fowler, therefore, he holds that 'to impute for righteousness' involves God counting our own faith and good works as if they were truly righteous, on account of the merit of Christ.[145] In other words, although he does not use

138 G. Bull, *Defence of the Nicene Creed*, 3 vols (Oxford, 1851), i p6.

139 S. Episcopius, *Disputationes Theologicae Tripartitae* (Amsterdam, 1646), p375.

140 Ibid., pp198–9, 372. Cf. Bull, *Harmonia Apostolica*, p95.

141 'Caeremonilia praecepta fuerunt multa, varia et sordida.' Episcopius, *Disputationes*, p198.

142 Episcopius, *Opera* (Amsterdam 1678), p272. Grotius takes a similar line. H. Grotius, *Criticorum Sacrorum*, 7 vols (London, 1660), vii p4447.

143 Episcopius, *Disputationes*, pp104, 215.

144 'Non itaque est justitia proprie Christi, nedum activa aut passiva, sed id quod Christus utraque promeruit, & nos per solum Christum Iesum consequimur. Non enim justitia Christi proprie id est quod imputatur, sed id propter quod imputatur nobis, credentibus in ipsam, justitia.' Episcopius, *Disputationes*, p394. See also Grotius, *Criticorum Sacrorum*, vii p2510.

145 Episcopius, *Disputationes*, p394.

the precise term, it is clear that, for Episcopius, Christ's death is what Bull calls the 'meritorious cause' of our justification.

Again, like Bull, Episcopius is clear that the essence of justification is a gratuitous judicial act of God, whereby he pardons sins, and accepts a sinner to eternal life.[146] He too holds that justification cannot be separated from the gift of salvation, even though the two things are conceptually distinct.[147] Whatever is the requirement for the first, he believes, must also be the requirement for the second.[148] And he is clear that the sincere obedience which is required under the New Covenant is properly described as a condition sine qua non, not as a cause of justification. It is, he writes 'the *condition* prescribed and required by the Evangelical Covenant, *without which* God does *not* wish to remit sins or impute righteousness'.[149] And he is convinced that this obedience is acceptable purely because of God's absolutely free and gracious decision to accept it, not because it has any merit or intrinsic efficacy.[150]

Episcopius is as clear as Bull, therefore, that when justification is ascribed to faith in the scriptures, this is not meant to exclude good works from the equation. Rather, he writes, 'That faith itself, by which believers are said to be imputed with righteousness, not only does not undermine good works, but by nature contains and comprehends them in itself.'[151] And this leads him to conclude, as it does Bull, that justification is not an instantaneous act but an ongoing process in the life of a believer.[152]

Like Bull, Episcopius denies that justifying faith can properly be described as an instrument of justification.[153] Faith is an instrument only in the sense that by it we apprehend Christ, through whom righteousness is to be sought, and not in the sense that through faith we apprehend a righteousness which is somehow imputed to us.[154]

Given the pronounced similarities between Episcopius's position on justification, and that which Bull advanced in the *Harmonia Apostolica*, and given the testimony of Robert Nelson to the influence of Episcopius on Bull's

[146] Episcopius, *Disputationes*, pp383–4. Cf. Bull, *Harmonia Apostolica*, pp6, 10.

[147] Episcopius, *Disputationes*, p394.

[148] Cf. Bull, *Harmonia Apostolica*, p12.

[149] Episcopius, *Disputationes*, p394. '*Conditio* foedere Evangelico praescripta et requisita, *sine qua* Deus remittere peccatum & imputare iustitiam *non* vult' (italics added).

[150] Ibid., p395. See also Grotius, *Criticorum Sacrorum*, vii p4451.

[151] Ibid., p395. 'Fides illa ipsa, quae credenti imputari dicitur in iustitiam, bona opera non tantum non tollit, sed ea ipsa... natura sua in se contineat & comprehendat.' See also Episcopius, Opera (1678), p179.

[152] Episcopius, *Disputationes*, pp395–6. Cf. Bull, *Harmonia Apostolica*, p44.

[153] Episcopius, *Disputationes*, p393.

[154] Ibid., p394.

theological formation, it seems reasonable to argue that Bull must have been significantly influenced by the earlier theologian in his understanding of the matter. This might account, of course, for the remarkable consistency of Tillotson's views with those of Bull, since we know that Tillotson, like the other Latitudinarians, held Episcopius in high regard.[155] It is also entirely consistent with the way Bull's contemporaries interpreted his work. As his biographer underlined, Bull was widely accepted to have adopted a 'Remonstrant' or Arminian position in the *Harmonia*.[156]

And this is important. Because it means that rather than being part of an essentially home-grown English movement, Bull should be seen as a product of the wider European tradition of anti-Calvinist thinking. And since Bull's theology bears the closest resemblance to that of Simon Episcopius, his views reflect Arminianism in its most systematic and sophisticated form. In other words, behind George Bull lurked the shadow of the Remonstrants.

By the 1660s and 1670s, of course, the struggle between Remonstrant and Contra-Remonstrant had been rumbling on for over half a century. And that hoary antagonism alone might be sufficient to account for the alarm which Reformed Anglicans felt at the publication of the *Harmonia*: the old enemy of Dort was rearing its head once more. But there was another school of thought which was, to the Reformed mind, even more pernicious than Arminianism. And that was Socinianism.

Socinus was the heretic who increasingly dominated the Reformed imagination as the seventeenth century wore on.[157] His heresy was so extensive that it became feasible to organize theological teaching around the rejection of his views. The volumes of Continental Reformed theology echo with the phrase, 'We affirm, against the Socinians.'[158]

Jonathan Edwards, who was Principal of Jesus College, Oxford, towards the close of the century, argued that Socinus had been so wrong, about so many things, that it was probably inaccurate to call him a heretic at all. He writes:

> Upon the whole matter, I think it may be reasonably doubted whether Socinus, any more than that grand impostor Mahomet, may be properly called a heretic, as being the founder of a new religion, rather than the author of a new name and sect among Christians. For as the Alcoran of the former, is . . . a fardel of errors and absurdities arising from the impure mixture of Christianity, Judaism and Paganism, together with some idle and extravagant notions of his own; so the doctrine of Socinus seems to be a composition of the errors of Arius, Photinus, and Pelagius & c. together with some

[155] M.I.J. Griffin, *Latitudinarianism*, p87.

[156] Nelson, *Life of Bull*, pp169, 189.

[157] Spurr, *Restoration Church of England*, pp254–5 underlines the constant fear of Socinianism within the Church of England after the Restoration.

[158] See Turretin, *Institutes*, passim.

additions of his own, not so seemingly absurd as those of Mahomet, but I am afraid no less dangerous to the Christian religion.[159]

Fausto Sozzini (Socinus) was an Italian, born in Siena in 1539. Early on in his life, he began to question whether Christ was truly divine. After a period of study in Basel, he worked out a fully fledged anti-Trinitarian theological system, whose cardinal principles were the primacy of reason in theology and the freedom of the human will.[160] In 1579 he moved to Poland, where, through a series of disputations and synods, he soon established himself as the leading reformer in a country already receptive to anti-Trinitarian views. During his lifetime, his ideas knew considerable success. An academy and printing house in Racow disseminated them and also attracted scholars from other parts of Europe. After his death in 1604, his followers published a Unitarian confessional statement on the basis of his manuscripts: the *Racovian Catechism.*

The elaboration of Socinus's views continued at Racow for the first few decades of the seventeenth century. Johann Volkel produced the authoritative systematic presentation of Socinian thought in 1630,[161] and Johann Crell complemented that work with an exposition of the Socinian understanding of God.[162] However, a Roman Catholic backlash against anti-Trinitarianism set in and, in 1638, Socinianism was prohibited at the Diet of Warsaw. The academy and printing house at Racow were closed and Socinian teachers were proscribed. Some Socinians travelled to Holland to escape the persecution, and it is there that they produced the comprehensive edition of Socinian writings,[163] and encountered the leading lights of the Remonstrant movement.

Although Socinianism was essentially a continental European movement,[164] both McLachlan and Spurr have pointed out that it had links with England, and that these links persisted into the Restoration period.[165] These points of contact enabled the dissemination of Socinian literature, some of which, including the *Racovian Catechism* itself,[166] was translated into English. All these factors combined to keep Socinianism alive as a threat in the minds

159 Edwards, *Preservative against Socinianism*, p7.

160 Expressed in two works, produced during that time but published later: *De Jesu Christe Servatore* (Basel, 1594) and *De Statu primi hominis ante lapsum* (Racow, 1610).

161 J. Crell and J. Volkel; *De Vera Religione* (Racow, 1630).

162 Crell, *De Deo et Attributis*, bound with Volkel's *De Vera Religione* in its first edition. McLachlan, *Socinianism*, p12. n. 3 has underlined the importance of Crell's influence in the development of Unitarianism in England.

163 The *Bibliotheca Fratrum Polonorum* (Amsterdam, 1656).

164 J. Biddle, *A Scripture Catechism* (London, 1654) was the first English writer to publish anti-Trinitarian views. In the 1691 edition of this work, it is prefaced by a life of Biddle which claims that he produced it before having encountered any properly Socinian writings. Its theological crudeness would seem to support this contention.

165 McLachlan, *Socinianism*, passim. Spurr, *Restoration Church of England*, p254–5.

166 *The Racovian Catechisme* (Amsterdam, 1652).

of Reformed English churchmen long after the Socinian movement itself had effectively collapsed.[167]

As Jonathan Edwards's remarks reveal, to the orthodox Protestant mind, Socinianism involved an astonishing number of seriously heretical assumptions. Since the Socinians held reason to be the arbiter of all human thought, they rejected all doctrine that did not seem to square with either human reason or natural ethics. They consequently considered the doctrine of the Trinity to be absurd and contradictory, though they allowed that Christ and the Holy Spirit might be called gods in an honorific manner. They considered the doctrine of the satisfaction of Christ to be morally abhorrent, and asserted that God had no need to be placated in order to forgive sins. They argued that human beings had been created free before the fall, and that they remained so, since freedom was, in their mind, the only foundation of moral responsibility. As a result, of course, they renounced any doctrine of predestination. They further rejected the doctrine of justification by faith also as being both unreasonable and not conducive to human goodness. This near comprehensive rejection of Reformed theological instincts accounts for the hostility which Socinian ideas met throughout the Reformed world. Socinianism was, to the Reformed mind, an intellectual abomination, and one which needed to be countered with particular vigour.

One of the accusations that Reformed writers frequently directed at their Arminian opponents was that some of the Remonstrant writers had been influenced by Socinian patterns of thinking. And there seems to have been some truth in this accusation. There were certainly many links of friendship between the two groups.[168] One prominent Remonstrant writer, Konrad Vorst (Vorstius), was repeatedly accused of Socinianism, and finally condemned for it at the Synod of Dort.[169]

The similarity between the Socinians and the Remonstrants was certainly not lost on the late seventeenth-century Unitarians,[170] nor on continental Reformed writers such as Francis Turretin.[171] And Jonathan Edwards noted, for example, that Episcopius 'agrees too well with Socinus in many of his

[167] Though it is noticeable that the anti-Trinitarians of the 1690s were aware of their intellectual pedigree. See *A Brief History of the Unitarians* (London, 1687), p3.

[168] L. Simonutti, 'Resistance, Obedience and Toleration: Przypkowski and Limborch,' in M. Mulsow and J. Rohls (eds.), *Socinianism and Arminianism: Antitrinitarians, Calvinists and Cultural Exchange in Seventeenth Century Europe* (Brill, 2005), pp187, 191. See also: McLachlan, *Socinianism*, p22.

[169] Ibid., p21 notes that Vorstius, though he denied being a Socinian, had read many Socinian works, and even encouraged their distribution in Holland. A more recent study confirms that: J. Rohls, 'Calvinism, Arminianism and Socinianism in the Netherlands,' in Mulsow and Rohls (eds.), *Socinianism and Arminianism*, p24.

[170] *A Brief History of the Unitarians*, p3. Edwards noted that the Unitarians had claimed Episcopius as an ally in *The Socinian Creed*, p27.

[171] E.g. Turretin, *Institutes*, Topic III qq7,8,9, 24. See also McLachlan, *Socinianism*, p23 n.5. Again, Edwards was also not unaware of this link: *The Socinian Creed*, p35.

other loose and dangerous notions',[172] whilst elsewhere referring dismissively to 'the Socinians themselves, and the Remonstrants, their friends.'[173]

On the doctrine of justification, it is certainly true that, at several points, Episcopius's position (and so also Bull's position) closely resembles that adopted by the Socinian theologian, Johann Volkel. Volkel, for example, asserts that the Old Covenant made only earthly and temporal promises,[174] and offered neither forgiveness of sins,[175] nor the promise of eternal life.[176] Like Episcopius, he argues that the New Covenant, just like the Old, is conditional in nature.[177] He also asserts that obedience to God's law is necessary for our salvation under the New Covenant.[178]

Volkel's understanding of the imputation of righteousness is similar, in significant respects, to that of Episcopius and Bull. Volkel is clear that Christ's righteousness is not imputed to the believer in any personal sense. Rather, God, simply on account of his own goodness and generosity, counts us as righteous, though we are not perfectly so.[179] So when scripture speaks of imputation, Volkel argues, 'It is certainly not meant, by these ways of speaking, that an alien justice or holiness is imputed to us, but that . . . God, on account of that faith which we offer to him, out of his sheer goodness treats us as though we were just.'[180]

Like Bull and Episcopius, Volkel believes that, when the scriptures ascribe justification to faith, 'that faith . . . includes obedience and piety in itself'.[181] And like the others he is also clear 'that faith is not indeed the meritorious or principally efficient cause, but the cause *sine qua non*, as they say, of our justification, and not by its own strength, but by the strength of the divine promises offered merely on account of [God's] goodness'.[182] Of course, since the Socinians flatly denied that Christ's death was in any way a source of merit that could be deployed elsewhere,[183] they could not describe it as the

[172] J. Edwards, *A Preservative against Socinianism* (Oxford, 1693–1703), p17.

[173] Ibid., p19. He makes the link between Remonstrant and Socinian thinking in his attack on Gilbert Burnet. J. Edwards, *The Exposition given by my lord bishop of Sarum of the Second Article of our Religion Examin'd* (London, 1702), pp6, 80.

[174] J. Volkel, *De Vera Religione* (Racow, 1630), p31.

[175] Ibid., pp34–5.

[176] Ibid., p56.

[177] Volkel, *De Vera Religione*, p361.

[178] Ibid., p568.

[179] Ibid., p565.

[180] Ibid., p565. 'His locutionibus, nequaquam significetur, alienam iustitiam seu sanctitatem nobis imputari, sed . . . Deum ob eam fidem, quam in ipso collocamus, pro sua benignitate ita nobiscum agere, ac si iustum essemus.'

[181] Ibid., p181. 'Fidem istam . . . obedientiam ac pietatem in se comprehendat.'

[182] Ibid. 'Fiduciam istam non quidem causam meritoriam aut principaliter efficientem, sed causam sine qua non, ut loquuntur, justificationis nostrae esse & non vi sua propria, sed vi promissi divini, ex mera benignitate profecti.'

[183] Ibid., pp563–4.

meritorious cause of this transaction. Indeed, justification was for them no more than the gracious decision of God to remit sins, without any reference to the work of Christ at all. But, that aside, their view was very close to the scheme adopted by Episcopius, and so, under his influence, by George Bull.

It is this evident proximity to Socinianism which probably accounts for the virulence of the Reformed responses to Bull. It certainly provided Barlow and Tully with some handy polemical ammunition: for all English Churchmen were (at least in public) united in their abhorrence of Socinianism. George Bull, by adopting the teaching of the Remonstrant theologian Simon Episcopius, had, wittingly or not, imported into England, and disseminated, some of the key propositions of Socinian doctrine. To an orthodox Reformed theologian, he was, as a result, a dangerous heretic, whose publication could under no circumstances be left unanswered.

## CONCLUSION

The publication of George Bull's *Harmonia Apostolica* in 1670 was a deliberate assault on Reformed orthodoxy, and it was an assault sanctioned by the Archbishop of Canterbury, Gilbert Sheldon. Bull was, in other words, the mouthpiece of a growing band of theologians who had no time for Reformed system, and who viewed the classic Protestant teaching on justification as both philosophically dubious and ethically perilous, liable to encourage the spread of sin and lawlessness within English society. The stated aim of the *Harmonia* was to discredit the Reformed position on justification, and so to sap the abiding influence which, to his mind, Reformed theology still held over the English Church.

Charles Allison argued that the axis of Bull's theological innovation was the reconfiguration of the formal cause of justification. More recently. John Spurr has followed his lead. They both assert that Bull takes the formal cause of justification to be God's acceptance, on account of the merits of Christ, of our imperfect good works as if they were perfect.

It has been argued here, by contrast, that Bull made a number of interlocking theological moves, which together contributed to a compelling alternative to the Reformed view of justification. Bull's new theology of justification involved re-conceiving not only the causality of salvation, but also the structure of the covenants, the role and nature of faith, and the imputation of righteousness. Contrary to Allison and Spurr's understanding of the matter, Bull insisted that human good works do not bear a causal relation to salvation, but are rather the necessary precondition for it, or condition sine qua non. This move was intended to put sufficient distance between Bull's position and that of the Roman Catholic writers on justification, and it was polemically vital if he was to deflect the inevitable charge of Popery.

The theology of justification which Bull advanced, though hotly contested by the Reformed, was becoming widespread within the Church of England. John Tillotson, Edward Fowler, and William Sherlock either reflected Bull's emphases, or extended, in some respects, his engagement with the Reformed position. Sherlock, in particular, sought to undermine the Reformed teaching on the union of the believer with Christ, a teaching which played a fundamental role in the solifidian scheme. His work on the subject may have been presented as an attack on the excesses of dissenting theology, but it was equally threatening to the Anglican Reformed.

Bull's theology, like that of others who thought as he did, has usually been understood as a home-grown reaction to Reformed divinity. It is certainly not to be denied that interregnum writers such as Jeremy Taylor and Henry Hammond did influence the post-Restoration critics of Reformed teaching. However, this type of theology also had roots amongst an earlier generation of continental theologians, namely the Dutch Remonstrants, and, in particular, in Simon Episcopius. As we have seen, Episcopius had advanced a teaching on justification which was substantially the same as that adopted by George Bull, and it is clear that Bull both read him and approved of a great deal of his theology. George Bull was, in other words, advancing an identifiably Remonstrant position on justification.

Unfortunately, many of Episcopius's positions on justification bore more than a passing resemblance to Socinian views on the subject. This presented a handy polemical weapon to Bull's Reformed opponents, who were consequently able to present him as yet another head of that heretical hydra. The English controversy surrounding Bull's *Harmonia* can, therefore, only be fully understood in the context of the wider European debate about the merits of Reformed soteriology.

# 3

# The Reformed Rejoinder

## THE REFORMED RESPONSE TO BULL

George Bull's biographer, Robert Nelson, leaves us in no doubt that the publication of the *Harmonia Apostolica* sparked a systematic Reformed campaign against its author. As he puts it, 'there were . . . men of some eminence in our Church, who with all their might opposed him'.[1] Bull's most zealous opponent, as we have underlined, was the Bishop of Winchester, George Morley, who, in Nelson's words, 'proceeded much further than any of the rest of his order,'[2] by issuing a pastoral charge prohibiting his clergy from reading Bull's work or preaching the doctrine it contained. But even the way Nelson phrases this indicates, of course, that Morley was not the only Restoration Bishop who received Bull's teaching with little enthusiasm.

Nelson also notes that

> some heads of houses in the two Universities were also of the bishop's mind: and there were some tutors too, that thought it incumbent upon them to guard their pupils from the danger of what appeared to them an innovation in the Church.[3]

And he indicated that Thomas Barlow and Thomas Tully were the key players in fostering this theological resistance to Bull's ideas within Oxford. Nelson's testimony is, of course, entirely consistent with what Barlow had told Lewis du Moulin about the key role he and Tully had played, in preventing the spread of Arminian and Socinian ideas within the University.[4]

Their work seems to have been successful, because when the time came to appoint a successor to Barlow as Lady Margaret Professor, another Reformed theologian, John Hall, was duly elected by Oxford's divinity faculty to replace him. And a few years further down the line, when the Arminian Regius Professor Richard Allestree eventually died in 1681, the King replaced him, too, with a Reformed theologian: Henry Compton's chaplain, William Jane. George Morley appears to have been influential in securing Jane's appointment to this key post.[5]

[1] Nelson, *Life of Bull*, p99. [2] Ibid., p101. [3] Ibid., p102.
[4] Du Moulin, *Short and True Account*, p31. See above. [5] *ODNB*, s.v. 'William Jane'.

According to Nelson, when Barlow began lecturing against the *Harmonia* in the Oxford Divinity School, Bull challenged the Lady Margaret Professor to a public disputation, but was declined. Instead, Barlow turned to his friend Tully and urged him to write against the *Harmonia*.[6] Their project soon became the talk of the University,[7] and although Bull repeatedly tried to discourage Tully, eventually the *Iustificatio Paulina* went to press with the permission of the leading men of the University.[8] Once again, Nelson discerned the hand of George Morley in these events, since it was he, and another unnamed prelate, who, having been shown a draft of the book, encouraged Tully to publish it. We have already pointed out how even Nelson admitted that many people felt Tully had carried the debate. And Anthony Wood records that 'since the publication of the said *Iustificatio Paulina*, the author thereof is characterized by some churchmen and fanatics to have been the main pillar of the Church in the defence of her true doctrine'.[9]

So when George Morley laid hands on Thomas Barlow, to consecrate him as the new Bishop of Lincoln on 27 June 1675, he could look back on a well managed campaign to counter the Arminian novelties which Bull had imported, and to defend the Reformed interpretation of the Anglican tradition. Barlow's lectures and Tully's book were acknowledged by their contemporaries to have played a significant part in stemming the tide of heterodox opinion.

As we shall see, however, this strategically minded group of men were not alone in maintaining the Reformed tradition within the English Church. They were but the visible tip of a far larger iceberg. In sermons, polemic, biblical commentaries, catechetical works, and expositions of the Church's Articles, clergy up and down the country were defending and promoting the Reformed view of justification. And they continued to do so well into the eighteenth century. Bull's views were increasingly influential, but they did not become the new Anglican orthodoxy.

## THOMAS BARLOW'S LECTURES

There is no doubt that Barlow intended his lectures to be the first official reply to Bull's work. Bull had offered the *Harmonia* to students in theology. Barlow, as Oxford's Lady Margaret Professor, and so self-conciously engaged in the

[6] Nelson, *Life of Bull*, p212. [7] Ibid., pp216–17.
[8] Ibid., pp218–19. [9] Wood, A., *Athenae Oxonienses*, 4 vols (London, 1817), iii. p1058.

business of elenctic theology,[10] was determined to ensure that Bull's heresy did not take root amongst the students in his care. Barlow's lectures are by far the most extensive and detailed treatment of the doctrine of justification which the Restoration period produced and, as Nicholas Tyacke has underlined, they merit an attention which has not previously been accorded them.[11]

In his opening lecture, Barlow gives a brief outline of the method he will adopt. Mirroring Bull's approach exactly, the focus of the lecture series is not merely justification, but the wider issue of the reconciliation of Paul and James. The points of departure for every lecture were James 2:24 and Romans 3:28, the very verses, of course, which provided the outline for the *Harmonia Apostolica*.

These verses are problematic, Barlow writes, because they appear to contradict each other, which is something the sacred scriptures should not do.[12] One way of resolving the problem would be to question the inspiration, and therefore the reliability of one of the verses. If one verse was not inspired, and so infallibly true, no problem actually arises. This, Barlow argues, is precisely what Luther did, as well as some of his followers, 'who, in order to safeguard Paul's teaching about the justice of faith without works, either wholly denied, or diminished the authority of James by saying it was less than infallible and divine.'[13]

By the time he was delivering his lectures, however, Barlow assumed that the canonicity of James had been established beyond reasonable doubt, even to the satisfaction of the more reasonable sort of Lutheran. More importantly, he states, there is no public doubt of it within the Church of England, for whatever private doubts there might be: 'our Church certainly pronounces the epistle of James to be undoubtedly canonical.'[14]

Apart from the Lutheran position, Barlow asserts that there remain three schools of thought on the correct way to reconcile Paul with James. First there are the Roman Catholics, 'who divide justification into two, ascribing our first justification to faith, and our second to works.'[15] Then there are the Socinians or neo-Photinians, 'who confuse faith and works, and assert that faith in Paul

[10] In his inaugural lecture as Lady Margaret Professor, Barlow defined this as the manner of doing theology which answers the objections raised against orthodox doctrine or apostolic discipline by the Church's opponents. MS QCL 235, pp11–12.

[11] Tyacke, 'Arminianism and the theology of the Restoration Church,' p70.

[12] Ibid.

[13] 'Qui ut doctrinam Pauli de iustitia fidei sine operibus ratam fixamque habeant, authoritatem Jacobi penitus negant vel (infra divinam et infallibilem deiiciendo) minuunt.' Barlow, MS QCL 239, 166r. Bull, of course, also briefly mentioned the Lutheran approach. Bull, *Harmonia Apostolica*, p4.

[14] 'Certe ecclesia nostra hanc Jacobi epistolam indubie canonicam pronuntiat.' Barlow, MS QCL 239, 149r.

[15] 'Qui iustitiam dividuunt, in primam et secundam, et fidei illam, hanc operibus attribuunt.' Ibid., 166v.

and works in James mean the same thing. They also say that the faith which justifies is not the act of one virtue, but consists in universal obedience to the gospel.'[16]

Barlow underlines that the Socinian authors had been condemned throughout the Reformed world when their views were first made public earlier in the century. Despite this, he writes,

> even in our own Britain, as I know and lament, they have their defenders and patrons. Not long ago there appeared a book called *Harmonia Apostolica*, in which the author expressly approved the said Neo-Photinian hypotheses, and incrusted and augmented them with even more errors.[17]

This recent resurgence of Socinian opinions made it all the more important, Barlow believed, to address their errors in particular. So it is clear that Barlow had discerned the points of contact between Bull's theology and that of the Socinian writers, and had drawn the inference that Bull's views came from the same unholy stable.

The remaining option for reconciling Paul and James is the position, as Barlow describes it, of the 'divines of the Church of England, with whom (as far as I know), in this article, all the Reformed Churches are in agreement'.[18] They, Barlow notes,

> whilst preserving the authority of James, the unity of righteousness and the distinction between faith and works, clearly indicate what the duties and what the proper roles of works and faith are in relation to justice and glory, and then demonstrate that effectively from the teaching and consensus of both Apostles.[19]

In a more positive vein, later in the series, he presents this Anglican and Reformed orthodoxy as being based on these five assertions:

1. That it is God who justifies the sinner.
2. That only the merit of Christ and his satisfaction alone is the formal motive, the morally impulsive cause, and that on account of which He justifies.

[16] 'Qui fidem et opera confundunt, qui fidem Pauli et opera Jacobi idem significare autumant. Ipsis enim fides illa quae iustificat non est unius virtutis actus, sed obedientia universalis evangelio praestita.' Ibid.

[17] 'Tamen etiam in Britannia nostra (quod scio et doleo) fautores habent et vindices. Prodiit non adeo pridem . . . *Harmonia Apostolica*, in qua author, dictas Neo-Photinianorum hypotheses approbat, et errore non uno incrustat cumulatque.' Barlow, MS QCL 239, 151r–151v.

[18] 'Ecclesiae Anglicanae Theologi, cum quibus, in hoc articulo, Ecclesiae Reformatae (quas scio) omnes consentiunt.' Ibid., 149v.

[19] 'Jacobi authoritate, iustitia unitate, fidei et operum distinctione salvis, quod munus, et quae sint propriae operum et fidei partes in ordine ad iustitiam et gloriam distincte indicant, et ex doctrina et consensu utriusque Apostoli efficaciter demonstrant.' Ibid., 166v–167r.

3. That faith which is true, living and working through love, and faith alone, both apprehends the merit of Christ and applies it to the soul of the sinner.
4. That all works are entirely excluded from the justification of a sinner; that is to say, they do not merit justice (as the papists pretend), nor are they the motive of justification, its impulsive cause, or that on account of which God justifies the sinner.
5. Our Church and all the Reformed Churches, mean by 'works of the law' not only works of the ceremonial or any other positive law given to the Jews by Moses, but also the works of the natural and moral law.[20]

Throughout his lectures, Barlow demonstrates a deep consciousness of the wider Reformed theological world, and the place of the Church of England within it. He does, of course, hold that the only properly authoritative sources of Anglican doctrine are the Anglican formularies, writing at one point:

the doctrine of the Church concerning the justification of the sinner in the eyes of God, is to be sought in the public formularies and authentic documents of the Church, the sum of which we acknowledge to be contained in four books (and not more), namely: 1. The Book of Common Prayer. 2. The book containing the Thirty-nine Articles of our religion. 3. The Book of Homilies put together during the reign of Edward VI and before the Articles. 4. The English Pontifical, or the book containing the solemn rites for the ordination of a deacon and a priest, and for the consecration of a bishop.[21]

Nonetheless, in argument, he repeatedly refers not only to the works of the older generation of English Reformed theologians, such as Jewel, Hooker, White, Rainolds, and Davenant,[22] but also to continental writers such as Huldrich Zwingli,[23] Francis Junius,[24] David Paraeus,[25] Gerhard Vossius,[26] and

[20] '1. Quod Deus est qui peccatorem justificat. 2. Quod Christi meritum tantum, et satisfactio eius sola, est motivum formale, causa moraliter impulsiva . . . et illud propter quod justificat. 3. Quod fides vera, viva, et per charitatem operativa, eaque sola, satisfactionem illam, et Christi meritum apprehendit, et animae peccatrici applicat. 4. Quod opera omnia in iustificatione peccatoris sunt penitus exclusa; ita est, nec sunt iustitia merita (quod pontificiis fabulantur), nec sunt justificationis motiva, causae impulsivae, aut illud propter quod peccatorem justificat Deus. 5. Ecclesia nostra et reformatae omnes, per opera legis, non solum legis ceremonialis aut cuiuscunque positivae, judaeis per Mosem datae, sed legis etiam naturae et moralis opera intelligunt.' Ibid. 234, 79r–79v.

[21] 'Doctrina ideo ecclesiae, de justificatione peccatoris coram Deo, ex tabulis ecclesiae publicis, et scriptis authenticis petenda est: quo in censu libros 4or (nec plures) habemus aut agnoscimus, Nempe. 1. Librum liturgicum seu precum publicarum formularum. 2. Librum qui Articulos religionis nostrae 39 comprehendit. 3. Homiliarum librum, sub Eduardo 6 et ante Articulos, conditum. 4. Pontificale Anglicanum, seu librum qui ordinationis diaconi et presbyteri, et consecrationis episcopi formulas solennes comprehendit.' Ibid., 91r–91v.

[22] Ibid. 230, p155. [23] Ibid. 233 pp158–9. [24] Ibid. 230, p51.

[25] Ibid. 239, 147v. [26] Ibid., 155v.

his near contemporary Francis Turretin,[27] as well as to the confessional documents of the continental Reformed churches.[28] For Barlow, the position he was defending was not merely the historic faith of the Church of England. It was the common faith of all the Reformed.

The four positions outlined above provided Barlow with the basic structure of his lecture series, and he dealt with each one in turn (although, ironically, his presentation of the Anglican or Reformed position was brought to a premature conclusion by his elevation to the bishopric of Lincoln). At first glance, this might seem a rather odd way of proceeding, since, as a result, Barlow spent fully two years dealing with positions other than that which he had been intending to combat. Certainly, the first year of lectures on the authorship and authority of the epistle of James which Barlow directed against the Lutherans does seem somewhat beside the point. After all, as Barlow himself said, by the 1670s most Lutherans actually accepted the canonicity of James, so lectures on the older Lutheran view were really an excuse for treating the wider issues of scriptural authority and canon. Barlow was perhaps influenced in his decision to treat the Lutheran position by a work of Francis Turretin on the reconciliation of Paul and James,[29] which Barlow cites in his lectures,[30] and which did the same.

On the other hand, dealing with the Roman Catholic position was highly relevant to the controversy with Bull. For although, in his summary, Barlow presented the Roman Catholics as simply dividing justification into two, he was aware that many other views existed alongside this within the Roman Catholic church,[31] and that some of the arguments used by Roman Catholics to defend these views were virtually identical to the arguments being deployed by George Bull and those who sided with him.

Some Roman Catholics, like Bull, argued that Paul only excluded ceremonial works, or works performed without grace from justification.[32] Others, like Bull, accused the Reformed of denying the necessity of works.[33] Most importantly, though, the Roman Catholic position implied, just as Bull's did, that works are, to some degree, necessary for justification.[34] Barlow was thus

[27] Barlow evidently had a high opinion of Turretin. In his own copy of Bull's *Harmonia Apostolica*, he noted that Turretin's treatment of the issues was much superior to Bull's. In this section, we will refer to Turretin's writings to underline Barlow's similarity to him.

[28] Ibid. 230, p42.

[29] Turretin, F., *De Concordia Pauli et Iacobi in Articulo Iustificationis* (Geneva, 1691), p385. This first appeared in his *De Satisfactione Christi Disputationes* (Geneva, 1666).

[30] Barlow, MS QCL 240, 95r.

[31] Ibid., 88r.

[32] Ibid. Cf. Bull, *Harmonia Apostolica*, p194.

[33] Ibid., 233r et seq. Cf. Bull, *Harmonia Apostolica*, p35.

[34] Barlow, MS QCL 240, 115r. Cf. Bull, *Harmonia Apostolica*, p11.

able, whilst purportedly responding to the Roman Catholics, to explore arguments which would be useful against the *Harmonia Apostolica*, and also, by implication, to discredit Bull's position by demonstrating its evident similarity to certain forms of popery.[35] This might have muddied the waters of Barlow's analysis of Bull, but it was a useful polemical stick with which to beat the hapless harmonist nonetheless.

Nonetheless, the substance of Barlow's criticism of Bull is to be found in the lectures against the Socinian position which Barlow gave between 6 November 1673 and 20 January 1675. He begins by giving a fuller outline of the position he was countering. The Socinians, he says, hold that justifying faith is really the same thing as obedience.[36] They consider obedience to be not merely the effect of faith, but the substance and form of it, and so included within its essential definition. Accordingly, they are able to reconcile Paul with James without difficulty, since they argue that both apostles believe that it is obedience which justifies. The difference between the apostles, to the Socinian understanding, is merely that Paul calls this obedience 'faith,' whereas James calls it 'works'.

Barlow cites Valentine Smalcius and the Racovian Catechism as propounding the Socinian hypothesis, but then writes: 'the recent author of the *Harmonia Apostolica* says the same thing as Socinus.'[37] Indeed, throughout his lectures, Barlow consistently associates Bull with writers who were widely accepted as heterodox, whether Socinus, Smalcius, Volkel or the positions of the Racovian Catechism, and shows how similar his views are to theirs. As far as Barlow was concerned, George Bull was the newest member of an international Socinian cabal.

Barlow begins by taking issue with Bull's interpretation of scripture, and in particular with his understanding of what Paul meant by works and faith. As we have seen Bull argued that Paul did not mean to exclude all good works from the process of justification, but only what he called the works of the Mosaic law.[38] Barlow disagrees.[39] Arguing from various passages in Romans, Barlow insists that Paul intended to exclude all works from the process of justification, even the works of the moral law.

[35] This is not to say that Barlow was not also really opposing the Roman Catholic view. That Reformed authors were still engaging with their Catholic opponents on these matters can be seen in Francis Turretin's *De Concordia Pauli et Iacobi in Articulo Iustificationis* (Geneva, 1691), pp385–8.

[36] Turretin, *Institutes*, Topic XV q.13.5 describes the Socinian position in the same way.

[37] 'Idem ait (quod Socinus) scriptor nuperus Harmoniae Apostolicae.' Barlow, MS QCL 233, p6. Cf. Bull, *Harmonia Apostolica*, p18.

[38] Ibid., p75. Of course, Barlow is guilty of oversimplifying Bull's position slightly here. Cf. Bull, *Harmonia Apostolica*, p174.

[39] As did Turretin: *Institutes*, Topic XVI q.2.11, 12.

Expounding Romans 3:19–20, for example, Barlow argues that 'Paul is speaking of that law to which not only the Jews but also the gentiles were subject, and according to which the whole world was exposed to condemnation.'[40] But that could only be the moral law, since the Mosaic law did not apply to gentiles. Indeed, as Barlow notes, the cleverer Roman Catholics agree with him on this, 'and whoever thinks differently, has either not read the scriptures seriously, or, if they have, has not understood very much'.[41]

Having disposed of the idea that Paul excluded only the works of the Mosaic law from justification, Barlow moves on to consider Bull's argument that faith, in the Pauline corpus, is equivalent to obedience.[42] Barlow rejects this view firmly: 'Universal obedience is not that faith which in the sacred scriptures, and most often by Paul, is said to be justifying.'[43]

On rational grounds, Barlow takes issue with Bull's view that obedience can be described as the form of faith.[44] Obedience is rather the effect of faith. This is clear, for example, from Hebrews 11, where Paul (as Barlow believes) expressly states that the good works of the patriarchs were the results of faith. Since a cause and its effect cannot be identical, works cannot be the same thing as the faith which produces them. Barlow writes: 'the effect of justifying faith cannot be the form of that faith, or identical to that faith; because an effect necessarily presupposes the thing and form of which it is the effect, and does not constitute it.'[45] Just as the acts of understanding, willing and knowing are the proper effects of a rational mind, but do not constitute that mind (since a mind is still a mind even when not actually thinking, willing or knowing), so obedience is properly the effect of faith, and does not constitute that faith.

Again, Barlow says, if good works were the form of faith, the question arises in relation to a Christian's first act of obedience, whether it arose out of faith or not? If it did not, then it was not an act of obedience at all, nor could it please God, since it is clear from Hebrews 11:6 that 'without faith it is impossible to please him.' If it did, then it must follow that faith was actually in the Christian before any act of obedience, and that by consequence, obedience cannot be an essential part of faith.

[40] 'De ea lege loquitur Paulus, cui non solum Judaei, sed et gentes suberat, et ex qua totus mundus erat condemnationi obnoxius.' Barlow, MS QCL 233, p10.

[41] 'Et qui aliter sentiunt, scripturas sacras vel serio non legunt, vel lectas, parum intelligunt.' Ibid., p14.

[42] Bull, *Harmonia Apostolica*, p58.

[43] 'Obedientia universalis . . . non est fides, quae in sacris literis, et a Paulo iustifica [*sic*] passim dicitur.' Barlow, MS QCL 233, p24.

[44] Bull, *Harmonia Apostolica*, pp25–6.

[45] 'Effectus fidei iustificantis, non est forma ipsius fidei, vel ipsa fides iustificans . . . quia effectus omnis rem et formam cuius effectus est necessario praesupponit, non constuit.' Barlow, MS QCL 233, p27. Cf. Turretin, *Institutes*, Topic XV q.13.

That faith and obedience are really different things can further be demonstrated by a careful analysis of the acts involved. Barlow takes the example of an act of charity. First, he says, the act of charity and the act of faith have different aims: 'they tend towards different objects (whence distinction arises in acts and habits): faith tends towards Christ, charity towards the neighbour.'[46] Secondly, they arise out of different faculties, and are motivated by different things: 'Charity is of the appetitive faculty, and is drawn towards what is good; faith is of the cognitive faculty, and is drawn towards what is true.'[47] But since faith and charity have different objects, arise from different faculties, and are drawn to different things, it is absurd to say that they are the same, or that one is a part of the other.

But Barlow's fundamental argument against Bull's equation of faith and good works is that scripture consistently treats them as different things. He writes:

> in the sacred scriptures, universal obedience shown to the commands of the law and the gospel is never called faith; neither explicitly, nor by some consequence (according to the rules of logic) which can be legitimately drawn from them: but true and living faith, to which our justice in the eyes of God is ascribed, is constantly distinguished from charity, hope, and the rest of the virtues.[48]

This, Barlow believes, is evident from passages such as 2 Peter 1:5 'Add to your faith, virtue; and to virtue, knowledge', for if faith were the sum of all the virtues, how could virtue be added to it? Even Bull's beloved Apostle James makes the distinction between faith and good works clear, Barlow says, and most clearly perhaps in the very verse Bull has cited: 'for by works is a man justified, and not by faith.' This statement, Barlow argues, evidently presupposes a real distinction between the two. Elsewhere, James says that Abraham's obedience worked with and perfected his faith (James 2:22). But, as Barlow writes: 'that which perfects and consummates presupposes the thing which is to be perfected and consummated. It follows that the faith of Abraham (as to its essence) came first, and that later he perfected it by his exemplary obedience.'[49]

[46] 'In objecta diversa (unde actuum et habituum distinctio) tendunt: fides in Christum, charitas in proximum.' Barlow, MS QCL 233, p43.

[47] 'Charitas est facultatis appetentis, et fertur in bonum; fides in cognoscentis, et fertur in verum.' Ibid.

[48] 'In sacris literis obedientia universalis evangelio et legis praestita nunquam dicitur fides, necque . . . expresse, nec consequentia aliqua (secundum logicae regulas) legitime deducta: sed fides vera et viva, cui iustitia nostra coram Deo ascribitur, a charitate, spe, et reliquis virtutibus perpetuo distinguitur.' Ibid., p42.

[49] 'Id quod perficit et consummat, rem perficiendam et consummandam praesupponit. Fides ergo Abrahami (quoad essentiam) praefuit, quam postea eximia illa obedientia perficit.' Ibid., p54.

Barlow argues that good works perfect faith not in that they contribute to or constitute its essence (as Bull would have it), but by a perfection which is purely extrinsic and accidental, as 'actions perfect the potentials and dispositions from which they arise.'[50] Faith is a habit, which, like all habits, is made stronger by its frequent exercise in the production of good works. Barlow writes: 'Since any habit is a quality which adds promptness and facility of operation to the potential to which it corresponds; and since frequent exercise of any habit, and frequently repeated actions, increase that facility, so they are said to perfect it.'[51] And just as one gets better at academic disputations by frequently disputing, so one's faith is rendered more certain and tranquil through frequent good deeds.

It follows that charity, the other virtues, and indeed all good works, are properly the fruits of faith.[52] They demonstrate the faith is living, and they strengthen it, but they do not constitute it.[53] Nor, indeed, can they make a man just. Barlow writes:

> He who acts justly is just; but it is not because he acts justly that he is just. A good tree is one that bears good fruit; it follows from the effect. However, the bearing of good fruit does not make the tree good; it presupposes that the tree is already good. In the same way, good works presuppose that a man is just, they do not make him so.[54]

When James writes (2:26) 'For as the body without the spirit is dead, so faith without works is dead', he is not using the Greek word *pneuma* for soul, but for breath. Bull is therefore wrong to use the image to assert that works are the form of faith, as the soul is the form of the body. What James actually means is that, just as you can tell that a body is living by the fact that it is breathing, so you can only tell that faith is alive, because it is fruitful in good works.[55] That does not mean, however, that faith and works are the same thing.

Having rejected Bull's understanding of the meaning of the terms faith and works, Barlow then turns to consider Bull's substantive doctrine of justification. He admits that the Reformed and the Socinians both agree (against the Roman Catholics) that justification is a judicial or forensic process, and does not involve an internal change in the believer. Reformed and Socinian alike can, therefore, agree that

[50] 'Actiones, potentiae suae et habituum perfectivas esse.' Ibid., pp56–7.

[51] 'Cum enim habitum omnis sit qualitas, quae potentiae suae promptitudinem operandi et facilitatem superaddit, cumque habitus cuiuscunque exercitium frequens, et actiones saepius repetitae, facilitatem illam augent et intendunt, ideo et perficiunt.' Ibid., p57.

[52] Ibid. 230, p44.

[53] Ibid., pp52–3.

[54] 'Qui facit iustitiam iustus est, agnosco, qui facit, non quia facit. Arbor bona est quae fructus fert bonos; sequitur ab effectu, sed fructus bonos ferre non constituit arborem bona, sed praesupponit. Ita bona opera praesupponit, non constituunt iustum.' Ibid., p146.

[55] Ibid., p94. Turretin interprets the passage in the same way: *De Concordia Pauli et Jacobi*, p399. Cf. Bull, *Harmonia Apostolica*, p50.

to justify is to absolve, and justification by judicial sentence is absolution from the guilt and punishment of the law, although the person thus justified is not formally and inherently just on account of some antecedent quality, or some quality imparted by the judge.[56]

Barlow also concedes, with Bull, that in this forensic process, God is the judge, man the accused, and the law by which the accused is judged is indeed the law of liberty mentioned in James; that is to say, the moral law.[57] He then analyses justification in terms of causality, and here the roots of his disagreement with Bull begins to appear. Barlow writes:

1. All agree about the efficient cause. It is the justification proper, the judicial absolution, and the act of the judge...
2. The final cause of justification is: 1. Intermediately, the salvation of man. 2. Ultimately, the glory of God who justifies.
3. The material cause of justification (since, according to the agreed principles of the schools, actions do not properly have a material out of which they are made) either is: 1. The material cause in which it arises; and since it is a divine action, it necessarily has God as its principle and subject. 2. The material cause about which it arises objectively and terminatively; and since the guilty man is pardoned by God as the object and end of justification, it is an action of God outside himself, and therefore limited to the creature.
4. About the formal cause, however, there is a question; that is to say, about the motive and formal reason which induces God to justify a man and, in some sense, moves Him, so that the justified man is not fictitiously, but really and truly righteous.[58]

Thus for Barlow, the key issue is the formal cause of justification. But Barlow's understanding of what a formal cause of justification might be is entirely different from Bull's. What Bull called the formal cause of justification, the divine act of pardon, Barlow has defined as the efficient cause of justification, thus enabling him to identify something else as justification's formal cause, namely whatever it is which impels God to act as he does.

[56] 'Justificare est absolvere, et iustificatio per sententiam iudicis, a culpa et poena legis absolutio: licet persona sic... iustificata, non sit, per qualitatem aliquam antecedentem, aut a iudice inditam, formaliter et inhaerenter iusta.' Barlow, MS QCL 233, pp63–4.

[57] Cf. Bull, *Harmonia Apostolica,* p19 and Turretin, *Institutes,* Topic XVI q.1.

[58] '1. De causa efficiente constat et inter omnes convenit. Est enim iustificatio, iudicialis rei absolutio, et actus iudicis.... 2.Causa finalis iustificationis 1. Inter media, hominis salus 2.Ultima, Dei iustificantis gloria. 3. Causa materialis iustificationis (cum ex receptis scholae placitis, materiam ex qua, actiones proprie non habeant) vel est: 1. In qua, cumque sit actio divina, et principium, et subjectum Deum habeat necesse est. 2. Circa quam, objective et terminative: sic homo reus a Deo absolutus est iustificationis objectum et terminus, est enim actio Dei ad extra, et ideo ad creatura terminata. 4. De causa formalis quaeritur; seu potius de motivo et ratione formali quae deum ad hominem iustificandum inducat, et modo aliquo moveat, at sic iustificatum, non ficte, sed realiter et vere iustum denominet.' Barlow, MS QCL 233, pp72–3.

Barlow discusses, in the following lecture, Bull's contention that works are not really the formal cause of justification in his scheme, but its condition sine qua non.[59] Barlow is not impressed with this move. Bull argued that works necessarily precede justification not in the manner of a cause, but in the manner of an indispensable condition. But, as Barlow makes clear, all sorts of things are necessary preconditions to our justification: the hearing of the gospel, for example, or the possession of an intellect and a will. However, just because they are indispensable conditions for justification, it does not follow that they justify us. Yet Bull thinks that our works do indeed justify us—they are both a necessary and a sufficient condition for justification in his scheme. They must, therefore, be rather more than a condition sine qua non.

Equally, if it is true that obedience, as it is defined by Bull, is the condition sine qua non of justification, then faith (which Bull acknowledges is part of Christian obedience) would have no causal relationship with justification either, when Paul explicitly states that it does.

Above all, Barlow argues, if obedience really is the necessary and sufficient condition for justification under the gospel covenant, as Bull clearly thinks it is, then it cannot properly be described as a condition sine qua non. It must instead be called a moral cause, and a truly and properly impulsive one at that. Because, under a covenant, an obligation arises by natural justice whenever its stipulated condition is fulfilled. Barlow writes:

> If universal obedience is the condition of the gospel covenant, and is accomplished by the faithful; it follows that the justice promised under this condition in this covenant, is owed in all justice, and that God (by virtue of the stipulated promises and conditions) is bound to keep his promise.[60]

As a consequence, a relationship of causality does, indeed, arise between our obedience and the divine act of justification, and Bull is guilty of special pleading when he describes it as no more than a condition sine qua non.

For these reasons, Barlow thinks that Bull's description of obedience as a condition sine qua non is a red herring. What is really at issue is the *ratio, causa, et illud propter quod* God justifies the sinner; in other words, justification's formal cause, as Barlow (but not Bull) has defined it. This, he says, could not possibly be obedience, since our obedience is imperfect.[61] The law

[59] Barlow, MS QCL 233, p88 et seq. Cf. Bull, *Harmonia Apostolica*, p11.

[60] 'Si ideo obedientia universalis sit foederis Evangelici conditio, et a fidelibus praestitur; inde sequitur, iustitiam in eodem foedere, sub ea conditione promissa, esse etiam ex iustitia debitam, Deumque (ex vi promissi et conditionis praestitae) teneri ut promissam redolat.' Barlow, MS QCL 233, p93.

[61] F. Turretin, *Institutes*, Topic XVI q.2.9.

by which we are judged is the moral law, Barlow argues, and this requires obedience which is both absolute in extent and perfect in degree. However:

Whilst they are in this life, not even the most holy can achieve this perfection. The reason for this is that, even in the regenerate there remain the concupiscence of the flesh and the relics of sin, which are not yet wholly defeated: hence the constant struggle between the Spirit and the flesh, which prevents us achieving the perfection required by the law.[62]

He had made this point in his lectures against the Roman Catholics as well, repeatedly citing Richard Hooker's *Treatise of Justification*. Perfection is ardently desired by the faithful in this life, but not attained until the next; it is of grace that we desire what is good, but our fleshly natures ensure that we cannot achieve it.[63] Indeed, these imperfect works are, to the extent of their imperfection, so far from being able to justify us, that they actually increase our guilt.[64]

Barlow considers an objection which might arise from this view, namely that it is unreasonable of God to make demands that human beings cannot fulfill. He answers this by making a distinction between the two sorts of possibility which are involved in moral actions. He writes:

In matters of morals, the possibility or potential to fulfil the law is twofold: 1. Physical and natural, which is grounded upon the intellect and the will, mutual and natural potentials of the rational soul; in this is found the end of the soul, that man is able to know God and the divine laws, and obey those laws rightly and perfectly.[65]

In this respect, human beings are always able to fulfil the law, since they retain the basic faculties required to do so. On the other hand '2. Other is the potential to fulfill the law which is called secondary and moral, and which consists in the correct disposition of the intellect and the will',[66] and considered this way, human beings lost the capacity to fulfill the law in the Fall, when they were afflicted with depravity of will and blindness of intellect as a result of original sin.

62 'Perfectionem autem hanc, dum sunt in via, ne sanctissimi quidem assequuntur. Ratio est; quia etiam in renatis manet concupiscentia carnis et peccati reliquiae, nondum penitus victae et triumphae: hinc perpetua Spiritus et carnis lucta, quae perfectionem ex lege requisitum, impedit.' Barlow, MS QCL 233, p79.

63 Ibid. 240, 263r. Turretin, *Institutes*, Topic XVII q.2.10, 11.

64 Barlow, MS QCL 233, p81.

65 'In moralibus, possibilitas seu potentia implendi legem, est duplex: 1. Physica et naturalis... quae fundatur in intellectu et voluntate, potentiis animae rationalis naturalibus et reciprocis, in hunc finem animae insitis, ut possit homo Deum et leges divinas cognoscere, cumque ex prescripto legis rite et perfecte collere.' Ibid. 234, 37r.

66 '2. Alia est potentia implendi legem, quam secundam et moralem dicimus, quae constit in debita intellectus et voluntatis dispositione.' Ibid.

But since that loss was itself culpable, it is not unjust for God to continue to exact from us a performance which, through our own free action, we are now no longer able to accomplish.[67] God therefore rightly demands of humanity a degree of moral perfection which it cannot possibly attain.

The only thing which actually does possess the highest degree of perfection is the meritorious death of Christ.[68] Barlow writes: 'That which takes away all sin, and which perfectly and completely absolves the sinful soul from all guilt and stain of sin, is the only adequate reason and formal motive on account of which we are justified in the sight of God.'[69] But only the death of Christ does these things, so only that death could be the motive of our justification. The debt we owed by our sins has been justly exacted from our sponsor. Barlow writes: 'God himself pays all our debt to the creditor, and nails the bond which was against us to the cross, completely destroying it.'[70] Nothing else either is, or could be required of us.

It should be noted here that Barlow, unlike most Reformed writers, considers that only the passive obedience of Christ is imputed to the believer, not the active, since his active obedience was already owed to God by virtue of his human nature.[71] Whilst conceding that many learned authors do not agree with him, he writes:

> The man Christ, in that he was an intellectual creature, was compelled by the indispensable law of nature, to offer the most perfect obedience that he could by himself and in person for himself.... Since, therefore, the most perfect active obedience of Christ was owed to God by the law, it follows: 1. That the active obedience of Christ was a service owed to God and the law, and that it cannot therefore be merit for us. 2. That he did not offer it in our place, but in his own, and that is is not, therefore, imputed to us.[72]

[67] Ibid.

[68] Turretin, *Institutes*, Topic XVI q.3.15.

[69] 'Illud quod peccatum omne tollit, et animam peccatricem ab omni culpa reatu et macula plene et perfecte abluit. Illud est sola adaequata ratio, motivum formale et illud propter quod coram Doe iustificamur.' Barlow, MS QCL 233, pp200–1.

[70] 'Omne debitum nostrum ipse... Deo creditori integre solvit, chirographum quod adversus nos erat, cruci affixit et penitus delevit.' Ibid., p228.

[71] Barlow is unusual, but not alone in asserting this. Cameron and Forbes do the same.

[72] 'Homo Christus, in quantum erat creatura intellectualis, ex lege naturali et indispensabili, ad obedientiam, quam praestare potuit perfectissimam per se, et personaliter pro seipso tenebatur.... Cum ideo obedientia Christi activa... perfectissima erat deo ex lege debita, sequetur: 1. Obedientia Christi activa erat obsequium legi ac Patri debitum ergo non potuit esse pro nobis meritum. 2. Quod vice et loco nostro non praestitit, sed suo, illud nobis non imputantur.' Barlow, MS QCL 233, p222.

The merit of Christ which is the motive of our justification is thus the merit of Christ's satisfaction, not the merit of his obedient life.

Since Christ's death is the only source of merit which could satisfy the demands of divine justice, the imputation of that merit to us must be the formal cause of justification.[73] Barlow writes:

> Christ alone is the meritorious cause; he indeed, who alone could, merited righteousness and salvation for us. Just as Christ is the sole meritorious cause, so his merit, the payment of our debt offered to the Father and imputed to us, is the sole external motive cause of justification, the unique formal reason, and that on account of which we are justified in the sight of God.[74]

So, following Davenant, Barlow resists the attempt to split the formal and meritorious causes of justification, and insists that the merit of Christ's death imputed to us, must be both. This imputation of Christ's merit to us, he believes, is accomplished through faith alone.

Barlow writes: 'Faith, in order to achieve this effect, grasps the merit. The merit of Christ is the plaster and medicine which heals our wounds, but faith alone (and not any work or other virtue) is the hand of the ailing soul, which applies the medicine.'[75] The merit of Christ is of no avail unless a living faith knows it, embraces it, and applies it to the sinful soul. Faith can therefore, Barlow believes, be properly described as the instrument of justification,[76]

> but the instrument (we say) not of God who justifies. For God to will is to accomplish, and since he is the judge, the pronouncement of his sentence is our justification; in which process God neither needs nor uses an instrument. But it is the instrument of the sinful soul, and like a hand which grasps the promises of God and the merits of Christ, and applies them to himself as a medicine.[77]

The merit of Christ is thus the *causa sola propter quam* God justifies us; but our faith is the *causa sola per quam*, albeit only from our point of view, and so can appropriately be called the instrumental cause of justification.

[73] Turretin, *Institutes*, Topic XVI q.3.

[74] 'Solus Christus est causa meritoria; is enim, qui solus potuit, iustitiam et salutem pro nobis meruit.... Sicut ipse Christus est sola causa meritoria, ita eius meritum, seu solutio debiti nostri Patri praestita et nobis imputata, est solum causa iustificationis motivum externum, ratio formalis unica, et illud propter quod solam coram deo iustificamur.' Barlow, MS QCL 233, pp98–9.

[75] 'Fides, ut in ordinem ad hunc effectum, meritum apprehendat. Meritum Christi est emplastrum et medicina quae morbos nostros sanat, sed fides sola (non opera aut alia virtus ulla) est animae aegrotantis manus, quae medicinam applicat.' Ibid., p99.

[76] Turretin, *Institutes*, Topic XVI q.7.

[77] 'Instrumentum (dicimus) non Dei iustificantis... Dei enim velle est efficere, et cum iudex sit, pronuntiatio sententiae suae est iustificatio nostro; quo negotio, instrumentis nec utitur, nec opus habet Deus. Sed est animae peccatricis instrumentum, et quasi manus, qua Dei promissa, et Christi merita apprehendit, et sibi in medelam applicat.' Barlow, MS QCL 233, p100.

Barlow underlines that all this is precisely what the Church of England asserts in her public confessions.[78] This is the authentic reading of the Anglican tradition. The Articles and Homilies make it quite clear that we are justified before God on account of Christ's merits, not our own works, and that it is our faith alone which apprehends and applies the merit of Christ to us. Since the time that the Articles were accepted, Barlow insists, the Church has defended these truths against all the enemies of the faith. Compiling a list in the process which would make a Victorian High Churchman blanch, Barlow writes: 'thus believed, thus taught and wrote Jewel of Salisbury... as also did Whitaker, Rainolds, Hooker, and until 1640... all others.'[79]

The foreign Reformed churches, Barlow notes, have also embraced this doctrine, as is abundantly clear from their own confessional statements. It is also the common teaching of Protestant writers of all shades of opinion, from Peter Martyr or Luther, all the way to Arminius, who, in other respects, disagreed with the Reformed.[80] Barlow writes: 'I know that reason deduced from the consent of the Church is not metaphysically or mathematically infallible; but it is nonetheless of great weight, and morally certain',[81] and Bull is certainly guilty of disregarding this weight of authority. For Barlow, therefore, by asserting that our own good works are the reason why God justifies us, Bull is opposing both the authority of the Church, and the consensus of her greatest teachers, and this is yet another reason for rejecting his opinions.

On the basis of this understanding of justification, Barlow takes issue with Bull's conception of the Mosaic law. As we saw, Bull established a dichotomy between the Mosaic law, with its many imperfections, and the perfect law of Christ. Christ not only expounded, but improved the Mosaic law, tempered it with evangelical grace, and made it his own, thereby establishing it as the condition of entry into the New Covenant, which all are now bound to fulfill.

Barlow firmly rejects this conception of the law. To say that the Mosaic law is imperfect in any way, he asserts, 'is not only wrong, but blasphemous of the law and the law-giver, God.'[82] For it would entail an imperfect divine act, which is unthinkable. As he states:

[78] 'Instrumentum (dicimus) non Dei iustificantis... Dei enim velle est efficere, et cum iudex sit, pronuntiatio sententiae suae est iustificatio nostro; quo negotio, instrumentis nec utitur, nec opus habet Deus. Sed est animae peccatricis instrumentum, et quasi manus, qua Dei promissa, et Christi merita apprehendit, et sibi in medelam applicat.' Barlow, MS QCL 233, p96.

[79] 'Sic credidit, sic docuit et scripsit Jewellus Sarisburiensis... sic Whitakerus, Rainoldus, Hookerus, et ad annum usque 1640... alii omnes.' Ibid., p103.

[80] Ibid.

[81] 'Scio, rationem a consensu ecclesiae deductam, non esse... metaphysice et mathematice infallibilem; magni tamen ponderis et moraliter certam.' Ibid., p123.

[82] 'Non solum erronee, sed in legum et legislatorem Deum blaspheme dicta esse.' Barlow, Ibid., p292.

Since it is necessarily true that every work of God should be wholly good, beautiful and perfect, given that an effect certainly bears a likeness to its cause: it is impossible that anything crude or imperfect might be produced by Him, the most perfect agent.[83]

In fact, to assert, as Bull does, that Christ perfected the law in any substantive way is absurd. Barlow says of the law:

since (following the accepted and correct opinion of the scholastics) the works of the Trinity *ad extra* are indivisible, and common to all persons of the sacred Triad: it follows that God the Father, the Son and the Holy Spirit (and one with human nature) originally delivered that law.[84]

So if Christ modified the law of Moses, he would be opposing what he himself, as God, had previously delivered.

The Mosaic law contained within it the precepts of the moral law, and for this reason too, Bull's scheme cannot be right. As Barlow says: 'the moral law is absolutely immutable, and capable of neither diminution nor extension.'[85] It is therefore inconceivable that Christ could have altered the moral law. It is also unthinkable that Christ could have tempered its severity. The moral law sets an absolute standard which is either attained or not, and when one is judged according to the moral law, one must attain that standard. Christ could not have modified the moral law without making it less perfect.[86] Christ's teaching served merely to expound the law in greater detail, and to clear it from the incorrect interpretations and glosses with which Jewish teachers had obscured it.[87]

Barlow is also clear, against Bull, that the law contained within it the promise of eternal rewards, and so was capable of bringing men to eternal life.[88] In common with other Reformed writers, Barlow believed that the Mosaic law could be understood in two ways.[89] First, it could be understood as the proclamation of the moral law, obedience to which was the condition of the Covenant of Works. Secondly, it could be understood as the legal expression of the Covenant of Grace, which contained the promise of salvation through faith in Christ, albeit in a more obscure way (e.g. through

[83] 'Cum omne opus Dei sit valde bonum, pulchrum et perfectum, certe ut effectus efficientem suam referat, necesse est: adeo ut impossibile sit, ut ausatum rude et imperfectum ab agente perfectissimo producat.' Ibid., p293.

[84] 'Cumque (ex recepta ac vera scholasticorum sententia) opera trinitatis ad extra sunt indivisa, et personis sacrae triadis omnibus communia: sequetur Deum Patrem, Filium et Spiritum Sanctum (una cum natura humana) legem illam primitus condidisse.' Ibid., pp292–3.

[85] 'Lex morale est... absolute immutabilis; nec diminutionis aut augmenti capax.' Ibid., p281.

[86] Ibid., p457 et seq.

[87] Ibid., p458.

[88] Ibid., p295.

[89] Ibid., p545.

the sacrificial cult which pointed to the perfect sacrifice of Christ) than the proclamation of the Church after the coming of Christ.[90]

Barlow argues that the law contains threats and promises which are eternal in nature under both of these considerations.[91] As a proclamation of the condition of the Covenant of Works, it offered salvation on the terms of perfect and complete obedience, terms which are, of course, impossible for fallen human beings to to fulfil.[92] As the legal, or Old Testament dispensation of the Covenant of Grace, the Mosaic law offered salvation on the terms of the gospel, though that offer was made in a more obscure way that it was after the coming of Christ.[93] Indeed, the New Covenant is called 'New', not because the gospel terms of salvation were not available under the Mosaic dispensation, but rather because, after the coming of Christ, those terms were more clearly preached, and became open to the gentiles as well as the Jews.[94]

As a consequence, Barlow's understanding of covenantal theology is entirely different from Bull's. For Barlow, the fundamental dichotomy is not between the Mosaic law and the law of Christ; but between the Covenant of Works and the Covenant of Grace.[95] And, as he underlines, 'from a true conception of the covenant of grace depends a genuine understanding of the law and the gospel, and our salvation'.[96] To Barlow's mind, Christ did not simply lighten the load of works to be performed, or promise divine assistance in bearing it: he is the source of an entirely different covenant.[97] The Gospel Covenant is not called a Covenant of Grace because through it we benefit from some assistance in meeting the requirements of divine justice, or some forbearance about our failings. Rather, it is called a covenant of grace because, under it, Christ has completely fulfilled the requirements of divine justice on our behalf, requirements which we could not fulfill. The Covenant of Grace is, therefore, a covenant based upon a promise, not a demand. Barlow writes:

> the covenant is said to be eternal as to its substance, as to the benefits and blessings which God promised in this covenant at the beginning, and which God eternally offers

[90] Ibid. p491. Francis Turretin observes an analogous distinction. Turretin, *Institutes*, Topic XII q.8.3,4, 8. I am grateful to Michael McClenahan for clarifying my thinking about the Reformed approach to covenant theology.

[91] Ibid., pp295, 545.

[92] Ibid., p279.

[93] Ibid., p507.

[94] Ibid., p557.

[95] Ibid., p463.

[96] Ibid., p507.

[97] Though salvation on the terms of the gospel was, as we have seen, open to believers even before the coming of Christ.

to the covenanted parties: that is to say eternal salvation and redemption; which Christ, the sponsor and mediator of the covenant, acquired by his blood.[98]

The only condition required from us in this covenant is the acceptance of what is offered under it, through faith.[99]

Barlow takes pains to underline that the faith of which he is speaking is a faith fruitful in good works, not a mere intellectual belief.

The faith which justifies, relative to its particular object, the merit of Christ, is not a sceptical faith which does not operate outside the intellect, but a practical one: and it 1. Illuminates and 2. Purifies the soul in which it is. It is a faith which produces Christ in the heart, not syllogisms in the head.[100]

This lively faith is the sole condition, on our part, of the New Covenant. But it is a condition, not in that it is something which we must do, but in that by it, we are united with Christ, and receive his merit as our own. It has, therefore, a double object: both a general object, as all divinely revealed truth is an object of faith; and a specific object, 'as the promise of God concerning the remission of sins, and the merit and satisfaction of Christ for those we have committed, is the special object of faith', and it is under this consideration that faith more particularly apprehends Christ, and so is the instrument, on our part, of our justification.[101]

Bull, of course, had accused the Reformed of encouraging libertinism by down-playing the role of good works,[102] and Barlow was keen to respond to that charge. As he has made clear, works do not and could not play any role in our justification, but he still asserts that they are necessary.[103] He writes:

We say that good works are necessary under the gospel, I. By necessity of precept. 1. The precepts of nature; because the law of nature eternally and indispensably obliges all people to the performance of all pious duties towards God, and of all charitable duties toward the neighbour. 2. The precepts of the gospel; because the

[98] 'Foedus aeternum dicitur, quoad substantiam, quoad beneficia et benedictiones, quas in hoc foedere ab initio promisit, et foederatis aeterno praestat Deus: salutem et redemptionem aeternam intelligo; quam foederis.. sponsor et mediator Christus suo sanguine acquisivit.' Ibid., pp484–5.

[99] Turretin, *Institutes*, Topic VIII q.3.4. This brief summary of his covenantal theology shows it to be virtually identical to Barlow's.

[100] 'Non sceptica illa quae ultra intellectum non operatur, sed practica, quae relative ad objectum suum speciali, nempe Christi meritum... justificat: et etiam animam cui inest. 1. Illuminat. 2. Purificat... fides quae Christum in corde, non quae capite in syllogismos solum progenerat.' Barlow, MS QCL 234, 88r–88v.

[101] 'Sic promissa dei de peccatis remittendis, et Christi meritum et satisfactio pro commissis est proprium fidei objectum.' Ibid., 112v. Turretin also thinks that faith has both a general and a specific object, and describes them in similar terms: *Institutes*, Topic XV q.11.13, 15.

[102] Bull, *Harmonia Apostolica*, 'Advertisement to the Reader.'

[103] Turretin, *Institutes*, Topic XVII q.3. He also distinguishes between necessity of precept and necessity of means (q.3.5).

gospel does not abrogate the moral law, nor relax or diminish its obligations. II. By necessity of means: they are the way to the Kingdom, though admittedly not the cause of the reign. The perfect fulfilment of the law is the duty of all Christian men; the law and the gospel both indicate this, and oblige us to obey.[104]

Christians are obliged to obedience, and whoever disobeys the least commandment has sinned, and so failed to do their duty. Nonetheless, this obedience, though necessary, is not required for justification under the gospel, since that can only come through faith.

In Barlow's view, good works are instrumental to sanctification, rather than to justification. This distinction must be maintained. He writes:

Infused grace sanctifies as both habit and act, but in neither manner (as a reason or motive on account of which) does it formally justify. To inherent grace (both habitual and actual), as the principle and formally sanctifying cause, we owe all our sanctification; but not our justification.[105]

All good works are the result of grace, arising as they do from the various virtuous habits which were infused into the soul at the same time as faith, and are productive of a real and inherent righteousness within us. The righteousness that these works produce in us is, however, an imperfect righteousness, and so we cannot rely upon it for our justification.

Barlow asserts, therefore, the need for a double righteousness in humanity: first the perfect, but external, righteousness of Christ, which satisfies the full rigour of divine justice, which is imputed to us through faith, and by which alone sinners can be justified before God; and, secondly, the imperfect, but internal and inherent righteousness of the sinner, which is the substance of our sanctification.[106]

Faith, he underlines, though it may be distinguished from the other virtues, can never be separated from them in the believing subject, since they are infused into the soul by the Holy Spirit in the same moment that faith is

[104] 'Bona opera sub evangelio necessaria dicimus, 1. Necessitate precepti. 1. Naturalis; quia lex naturae omnes, ad omnia pietatis officia erga Deum, et charitatis erga proximum, aeterno et indispensabiliter obligat. 2. Evangelici: evangelium moralem non abrogat, nec obligationem eius laxat aut minuit. 2. Opera bona sunt necessaria, necessitate medii: sunt via regni, licet non causa regnandi. Praestantia enim legis perfecta, est hominis Christiani officium; lex et evangelicum hoc indicant et ad praestandum obligant.' Ibid. But note that Barlow describes some works (baptism, the eucharist, repentance) as necessary by divine prescription only, and not by natural law. Barlow, MS QCL 240, 267r–267v.

[105] 'Gratia infusa, et quoad habitum et actum sanctificat, sed neutro modo (ut motivum et ratio propter quod) formaliter iustificat. Gratiae (habituali et actuali) inhaerenti, tanquam principio et causae formaliter sanctificanti, omnem sanctificationem debamus; sed non ita iustitiam.' Ibid., 116r–116v.

[106] Ibid. 234, 135r.

given. Of faith, hope, and charity, Barlow writes: '(according to the opinion of our Church) all three are infused at the same time, and coexist perpetually. So faith is said to be alone, not in the subject, but in the process of justification.'[107]

Barlow is also clear that the faith which justifies, justifies as a habit, prior to any act which it produces (i.e. we are justified by the divinely infused propensity to believe, rather than any particular act of belief). He writes: 'The believing itself, or act of faith, inasmuch as it is our own action, and prompted by grace, does not justify.'[108] As he later clarified in a letter to one of his diocesan clergy, who had the temerity to question Barlow's doctrine,

> the habit alone many times justifies when the act is absent. For as a man may be (and many times is) just, charitable or temperate by the habits only, when he exerciseth no act of justice, charity or temperance. So a man (by the habit or grace of faith) may be a faithful and justify'd person, when he does not *in acto exercito* believe.[109]

Since he holds that it is faith considered as a habit which justifies, Barlow is able to escape the accusation that the Reformed simply make one act necessary for justification, rather than many. Barlow, of course, does not think that any act justifies, even the act of faith. And just as the acquisition of the habit of faith first justifies us, so the persistence of this habit continues to justify us throughout our lives.

Barlow gives such significance to the habit of faith because he believes that it is the index and instrument of our union with Christ. He writes:

> The justice of Christ is imputed at the same time as the Spirit and his sanctifying habits are given to us, and so the sinner is justified by the habit of faith, before any act of it. Because it is through the indwelling of the Spirit, and the immediate effects of that, namely sanctifying graces, that we are made a member of the body of Christ; because by the Spirit is given union and grace, for Christ only offers the Spirit and grace to his members. But whoever has the grace and the Spirit of Christ, has also his merit, and justice, and is therefore justified.[110]

107 'Omnes (ecclesiae nostrae sententia) simul infunduntur, et perpetuo coexistunt. Adeo ut fides dicitur sola, non in subjecto, sed justificationis officio.' Ibid., 134r.

108 '*To* credere, seu actus fidei, in quantum actio nostra, a gratia proveniens, non iustificat.' Ibid. 230, p100.

109 Barlow, *An Answer to Mr. Wrexham's Letter*, MS QCL 267, p14.

110 'Simul cum Spiritu et habitus illis sanctificantibus, iustitia Christi imputatur, at sic peccator iustificatur per habitum fidei ante actum eius aliquem. Quia per Spiritum inhabitantem, et immediatos eius effectos, scilicet gratias illas sanctificantes, fit membrum corporis Christi; quia per Spiritum unionem dacipit [*sic*] et gratiam, spiritum enim et gratiam solis membris suis communicat Christus, sed quicunque gratiam et spiritum Christi habent, habent et meritum, et iustitiam ergo iustificatur.' Barlow, MS QCL 234, 133r.

Thus for Barlow, sanctification (i.e. the infusion of gracious habits) is prior to justification in logical order, though not in time.[111]

Having established this clear distinction between the respective roles of habits and acts, Barlow is also able to carry it through to his discussion of the respective conditions for justification and salvation: the habit of faith only is needed for justification, but acts of obedience are needed for salvation. The prior condition of sanctification is the same as the prior condition of final salvation. Persistence in the first leads ultimately to the second. Barlow writes: 'Perseverance in faith and justice, are required in the gospel for salvation (because you will not be saved, unless you persevere).'[112] Good works and all virtues are, therefore, prior conditions to salvation, though not to justification, in that they are means to holiness, without which it is impossible to see God.

The same can be said of repentance. Barlow writes: 'the good works of repentance, and obedience, habitual and actual holiness are, in adults, the necessary prior conditions, the way and causes *sine qua non* in order to salvation and glory.'[113] For Barlow, of course, even this limited role for works is dependant on faith. As he writes of repentance: 'true repentance, when it pleases God, necessarily presupposes faith (and therefore justice). Without faith it is impossible to please God: Hebrews 11:6. Therefore before faith (and consequently before justice) you will not truly repent.'[114]

Thus, by clearly distinguishing between salvation and justification, Barlow ends up saying that works are necessary to salvation, in exactly the same respect in which Bull argued that they were necessary to justification, as a *causa sine qua non*. Indeed, considered as such, the works God requires are not perfect, but sincere. Barlow writes:

[111] In this, Barlow is following Richard Hooker, who wrote: 'If it be here demanded which of these we do first receive; I answer that the Spirit, the virtues of the Spirit, the habitual justice which is engrafted, the external justice of Jesus Christ which is imputed: these we receive all at one and the same time; whensoever we have any of these we have all; they go together. Yet seeth no man is justified except he believe, and no man believeth except he have faith, and no man hath faith except he receive the Spirit of adoption... forasmuch as they do necessarily infer justification, and justification doth of necessity presuppose them: we must needs hold that imputed righteousness, in dignity being the chiefest, is notwithstanding in order last of all these.' *A Learned Discourse of Justification* (Oxford, 1612), pp26–7. Turretin holds, in effect a similar view: *Institutes*, Topic XV q.4.13. However, by defining sanctification more narrowly, as the growth in grace which follows regeneration, he is able to assert that sanctification, so described, is subsequent to justification.

[112] 'Perseverantia in fide et iustitia, in evangelio, necessario requiritur ad salutem (quia salvis non eris, si non persevaveris).' Barlow, MS QCL 234, 116r.

[113] 'Bona opera paenitentiae ac obedientiae, sanctitas habitualis et actualis in adultis sint media, conditiones previae ac necessariae, seu via et causae sine qua non, in ordine ad salutem et gloriam.' Ibid., 124r.

[114] 'Vera paenitentia, cum Deo placeat, fidem (et ideo iustitiam) praesupponit necesse est. Sine fidem impossibile est ut Deo placeas. Heb. 11:6. Ergo ante fidem (et consequenter ante iustitiam) vere non paeniteas.' This remark is made in the marginal notes to Barlow's own copy of the *Harmonia Apostolica*: Bodleian Library B.7.11 Linc.

Although good works and perfect obedience are only necessary by the necessity of precept, sincere obedience and unfeigned piety is necessary both ways, by necessity of precept and by necessity of means. 1. By necessity of precept; because the precept requires perfect obedience (which is greater), and therefore requires all the more sincere obedience (which is lesser). 2. As a means; because without sincere obedience and unfeigned piety we shall not attain salvation.[115]

Thus Barlow requires from the believer exactly what Bull required, but he requires it for salvation, not for justification.

Ironically, Barlow never made clear in his lectures exactly what his way of reconciling Paul with James was. He was elevated to the see of Lincoln before he could complete his task. He did, however, make it clear in the notes which he had prepared for the lectures. James, he says, meant that works justify us in that they declare, to others and to ourselves, that we are truly justified, since they are the fruits of that faith which is instrumental to it. He writes: 'works reveal and declare faith and justice. 1. To ourselves. 2. To others.'[116] Charity is the sign and symbol of true Christianity, the proof that we are the sons of God. But by faith alone, and only on account of the merit of Christ imputed to us, are we justified in the sight of God.

## THE *IUSTIFICATIO PAULINA*

Published at the behest of one of the most powerful clergymen of the day, licensed by the grandees of Oxford University, produced in collaboration with a celebrated theological expert, and written by a chaplain to the King, Tully's *Iustificatio Paulina* was indeed conceived, as Nelson puts it, as 'a battery from the side of the Church of England'.[117] It won its author, as we have already pointed out, a lasting reputation amongst Reformed theologians. A century after its publication, the Reformed controversialist Augustus Toplady could still refer to 'the famous Dr. Tully', who had conclusively answered the Arminian arguments of the wicked George Bull.[118]

[115] 'Licet bona opera, et obedientia perfectissima, sit necessitate praecepti solum necessaria, obedientia tamen sincera et pietas non simulata est utroque modo, et necessitate praecepti, et medii necessaria. 1. Necessitate praecepti; quia praeceptum requirit obedientiam perfectam (quod maius) ergo a fortiori sinceram (quod minus). 2. ratione medii, quia sine obedientia sincera et pietate non simulata, salutem non assequimur.' Barlow, MS QCL 240, 266v.

[116] 'Opera ostendunt et declarant fidem et iustitiam. 1. nobis. 2. aliis.' Ibid., 230, p47.

[117] Nelson, *Life of Bull*, p214.

[118] A. Toplady, *The Church of England Vindicated from the Charge of Arminianism* (London, 1769), p15.

Tully opens his book with a formal 'outline, or statement of the question.'[119] His aim is to eliminate the extraneous matters with which, he says, the opponents of Reformed divinity have clouded the issue. So he writes:

We say:

1. That the Reformed are not in disagreement amongst themselves or with others about whether the faith which justifies is sterile and unfruitful, or devoid of good works when there is an opportunity for them.
2. Neither is it questioned whether, with justifying faith, the roots of other virtues, or habits, if you will, are simultaneously infused. For this is conceded by both sides; though, on our side, it is maintained that each virtue individually devotes its energy to its own task, and does not obtrude upon that intended for another. Thus it is given to righteousness that it justifies, and it is given to holiness that it sanctifies. In the same way, sight and hearing, as to habit or faculty, are born together in a sentient soul; yet the eye does not hear, nor the ear see.
3. Nor do we take issue with the necessity of works for salvation in the manner, place, order and on the basis proper to them. We abhor the merit of works, but we embrace their necessity with open arms.
4. Nor is it in dispute whether justification in a declarative sense is to be ascribed to good works; for whether in oneself and at the court of one's own conscience, or before the bar of public opinion, a tree is known by its fruits.[120]

So he focuses the issue more narrowly than Barlow, but in such a way as indicates his agreement with the Lady Margaret Professor on all these matters he is excluding from the debate.

The justifying faith Tully will be talking about is fruitful in good works, not a dead or merely speculative faith.[121] It also cannot be separated, in the subject, from the other virtues of which it is the root; yet it must be distinguished from them in terms of both its nature and its function.[122] Good works are necessary to

[119] 'Conjectio, sive status questioni.' T. Tully, *Iustificatio Paulina* (Oxford, 1674), p8.

[120] 'Dicimus: 1. Nullam esse Reformatis vel secum, vel cum aliis controversium, an fides quae iustificat sit res sterilis et infructuosa, ceu bonis operibus, uti fert occasio, nudata.... 2. Necque quaeritur an cum fide justifica reliquarum quoque virtutum semina radicalia, ceu mavis, habitus, simul infundantur. Hoc enim utrique conceditur; ita tamen ex parte nostra, ut muneri suo virtus unaquaeque in solidum incumbat, non alieno se ingerat. Iustitia detur quae justificat, sanctimonia, quae sanctum faciat. Visus et auditus quoad habitum, sive facultatem, animae sensitivae ab initio simul inascuntur [*sic*]; necque tamen aut oculus ausit, aut videt auris. Nec 3. Litem movemus ipsi, an bona opera sint ad salutem necessaria, modo, scilicet, loco, ordine et ex fundamento sibi proprio.... Operum iustitiam merito exhorrescimus, necessitatem ambabus ulnis amplectimur.... Nec 4. Controvertitur, an sensu declarativo sua bonis operibus tribuenda sit iustificatio, tum domi scilicet et in foro conscientiae apud ipsum justificatum, tum foris ab alius, arbor enim cogniscitur ex fructibus.' Tully, *Iustificatio Paulina*, p8.

[121] See Barlow, MS QCL 234, 88r–88v.

[122] See Ibid., 134r.

salvation in their proper manner, yet not sufficiently meritorious as to deserve it.[123] They also justify us to ourselves, and before others, though not, of course, before God.[124]

Tully goes on:

> This, therefore, is the genuine statement of the question (as it is defended by the Reformed Churches): on account of what exactly does God receive a sinful man, a son of wrath and punishable by the curse of the law, into grace, absolve him from the denunciation of the law, and finally make him an heir of eternal life?[125]

So Tully may not immediately use the terminology of formal cause, but he is at one with Barlow in defining the central issue: what is it that enables God to pardon a sinner?[126]

Tully further notes that, even on this question, there seems to be some agreement between the Reformed and the Socinians, in that all parties apparently agree that the only merit involved in justification is Christ's. So, it would appear that

> the disagreement arises concerning the application of this merit, namely what is it which, by applying it to us, makes this inestimable treasure ours; our domestic adversaries say, with the papists, that it is faith and works; we say that it is faith alone, and that, not considered as a human work however good, but as taking hold of, sealing us with, and applying to us the justice of the one Christ: not absolutely and in itself, but relatively, as you might say, to Christ.[127]

Once again, the substantive agreement with Barlow is clear: faith alone justifies, not as a work, but as an instrument which applies the justice of Christ to the sinful soul.[128]

Tully begins his discussion of the issue by spending three chapters outlining first the view of the patristic authors, then the position of the Church of England, and finally the opinion of the foreign Reformed churches. He rejects Bull's claim that all the fathers before Augustine held the Socinian view of justification.[129] As

123 See ibid. 240, 267r–267v. 124 See ibid. 230, p47.

125 'Hoc itaque est . . . status quaesiti genuinus (prout ab Ecclesiis Reformatis defenditur) quod nimirum illud sit . . . propter quod hominem peccatorem, irae filium et legis maledictione obnoxium, Deus in gratiam recipiat, ab execratione legis absolvat, vitae demum aeternae haeredem faciat.' Tully, *Iustificatio Paulina*, p9. This is very similar to Davenant's explanation of what he means by the formal cause of justification. Cf. Davenant, *Disputatio*, p162.

126 Cf. Barlow, MS QCL 233, pp72–3.

127 'Dissidium ex huius meriti applicatione oritur, nempe quid illud sit quod inaestimabilem hunc thesaurum applicando nostrum facit; fidem et opera cum pontificiis aiunt adversarii domestici, nos fidem solam, idque non ut opus humanum, etsi bonum, sed ut apprehendens, obsignans et applicans unius Christi iustitiam: non absolute et in se, sed relative, ut dicunt, ad Christum.' Tully, *Iustificatio Paulina*, p9.

128 Cf. Barlow, MS QCL 233, p100.

129 Tully, *Iustificatio Paulina*, p13. Cf. Bull, *Harmonia Apostolica*, p99.

Tully notes (without citing them specifically), the Book of Homilies demonstrates that this is not so, by itself citing various ancient authors, to which Jewel and Downham later added more. He does, however, underline that

it should not be concealed, and indeed must be noted in any reading of the Fathers on justification, that although in this controversy they profess absolutely the same opinion as us a thousand times, nonetheless, most of them use, in the vocabulary of justification, a greater liberty of expression than we ordinarily do.[130]

Thus patristic authors need to be handled with care, as they have a tendency to elide the distinction between justification and sanctification. Nevertheless, Tully does believe that careful analysis will disclose which one they were really talking about.

Much clearer than the patristic writers, though, are the official formularies of the English church, famed as they are, Tully notes, for their moderation and clarity.[131] These documents, he argues, clearly advance the Reformed view that man is justified on account of the righteousness of Christ imputed to the believer through faith. He sets out Article XI, and exclaims: 'What could be clearer? Not even the midday sun.'[132]

Similar clarity obtains, Tully believes, in the formularies of the Reformed, and even, in this respect, the Lutheran churches abroad. He writes:

it is certainly worthy of note that all the Reformed everywhere sound the same note: since they deny (against Socinus) that faith justifies as a human work or act, but assert that it justifies as it accepts (that is, by metonymy of effect) the divine favour (it is God who justifies, and faith is the gift of God).[133]

He goes on to cite the Augsburg Confession,[134] then successively the confessions of the Swiss, French, Belgic, Saxon, and Bohemian Churches, showing that all of them hold to his view.

So, Tully concludes, either all the Protestant Churches are wrong, which seems unlikely, or Bull is. Once again, it is important to note that Tully clearly feels that

[130] 'Illud vero dissimulandum non est et in lectione Patrum de justificatione cum primis notandum, quod licet in hac controversia eandem prorsus nobiscum sententiam millies profiteantur, in vocabulo tamen justificationis majori saepe libertati uti, quam solemus ipsi.' Tully, *Iustificatio Paulina*, p16.

[131] Ibid., p20.

[132] 'Ecquid clarius? Ne sol quidem meridianus.' Ibid., p21. Bull had cited Article XI in defence of his own view. Cf. Bull, *Harmonia Apostolica*, p196.

[133] 'Quippe notissimum est, Reformatos omnes idem ubique personare, cum negant (contra Socinus) fidem justificare ut actum aut opus humanum, sed ut accipiens (per metonymiam scilicet effecti) beneficium divinum (Deus est qui justificat et fides est donum Dei).' Tully, *Iustificatio Paulina*, p32.

[134] Bull also discussed the Augsburg Confession, again claiming it for his own position. Bull, *Harmonia Apostolica*, p197 et seq.

the orthodoxy which he has set out to defend is the common doctrinal heritage of all Protestant Churches whether English or continental. To Tully's mind, Bull's views are not an authentic statement of the Church of England's theological tradition, because that tradition was and always had been Reformed in nature.

Tully then outlines what he considers to be the roots of Bull's error in the matter. The most important, he thinks, is Bull's fear of antinomianism.[135] But, as Tully says, 'what sober man will assess whether an established doctrine should be preached on the basis of an entirely accidental side-effect?'[136] Some people may well use the doctrine as an excuse for immorality, but they do so against the clear teaching of Reformed orthodoxy. As he says:

> These same, i.e. the fathers and all the Reformed churches, who themselves deservedly affirm and teach justification in the sight of God by faith alone; the very same men indeed deny that a faith which lacks holiness of heart and of life is a true and saving faith. Without which, as they assert with the Apostle, no one will see God.[137]

Accordingly, there is no refuge for hypocrites in this doctrine, and Bull is unwarranted when he calls the Reformed 'Solifidians,' as if they taught that good works were not necessary to the Christian life.[138]

Tully then addresses several substantive theological problems with Bull's view. The first, he says, is the 'distinction between justifying works, and their merits.'[139] Bull uses this distinction in order to assert that one can be justified by works as a condition, but without making works thereby meritorious. Tully argues that there is no warrant in scripture, and no authoritative precedent for this distinction. He writes:

> This we nonetheless assert, that in all the Pauline epistles, and the writings of the Reformed Churches, whenever the matter of justification is dealt with in the sight of God, to justify by works means the same thing as to justify on account of the dignity of works; so that whoever is justified by works as the Apostle understands it, is necessarily justified by the merit and dignity of works[140]

[135] As, for example: ibid., p21.

[136] 'At quis unquam vir sobrius de praestantia doctrinae ab effectu plane accidentali pronunciandum censuit?' Tully, *Iustificatio Paulina*, p40.

[137] 'Ii ipsi i.e. patres et reformatae omnes ecclesiae, qui justificationem in foro Dei per solam fidem merito astruunt et inculcant; ii, inquam, ipsi veram et salvificam fidem esse negunt, quae cordis et vitae sanctimonia careat. Sine qua cum Apostolo statuunt neminem visurum Deum.' Ibid.

[138] Bull, *Harmonia Apostolica*, p208.

[139] 'Distinctio inter opera justificantia, eorumque meritum.' Tully, *Iustificatio Paulina*, p44. Cf. Bull, *Harmonia Apostolica*, p207.

[140] 'Hoc tamen asserimus, quod in epistolis omnibus Paulinis, immo et Ecclesiarum Reformat. [sic] scriptis, quandocunque de justificatione agitur in conspectu Dei, justificare ex operibus et propter operum dignitatem, idem omnino valent, ita ut qui ex operibus sensu Apostolico justificatur, ex operum merito et dignitate justificare necesse est.' Tully, *Iustificatio Paulina*, p45.

In the matter of justification, he argues, Paul consistently opposes the works of the law to grace. And whatsoever is not the result of grace is spoken of as earned, i.e. merited.

Furthermore, Tully asserts, if it were possible to be justified by works, yet so as not to be justified by their merit, it would be possible to be justified by works that are *adiaphora*, that is, neither morally good nor morally bad. And that would be absurd, for how could works that have no goodness in them justify us before God?[141] He repeats: 'For Paul, as for the fathers and the Churches, to justify by works and to justify by merit are the same thing. Our adversaries' subterfuge is therefore a vain one.'[142]

The next problem with Bull's argument, Tully thinks, is his assertion that Paul excludes only some works from justification, not all. This is clearly against the mind of the apostle.[143] With Barlow, Tully argues that St Paul cannot simply be excluding the works of the Mosaic law considered as such, since that did not apply to gentiles. Echoing Barlow, he cites Romans 3, 'where [Paul] proves that the whole world, the gentiles as much as the Jews, is liable to divine justice; which he would have unsuccessfully attempted on the basis of the ceremonial law, since that only applied to the Jews.'[144]

Tully notes that Bull builds his case for the necessity of evangelical works upon a criticism of the Mosaic law. He writes: 'the Harmonist argues with much intricacy about the shortcomings of the law, by which he hopes to construct his doctrine of justification by evangelical works.'[145] Like Barlow, Tully is not impressed with what Bull has to say. He admits that remission of sins, and the assistance of the Holy Spirit were not available through the Mosaic law considered as law (i.e. as the condition of the Covenant of Works), but they were available through the Mosaic law considered as a different dispensation of the gospel.[146] He admits that, with the coming of Christ, the gospel promises are 'more distinct, more clear, fuller of sweetness and

[141] Tully, *Iustificatio Paulina*, pp47–8. Tully admits that even imperfect works have some goodness in them (though no merit), which indifferent actions do not.

[142] 'Paulo itaque, patribus et ecclesiis ex operibus justificare, et ex merito idem sunt. Vanum itaque est adversariorum subterfugium.' Ibid., pp51–2.

[143] Bull, *Harmonia Apostolica*, p142.

[144] 'Ubi totum probat mundum, qua judaicum, qua gentilem, justitiae divinae obnoxium; quod ex lege ceremoniali frustra tentasset, utpote quae ad solos Judaeos petinebat.' Tully, *Iustificatio Paulina*, p56. Barlow makes exactly the same point as Tully and, like him, cites Romans 3 to that effect. Barlow, MS QCL 233, p10.

[145] 'Multa quidem perplexe disputat Harmonista de legis infirmitate, quo justificationem suam per opera evangelica aedificat.' Tully, *Iustificatio Paulina*, p59. Bull spends four chapters doing this. Bull, *Harmonia Apostolica*, p87 et seq.

[146] Tully, *Iustificatio Paulina*, p64.

comfort'.[147] However, he insists that spiritual and eternal promises were made under the law. Indeed, he argues that those promises were not even terribly obscure, but manifest and obvious, so that many prophets and holy men believed in them.[148]

Tully asserts, again with Barlow, that Paul excludes all works, not just the works of the Mosaic law considered as such, from justification. His reasoning is the same as Barlow's too. He writes:

> [Paul] allows no human work to have even the smallest part in justification. The reason is that whatever justifies the sinner before God, must have justice in accord with the strict rule of justice, i.e. must be in exact conformity with the divine law. But this is not true of any of the sinner's works. Therefore there can be no justification in the sight of God by works.[149]

All human works are tainted with sin, and so fall short of the demands of divine justice; we simply cannot rely on them for justification. Furthermore, the demands of divine justice mean that God cannot accept an imperfect work as though it were a perfect one, nor overlook our past sins.[150]

Tully believes that Bull's misunderstanding about the doctrine of imputed righteousness is another root of his mistaken teaching.[151] He writes: 'a great cause of error in this matter is the imputed justice of Christ, whether because it is rejected as a doctrine, or because it is misunderstood.'[152] The Church of England, Tully argues, teaches the imputation of both Christ's passive and his active obedience (parting company here, of course, with Barlow);[153] yet many Anglican clergy see fit to ridicule the doctrine in print and from the pulpit.[154] Clearly, the doctrine of imputation needs to be properly explained. Tully writes:

> To impute, if we have regard to the origin of the expression, means nothing other than, to reckon, for whatever reason, something to the account of an individual, whether something rightly his or not, whether something good or something bad. Amongst churchmen it has this use: that is said to be imputed which, whilst it is not ours, properly speaking, personally or physically, is nonetheless attributed to us as ours in a forensic or political sense. Thus our sins are imputed to Christ, and his

[147] 'Distinctiora, clariora, suavitatis et solatii pleniora.' Ibid. [148] Ibid., pp63–4.

[149] 'Nulla enim opera humana ... ad partem justificationis vel minimam admisit. Ratio autem est, quia quicquid peccatorem justificat coram Deo, justitiam habere debet regulae justitiae, i.e. legi divinae per omnia parem et conformem. Talia vero nulla sunt peccatorum opera ... ergo coram Deo nulla erit ex operibus justificatio.' Ibid., p66. Cf. Barlow, MS QCL 233, p79.

[150] Tully, *Iustificatio Paulina*, pp85, 87.

[151] For example, in discussing imputation, Bull makes no mention of Christ's righteousness, but instead equates imputation with divine acceptance. Bull, *Harmonia Apostolica*, pp8, 156.

[152] 'Imputata Christi justitia, aut prorsus explosa, aut secius intellecta, permagna in hoc negotio erroris causa.' Tully, *Iustificatio Paulina*, p76.

[153] Cf. Barlow, MS QCL 233, p222. [154] Tully, *Iustificatio Paulina*, p76.

righteousness is imputed to us. And this [righteousness] is commonly distinguished into active and passive, or penal, though both are denoted by the term obedience.[155]

He admits that there is some disagreement amongst the Reformed about active obedience, but he asserts that the *Homily on Salvation* makes it clear that both are involved, saying as it does that Christ fulfilled the law for us.

The believer, Tully argues, is formally righteous only on account of the imputed righteousness of Christ.[156] And this happens in a way analagous to the way in which we became guilty in Adam: just as we were in Adam as the head of our race, so believers are in Christ as members of his spiritual body. Tully writes:

We confess that the faithful are engrafted into their head, Christ, to a supernatural justification, in exactly the same way as all are born in Adam to their condemnation, in whom was the entirety of his descendants, potentially or virtually and as to the root, and that in a twofold respect: 1. Naturally, since he was the first man and father of all. 2. Legally, in which respect Adam, with all the descendants to be born of him, constituted one person only. In exactly the same manner... all the faithful are included in Christ; both as to the heavenly and regenerate nature, of which he is the first and, so to speak, the father, who produces, in his own time, sons in his image by the Spirit and the seed of the word; and also as to the derivation from him of justice by imputation.[157]

Some, he notes, object to this doctrine on the grounds that a quality which belongs to one person cannot be shared with another. Christ's justice cannot be both his and ours, they would say, since we are not the same person. Tully rejects this argument, saying that although this might be true of physical identity, it is not when talking about such a forensic identity as he has in

[155] 'Imputare, si vocis originem spectemus, nihil aliud est, quam rationibus alicuius in computo adscribere, sive proprium fuerit, sive alienum, sive bonum, sive malum. At usis inter ecclesiasticos obtinuit, ut id tantum imputari dicatur, quod cum nostrum proprie, personaliter, et sensu physico non sit, nobis tamen, ut nostrum, tribuitur, sensu nimirum forensi ceu politico. Ita Christo nostra imputatur peccata, nobis illius justitia. Haec autem vulgo distinguitur in activam et passivam, ceu paenalem, utraque consimilis obedientiae nomine dignoscitur.' Ibid., p77.

[156] Ibid., p80.

[157] 'Fatemur quidem fideles eodem modo capiti Christo ad justificationem supernaturalem insertos, quo ad condemnationem omnes innascebantur Adamo, cuius universa progenies illi inerat potentia, sive virtualiter et quoad radicem, idque duplici nomine, 1. Naturaliter, cum fuerit primus omnium homo et pater.... 2. Legaliter... quo nomine Adam cum tota sobole nascitura unam duntaxat personam constituebat. Eodem plane modo... Christo insunt fideles omnes, tum quoad naturam caelestem, et regenitam, unius ille primus quasi pater, qui filios suo tempore sibi generat a Spiritu et semini verbi ad imaginem suam; tum quoad derivatam ab eo justitiam per imputationem legalem.' Ibid., p81. Cf. Barlow on the importance in the process of justification of our union with Christ. Barlow, MS QCL 234, 135r.

mind. Just as a teacher and pupil may have one will, so Christ and the believer may have one justice.

Tully insists that a correct grasp of imputation is essential to understanding the role of faith in justification. For our faith justifies only relatively, not in and of itself. As he explains: 'If faith is imputed only relatively, as it applies to the sinner the justice of Christ, then it is clear that it is Christ's justice only which is imputed, and that faith avails no more to justice, than an empty hand to the reception of alms.'[158] Faith could not itself be imputed as righteousness, since it is as defective as other human works. Thus the righteousness which is ours by faith is only called the righteousness of faith improperly. Again Tully writes:

> The justice which is imputed cannot formally and absolutely be said to be of faith (since, as such, it is a human work which, however good it may be, is marred by many defects, and is consequently useless for the justice of which we speak) and is only called the justice of faith by metonymy, in its relation to Christ. Properly speaking, the justice is Christ's, and accepted by faith which is in itself devoid of justice; whence it follows that the justice is properly said to be only of Christ, and is said to be of faith in no sense save metonymically.[159]

Tully then analyses how we are justified by the imputation of Christ's righteousness to us, i.e. in what causal relationship does the imputation of Christ's justice stand to our own. It is not the ultimate aim of our justification, he says, since the justice of Christ is not our ultimate end: heaven is. And although Christ's justice is the material cause of our justification—it is the 'stuff' which makes us just—its imputation to us is not the material cause of our justification. The imputation of Christ's justice is equally not the efficient cause of our justice, since God himself initiates the process. It must follow, Tully argues, that the imputation of Christ's righteousness to us is the formal cause of our justification.[160] It is the defining characteristic, the essential definition of what constitutes the act, rather than being causally related to it in any other way.

158 'Si imputatur fides relative solum, ut applicat peccatori justitiam Christi, constat profecto justitiam unius esse Christi quae imputatur, necque plus valere fidem ad justitiam, quam vacua manus ad percipiendam eleemosynam.' Tully, *Iustificatio Paulina*, p82. Cf. Barlow, MS QCL 233, p99. He prefers the image of applying medicine to a wound, but the implication is surely the same.

159 'Justitia fidei formaliter et absolute sumptae, quae imputatur, esse non potest (cum, ut talis, sit opus humanum, quod etsi bonum, multis tamen defectibus hideum, et consequenter ad justitiam, quam loquimur, ineptissimum) et relate ad Christum non est nisi metonymice justitia fidei, sed proprie Christi per fidem in se justitia vacuam, accipit enim justitiam, quam non habet; unde sequitur justitiam . . . proprie unius esse Christi; fidei sensu nullo nisi metonymice.' Tully, *Iustificatio Paulina*, p83.

160 Ibid., p91.

Tully points out, that the imputation of Christ's righteousness to us destroys sin in us as to guilt, but not as to existence (only sanctification does that), and, further that, since we are just by imputation, we are just by extrinsic denomination only, and so we are not, of course, as just as Christ himself.

The next Socinian error Tully finds in Bull, is the mistaken argument from the presence of good works *with* justifying faith, to its role *in* the process of justification.[161] With Barlow, and for similar reasons, he rejects Bull's view that justifying faith is the same thing as obedience, writing: 'the Socinians absurdly confound faith and universal obedience. Works which precede justifying faith cannot justify, much less those that follow it.'[162] Works performed without justifying faith cannot please God, and indeed have the nature of sin, he argues, citing Article XIII as authority for this. Works produced by that faith are clearly subsequent to justification, and therefore cannot possibly be conditions for it 'because it is completely impossible that what follows a thing as caused by it should also be the condition for that thing's existence.'[163] Good works, Tully asserts, are always present with faith, and so can properly be said to be coexistential with it—they exists wherever it exists. But they are not part of its formal definition, so cannot be said to be coessential with it—they are not of the same essence with it. 'How absurdly fantasize those who have been educated in the school of Socinus!'[164]

Tully believes that Bull has misunderstood the nature of justifying faith. With the Roman Catholics and the Socinians, Bull understands faith to be no more than an intellectual assent to what is revealed. He then assumes that the Reformed share his erroneous understanding of faith, and criticizes orthodox belief on that basis.[165] However, as Tully makes clear: 'a notional faith is not what we mean. Justifying faith is not merely assent, or even some sort of trust. It is an act of the will.'[166] Faith, for the Reformed (and, Tully notes, for medieval writers such as Bonaventure and Hugh of St Victor as well) cannot be defined merely as an intellectual assent to revelation, much less as mere reliance on God for salvation. Tully writes: 'to the constituting of justifying faith, two things above all must work together: 1. On the part of the intellect,

161 Bull makes this deduction in *Harmonia Apostolica*, p33.

162 'Fides cum obedientia universali a Socinianis ridicule confunditur.... Opera fidem justificam [*sic*] praecedentia justificare non possunt, subsequentia multo minus.' Tully, *Iustificatio Paulina*, p96.

163 'Cum prorsus impossibile est ut quod rem sequitur aut causa sit aut conditione quod sit.' Tully, *Iustificatio Paulina*, pp103–4. Cf. Barlow, MS QCL 233, p27.

164 'Quam ridicule hallucinantur in Socini schola educati.' Tully, *Iustificatio Paulina*, pp96–7.

165 Bull, *Harmonia Apostolica*, p22 et seq.

166 'Fides notionalis... non nobis est. Fides iustifica necque solus est assensus, necque quaevis fiducia.... Est actus proprie voluntatis.' Tully, *Iustificatio Paulina*, p104.

an assent to what is known. 2. With respect to the will, consent, or willing acceptance.'[167] Thus faith is a composite act of the whole soul, involving both intellect and will, just as walking is a composite act of the whole body, involving all its members.

Tully admits that strict philosophy has a problem conceiving of composite acts. Powers or capacities, as he says, are distinguished by their proper acts and objects, so one and the same act cannot be said to arise from two different powers (as hearing may not be said to arise from the power to see). However, he argues: 'the problem can be easily solved if we distinguish between the two aspects of faith, the first is its origin and principle, the second its end and complement. The first provides, as it were, the matter of faith, the second its form.'[168] As he goes on to say, the intellect provides the material of faith, and the will its form; faith is materially in the intellect, but formally in the will. And for this reason, faith cannot be defined merely as one act of the soul, to the exclusion of others:

> From what has been said, it follows that it is wrong to define faith by only one act of the soul, to the exclusion of other pertinent acts: because although, formally, the act is one, other acts are nonetheless required for the completion of its essence. Hence it is incorrect to define faith by the bare assenting habit of the mind to the gospel, no matter how sure, or by trust, no matter how reliant; the reason being that assent includes the devil, and trust the hypocrite.[169]

The assent of faith, Tully argues, is not merely a speculative assent (i.e. to a truth which must be known), but a practical assent (i.e. to a good which must be embraced). The devil, for example, understands the Gospel and accepts that it is true, but does not wish to embrace Christ, so is not justified. The grasp of the intellect does not automatically incline the will, Tully believes, so justifying faith must involve an act of both faculties. And since faith is not complete without the inclination of the will, it can be said to be, formally, an act of the will rather than an act of the intellect. Tully writes:

[167] 'Ad constituendam fidem justificam... duo potissimum necessario concurrere, 1. ex parte intellectus, assensum notitiae, 2. Respectu voluntatis, consensum, sive acceptationem complacientiae.' Ibid., p107. Turretin also insists that faith is more than mere knowledge: *Institutes*, Topic XV q.10.5.

[168] 'Res facile conciliari poterit, si distinguatur de gemino fidei respectu, primus est originis et principii; alter finis et complementi. Et ille quidem fidei quasi materiale, hic ipsum fidei formale dabit.' Tully, *Iustificatio Paulina*, p107.

[169] 'Ex dictis sequitur prave definiri fidem per actum animae unum ullum, qui reliquos eo pertinentes excludet, imo qui non inferat: quia etsi formaliter unus tantum sit actus, alii tamen ad essentiam eius complendam requiruntur. Hinc male definiri constat per nudum mentis assensum evangelio habitum, etsi certissimum, sive per fiduciam, etsi fidentissimum; ratio est, quoniam diabolos includit assensus, hypocritas fiducia.' Ibid.

From all this it is argued that justifying faith, taken formally, is an act of the will and not the intellect. Formally, I say, not by itself and excluding any intellectual acts, but necessarily presupposing them; just as in all moral acts, though they are moved by the counsel of the mind, yet they are not called acts of the mind, but of the will.[170]

Furthermore, since act and motion, according to Aristotle, are identical; and motion is specifically distinguished by that at which it terminates; faith, as an act, must be proper to that faculty where it terminates, not that faculty whence it originates. And since faith is completed, through the acceptance by the will of the salvation which is offered in Christ, it properly terminates in the will rather than the intellect. The Socinians are, therefore, simply wrong to define faith as a purely intellectual act.

Tully goes on to underline (as, of course, Barlow had done) how close Bull is in his thinking to the Roman Catholics. Both accuse the Reformed of antinomianism. Both argue that the merit of Christ is what enables our imperfect works to be accepted, but have no place in their scheme for the personal imputation of Christ's righteousness to us. Both agree, in effect, that formally speaking our justification is due to our works, in that they stand in a causal relationship to it. Both refuse to ascribe to faith in justification any more than the other virtues. And both, as a consequence of all this, ascribe both justification and sanctification to our own works, and so effectively confound the two.[171]

In his final chapter, Tully moves on to consider the correct way to reconcile Paul and James. He notes that Bull interpreted Paul by James, not vice versa.[172] This is absurd, he argues, since Paul expounds his view that justification is by faith without works quite clearly across several chapters of Romans and Galatians, whilst James only mentions the issue in one small section.

Indeed, Tully exclaims, Bull is acting quite contrary to all the accepted canons of hermeneutics:

If a comparison of the two is to be made, would it seem reasonable to anyone sober (let alone anyone learned or attentive to theology) to interpret Paul by James? It hardly seems possible, since it militates against all canons of interpretation (and especially those of biblical hermeneutics), which require us to shed light on the more obscure by the more evident, on the fewer by the more frequent, on the parts

[170] 'Hinc itidem toto arguatur fidem justificam [*sic*], formaliter sic dictam, actum esse voluntatis non intellectus. Formaliter inquam, non simpliciter exclusis actibus intellectus, sed necessario praesuppositis, sicut in omni actus voluntatis morali qui de mentis licet consilio semper peragatur, non tamen mentis actus dicitur, sed voluntatis.' Ibid., p110.

[171] Ibid., p120. [172] Bull, *Harmonia Apostolica*, p56.

by the whole, and finally on those things which were said in passing and on a particular occasion, by those things aired plainly and with authority.[173]

In truth, Tully says, there is no real conflict between the apostles, since they are not talking about the same sort of faith, or the same sort of justification. As he says:

Paul always speaks of true and justifying faith, whereas James speaks of a lying faith, or a dead faith, or one that is notional and lies only in the brain, or one that is hypocritical and is only found shining on the surface of one's behaviour.[174]

This is clear from the whole thrust of the passage in James, Tully notes, as Beza pointed out.[175] And indeed, he says, all the Reformed concede that an unfruitful faith is dead, and worthless for salvation. He also grants that works are necessary for salvation, though not for justification, and (again like Barlow) criticizes Bull for eliding the difference between the two. He writes:

Justification is the cause, and eternal salvation (or glory) the effect; but the cause and the effect are mistakenly confounded as to their forms. Nothing prevents works, which avail nothing to our justice, from availing to our glory in their own way, that is to say, as the path the faithful must tread.[176]

Tully also argues that the justification of which James speaks, is also not the same as Paul's. Tully writes:

Justification is understood by the theologian in two ways, constitutively and declaratively, the first in the sight of God, the second in the sight of creatures; which is, therefore, not justification in the strict sense (that was the previous use) but only figuratively, where the sign is taken for the object signified.[177]

[173] 'An ergo, si comparatio instituenda est, Paulum ex Jacobo interpretandum viro cuipiam sobrio (nedum docto et attento Theologo) rationi consantaneum videbitur? Fieri vix potest, quia pugnat cum omni interpretationis lege (in sacris maxime) quae exigit ut obscuriora ex luculentioribus, pauciora ex pluribus, partes ex toto, denique in transitu et per occasionem dicta, a plene et ex professo ventilatis, lucem accipiant.' Tully, *Iustificatio Paulina*, p132.

[174] 'Paulus de fide vera et justificante semper loquitur... Jacobus de fide ementita, sive mortua, quae assensum, sive notionalem et in solo cerebro torpentem, sive hypocriticum et in sola conversationis cute nitentem complectitur.' Ibid., p133.

[175] Ibid., p135.

[176] 'Justificatio est causa et salus aeterna (sive gloria) est effectus; causa autem et effectus in suis... formalitatibus indecore confunduntur. Opera quae non valent ad justitiam, ad gloriam valere, suo modo, ut viam scilicet fidelibus calcandam, nihil impedit.' Ibid., p139. Cf. Barlow, MS QCL 240 116r–116v.

[177] 'Justificatio ad theologus duplicem esse notum satis, constitutivam scilicet et declarativam, illam in foro (sive conspectu) Dei, hanc in foro creaturae, quae ideo non est justificatio stricte sumpta (uti prior) sed figurata tantum, ubi signo pro signato positur.' Tully, *Iustificatio Paulina*, p144.

Accordingly, Paul consistently discusses the justification which is properly constitutive of our justice, and James of the justification which is merely declarative of it. Tully is in agreement with Barlow on this point, as he also is, in seeing declarative justification as being concerned not only with what others think of us, but also with how we see ourselves. He writes:

Faith is shown to men by works, and that: 1. To the faithful themselves, in the court of the conscience; for by them, they know that their faith is not an illusion, or a figment of their imagination, but rather a solid trust in Christ, to which the remission of sins is conjoined. 2. By works it is revealed to other men, and above all to good men.[178]

Obedience, Tully believes, can be called a condition of the Gospel Covenant, but only if it is recognized that the Gospel Covenant has many aspects, and that what is necessary under it for one thing, is not thereby necessary for anything else. A human body has different members, each of which has a different function and a different constitution, Tully argues:

In the same way, the evangelical covenant has different branches; what is necessary to one part is not necessary to another; we are not formally justified by that by which we are sanctified, nor are we formally sanctified by that by which we are justified: imputed justice accomplishes the former, inherent justice the latter (yet both are given us by the Divinity).[179]

Furthermore, one must distinguish between different sorts of condition under the Covenant. Some conditions are causal, such as faith (though only relatively to its object, the merit of Christ); others are declarative (in that they show what the covenant has effected), or are means and ways to an end (i.e. salvation), and that is the sense in which good works can be said to be a condition of the Covenant.

Just because true faith is never without charity, Tully underlines, does not mean that it is charity which justifies, or indeed that it has any role in justification at all. Faith cannot be separated from charity, but it must be distinguished from it in the matter of justification. Indeed, Tully is willing to concede that when Paul talks of faith, he does include evangelical obedience in his meaning, but only as the fruit or effect of that faith. And, once again with Barlow, Tully asserts that the sort of obedience which is required under the Covenant, in the declarative or instrumental sense he has outlined, is not

[178] 'Ostenditur fides per opera hominibus, idque 1. Ipsis fidelibus, ceu in foro conscientiae; hinc enim colligunt earum fidem non esse spectrum, aut umbram phantasiae, sed potius solidam in Christo fiduciam, cum peccatorum remissione conjunctam.... 2. Ex operibus innotescit hominibus aliis, praesertim bonis.' Tully, *Iustificatio Paulina*, p147.

[179] 'Perinde habet in Foederis Evangelici membris; aliorum alia sunt munia; non justificamur formaliter per illud quo sanctificamur, nec sanctificamur formaliter per illud quo justificamur; illud justitia efficit imputata, hoc inhaerens (sed utraque divinitu indulta).' Ibid., p155.

perfect, but sincere: 'legal obedience is one thing, evangelical obedience another; the former requires complete perfection, the latter requires only the sincerity of the soul, though it be tainted by many defects and imperfections.'[180]

Tully ends his work with a brief explanation of what exactly he means when he says that good works are a condition of salvation. He writes:

We say:

1. No works are conditions of salvation conferring a *ius ad rem*, i.e. as if conferring an entitlement to glory; the reason being that this whole entitlement is completed in justification by faith alone (as applying to the faithful the justice of Christ), which is why faith is everywhere acknowledged by the Reformed theologians to be the sole condition of the new covenant on the part of the man to be justified. The whole entitlement to glory, I say, is conferred in this justification, so it certainly cannot arise through works.
2. Yet we do not resist the idea that holiness confers some sort of *ius in re* (I mean to the possession and property of glory) on the justified, for without holiness no one will see God.[181]

Thus good works do not give rise to any new entitlement, but are rather the completion of the original entitlement; God, of his grace, glorifying the justified person through good works. As he says:

Briefly, and as far as possible, most clearly, we deny that works (even the best) are properly called conditions for the possession of glory, because before any works, i.e. in justification, the faithful enjoy this right to eternal salvation. Possession is given by works, rather than an entitlement.[182]

In this, Tully is again close to Barlow. The older theologian had maintained that good works are conditions sine qua non of salvation,[183] that is to say,

[180] 'Alia scilicet est obedientia legalis, alia evangelica, perfectionem illa omnimodam postulat, haec unam animi sinceritatem, quamquam multis imperfectionibus et maculis inquinatam.' Ibid., p166. Cf. Barlow, MS QCL 240, 266v.

[181] 'Dicimus 1. Opera nulla tales esse conditiones ut ius ad rem, i.e. ad gloriae mercedem conferant; ratio est quia jus hoc omne totam ante peragitur in justificatione per fidem solam (quatenus applicantem credentibus justitiam Christi) quae igitur novi Foederis conditio unica (ex parte hominis justificandi) a theologis reformatis passim agnoscitur. Totam, inquam, jus ad gloriam in ipsa justificatione confertur, proinde ex operibus oriri non potest.... 2. Non reluctamur, sanctimoniam jus aliquod in re (gloriae possessionem et proprietatem loquor) conferre justificantis, quia nemo sine sanctimonia videbit Deus.' Tully, *Iustificatio Paulina*, pp170–1.

[182] 'Breviter, et qua licet apertissime, negamus opera (etiam optima) humana potiundae gloriae esse conditiones proprie dictas, quoniam ante opera, i.e. in ipse justificatione, jure isto ad salutem aeternam fruuntur fideles. Possessio potius ab operibus datur, quam jus.' Ibid., p176.

[183] Barlow, MS QCL 234, 124r.

conditions without which there is no salvation, but not conditions with a causal link to salvation (which, he made clear elsewhere, meant conditions, the fulfilment of which conferred a right to the reward); and Tully, for his part, is arguing that good works are the marks of salvation, but confer no new right to it. The gulf between them is, once again, not a wide one.

## THE WIDER REFORMED CONSENSUS

Barlow and Tully certainly led the charge in defence of the Reformed teaching on justification, but they were far from being alone. Many Anglican clergy continued to adhere to Reformed orthodoxy. Some did so in explicit opposition to the new ideas, such as John Wallis, in his unpublished letter to Richard Baxter of 28 June 1652,[184] or John Edwards in a work primarily directed against Tillotson, *The Doctrine of Faith and Justification set in a True Light* (1708). More often, however, they simply continued to expound the Reformed faith as the uncontroversial norm of Anglican belief.

Before we turn to consider this general Reformed consensus, it might be helpful to set out the main lines of the Reformed position, as Barlow and Tully had defended it. The Reformed asserted, against George Bull, that:

1. The Gospel Covenant is not a covenant of law, it is a covenant of grace.
2. The covenant of works offered eternal life and salvation, upon condition of a perfect and sinless obedience to the law.
3. The moral infirmity of human beings after the Fall meant that no one could actually fulfill the conditions of the Covenant of Works. This moral infirmity also means that all human works are inherently defective and sinful, and so cannot merit justification.
4. Under the Gospel Covenant, Christ has fulfilled the requirements of the law on behalf of believers.
5. Under the Gospel Covenant, believers are justified, not by their own righteousness, but by the righteousness of Christ, which is imputed to them in such a way that it truly becomes their righteousness.
6. The righteousness of Christ is the sole motive which inclines God to pardon a sinner. It is, therefore, the formal cause of justification, by which is meant, that the rightousness of Christ is that on account of which God justifies a sinner.

[184] P. Beeley and C. Schriba, (eds.), *The Correspondence of John Wallis* (Oxford, 2005), pp42 et seq.

7. It is the believer's mystical union with Christ which enables the righteousness of Christ to be considered as if it were the believer's own rightousness.
8. Faith alone unites the believer to Christ, so faith alone is the instrument of the believer's justification.
9. Faith is not the instrument of justification in that it is a work, but in that it is the sole virtue which apprehends Christ and his righteousness.
10. Justifying faith is not a dead faith, but a living faith which produces good works. Accordingly, although faith is without works, when considered as the instrument of justification, it is never without works, when considered as existing in the believing subject.
11. When Paul writes that justification is by faith alone without works, he intended to exclude all works, not merely ceremonial works, or works considered as performed without the assistance of grace.
12. When James writes that justification is by works, he means justification in a declarative sense, namely, that the believer is shown, by her works, to have a living faith, and so to be justified.
13. Good works, while not necessary to justification, are nonetheless necessary to salvation. They are the condition sine qua non of salvation in that, although they confer no right to salvation, no one will enjoy salvation who has not performed good works.
14. Good works are also necessary to be performed by the believer, since God commands her to perform them.
15. The antinomian inference cannot, therefore, be drawn from the Reformed teaching on justification.

Barlow and Tully certainly gave the most detailed exposition of the Reformed scheme. But it is a pattern of doctrine which we find, again and again, through the writings of the Reformed Anglicans of the late seventeenth and early eighteenth centuries. It is to that broad Reformed consensus which we must now turn. And, for the purpose of clarity, we shall present that consensus in the order indicated by the summary outline above.

Edward Reynolds enunciates with clarity the Reformed understanding of the relationship between the covenants. The fundamental distinction lies between the Gospel covenant and the covenant of works. He writes, of the Gospel covenant, that 'The covenant and grace thereof is free and absolute, not conditional and suspended upon the unstable will of man.'[185] He argues that, under the Gospel covenant, believers are delivered from the law, and that in two respects.

[185] E. Reynolds, *Works* (London, 1679), p923.

First, we are delivered from the law as a covenant of righteousness, and expect justification and salvation only by faith in him who is the Lord our Righteousness. . . . We are righteous by the righteousness of God without the law; that is, not that righteousness by which God, as God, is righteous, but by a righteousness which we have not by nature, or in ourselves, or from any principle of our nature . . . but from the mere grace and gift of God. Secondly, hereupon consequently, we are delivered from the rigour of the law which consisteth in two things: first it requireth perfect obedience: secondly perpetual obedience. . . . Now from this we are delivered, though not as a duty, yet as such a necessity as brings death upon the fail of it.[186]

Ezekiel Hopkins agrees, writing:

Now the moral law may be considered by us either as a Covenant of Works, or as a rule of life. In the former sense it is superseded to all believers by the mercy and grace of the gospel: in the latter it is explained, corroborated, and protected by the gospel; and though it be no longer the measure of God's proceedings to us, yet still it is the measure of our duty to him.[187]

John Wallis, for his part, writes succinctly of the terms of the Gospel covenant: 'no other terms are required but a condition of want, not a condition of worth.'[188] For the Reformed, in other words, the Gospel covenant is fundamentally different from the covenant of works: it is a covenant based upon divine promises, not upon human conditions,[189] it is an offer of free grace, not a demand for obedience.[190]

That said, the Reformed are clear that their understanding of the covenants does not mean that the Mosaic law was defective. Expounding the Sermon on the Mount, and, in particular, Jesus's exposition of various instructions in the law, Robert South writes: 'Christ does by no means here set himself against the law of Moses, as a law faulty or imperfect, and upon those accounts needing either correction or addition, but only opposed the corrupt comments of the scribes and pharisees upon the law.'[191] South is clear, as Barlow and Tully were, that the law contained spiritual, and not merely temporal promises.[192] South also argues that the Arminian idea that Christ published a new and

[186] Reynolds, *Works*, p155. See also: John Conant, *Sermons*, 6 vols (London, 1693–1722), i p128; J. Hacket, *A Century of Sermons* (London, 1675), p43; W. Burkitt, *Expository Notes with Practical Observations on the New Testament* (London, 1760), p407; P. Newcome, *A Catechetical Course of Sermons*, 2 vols (London, 1712), i p436; Edwards, *Doctrine of Faith and Justification*, p345–6; T. Marshall, *The catechism set forth in the Book of Common Prayer* (Oxford, 1679), p7; B. Jenks, *Submission to the Righteousness of God* (London, 1700), p49.

[187] E. Hopkins, *Works*, 4 vols (London, 1809), ii p306.

[188] J. Wallis, *Sermons* (London, 1791), p47.

[189] Ibid., p233.

[190] S. Crossman, *The Young Man's Monitor* (London, 1664), p24. Parkhurst, N., *A Second Volume of Select Discourses* (London, 1707), p59. Hacket, *Sermons*, p43. Hopkins, *Works*, p206.

[191] R. South, *Sermons*, 5 vols (Oxford, 1842), ii p123.

[192] Ibid.

different law is absurd. He writes: 'If Christ opposed his precepts to those of the Mosaic law; then God speaking by Christ must contradict God speaking by Moses.'[193] The law is not something which is susceptible to modification, any more than God is susceptible to modification.

The Reformed are clear that the covenant of works did offer eternal life. Reynolds writes: 'God did out of mercy propose salvation unto Adam, as an infinite reward of such finite obedience, as Adam was able by his own created abilities to have performed.'[194] But the condition required by the Old Covenant for salvation, was one of perfect righteousness. As Edwards puts it, 'the divine justice requires a perfect righteousness and obedience of us. And the law... requires the same'.[195] And, as Hopkins argues, 'this covenant makes no allowance for transgressions, nor any admission of repentance'.[196]

The Reformed are all agreed that it is the moral weakness of humanity after the Fall that has prevented us acquiring salvation through the covenant of works. Human beings not only commit sin repeatedly, of course, but their nature is now so vitiated by the Fall that even their best works are in fact corrupt.[197] And so, far from earning salvation by such works as they perform, they only require further forgiveness. Thomas Horton writes that 'All a man's external righteousness, it will never make a satisfaction to God's justice, neither to God's preceptive justice in commanding, nor to God's vindictive justice in punishing. This righteousness, it falls short of both.'[198] For, he says, 'The best works of any which live here in this world, they are imperfect and come short of the rule; and so are so far from justifying, as that they need a great deal of pardon and forbearance themselves.'[199]

The other Reformed writers take a similarly bleak view of the chances of human beings earning their justification by their works.[200] Sin corrupts even those works which we perform with the aid of God's grace. As Reynolds puts it:

> this we affirm constantly, unto the best work that is done by the concurrence and contribution of our own faculties, such a viciousness doth adhere, such stubble of ours is super-induced, as that God may justly charge us for defiling the grace he gave.... Sin

[193] Ibid., p124. [194] Reynolds, *Works*, p3.

[195] Edwards, *Doctrine of Faith and Justification*, p295. See also Wallis, *Sermons*, p142.

[196] Hopkins, *Works*, ii p308. See also Jenks, *Submission*, p11.

[197] W. Delaune, *Twelve Sermons* (London, 1728), p252; S. Ward, *Seven Sermons* (London, 1674), p83; Jenks, *Submission*, p11.

[198] T. Horton, *One Hundred Select Sermons*, 2 vols (London, 1679), ii p3.

[199] Horton, *Forty-Six Sermons* (London, 1674), p30.

[200] E. Welchman, *The XXXIX Articles of the Church of England* (London, 1743), p31. Burkitt, *Expository Notes*, p405. Newcome, *Catechetical Course*, ii pp345–6. W. Beveridge, *Works*, 12 vols (Oxford, 1842), vii p295. R. Boyle, *Works*, 14 vols (London, 1999–2000), i pp101, 102. Parkhurst, *Second Volume*, p18. H. Compton, *The Bishop of London's Tenth Conference with his Clergy* (London, 1701), p10.

in the faculty, is poison in the fountain, that sheds infection unto everything that proceeds from it.[201]

Since human beings cannot fulfill the requirements of God's law, a substitute was found who could fulfill the law on our behalf. And that is the work of the mediator, Jesus Christ. Thomas Horton writes: 'Whatsoever the law could demand and require of us, the same is fully satisfied and fulfilled by Christ. He has fulfilled the righteousness of the law on our behalf.'[202] William Delaune agrees, writing of God's new way of dealing with man:

A new covenant is made with him, agreeable to the present frailty of his nature: the Son of God himself takes his flesh, that in it he may undergo his penalty by dying for him, and in his life of sorrow upon earth, performed the whole law, that man who had lost his own righteousness, might now be clothed with his.[203]

John Wallis writes along similar lines, saying,

as for that obedience, we grant that there is nothing required of us, either in way of satisfaction for our former sins, or in way of merit for future happiness: for whatsoever is required of us, either in way of satisfaction or in way of merit, is already done and performed by Christ.[204]

Since Christ has completely fulfilled the law, both satisfying the divine justice by suffering for human sin, and earning salvation by a life of perfect righteousness, salvation can now be offered to human beings unconditionally. Whatever needed to be done by humanity has been done by the God-man. It follows that, under the gospel covenant, human beings are justified by having the righteousness of Christ imputed to them.[205] What Christ has done and earned on the cross becomes the believer's, by God's graciously reckoning it as theirs. Horton describes the righteousness upon which a believer depends for her justification, as 'the righteousness of Christ himself imputed to us, both of his nature, life and death. This is our righteousness so far forth as it is accounted for ours, and we have a share and interest in it'.[206] Or as William Beveridge puts it:

201 Reynolds, *Works*, p56. John Conant, MS Bod Add A 260, 14v.

202 Horton, *Forty-Six Sermons*, p50. See also: Burkitt, *Expository Notes*, p405; J. Wilkins, *Sermons* (London, 1682), p207; Nathaniel Parkhurst, *The Faithful and Diligent Christian Described and Exemplified* (London, 1684), p10; Hopkins, *Works*, ii p319; Reynolds, *Works*, p211; Hacket, *Century*, p220; Jenks, *Submission*, p146.

203 Delaune, *Twelve Sermons*, p26. See also p254.

204 Wallis, *Sermons*, p204.

205 Edwards, *Doctrine of Faith and Justification*, p244.

206 Horton, *One Hundred Sermons*, p5. See also Newcome, *Catechetical Course*, p353; Reynolds, *Works*, p176; Jenks, *Submission*, p50.

we cannot be accounted righteous but by Christ's merits imputed to us . . . whatsoever we lost we gained in the second Adam. Are we accounted sinners by Adam's sin imputed to us? We are accounted righteous by Christ's righteousness laid upon us.[207]

And Hacket speaks of 'the robe of justification, when God looks upon us, not as we are in ourselves, but as we are clothed with the merits of Christ'.[208]

Hopkins, for his part, is anxious to underline that the imputation of Christ's righteousness actually makes us just, so long as we understand that justice in a forensic sense. He writes: 'Christ's righteousness being made ours by faith, God doth then actually impute it to our justification. And therefore, the righteousness of Jesus Christ is not by God only thought to be ours; but it is ours really and truly, in a law sense.'[209] Reynolds employs a pretty analogy to describe the process, writing that

As the colour of the glass is by the favour of the sunbeam shining through it made the colour of the wall, not inherent in it, but reluctant upon it by extrinsical affection; so the righteousness of Christ, by the favour of God, is so imputed to us, as that we are *quoad gratiosum Dei conspectum* [with regard to the gracious regard of God] righteous too.[210]

Several authors point out that, to this imputation of Christ's merits to the believer, there corresponds an imputation of the believer's sins to Christ. Edwards argues that Scripture shows us 'a double imputation, one on our part, and another on Christ's. Our sins are imputed to him, and his righteousness to us'.[211] And Conant holds a similar view: 'Christ's righteousness ours, as our sins his.'[212] This explains, to the Reformed mind, how our personal guilt is paid for by Christ: he took it upon himself, just as he graciously offers the believer his own righteousness.

Since the believer is counted righteous by the imputation of Christ's righteousness to her, that divine righteousness must be the motive or reason why God justifies her.[213] The imputation of the merit or righteousness of Christ is thus the 'formal cause' of justification. Most writers prefer to use less technical phrases to describe it. John Edwards, who is happy to use the technical term, writes:

If we will conceive of justification as it may be run thro' the distinct causes which logicians are wont to assign, then we may set it forth thus: the efficient cause of it is either principal or instrumental; the principal efficient cause is God, the whole Blessed Trinity: the instrumental cause is faith. Christ's satisfaction or righteousness is the

207 Beveridge, *Works*, vii p286.
208 Hacket, *Century*, p426.
209 Hopkins, *Works*, ii p322.
210 Reynolds, *Works*, p382.
211 Edwards, *Doctrine of Faith and Justification*, p244.
212 Conant, MS Bod Add A 260, 38v.
213 Burkitt, *Expository Notes*, p11.

material cause of it. The imputation of it is the formal one. And the redemption or salvation of man is the final one.[214]

And Robert South, when describing the process of justification, writes of God, 'he freely imputes to us Christ's righteousness, which is the sole, proper and formal cause of our justification.'[215]

The imputation of Christ's righteousness to the believer is only possible because the believer is spiritually one with Christ. So, to the Reformed mind, the believer's union with Christ is an essential foundation to the right understanding of justification. Thomas Horton writes:

in regard of our interest and mystical conjunction, there is such a near tie and union betwixt Christ and every believer, as of head and members, so that that which is done by him is accounted as done by them; and that which is fulfilled by him, is said to be fulfilled in us: in us so far forth as we are ingrafted and incorporated into him, and by faith are made one with him. He hath taken our nature upon him and imputed his righteousness to us.[216]

John Edwards waxes similarly lyrical about the union with Christ which is enjoyed by the believer. He writes, that by virtue of union with Christ:

Believers are virtually the same with Christ: they are accounted as one person with him, and he with them.... This near and intimate conjunction between Christ and his chosen, is the foundation of the reciprocal transferring of sin and righteousness. For Christ and the faithful being by their near union become one mystical person, there must needs flow from thence this interchangeable communication. By virtue of this coalition it is, that believers are reckoned to have done and suffered the very same things that Christ did and suffered. Not only their sins transferred on him, but this obedience and death are esteem'd theirs. This is the natural result of Christ's being made, by the divine appointment and constitution, one person with us.[217]

All the Reformed are in agreement that faith is the only virtue which unites a believer to Christ. And since union with Christ is essential to the process of justification, it follows that faith is the sole instrument of our justification. So John Conant writes: 'Faith is that grace by which alone we apprehend Christ to our justification.'[218] Delaune echoes his view. 'Our very salvation is attributed

[214] Edwards, *Doctrine of Faith and Justification*, p388.

[215] South, *Sermons*, ii p148. See also Burkitt, *Expository Notes*, p406. Burkitt uses the phrase 'meritorious cause' rather than 'formal cause'.

[216] Horton, *Forty-Six Sermons*, p53. See also South, *Sermons*, iv p242; Reynolds, *Works*, p172; Jenks, *Submission*, p61.

[217] Edwards, *Doctrine of Faith and Justification*, p294. See also Beveridge, *Works*, x p463.

[218] Conant, *Sermons*, iv p365.

to faith alone; and faith is declared to be the principle of that union between God and man without which there can be no happiness.'[219]

With Barlow, Wallis is insistent that it is only faith considered as a virtue, as the disposition to believe, not faith considered as an act, that justifies. He writes:

If it should be urged, that it is not habitual, but actual faith which justifies; I think there is no necessity of granting that: but rather that it is such a habit, which acts as there is occasion . . . or else it would seem to follow, that our justification is as often intermitted as our actings of faith, and that a believer, when asleep, is not in like justified state as when awake.[220]

Like Barlow and Tully, Beveridge thinks that the Socinian understanding of faith, as meaning the same thing as obedience, is a dangerous opinion, and one which must be resisted. He writes: 'The Socinians hold, that justifying or saving faith is nothing else but obedience sincerely performed to the law of God; so that good works are not the fruit of faith, but constitute the very form and essence of it.'[221] This, he argues, is contrary to the normal usage of the word in scripture. Like Barlow, Beveridge is insistent that faith and obedience differ, as cause and effect differ.[222]

The Reformed are, without exception, happy to describe faith as the instrument, or instrumental cause of justification. And they are insistent that it justifies, not as it is a work, but as it is the virtue which apprehends Christ and accepts his promises. Edwards writes of faith:

It is the direct means in order to such an end, to wit, justification. But the most proper expression or term is that of instrument. And this is a very intelligible notion, one would think; for an instrument is that which is made use of by the efficient cause to produce an effect: and accordingly, this may rationally be applied to faith which God hath ordained as the organ, yea as the proper and peculiar organ on our part of effecting justification.[223]

Edwards notes that various writers have opposed this description of faith as the instrument of justification. He notes, in particular, the views of Episcopius, Hammond, Fowler, and Tillotson. Tillotson, he notes, pours liberal scorn on the idea of moral (as opposed to physical) instruments generally. Yet, Edwards notes, the Archbishop seems happy to conceive of prayer, the scriptures, and the sacraments as instruments of religion.[224] Edwards defends

[219] Delaune, *Twelve Sermons*, p230. See also: Wallis, *Sermons*, pp235–6; Beveridge, *Works*, vii p304; Burkitt, *Expository Notes*, p406; Horton, *Hundred Sermons*, ii p94; Reynolds, *Works*, p10.

[220] Wallis, *Sermons*, p265. See also Jenks, *Submission*, p14.

[221] Beveridge, *Works*, vi p83.

[222] Ibid. p84. See also: Edwards, *Doctrine of Faith and Justification*, p83.

[223] Ibid., pp318–19. [224] Ibid., p320.

the coherence of the Reformed view, arguing that they are using the term 'instrument' in a philosophically acceptable way. He writes:

> The instrumental cause is that which is subservient to the principal cause, and on that account faith may truly be said to be an instrumental cause. . . . There is some power to work in an instrument, but it can't produce the effect unless actuated and managed by the principal cause. So it is here, faith hath all its power to act from God, the efficient and principal cause.[225]

He therefore concludes that 'Faith is a proper moral instrument, as it is subservient in receiving Christ and applying his righteousness.'[226]

Edwards's views find frequent echoes in the writings of other Reformed figures. Faith, to the Reformed mind, has no inherent value that accounts for its role in justification. It is only significant because of its relation to Christ. Reynolds writes: 'we must note that the strength of faith doth not arise out of any formal quality thereof (for faith in itself, as a habit and endowment of the soul, is as weak as other graces), but only out of the relation it hath to Christ.'[227] Conant thinks the same. Faith is significant, he argues, not because of any inherent strength in it, but because it takes hold of Christ and makes his righteousness ours. 'Now of all the graces, faith alone takes hold of Christ and so makes him and his righteousness ours to justification.'[228] And that is why we are said to be justified by faith alone.

But if faith is alone, considered as the instrument of justification; it is not alone as it exists in the believer. In the Reformed view, that faith which is the instrument of justification, is a living faith, a faith that naturally and automatically produces good works. And as a result, although, with regard to its role in justification, it can be separated from the other Christian virtues, and the obedience which characterizes the Christian life; it is never found where they are not also present. Peter Newcome writes: 'That which crowns and perfects the act of believing, is a suitable practice of repentance and obedience, whereof it is naturally productive, without which effect none can be saved, and without which it ought not to be accounted faith.'[229]

Robert Boyle deployed an unusual scientific analogy to explain the relationship between faith and works in his *Some Motives and Incentives to the Love of God* (1659). He writes:

225 Beveridge, *Works*, p84. See also: Edwards, *Doctrine of Faith and Justification*, p321.

226 Ibid., p321.

227 Reynolds, *Works*, p169. See also: Welchman, *XXXIX Articles*, p32.

228 Conant, MS Bod Add A 260, 15r. See also: Hacket, *Century*, p524; Beveridge, *Works*, vii p290; Wallis, *Sermons*, p200; Burkitt, *Expository Notes*, p237.

229 Newcome, *Catechetical Course*, pp60–1. See also: Marshall, *Catechism*, p7; Burkitt, *Expository Notes*, p498; Parkhurst, *Ten Select Discourses*, pp37, 38; Wallis, *Sermons*, p213; Beveridge, *Works*, vii p289.

I said, Lindamor, that faith was the grand condition required, in God's free grant of eternal life. Not that I would ascribe anything to a lazy, speculative; & barren faith, in opposition to the lively one, which is called by the Apsotle . . . faith operating by love; since I am informed by St James, that the divorce of faith and works is as destructive to religion, as that of soul and body is to life; but that I was willing to mind you, that though true faith . . . be ever the pregnant mother of good works; yet are not those works the cause, but the effects of God's first love to us. . . . As, though a needle's pointing at the pole be, by being an effect, an argument of its having been invigorated by the lodestone, or received influence from some other magnetic body; yet is not that respect unto the north the cause, but the operation of the iron's being drawn by the attractive mineral.[230]

For, as Edwards puts it, 'Faith naturally produces inherent (tho' imperfect) righteousness. A man must trust in Jesus, and not in his works; yet everyone that trusts in him is careful to do good works. For the grace of faith begets not only a new disposition of mind, but a new course of life.'[231] Which is why, Edwards believes, Paul 'separates works from justification, yet he doth not separate them from justifying faith'.[232]

The Reformed remain adamant, despite this, that Paul intended to exclude all human works from the process of justification. He did so, so as to make clear that justification is by grace alone, and that no human action contributes anything to it. As Burkitt writes, in his commentary on Paul's epistles, 'It is evident, that the antithesis, or opposition, runs all along, not between ceremonial works and moral works, but between works in general and faith: the law of works and the law of faith, are opposed to each other.'[233] Wallis agrees, writing of Paul that 'He makes justification by grace to be inconsistent, not only with justification by an adequate merit, but by any works at all; nay, if at all by works, it cannot possibly be by grace.'[234]

When they turn their attention to James, the Reformed agree with Barlow and Tully, that he is discussing justification only in a public and declarative sense. He is talking about how the believer demonstrates to herself, and to her neighbours, that her faith is a living one, and that she is, therefore, truly justified.[235] In explanation of how Paul and James should be understood, Beveridge writes of the believer that,

As his person is justified by faith only before God, so is his faith justified by works only before men and his own conscience. It is by faith only, and not by works, that a man is

[230] Boyle, *Works*, i p95. [231] Edwards, *Discourse of Faith and Justification*, p197.
[232] Ibid. [233] Burkitt, *Expository Notes*, p406.
[234] Wallis, *Sermons*, p215. See also: Beveridge, *Works*, vii p292 and vi p84; Edwards, *Discourse of Faith and Justification*, p325; Jenks, *Submission*, p10.
[235] Burkitt, *Expository Notes*, p763.

accounted righteous in heaven; but it is by works only, and not by faith, that a man is esteemed righteous upon earth.[236]

Edwards says much the same.[237]

But although good works only justify the believer in this external and declarative sense, nonetheless, they can be described as necessary to salvation. For unless believers' lives are marked by good works, they will not get to heaven. Good works are the means of salvation, though they are not its cause. They are a necessary instrument to attain eternal life, but they do not convey the title to eternal life. Henry Compton writes: 'It is agreed by all sober men, that a virtuous and holy life is necessary to salvation; not as giving a right, but as the necessary means to obtain that right, which is purchased by Christ's blood.'[238]

Reynolds, when discussing the necessity of works, distinguishes between the necessity of cause, and the necessity of means. The payment required for the purchase of anything is necessary with the necessity of cause, he argues, since a customer who pays the required price for the object acquires the title to it. But, he says, in the case of a customer who buys some property which is at a distance, the journey to that property is necessary only by the necessity of means. The journey does not give rise to the ownership of the property, but is required for the purchaser to enjoy the property.[239] Good works, Reynolds then argues, are necessary to salvation with this second, lower sort of necessity. He writes:

The only cause of salvation is the free grace of God, and price of the blood of Christ, deriving a property thereunto upon us.... But we cannot come to the actual possession of that inheritance, without running the race of evangelical holiness which is the way thereunto.

That holiness is, therefore 'necessary to the *ius in re*, to the actual possession of this inheritance, as the only way which leads thereunto. For without holiness, no man shall see the Lord. It is a *gradus* and an inchoation of glory.'[240]

Beveridge, too, is insistent upon the need for good works, writing:

Although it hath pleased God of his infinite mercy, in the covenant of grace, to entail justification upon our faith in his promises only, and not upon obedience to his precepts; yet it doth not follow that we are freed more from our obedience than we were before.[241]

236 Beveridge, *Works*, vii p292.
237 Edwards, *Discourse of Faith and Justification*, p424.
238 Compton, *Tenth Conference*, p9. See also Parkhurst, *Second Volume*, p58.
239 Reynolds, *Works*, pp1105–6.
240 Ibid., p1106. See also: Edwards, *Discourse of Faith and Justification*, p362.
241 Beveridge, *Works*, vii p299. This is what Barlow and Turretin called the necessity of precept: Barlow, MS QCL 240, 267r–267v and Turretin, *Institutes*, Topic XVII q3.5.

Works are thus to be performed as commanded by God, and, therefore, as pleasing to him. They are also, Beveridge notes, necessary for our salvation. With Barlow, he is prepared to describe good works as the condition of it. He writes: 'doing the will of God, or universal obedience to all his commands revealed to us, is the condition of our salvation, or entering into the kingdom of heaven, i.e. glory and eternal happiness.'[242] And, in fact, in one sermon, he even makes it clear that, like Barlow, he sees the fulfilment of this condition as working in the manner of a cause sine qua non, saying of Christian obedience: 'it is by this that we are qualified for that salvation which the grace of God in Christ hath brought to us, insomuch that our salvation depends upon that too, as *causa sine qua non*, as without which we shall never be saved'.[243]

So believers must perform good works, because they are necessary to the attainment of salvation: they are the way to heaven. But believers are also bound to perform them simply because they are commanded to do so by God. Reynolds writes, of Christian obedience, that, 'Necessary is the observance of it as a fruit of faith, not as a condition of life or righteousness. Necessary, *necessitate praecepti*, as a thing commanded, the transgression whereof is an incurring of sin.'[244] In other words, believers ought to perform good works, not because that performance gains them anything, but merely because God has instructed them to, and the performance of them is pleasing to him.[245]

For all these reasons, the Reformed deny categorically that an antinomian inference can be drawn from their view of justification. Jenks is adamant: 'The doctrine has no tendency to Antinomianism, and carnal liberty; or to throw out repentance, good works and holiness of life.'[246] As Welchman puts it,

A true faith has always love joined to it, and consequently is neither inactive nor unfruitful. And further, he who truly believes the gospel, will be careful to maintain good works, which he who neglects to do has only a dead faith, or even none at all.[247]

Beveridge writes along similar lines. He argues that:

Our being justified by faith, and not by works, should not at all lessen our endeavours after good works, but rather heighten them, seeing that Abraham, who was justified by faith, was also full of good works; though it was not by these good works, but by faith, that he was justified. And so any man, though it be not for his good works he doth that he is justified, yet if he is justified, he will do good works.[248]

[242] Beveridge, *Works*, ix p369. This is what Barlow and Turretin described as the necessity of means: Barlow, MS QCL 240, 267r–267v and Turretin, *Institutes*, Topic XVII q.3.5.
[243] Beveridge, *Works*, iv p230. Barlow, MS QCL 234, 124r.
[244] Reynolds, *Works*, p162. See also p383.
[245] Welchman, *XXXIX Articles*, p33. See also: Wallis, *Sermons*, p372.
[246] Jenks, *Submission*, p36.
[247] Welchman, *XXXIX Articles*, p34.
[248] Beveridge, *Works*, vii p291.

Wallis puts it succinctly. 'Sanctification, or holiness, is agreeable to the will of God, as a thing by him commanded, and consequently, is the duty of man.'[249]

## THE RESILIENCE OF THE REFORMED TRADITION

The publication of George Bull's *Harmonia Apostolica* was an officially sanctioned attack on the Reformed understanding of justification. It was met by a vigorous and highly successful campaign of resistance by Anglican churchmen of reformed sympathy.

The counter-attack was organized by George Morley, Bishop of Winchester, and by the 1670s he was probably a more influential cleric that the Archbishop. Morley fostered opposition to Bull's theology, encouraging the Lady Margaret Professor, Thomas Barlow, to lecture against Bull in the Divinity School, and persuading the Principal of St Edmund Hall, Thomas Tully, to defend the Reformed understanding in print. In both Universities, influential academics warned the students in their charge of the dangers of Bull's theology. And in the diocese under Morley's direct control, clergy were directed neither to read Bull nor to teach his doctrine from their pulpits. When, in due course, Barlow was made a bishop, he too used his episcopal authority to guard against those who adopted heterodox views on the subject of justification.[250]

Between them, Barlow and Tully mounted a powerful exposition and defence of the Reformed view, whilst exposing the weakness of its alternative. Their key guiding principle was that if justification was by grace, then all human works had to be excluded from the process. They embraced a view of the covenants which made a sharp distinction between the covenant of works, in which the believer was justified by perfect and consistent obedience to the moral law, and the covenant of grace, in which the requirements of the law were fulfilled in the believer's stead by Christ. Since all human actions are riddled by sin, they argued, no human being could offer the complete obedience which the covenant of works requires. Salvation could, therefore, only ever be a gift, not something earned.

The believer is justified, in their scheme, by the righteousness of Christ being imputed to her. This imputation is founded on the mystical union between the believer and Christ, of which faith as a sole virtue is the instrument.

[249] Wallis, *Sermons*, p372. See also Jenks, *Submission*, p34.
[250] T. Barlow, *An Answer to Mr Wrexham's Letter*, MS QCL 267, p48.

a lot of Bull

Accordingly, the formal, or morally impulsive cause of justification—that on account of which God justifies the sinner—is the righteousness of Christ imputed to her. Whereas faith is the means or instrument of justification, in that it applies to the believer the only medicine that can heal her sickness: namely the merits of Christ.

Barlow and Tully strongly resist the Arminian charge that the Reformed view of justification will lead to immorality. They insist upon the necessity of works for salvation, both in that they are commanded by God, and in that only those who do good works will come to salvation. Good works are, therefore, the condition sine qua non of justification. And they bring a believer into possession of salvation, though they do not confer a right to it.

Furthermore, Barlow and Tully insist that the faith which is the instrument of justification in their scheme, is a living faith, and so one which is naturally productive of good works. As a result, although faith is separate from good works, considered as the instrument of justification, it is never separate from them, considered as it is a virtue in a given believer.

Barlow and Tully contend that Bull's scheme makes good works necessary for justification, and so falls into the trap of Socinianism and Popery. They are entirely unimpressed with Bull's claim that good works are only the indispensable condition of justification in his view of the matter. For, they argue, when God appoints a condition in such a way that, if it is fulfilled, justification follows (i.e. if it is both a necessary and a sufficient condition for justification), then it bears, whatever Bull may say, a causal relationship to justification.

Barlow's lectures and Tully's book are without doubt the most important statements of the Reformed position on justification to have been produced by Anglican writers after the Restoration. Nevertheless, the views they enunciated were actually quite widespread within the Church. Even George Bull's biographer admitted that many Anglicans were not happy with the theology of the *Harmonia Apostolica*, and were delighted to see it so coherently rebutted. Barlow and Tully are in fact the visible tip of a far larger Reformed iceberg. Up and down the land, in sermons, tracts, catechisms, and commentaries, Reformed Anglicans were articulated their views on justification in a public manner.

It would be foolish to claim that, by the dawn of the eighteenth century, Reformed theology was still the dominant theology of the English Church. Even its devoutest adherents admitted that their views were no longer desperately fashionable. Nonetheless, the Reformed teaching that justification was by faith alone, remained a serious theological option in the reign of Queen Anne and beyond. And, pace J.C. Ryle, we can find Anglican adherents of that position well into the eighteenth century. That Reformed theology remained a compelling alternative, was the fruit of the many Reformed Anglican writers of the post-Restoration period. For they articulated the Reformed understanding of justification in a new theological environment, adapting it to the wider Church's growing preoccupation with lawlessness and immorality,[251] not least by emphasising the important place which works held even in the solifidian scheme. And they repeated, again and again, that the Reformed view of justification was the authentic tradition of the English Church.

Sheldon's attempt to sideline the Reformed inheritance of the English Church ultimately failed. The Reformed tradition was simply too firmly anchored within the English Church, even after the Great Ejection, to be rooted out. As a result, Augustan clerics, though now a minority, could still be heard proclaiming a doctrine of justification which linked the Church of England to its Reformed past, and to the wider world of European Protestantism.

[251] Spurr, *Restoration Church*, pp234 et seq.

# 4

# The Reformed Defence of Trinitarian Orthodoxy

## THE TRINITARIAN CONTROVERSY

> Most Reverend and Right Reverend Fathers in God, we greet you well. Whereas we are given to understand, that there have been of late some differences among the clergy of this our realm about their ways of expressing themselves in their sermons and writings, concerning the doctrine of the Blessed Trinity, which may be of dangerous consequence if not timely prevented; we therefore, out of our princely care and zeal for the preservation of the peace and unity of the Church, together with the purity of the Christian faith, have thought fit to send you the following directions, which we straightly charge and command you to publish, and to see that they be observed within your several dioceses.[1]

So began a remarkable set of injunctions issued by King William III on 3 February 1696.

The King had taken the unusual step of intervening in a theological debate, at the request of Henry Compton, Bishop of London. As Compton's chaplain, William Whitfield, recalled, in a sermon commemorating the Bishop's death, 'when the dispute about the Holy Undivided Trinity was managed by some in new and unusual terms, a royal letter was procured to forbid the bringing in such terms into that controversy, as were unknown to antiquity or to scripture'.[2] And, sure enough, the first two directions order:

I. That no preacher whatsoever, in his sermon or lecture, do presume to deliver any other doctrine concerning the Blessed Trinity, than what is contained in the Holy Scriptures and is agreeable to the three creeds, and the Thirty-Nine Articles of Religion.

[1] William III, *Directions to our Archbishops and Bishops for the preserving of unity in the Church, and the purity of the Christian faith concerning the Holy Trinity* (London, 1695), pp3–4.

[2] W. Whitfield, *A Sermon on the Death of the Late Lord Bishop of London* (London, 1713), p15.

II. That in the explication of this doctrine they carefully avoid all new terms, and confine themselves to such ways of expression as have been commonly used in the Church.[3]

But the injunctions then go on to give an intriguing insight to the way the controversy had been managed, because the third direction orders:

III. That care be taken in this matter, especially to observe the fifty-third Canon of this Church, which forbids public opposition between preachers, and that above all things, they abstain from bitter invectives and scurrilous language against all persons whatsoever.[4]

The injunctions were principally intended to bring an end to the exceptionally acrimonious battle that had broken out between two men we have already encountered: William Sherlock and Robert South. A few years previously, Sherlock had attempted to defend the doctrine of the Trinity against the attacks of Socinian pamphleteers, by publishing the *Vindication of the Doctrine of the Holy and Ever Blessed Trinity* in 1690. In that work, Sherlock attempted to strengthen the Church's Trinitarian teaching, by re-expressing the doctrine in what he saw as a more comprehensible vocabulary than the unwieldy terms of art bequeathed by the patristic and medieval periods. For all Sherlock's good intentions, however, the *Vindication* left him wide open to an accusation of heresy. More to the point, it gave Robert South just the opportunity he had been waiting for.

South and Sherlock had once been good friends, but the Glorious Revolution had put an end to that. The two men had fallen out over the issue of taking oaths of allegiance to the new sovereigns. They had discussed the matter together in private, but South had then circulated a draft paper of Sherlock's, which undermined the public position the latter had adopted against taking the oaths. Sherlock responded to this breach of confidence by holding South's own reasons for taking up the oaths to open ridicule.[5] When Sherlock published his defence of the Trinity, the aggrieved Canon took his revenge.

South fired a first salvo at Sherlock with the *Animadversions on Dr Sherlock's Book* (1693). Sherlock replied in similarly caustic terms with the *Defence of Dr Sherlock's Notion of a Trinity in Unity* (1694). South then published a studiedly offensive, but exceptionally witty, rejoinder, *Tritheism Charged upon Dr Sherlock's Notion* (1695). Even by the standards of the seventeenth century, the debate was an acrimonious one; and it is probably worth setting out a couple of the choicer passages, to demonstrate why the controversy caused both so much scandal and so much entertainment.

[3] William III, *Directions*, p5. [4] Ibid. [5] *ODNB*, s.v. 'William Sherlock'.

In a passage of the *Defence* which was purportedly discussing South's understanding of the communion between the divine persons, Sherlock accused South, none too subtly, of having made homosexual overtures to him at some time in the past. He wrote:

> But this severe censurer of other men ought to have been more cautious than to have said, that all acts of several persons on one another, are acts of communion, which makes boys in a state of communion with each other at boxing; and a match at scolding another state of communion; and had the Dean but been pleased to have returned mutual acts, he and the Animadverter might long before this have been in very strict communion with each other.[6]

If Sherlock surpassed South in the art of innuendo, South was easily his match in the field of the arch jibe. Early on in the *Tritheism Charged*, South gave a brief list of all the personal insults which had been directed at him in Sherlock's *Defence*. He then wrote, every sentence dripping with disdain:

> All the foregoing oyster-wife-kennel-rhetoric [*sic*], seems so naturally to flow from him who had been so long Rector of St Botolph's (with the well-spoken Billingsgate under his care) that (as much a teacher as he was) it may well be questioned whether he has learned more from his parish, or his parish from him. But after all, may I not ask him a short question? Where is the wit and smartness of thought? Where are the peculiar graces, and lucky hits of fancy, that should recommend the foregoing expressions to the learned and ingenious? No, nothing of all this is to be found in this man's words or way of speaking. But all savour of the porter, the car-man and the water-man, and a pleasant scene it must needs be to the reader, to see the Master of the Temple laying about him in the language of the Stairs.[7]

While the principal conflict was being waged in print, other forces were moving against Sherlock in the background. On 28 October 1695, a fellow of University College, Oxford, Joseph Bingham, had preached a sermon in which he employed language about the Trinity similar to Sherlock's. The sermon was denounced to the Vice-Chancellor as heretical, and after a meeting of the hebdomadal board, the hierarchy of the University issued a decree of condemnation.

The Oxford decree pronounced Sherlock's teaching on the Trinity to be 'false, impious and heretical, disagreeing with, and contrary to, the doctrine of the Catholic Church, and specifically to the publicly received doctrine of the Church of England,'[8] and instructed the members of the University to refrain

[6] W. Sherlock, *A Defence of Dr Sherlock's Notion of Trinity in Unity* (London, 1694), p73. Sherlock was promoted to the deanery of St Paul's Cathedral in London half-way through the dispute. I am grateful to Kenneth Padley for directing me to this particular exchange.

[7] R. South, *Tritheism Charged upon Dr Sherlock's New Notion of the Trinity* (London, 1695), p3.

[8] W. Sherlock, *A Modest Examination of the Oxford Decree* (London, 1696), p4. The decree pronounced the word to be 'falsa, impia et haeretica; dissona & contraria doctrinae Ecclesiae Catholicae & speciatim doctrinae Ecclesiae Anglicanae, publice receptae'.

from using such language in sermons or elsewhere. Sherlock clearly saw South's hand in this, and accused him of having preached a deliberately inflammatory sermon on the Sunday prior to the hebdomadal board's meeting.[9] Sherlock then belittled those who had issued the decree, noting that 'some of the wisest heads of house among them, and who were most concerned in a decree of heresy, were absent,'[10] before criticizing the quality of their Latin.

John Wallis, who had written on the Trinity since the publication of Sherlock's *Vindication*, but had thus far avoided getting drawn into a sparring match with him, now took up cudgels on behalf of the University. In his *An Answer to Dr Sherlock's Examination of the Oxford Decree* (1696), he made clear that Robert South had not instigated the original complaint against Bingham's sermon,[11] though he did not deny that South had urged the University to be zealous in the extirpation of heresy on the Sunday before the hebdomadal board's meeting. Responding to Sherlock's implication that some of the absent heads of house would not have condemned him, and that, therefore, his views had some support amongst the more discerning dons, Wallis remarked that 'as I do not hear that anyone dissented in the meeting of heads, so I believe there would have been few in Convocation, if it had been proposed there.'[12] For, as he puts it, 'I do not find that his new doctrine doth make so many proselytes.'[13] From Wallis's perspective, in other words, the University of Oxford was virtually unanimous in its opposition to Sherlock's views.

Further pressure was brought to bear on Sherlock in the same year that Wallis produced his *Answer*. Despite having been Bishop of London since 1675, Compton had not yet conducted a visitation of St Paul's Cathedral. He chose this tense moment to begin one, serving notice of his intention to do so on 16 July 1696.[14] Sherlock, who had become Dean of St Paul's in 1691, tried to persuade Compton that an attendance at chapter (which would not, of course, suspend the Dean's jurisdiction) would be sufficient, but Compton was unmoved.[15] The visitation was both prolonged and hostile—Compton was still conducting it in October of 1698[16]—as well as being marked by periodic confrontations between Compton and Sherlock.[17] Of course, it is possible that the timing of Compton's visitation was entirely coincidental (and there is no record that the Trinity was discussed), but Sherlock could

[9] W. Sherlock, *A Modest Examination of the Oxford Decree* (London, 1696), p3.

[10] Ibid.

[11] J. Wallis, *An Answer to Dr Sherlock's Examination of the Oxford Decree* (London, 1696), p9.

[12] Ibid., p6.

[13] Ibid., p9.

[14] E. Carpenter, *The Protestant Bishop* (London, 1956), p244.

[15] Ibid., p245. [16] Ibid., p246. [17] Ibid.

certainly have been forgiven for thinking that he was now facing hostility on all fronts.

Several other Anglican clerics were prompted by the confrontation between Sherlock and South to publish on the Trinity in a somewhat more irenic vein; but the impression was undoubtedly given, that the Anglican clergy were at loggerheads over the central mystery of the Christian faith. The bitterness of the dispute even became something of an international scandal.[18] Of course, the Socinian pamphleteers whose writings had originally sparked the fight, looked on from the sidelines with glee, as the Church of England tore itself apart. One commentator wrote:

> They all cast up their caps and cry, Trinity, Trinity, and consequently their faiths concerning this (pretended) mystery, are so many and so contrary; that they are less one party among themselves, than the far more learned, and far greater number of them . . . are one party with us.[19]

The royal instructions certainly had a calming effect on the dispute: South published nothing more on the Trinity, and, as the visitation of his cathedral stretched on, Sherlock beat a steady theological retreat from his more avant-garde positions.[20] Henry Compton, however, remained concerned lest Sherlock's new ideas infect the clergy in his diocese. So he dedicated one of his regular diocesan conferences[21] to a discussion of the royal injunctions. He then published, as was his wont, a pamphlet summarizing the points he wished his clergy to take away from the meeting which they had had. This was Compton's *The Bishop of London's Tenth Conference with his Clergy* (1701).

Compton is clear that intellectual arrogance was the true source of the controversy. As he put it,

> when the overweening opinion of our own accomplishments has once possessed our minds, the false flashes of such conceits, like an *ignis fatuus*, leads us into all error; so dazzling our eyes, that we cannot discover our miserable defects. We fancy ourselves to be rich, and clothed, and to abound in all things, whilst we are indeed poor and naked, and have nothing.[22]

He does not mention Sherlock by name, and he is careful to condemn public opposition between his clergy; but there is little doubt at whose door

18 *ODNB*, s.v. 'William Sherlock'.

19 Anon., *A Discourse Concerning the Nominal and Real Trinitarians* (London, 1695), p3.

20 Sherlock, *The Present State of the Socinian Controversy and the Doctrine of the Catholick Fathers concerning a Trinity in Unity* (London, 1698).

21 On Compton's diocesan conferences: Carpenter, *Protestant Bishop*, pp208–9.

22 Compton, *The Bishop of London's Tenth Conference with his Clergy* (London, 1701), p2.

Compton laid most of the blame. He underlines that all clergy should take pains

carefully to avoid all new terms or notions in the handling of this doctrine, and to confine ourselves to the usual expressions of the Church. To do otherwise, in so high and unfathomable point, would be too bold an attempt, and might sometimes endanger running ourselves, through unskillfulness or daring presumption, into that heresy, from which we would seem, and perchance really intend to flee.[23]

Predictably, Compton takes the opportunity of his letter to attack Socinianism.[24] Much less predictably, however, he launches a ferocious assault on Arminian theology as well. Without initially mentioning anyone by name, he points out that some writers, whilst not openly asserting Socinianism, lend it effective support by undermining the traditional teachings of the Church in subtle and devious ways. He writes:

They pretend to go hand in hand with us, and set up for champions of the fundamental articles of our faith; and in the meantime so order the matter as to betray all into the enemies' hands. Sometimes they bluster with their *eurekas* as if all the world had been asleep, till they arose; they reject all reasons that have been given before, and vouch for one of their own coining, which they can invalidate at their pleasure. Sometimes they will have the high mysteries of our religion bare speculative notions, true indeed, but of little or no weight in the concern of our salvation. At other times, they will set the whole frame of our confession so loose, that a small blast may blow it down.[25]

He then goes on to make clear who exactly he has in mind. He writes:

I take Episcopius, Curcellaeus, Limborch and such like writers, to be the great fomenters of this loose sort of divinity. They do indeed make a show of asserting the Trinity, but (alas!) it comes to nothing. For when they should set it forth the excellency of it from the gracious influence it has upon the means of our salvation, they sink into the beggarly constructions of Pelagius and Socinus.... Therefore it is not safe to tamper with such authors, who assume to themselves a privilege of altering the stated phrases and expressions of the Church; which has been the first practice of most heretics for insinuating their errors.[26]

So Compton felt that the pernicious influence of the leading Arminian theologians had been a significant factor in undermining Trinitarian orthodoxy within the Church of England. The Remonstrants were, in other words, ultimately responsible for the theological clumsiness of William Sherlock.

Philip Dixon has recently published an account of the Trinitarian debates on the Seventeenth Century: *Nice and Hot Disputes* (2003). It is a considerably

[23] Compton, H., *The Bishop of London's Tenth Conference with his Clergy* (London, 1701), p3.
[24] Ibid., p8. [25] Ibid., p15. [26] Ibid., p17.

more reliable guide to the controversy than some earlier discussions of the matter.[27] Dixon focuses his discussion on the meaning attached to the word 'person' in the seventeenth-century debates.[28] He argues that problems began to arise in relation to Trinitarian doctrine, partly because theologians lost the sense that all language about God is inherently problematic,[29] and partly because the central importance of Trinity to Christian life began to be less confidently celebrated.[30]

Dixon's presentation of the discussion is helpful, but does need to be enriched and perhaps qualified in a couple of directions. First, he consciously eschews any detailed consideration of the continental European dimension of the Trinitarian debate.[31] This is regrettable given that contemporaries, such as Henry Compton, were clear that the influence of the foreign Remonstrant writers were a major contributor to the Church's problems over this doctrine. Secondly, the Reformed writers, at least, show no sign of believing that theological language about God was straightforward, nor do they downplay the significance of the Trinity in the believer's everyday life—so Dixon's analysis of the problem is only partially accurate.

Henry Compton, for example, is absolutely convinced that the doctrine of the Trinity is central to the believer's spiritual progress. He underlines that Christians must believe in the Trinity:

> Because through the whole progress of our pilgrimage here on earth, there is no step we make towards our salvation, but is directed by one or more of those blessed persons under some distinct notion; there is no consolation, no hope, no confidence, but what is particularly attributed to one of the three persons. So that all the good we do or receive, all our religious actions and performances, have some special relation to Father, Son or Holy Ghost.[32]

Compton is emphatic: the doctrine of the Trinity is not to be relegated to the rank of an irrelevant theological speculation. He underlined that the clergy must not

> reduce it to a speculative piece of ornament to our religion, which may be laid aside without impairing the substance. For it is as much as our religion is worth to lay aside this doctrine. Let us not deceive ourselves: God has not discovered so great a mystery to us, only that we should be amused with the contemplation of it.[33]

27 E.g., J. Redwood, *Reason, Ridicule and Religion* (London, 1976).

28 P., Dixon, *Nice and Hot Disputes: The Doctrine of the Trinity in the Seventeenth Century* (London, 2003), p3.

29 Ibid., p136.

30 Ibid., p212.

31 Ibid., pxiii.

32 Compton, *Tenth Conference*, pp5–6.

33 Ibid., p5. See also: J. Edwards, *Theologia Reformata*, 2 vols (London, 1713), i p326.

Other Reformed writers also underline the engagement of the whole Trinity in the work of creation and redemption. William Delaune, for example, underlined that the salvation of humanity required the involvement of all the persons of the Trinity. He writes, of the story of human redemption:

> This it was that made it necessary for the ever-blessed Trinity to unfold itself; for to vindicate the honour of God's laws, and at the same time to save man, no less than all the three persons in the divine essence must be employed. God's authority must have been trampled on, or man lost forever, had not the Son undertaken to be his proxy, the Father accepted of the substitution, and the Holy Ghost completed all by renewing and sanctifying his nature.[34]

In other words, if there was a loss of Trinitarian imagination within the English Church, the Reformed show little sign of it. This is not, perhaps, so surprising, given the central role the Reformed tradition gives to the Holy Spirit in the process of redemption. But it does mean that Dixon's account needs to be complemented by a more detailed consideration of the way in which Reformed writers approached the Trinitarian debates, and their defence of a more traditional theological language against the forces of Arminian innovation.

## WILLIAM SHERLOCK'S TRINITARIAN THEOLOGY

Sherlock's *Vindication* was written in response to two Socinian pamphlets, *A Brief History of the Unitarians* (1687) and *Brief Notes on the Creed of St Athanasius* (1690). It was intended to defend the orthodox doctrine of the Trinity from Socinian accusations that it was absurd and contradictory.

Sherlock begins by discussing the nature of contradictions in general, asserting that 'a contradiction is to deny and affirm the same things in the same sense; as to say that a thing is, and is not, in the same sense, that there is but one God, and that there is three Gods'.[35] He underlines however, that in order to pronounce that an assertion about any given being involves a contradiction, it is necessary to understand the nature of that being accurately and comprehensively. Otherwise the contradiction might only be apparent: the assertion might appear, to our partial understanding, to involve a contradiction; but a deeper grasp of the object under consideration will reveal that it does not.

[34] Delaune, *Twelve Sermons*, p28; see also pp259–60; Hacket, *Century*, p189; Newcome, *Catechetical Course*, p99.

[35] Sherlock, *Vindication*, p2.

As Sherlock underlines, 'all men confess, that they have not a clear and comprehensive notion of the nature and essential properties of a spirit, especially of an infinite spirit, as God is'.[36] In other words, asserting that any statement about God involves a contradiction is inherently problematic: we simply do not understand the nature of God well enough to be absolutely certain about what is, and is not, inconsistent with his being.

There is also, Sherlock thinks, a further complication in our attempt to consider the essence of God, in that the essences of things are never directly knowable. The essence of anything, he argues, is apprehended only through its properties and qualities; it is not the direct object of our understanding. He underlines that there are, as a result, strict limits to human knowledge. We can discover the existence of things that fall within our knowledge (by sense, reason or revelation), and we can know what are the essential properties which distinguish things from each other,[37] 'but the essence of things, and the philosophy of their natures, the reasons of their essential properties and powers... are mysterious to us'.[38] And as a result, all discussions about the essences of things are rather too speculative to be illuminating.

With these prefatory remarks made, Sherlock then turns to consider the Athanasian Creed, and its assertion that, 'The Father is God, the Son is God and the Holy Ghost is God. And yet they are not three Gods but one God.' Sherlock is clear that the persons of the Trinity must be real, substantial beings, if they can each be described as God. Because a person cannot easily be separated, in our way of thinking, from its particular essence or substance.[39] Sherlock rejects the traditional scholastic idea that the persons are only modally distinguished from one another. As he puts it, 'there are no modes, no more than there are qualities and accidents in the deity, much less can a mode be God'.[40] So the distinction between the person must be more substantial than that. But although the three persons are, in his view, real, and distinct, substantial beings, the divine essence is nonetheless numerically one, because there is only one God. Consequently, 'the difficulty is, how three distinct substantial persons can subsist in one numerical essence'.[41] Sherlock confesses that he cannot fathom this mystery completely, but he sets out to show that it does not involve a necessary contradiction.

He starts by asking what it is that makes anything properly one with itself. In material things, he argues, it is a union of their parts into the whole; but this will not work as a way of conceiving the unity in God, because God does not have any parts. So Sherlock considers spiritual things instead, and here he starts to find some fruitful notions. He writes:

[36] Ibid., p7. [37] Ibid., p9. [38] Ibid., p10.
[39] Ibid., p47. [40] Ibid., p84. [41] Ibid., p48.

In finite created spirits, which have no parts and extension either... their numerical oneness can be nothing else, but every spirit's unity with itself, and distinct and separate subsistence from all other created spirits. Now this self unity of the spirit, which has no parts to be united, can be nothing else but self-consciousness: that it is conscious to its own thoughts, reasonings, passions, which no other finite spirit is conscious to but itself: this makes a finite spirit numerically one, and separates it from all other spirits, that every spirit feels only its own thoughts and passions, but is not conscious to the thoughts and passions of any other spirit.[42]

So, by eschewing any discussion of the essence of spirits (which, as we have seen, he believes to be unknowable), Sherlock is able to home in on the one property which is characteristic of all individual spirits, and which demonstrates that they are one particular spirit and not another. This, he thinks, is self-consciousness—because each individual spiritual being is conscious of the workings of her own mind, and not conscious of the workings of anyone else's mind.

Sherlock argues that this turns out to be a useful notion when contemplating the Trinity. Because, he urges:

If there were three created spirits, so united as to be conscious to each others thoughts and passions, as they are to their own, I cannot see any reason, why we may not say, that three such persons are numerically one, for they are as much one with each other, as every spirit is one with itself; unless we can find some other unity for a spirit than self-consciousness.[43]

In other words, if we abandon abstract discussions about essences, and concentrate instead on the property that shows any given spirit to be one, it becomes possible to imagine three spirits that have equal access to each other's consciousness as they do to their own, and so are as one with each other (as far as we can understand the matter) as each individual is one with herself.

This, Sherlock thinks, is the best way of understanding the mystical union of the persons within Trinity. As he puts it, 'the three divine persons, Father, Son and Holy Ghost, are three infinite minds'.[44] As a result, 'if we can suppose three infinite minds and persons, thus conscious of whatever is in each other, as they are of themselves, they can be but one numerical God'.[45] Because the union of pure and infinite minds can only be founded upon 'a mutual consciousness, and if I may so speak, an inward sensation of each other, as they know and feel themselves'.[46] Indeed, Sherlock opines, this mutual consciousness is what the Patristic writers must have had in mind when they talked about the *perichoresis* of the persons within the Trinity.[47]

[42] Sherlock, *Vindication*, pp48–9. [43] Ibid., p49.
[44] Ibid., p50. [45] Ibid.
[46] Ibid., pp51–2. [47] Ibid., p50.

Sherlock believes that this way of conceiving the divine unity also preserves the distinctness of the three persons. And this, he thinks, is vital if we wish to preserve Trinitarian orthodoxy. Casually writing off St Augustine's preferred image for the Trinity, he says:

It is plain the persons are perfectly distinct, for they are three distinct and infinite minds, and therefore three distinct persons; for a person is an intelligent being, and to say that there are three divine persons, and not three distinct infinite minds is both heresy and nonsense: the Scripture, I'm sure, represents Father, Son and Holy Ghost, as three intelligent beings, not as three powers or faculties of the same being, which is downright Sabellianism.[48]

So, in addition the mutual consciousness which each divine person has of the mental worlds of other two persons, 'each person has a self-consciousness of its own, and knows and feels itself (if I may so speak) as distinct from the other divine persons'.[49]

This notion of three self-conscious infinite minds, united by their mutual consciousness of each other is, Sherlock insists 'a very plain and intelligible account of this great and venerable mystery'.[50] And this, he thinks, is timely, because the traditional Trinitarian vocabulary of 'essence, and hypostasis, substance, subsistence, person, existence, nature, &c. which are terms very differently used by Greek and Latin fathers in this debate . . . have very much obscured the doctrine instead of explaining it'.[51] This is, he thinks, not entirely surprising, because all these terms were derived from material beings, and we tend to make inappropriate assumptions about them based on their use in the material sphere.[52] As he puts it, 'The truth is, that which has confounded this mystery, has been the endeavour of reducing it to terms of art.'[53]

Although Sherlock does ground the unity of the three persons on their mutual consciousness of each other, there is clearly another explanation of that unity at play in his mind. Because the three persons of the Trinity are not only united by their mutual consciousness; they are also united in their cause, namely the Father, from whom the other two persons are eternally produced. Sherlock writes:

The natural order in the Trinity is to reckon from the Father as the Fountain of the Deity, that Father, Son and Holy Ghost are one God, for the Son and the Holy Spirit are in the Father, not only by mutual consciousness, as the Father and the Son are in the Holy Ghost, but as in their cause (if I may so speak, and the ancient fathers were

[48] Ibid., p66. [49] Ibid., p67. [50] Ibid., p68.
[51] Ibid., p101. [52] Ibid., p68. [53] Ibid., p138.

not afraid to speak so) as in their root, their fountain, from whence they receive the communications of the divine essence and Godhead.[54]

In other words, Sherlock envisages a twofold manner of conceiving the unity that exists within the Trinity. For 'all these divine persons are naturally united in the Father, who is the Fountain of the Deity, and all essentially in each other by a mutual consciousness'.[55] In other words, Father, Son and Holy Spirit are properly one, not only because each person is as conscious of the other two, as he is of himself, but also because the Son and the Holy Spirit derive their existence from the Father, and not vice versa. This, of course, leads Sherlock to have a distinctly subordinationist view of the relations between the persons of the Trinity.[56] In this he reflects a wider tendency within the Church of England, which we shall discuss in due course.

Whatever his faults, William Sherlock can certainly be credited with creating an original synthesis of Trinitarian theology. No writer either before or after him put things together quite as he did. That is not to say that his approach had no precedents at all, and Dixon has pointed out how both John Turner and Ralph Cudworth had previously deployed the concept of self-consciousness in relation to the Trinity.[57] However, the key influences on Sherlock, as Compton hinted and Robert South explicitly pointed out, were the leading Remonstrant theologians. South pointed the finger specifically at Etienne de Courcelles (1586–1659)[58] and Jean Leclerc (1657–1736).[59]

Courcelles (or Curcellaeus—as he appears in Compton's letter) is quite as dismissive as Sherlock about the technical vocabulary of Trinitarian orthodoxy. He writes:

those expressions and ways of speaking, which have been devised for the explanation of the dogma of the Trinity, are more inconvenient by a long way, than those which we have in the scriptures, as being ambiguous, and about the true meaning of which, the doctors are not in agreement.[60]

Since the traditional theological vocabulary is both obscure and misleading, it is imperative that those terms be abandoned, because, Courcelles thinks, there will be no peace in the Church if they are not.[61]

[54] Sherlock, *Vindication*, p99. [55] Ibid., p100. [56] Ibid., p89.

[57] Thiel U., "The Trinity and Human Personal Identity" in M.A. Stewart (ed.) English Philosophy in the Age fo Locke (Oxford 2000) pp 228–231.

[58] South, *Tritheism Charged*, p47.

[59] Ibid., pp82, 84.

[60] Curcellaeus, *Opera Theologica* (Amsterdam, 1675), p73. 'Istae voces et loquendi formulae, quae ad explicandum Trinitatis dogma sunt inventae, longe incommodiores sunt iis, quas in Scriptura habemus, utpote ambiguae, & de quorum genuino significatu non consentiunt inter se doctores.'

[61] Ibid., p836.

Courcelles certainly has no time for the scholastic idea that the persons of the Trinity can be described as modes of subsistence of the divine being. That, he thinks, is to ascribe to the persons of the Trinity no more substantial existence than an accident or quality of a being.[62] It gives the persons of the Trinity, in other words, no more substantial existence, than the colour of something. So, just like Sherlock, he insists that the persons within the Trinity must be described as substantial beings. He writes:

> All that is, or exists, has its proper essence, by which it is what it is, and is distinguished from all other things: but the persons of the divinity are, or exist; therefore each person of the divinity has his proper essence, by which they are what they are, and are distinguished from all other things.[63]

Anyone who does not accept this axiom, Courcelles thinks, is guilty of Sabellianism.

Courcelles certainly goes beyond Sherlock in rejecting the description of the Son as being 'of one substance' with the Father,[64] and in abandoning the idea that the persons of the Trinity enjoy a numeric, rather than merely a specific unity.[65] For Courcelles, Father, Son, and Holy Spirit are only one God in the same way that Peter, James, and John may be said to share one humanity: namely they are three specific instances of the generic divine essence. Sherlock, by contrast, is quite insistent that the three persons do have a numeric unity of essence (though he is not able to demonstrate how they do). But although Courcelles does go beyond Sherlock, it is possible to see in his insistence that each person of the Trinity must be a substantial being in its own right, the seeds of Sherlock's later difficulties.

Leclerc had certainly read Courcelles. Indeed he cites him in relation to the doctrine of the Trinity.[66] He followed Courcelles in emphasizing the distinctness of the persons within the Trinity, but developed his thought by elaborating the intellectual nature of personhood within the Godhead. He writes: 'A person is an understanding subject. Now, that is called a subject, which is neither part of, nor an adjunct to another thing, and it is also called a complete being.'[67] He underlines, however, that each person need not

[62] Ibid., p796.

[63] Ibid., p879. 'Omne quod est, seu existit, habet suam essentiam propriam, per quam est id quod est, et ab aliis omnibus distinguitur: personae autem divinitatis sunt, seu existunt; ergo personae singulae divinitatis habent suam essentiam propriam, per quam sunt id quod sunt, et ab aliis omnibus distinguuntur.'

[64] Ibid., p881.

[65] Ibid., p883.

[66] J. Leclerc, (Liberius a Sancto Amore), *Epistolae Theologicae* (Saumur, 1679), p105.

[67] Ibid., p3. 'Persona est suppositum intelligens. Suppositum autem id dicitur, quod neque est pars neque adjunctum alius rei, idque aliter vocatur, ens completum.'

necessarily have its own distinct and individual essence: three persons might well coexist in one essence. It is sufficient to establish a distinction between the persons, if there is some respect in which each person exists in a different way from the others, and a way which is not consistent with them being totally conflated.[68]

Leclerc is clear that God is an infinite spirit, and that spirits are thinking substances.[69] A thought, he underlines, is 'whatever is in our minds, of which we are conscious'.[70] So, like Sherlock, he believes that self-consciousness is an essential property of all spiritual beings. Leclerc then goes on to consider what it is that might unite spiritual beings. He underlines that, 'things are not made one, except by that by which they agree between themselves.... [and] spirits agree between themselves by this [act of] thinking.'[71] As a result, Leclerc believes, two spirits can be personally united 'if they make all their thoughts mutually manifest to one another, such that each follows the conclusions of the other'.[72] In other words, like Sherlock, Leclerc considers that two spirits which are mutually aware of each other's thoughts can properly be described as one.

When he turns to consider explicitly the doctrine of the Trinity, Leclerc too asserts that the matter can be explained with perfect clarity, so long as the technical language of Trinitarian theology is abandoned, because, like Sherlock, Leclerc is of the view that it is the technical language, not the Trinity itself, which is inherently incomprehensible.[73] Leclerc instead advances that idea that the three persons of the Trinity can most coherently be understood as the divinity thinking in three different ways. And given that he has defined thought as that of which we are conscious, this comes very close to Sherlock's idea that the Trinity is three distinct centres of self-consciousness. And like Sherlock, Leclerc considers that his approach to the Trinity preserves a clear enough distinction between the persons, because to his mind the thought processes of the Father are not those of the Son or of the Holy Spirit, though there is no dissension between them.[74] And whereas a finite being cannot sustain more than one set of thought processes at the same time, an infinite being can.[75]

Neither Courcelles nor Leclerc offers a perfect facsimile of Sherlock's theology. But there are sufficient points of contact between the three writers to conclude, as Compton implicitly and South explicitly did, that Sherlock

[68] Leclerc, J. (Liberius a Sancto Amore), *Epistolae Theologicae* (Saumur, 1679), p103.

[69] Ibid., p6.

[70] Ibid., p5.

[71] Ibid., p6. 'Res non uniuntur nisi per id quo inter se conveniunt.... Spiritus conveniunt inter se per cogitationem tantum.'

[72] Ibid. 'Si omnes suas cogitationes sibi invicem manifestas faciant, adeo ut alter alterius sequatur determinationes.'

[73] Ibid., p102. [74] Ibid., p106. [75] Ibid., p103.

had drunk a little too deeply of the Arminian well. Certainly, there is in the Trinitarian teaching of the two Remonstrant writers, a strong tendency to emphasize the distinctness of the three persons within the Trinity, rather than their unity, a tendency which was bound up with their rejection of the technical terminology of Trinitarian orthodoxy, and which leaves an open door to Tritheism.

## THE CHARGE OF TRITHEISM

Robert South's two attacks on Sherlock are, without doubt, the most detailed Reformed discussions of Trinitarian doctrine to appear after the Restoration. His mind honed perhaps by personal antipathy, he took issue with virtually every point that William Sherlock had made, starting with Sherlock's conception of human knowledge.

South opens his discussion by establishing a difference between understanding something and comprehending it. He writes:

> To understand a thing, is to know it in any respect or degree in which it is knowable; and to comprehend a thing, is to know it in every respect in which it is knowable. And as it is certain that we cannot know God in this latter way, so it is certain that we may know him in the former: for we do, and may know him, by inadequate and imperfect and uncommensurate conceptions, as that he is just, wise, good, and the like, which are several ways of representing him to our mind.[76]

On this basis, he takes issue with Sherlock's assertion that we cannot understand the essences of things. South admits that we cannot exhaustively comprehend them, but that does not mean that we cannot have any true knowledge of them. Because, as South argues, to know something through the properties and operations by which it is distinguished from other things, is to know it truly and (to that extent) as perfectly as we are able.[77] In other words, some knowledge of the divine essence, like all essences, is, in principle, open to us. So we can, to some extent, both understand it and discourse rationally about it.

That said, South emphatically rejects Sherlock's search for a plain, easy, and intelligible notion of the Trinity. This quest, he asserts, is utterly inconsistent with the nature of a mystery—and the Trinitarian being of God is certainly that.[78] Human beings can never have a clear grasp of what God is, because, 'nothing but infinite knowledge can adequately comprehend an infinite

[76] South, *Animadversions*, p7. [77] Ibid., p15. [78] Ibid., pp19–20.

object. For which reason God alone can comprehend himself, and he does it by one simple indivisible act, incapable of parts or degrees.'[79]

South views Sherlock's contention that the Trinity has been obscured by the traditional technical language which is used by theologians to discuss it, as utterly mistaken. The difficulty lies, South argues, not in the vocabulary which is being used, but in the object which is being studied. We find it difficult to think accurately about God because the divine nature is unlike any other: it is spiritual, infinite, and therefore incomparable. In other words, the real reason for all the difficulty in our attempts to think about God is 'founded upon the essential disparity which the mind of man bears to so disproportionate, so transcendent an object'.[80]

Although God infinitely transcends human understanding, South believes, it is nonetheless necessary for us to discuss God in accordance with the normal rules of philosophy. In particular, there is a proper conceptual order which must be observed when discussing the divine essence. South admits, of course, that since God is an uncompounded being, there is, strictly speaking, no order within God: there is only the utterly simple act of his existence. Nonetheless, in our conceiving of God, an order must be respected, 'forasmuch as without our admitting this rule it is impossible for any human understanding either to conceive, or discourse intelligibly of him at all'.[81]

Human beings, in other words, can only think about God coherently if they impose an appropriate hierarchy on their thoughts, even though that order does not correspond to the way God exists in himself. In particular, human beings have to grasp the being or essence of anything, before they can discuss any of its attributes or qualities. Consequently, human beings must first understand what God is, before they can turn their minds to God's properties or attributes, such as knowledge or consciousness. As he concedes, this order of thinking does not correspond to an order in God himself; but since, to the human mind, the properties of anything depend upon its being, and not vice versa, the being of God has a necessary priority in our conception of him, over his other properties or attributes.[82]

South accuses Sherlock of breaking this rule in spectacular fashion when he asserts that self-consciousness is the reason why a given spirit is properly one person. That is simply not coherent, South argues, because 'self-consciousness in persons presupposes their personality, and therefore is not, cannot be the reason of it.'[83] Any act, South argues, assumes the existence of the agent which performs it. And since self-consciousness is properly a reflex act upon the thought processes of the person to whom they belong (in that it is a conscious

[79] South, *Animadversions*, p23. [80] Ibid., p54. [81] Ibid., p92.
[82] Ibid., p93. [83] Ibid., p71.

recognition that those thought processes are properly hers), self-consciousness cannot be the real explanation for why a person is one. Rather, self-consciousness is the consequence of that person being one. As South puts it,

> consciousness or sensation is not properly nature, but an affection of nature, or an act springing from it; and therefore unity of consciousness or sensation cannot be properly unity of nature, nor consequently can it constitute the subject it belongs to numerically one.[84]

South contends that Sherlock has carelessly confounded the principle of knowledge with the principle of being. He has confused the reason why a person knows that she is one, with the reason why she actually is one. He writes of self-consciousness,

> although this conscious sensation be that whereby a spirit knows itself to be one and distinct from all others, yet it is not that which makes it so... and consequently whatsoever is argued from this supposition, towards the proving the same of mutual consciousness with reference to three spirits, which has been asserted of self-consciousness with reference to one, must fall to the ground with it.[85]

Sherlock's whole scheme depends upon the act of mutual consciousness between the persons being numerically one—for that is where he locates the essential unity of the Trinity. South contends, however, that if the three persons are three infinite minds, as Sherlock says they are, their mutual consciousness is not numerically one at all, but only collectively so. As he puts it, Sherlock's mutual consciousness, upon which the numerical unity of the Trinity depends in his scheme, is

> only a complex and collective unity consisting of and containing in it three distinct acts of consciousness, whereof one belongs to each of his three spirits, and that whereby each spirit knows or feels (let him call it what he will) all that is in, or is known or felt, by the other two spirits.[86]

In other words, just as there are three distinct acts of self-consciousness, so there will be three distinct acts of mutual consciousness, each originating from one of the divine persons; and that is clearly an insufficient explanation of their essential unity.

South also has no time for Sherlock's other explanation of the unity in the Trinity, namely that, since the Father is the source and fountain of the whole Godhead, the three persons are one, when considered as originating in the Father. Sherlock, to South's mind, has here mistaken metaphor for metaphysics. He writes: 'And as for [the Father's being the fountain of the Deity], I hope

[84] South, *Tritheism Charged*, p26.
[85] Ibid., pp25–6. [86] Ibid., pp27–8.

he looks upon this expression only as metaphorical, and such as ought not to be stretched to the utmost of its natural sense.'[87] It will certainly not do as an explanation of the numerical unity of the divine essence.

To South's mind, the key weakness in Sherlock's scheme is his insistence that the persons of the Trinity are three distinct infinite minds. Three infinite distinct minds are, South believes, 'three absolute, simple beings, and so stand distinguished from each other by their whole beings or natures.'[88] As a result, South avers, three distinct infinite minds are necessarily three Gods. Sherlock is effectively promoting Tritheism.[89] Since a mind is nothing other than an intelligent substance, if there are three distinct minds, there are three distinct intelligent substances. And three distinct substances cannot be numerically one.

On the contrary, South insists, there is only one mind in God. In his words, the 'one and the same infinite mind or spirit is Father, Son and Holy Ghost'.[90] Indeed, he argues, the word 'God' is effectively interchangeable with the phrase 'Infinite Eternal Mind';[91] because whatever can be asserted of one can also be asserted of the other.

Since there is only one mind in the Godhead, there is only one act of knowledge within the Godhead as well. That one act of knowledge is common to all three persons, because knowledge is an attribute of the divine essence as a whole. But it does not belong to the persons considered separately from that essence. As South puts it, knowledge 'is an attribute springing from the divine nature, which is in the person, and not from his personality or personal distinction'.[92] In other words, the Father, the Son, and the Holy Ghost know things, not because they are Father, Son, or Holy Ghost, but because they are God.

As we saw, Sherlock felt that it was not really feasible to consider the persons in the Trinity as distinct from their essence. South, by contrast, argues that it is impossible to think accurately about the Trinity unless we do observe that distinction. As he insists,

> all the ancient orthodox divines and doctors of the Church distinguish in each person two things, though intimately and inseparably united, viz. the Godhead, or divine nature, and the personal distinguishing relation, so that what agrees to the person upon one account, does not properly belong to him upon another.[93]

It follows that nothing which is properly an attribute of the divine essence (the divine knowledge, for example) and which all the persons of the Trinity share, can be an explanation for the distinction which exists between them.

[87] South, *Animadversions*, p138. [88] Ibid., p120. [89] Ibid., p119.
[90] Ibid., p124. [91] South, *Tritheism Charged*, p32.
[92] Ibid., p33. [93] Ibid.

Indeed, the self-consciousness which Sherlock ascribes to each person, and the mutual consciousness which he ascribes to all of them, are merely different aspects of the one, undivided act of divine knowledge, which is in turn an attribute of the common divine essence. South writes:

I do here observe that there is but one single act of knowledge in all the three divine persons; that is to say, single as to the substance of the act, though diversified by the several modifications which it receives from the person whom it proceeds from; and from the several respects it bears to the several objects it terminates upon. Which different modifications and respects do by no means infer diverse or distinct acts of knowledge, but only variously modify, determine and distinguish one and the same act. Accordingly in the present case, I do here affirm to this author, that mutual-consciousness is nothing else but one and the same act of divine knowledge, differently modified, and, as it proceeds severally, and after a different manner from Father, Son and Holy Ghost as the persons knowing, and jointly terminated in them as the objects known; as on the other side, self-consciousness is no more than this one and the same act of knowledge as it issues only from one of the same persons, and terminates upon the same too.[94]

To put it in simpler terms, the self-consciousness of the Son (for example) is merely the one divine act of knowledge considered as proceeding from and directed to the Son: it is God's knowledge of himself as the Son, in the Son. It is therefore an aspect of God's total and undivided knowledge of himself: it is not a distinct act of knowledge. So it will not suffice to establish the distinct identity of the Son.

So South is clear that Sherlock's talk about three divine minds, and their acts of self-consciousness and mutual consciousness is an entirely inadequate, indeed a dangerous and heretical way of understanding the Trinity. He also feels, incidentally, that Sherlock is being inconsistent. He condemns the old theological terms of art, but all he does is substitute some new and less coherent ones.[95] It is far better, South thinks, to stick to the traditional vocabulary of the schools, to the 'old peripatetic philosophy, which, for ought I see, (as to the main at least) has stood its ground hitherto against all assaults.'[96]

South introduces and explains all the traditional metaphysical terms one by one. He then explains why metaphysical considerations should take precedence in our discussion of the Trinity, over other matters, such as the divine attributes. He writes

the terms essence, subsistence, existence and others synonymous to them ought to have the precedence of the other divine perfections commonly called attributes, in

[94] Ibid., p190. [95] South, *Animadversions*, p222. [96] Ibid., p30.

their application to God, and that upon a three-fold account, viz. 1. Of priority. 2. Of simplicity. 3. Of comprehensiveness.[97]

Considering God as a self-existent being is, South argues, the first and most basic way we can conceive of him—so it is prior to other ways of thinking about God. Considering God as a self-existent being also presupposes nothing else about him, whereas, for example, considering him as knowing presupposes his existence—so it is also simpler than other ways of thinking about God. And whereas all the divine attributes are included in any consideration of the divine being as a whole, they are not included when we direct our attention to one specific attribute—so it is finally a more comprehensive way of thinking about God.

Consequently, if the Trinity is to be coherently discussed, and (so far as is possible) understood, there is no escaping the use of metaphysical vocabulary. South accordingly presents the correct way to understand the doctrine of the Trinity in metaphysical terms, though he is emphatic that the employment of any philosophical terms in relation to God is done on the basis that they are analogous, not univocal, descriptions of God's being.[98] The Catholic faith is, South asserts:

That there is one, and but one, self-existing, infinite eternal being, nature or substance, which we call God. And that this infinite, eternal, self-existing being, or nature or essence, exists in and is common to three distinct persons, Father, Son and Holy Ghost . . . which three persons super-add to the divine nature or deity, three different modes of subsistence, founding so many different relations, each of them belonging to each person in a peculiar uncommunicable manner, so that by virtue thereof each person respectively differs and stands distinguished from the other two: and yet by reason of the same numerical divine nature or Godhead, equally existing in, and common to all the three persons, they are all but one and the same God, who is blessed for ever.[99]

So South describes the Trinity as being one united essence, which sustains three distinct modes of subsistence. The distinction between the persons within the Trinity is thus a modal distinction, rather than a distinction between different substances. This, he asserts, is the common teaching of all orthodox divines, whether Protestant or Roman Catholic. Of the former, he cites Melanchthon, Chemnitz, Peter Martyr, Musculus, Ursinus, and Turretin. Of the latter, he cites Lombard, Durandus, Aquinas, Cajetan, Estius, and Suarez; and he underlines, against Sherlock's carping to the contrary, that 'the Romish writers are as orthodox about the article of the Trinity as any Protestant writers whatsoever.'[100]

[97] South, *Animadversions*, p51.
[98] South, *Tritheism Charged*, p200.
[99] South, *Animadversions*, pp246–7.
[100] South, *Tritheism Charged*, p256.

A mode, South explains, is an aspect or affection of being. It does not alter the essence of the being, but it determines that essence in a specific way. As he puts it, a mode of being is 'an affection of a thing, or being, by which the nature of it, otherwise indeterminate and indifferent, is determined to some certain respect, state or condition'.[101] Modes are not beings, properly so called, rather they are 'appendages' of being, that depend upon the prior existence of the being which they modify. Different modes give rise to modal distinctions—which again are not distinctions between distinct beings, but distinction between the particular ways in which those beings exist. As South insists, however, a modal distinction, though not a distinction between two different substances, is nonetheless a distinction which is more than conceptual, a distinction in the thing itself and not merely in our minds.[102]

It may be helpful to clarify South's meaning by looking at the writing of perhaps the most eminent metaphysician of the early modern period, Francisco Suarez. Suarez gave a concrete example of a modal distinction in his influential *Disputationes Metaphysicae*. He imagines there a ray of light. The ray of light, he argues, is dependent on the sun for its existence: the way it exists, its mode of being, in other words, is dependent. The specific dependence of the light from the sun is clearly not an entity distinct from the ray of light, because it cannot be conceived of as existing on its own without the light. Yet, this dependence is more than a creation of the human mind; it makes a difference to what the ray of light really is, because it determines its mode of existence. For, Suarez argues, one could imagine God creating the ray of light directly, without using the intermediary of the sun. It would be substantially the same ray of light, but the way in which it exists, its mode of being, would be different: it would have an independent, not a dependent existence. This, he argues, is a modal distinction.[103]

South underlines that although the orthodox consider the persons of the Trinity to be modally, not substantially distinguished, they do not assume that the persons are no more than modes, as Sherlock had accused them of doing. He writes:

> To affirm the three divine persons to be only three modes of deity is one thing, and to affirm them to be only modally distinguished is quite another. The former we absolutely deny, and as positively hold the latter. For we do not say that a person is only a *modus*, but that it is the divine nature, or Godhead, subsisting under such a *modus*, so that the Godhead is still included in it, joined to it, and distinguished by it.[104]

[101] South, *Animadversions*, p31. [102] Ibid.
[103] F. Suarez, *Omnia Opera*, 26 vols (Paris, 1856–66), xxv p256.
[104] South, *Animadversions*, p291.

The persons of the Trinity are, in other words, the divine essence, considered as subsisting in a particular manner. As such, they are complete beings, in the sense that they do not complete, nor are they a part of any other being.[105]

The modes of subsistence of the divine being, South argues, are inseparably bound up with the relations between the persons of the Trinity—indeed they are constituted by those relations. The Father's particular mode of subsistence is that he begets the Son, and together with the Son sends forth the Holy Spirit. The Son's particular mode of subsistence is that he is begotten by the Father, and joins with him in sending forth the Holy Spirit. The Holy Spirit's particular mode of existence is that he proceeds from both the Father and the Son. Their relationships to each other are the modes under which they subsist.

As South puts it of the divine persons:

> They are so entirely relative, that their very *subsistere* [subsistence] is *referri* [relation], and their *referri* not only consequent and supervenient upon their substance (as it is in created persons) but one and the same with it; so that by virtue thereof they are indifferently termed by all Schoolmen and Divines either relative subsistences, or subsisting relations. The concrete and abstract terms in all the divine persons being, by reason of the particular condition of their personality, as well as the absolute transcendent simplicity of the divine nature, only different ways of expressing the same thing.[106]

So, for example, the Father is and subsists by begetting the Son, not (as Sherlock has it) by knowing himself to be the Father. The Father is and subsists by communicating his essence to the Son, not by thinking about himself.

And since the divine nature is common to all three persons, we must consider it as formally one, before we consider it as it is affected or modified by the particular ways it subsists in Father, Son, and Holy Spirit. The unity, the essential oneness, of the divine nature is thus logically the first attribute of the divine being, and antecedent to the modes of subsistence of that being in each of the three persons. Consequently, 'the formal reason, that the three divine persons are essentially one God, is the community of one and the same individual nature to the three persons'.[107]

## OTHER REFORMED VOICES

Robert South was truly unusual amongst the Reformed, in the technicality and precision with which he approached the Trinity. Most theologians of his persuasion steered clear of these rocky theological waters altogether.

105 South, *Animadversions*, p34.

106 South, *Tritheism Charged*, pp156–7.

107 Ibid., p180.

Thomas Barlow, for example, in his inaugural address as Lady Margaret Professor, made it very clear that the doctrine of the Trinity was not a subject which he would be treating during his lectures. He writes:

There are several heads of divinity which, though most true, and not doubted amongst the orthodox professors of the Christian faith, I am nonetheless not going to touch on during the forthcoming lectures, except it be unwillingly. 1. The stupendous mystery of the Sacred Trinity, the eternal generation of the Son, the procession of the Holy Spirit, what (in the economy of the Divine Trinity) godhead, essence, subsistence signify, how the persons are distinguished from the nature, and how they are distinguished from one another? About which the synod of Nicea, Athanasius, and the fathers for a few centuries after them disputed modestly and in an orthodox way; [but about which] Lombard and his successors disputed more often curiously and even sometimes irreverently. These and things similar to them, I would rather wonder at than investigate. For it is dangerous even to speak the truth about God, the light is unapproachable, and not to be neared without peril, and the eyes fail through such brightness.[108]

In fact, Barlow seemed to think that even the Athanasian Creed was sufficiently complicated to cause problems for ordinary believers, though he believed that all it contained could be deduced from scripture.[109] He was nonetheless quite clear that it was possible to be saved without explicitly believing everything it contained.[110] Thomas Tully was scarcely more forthcoming.[111]

One writer who was a little more expansive on the subject was John Wallis, though his approach was distinctly more reserved than South's. He published a series of letters on the subject of the Trinity, which in turn provoked some replies and queries from other authors. He eventually put together both his and his correspondents' letters together as the *Theological Discourses* (1692).

Although Wallis has clearly read Sherlock, he states that he does not fully comprehend what Sherlock meant[112] and refuses to engage with him polemically.[113] He does confess, however, that he agrees with one of his correspondents

[108] 'Nonnulla sunt ss. theologiae capita, verissima quidem, et apud orthodoxos fidei Christianae professores indubitata, a me non tamen futuris praelectionibus non nisi invito sollicitanda. 1. Stupenda illud Sacrae Trinitatis mysterium, generatio Filiis aeterna, processio Spiritus Sancti, quid (in Divina Trinitatis oeconomia) *theotes, ousia, hypostasis,* significant, quomodo persona a natura, et personae inter sese distinguuntur? De quibus synodus Nicenae, Athanasius, patresque pro aliquot secula subsequentes, modeste et orthodoxe; Lombardus et sui sequaces saepius curiose nimis, aliquando impie disputarunt. Haec et his similia mirari mallem, quam scrutari. Periculosum enim est de deo vel vera dicere, lumen est inaccessum, non sine periculo adeundum, suntque oculis tenebrae pro tantum lumen abortae.' Barlow, MS QCL 235 pp13–14.

[109] Barlow, *Analecta de Symbolo Athanasii,* MS QCL 279, p449.

[110] Ibid., p353.

[111] T. Tully, *Praecipuorum Capitum Enchiridion Didacticum* (London, 1700), p15.

[112] J. Wallis, *Theological Discourses* (London, 1692), p9.

[113] Ibid., 3rd letter, p42.

that Sherlock said 'more . . . than that learned author needed to have said'.[114] In particular, Wallis admits that he has great difficulty with Sherlock's assertion that the Trinity can be understood as three substances or three spirits. Rather, he urges, 'the three persons are one being, one substance, and one spirit',[115] because 'these three whos are one what. They are one thing, one substance, one God.'[116] And, as he makes clear in his rather more pugnacious *Answer to Dr Sherlock's Examination of the Oxford Decree*, Wallis is certainly not prepared to concede that, in relation to the Trinity, person and mind are equivalent terms.[117]

Wallis begins his own presentation of the matter by underlining that, within the Trinity, Father, Son, and Holy Spirit are clearly distinct, yet so united as still to be one God. He immediately strikes the somewhat agnostic tone which characterizes all his letters, writing,

> that these are three, distinguished each from each other, is manifest: and, that this distinction amongst themselves is wont to be called personality. By which word, we mean that distinction (whatever it be) whereby they are distinguished from each other and thence called three persons.[118]

Wallis argues that the word person is not itself vital to Trinitarian doctrine; but it is sanctioned by its use in the scriptures,[119] and 'we have no reason to waive the word, since we know no better to put in the place of it'.[120] Wallis notes that the scriptures say very little about what the characteristics of the persons are, except that the Father begets, the Son is begotten, and the Holy Ghost proceeds—and even these, he feels, are metaphorical statements.[121] As a result, he does not think that there is any need to press our investigations further: for 'where the scripture is silent we may content to be ignorant'.[122]

The scriptures are, however, clear in ascribing divinity to each of the persons of the Trinity.[123] Those who oppose the doctrine of the Trinity say that this is impossible, but Wallis thinks that their opinion is unjustified: they simply cannot pronounce so confidently on what is and is not possible within the divine nature. He underlines ' 'Tis hard, I say, for us . . . to determine . . . that it is impossible, or inconsistent with his essence, which essence we cannot understand.'[124] He suggests that one reason why people have such problems with conceiving of the Trinity is that they assume that the word person is used in the same sense when applied to the Godhead as it is when applied to

[114] Wallis, *Theological Discourses* (London, 1692), 7th letter, p2. [115] Ibid., p18.
[116] Ibid., 3rd letter, p9. [117] Wallis, *Answer*, p18.
[118] Wallis, *Theological Discourses*, 1st letter, p3.
[119] Hebrews 1:3 'Who being the brightness of his glory and the express image of his person . . .'
[120] Wallis, *Theological Discourses*, 1st letter, p3.
[121] Ibid. [122] Ibid., p4. [123] Ibid. [124] Ibid., p9.

human beings. But this is not the case, he points out, echoing South, 'nor doth any word, when applied to God, signify just the same as when applied to men, but only somewhat analogous thereunto.'[125] Wallis also believes that it is not necessary for us to know what exactly the distinction between the persons is.[126]

Wallis is occasionally a little more enlightening about his own view of what personhood within the Trinity might be. He makes clear, for example, that personhood denotes a relative rather than an absolute identity. He writes: 'the true and proper sense of the Latin word *persona*, is not to denote man simply (for this with them was *homo* not *persona*) but such quality, state or condition of a man, whereby he is distinguished from, or stands related to other men.'[127] In his *Answer*, Wallis makes clear that this is a major reason why Sherlock's contention that the persons of the Trinity are three distinct substantial beings must be rejected. He writes 'mind, spirit, substance are (in their proper signification) absolute; but person (in its proper signification) is relative'.[128] And so Wallis is here close to South's view that the persons in the Trinity are relative subsistences—their relationships with each other are their specific ways of being.

Wallis also underlines that 'there is, in truth, a distinction, and that more than imaginary, or what depends only upon our imagination; and greater than that of what we call the divine attributes'.[129] But he has already ruled out the idea that the distinction between the persons is a distinction between substances: so the distinction between the divine persons must be something between a substantial distinction, and a purely conceptual distinction. This of course, leaves him very little metaphysical room;[130] and, sure enough, he does confess that his understanding of the matter is that the distinction between the persons in the Trinity is probably closest to a modal distinction. He writes that the distinctions between the persons within the Trinity are 'somewhat analogous, in the deity, to what, in created beings, is called *distinctio modalis* [modal distinction], or *distinctio a parte rei, sed non ut res et res* [a distinction on the part of the thing, but not as between one thing and another]'.[131]

Wallis is much more reticent than South about deploying the full panoply of the scholastic terminology in relation to the Trinity. Nevertheless, he is in full agreement with South, and against Sherlock, that the Godhead is fundamentally one substance, being or spirit, not three. As we have seen, Wallis

[125] Ibid., p10. [126] Ibid., 2nd letter, p8.

[127] Ibid., 6th letter, p6. [128] Wallis, *Answer*, p17.

[129] Wallis, *Theological Discourses*, 4th letter, p11.

[130] Francisco Suarez is clear that the only sorts of distinction that exist are real distinctions, conceptual distinctions and modal distinctions. Suarez, *Omnia Opera*, xxv p257.

[131] Wallis, *Theological Discourses*, 7th letter, p21.

thinks that Sherlock's most problematic assertion is that the Trinity is three spirits. Furthermore, although he did not attack Sherlock himself in the *Theological Discourses*, Wallis reprinted one letter he had received, which was deeply critical of him. Wallis's correspondent W.J. asserts that Sherlock's views were tantamount to Tritheism,[132] and attacks Sherlock's conception of mutual consciousness on exactly the same grounds as South: namely that it was insufficient to establish the divine unity.[133] Wallis, in his reply to W.J., expresses no disagreement with these views.

Wallis's own view of the Trinity is consciously veiled. But it is telling that Wallis believes that a person is a relative, not an absolute term—indicating that, like South, he believes the distinction between the persons in the Trinity to be grounded upon their relationships with the other persons. More significantly still, when pushed, Wallis does concede that he considers the persons to be modally distinguished (though, again, like South he does not maintain that the persons are themselves modes). In other words, though he is less exuberant with his vocabulary, his conception of the Trinity is effectively the same as Robert South's.

The other Reformed writers, where they touch on the Trinity, are also in broad agreement with South. Beveridge, like South, believes that the Trinity is an inherently difficult thing to discuss: 'If I speak of it, how difficult it is to find out fit words for the explication of it.'[134] But he is clear enough that there is but one numerical and individual substance within the Trinity.[135] The distinction between the persons, he argues, lies in their particular manner of subsisting. He writes of the persons:

> And though these be really thus among themselves distinct from one another, yet are they not distinct in the divine nature; they be not distinct in essence, though they be distinct in the manner of subsisting in it.[136]

So, with South, he believes that the persons are distinguished by the way they exist rather than by what they are. For, unlike three human beings, the persons of the Trinity cannot be described as three individuals. As Beveridge puts is, 'the divine nature is not distinguished into several Gods, as the human is into several men; but only distinguished into several persons; every one of which hath the same undivided Divine nature, and is the same individual God.'[137]

Conceiving of the Trinity is, Beveridge argues, beyond the reach of human reason. He writes, having presented the scriptural authorities for Trinitarian belief,

[132] Wallis, *Theological Discourses*, 7th letter, p7. [133] Ibid., p9.
[134] Beveridge, *Works*, vii p59. [135] Ibid. p61. [136] Ibid. [137] Ibid.

if we proceed to reason, here also, though the unity of the Godhead be a truth which from natural principles may easily be demonstrated, yet the Trinity in the unity is a mystery which by the light of nature could never be discovered: forasmuch as our senses cannot perceive it, our tongues cannot express it, our experience cannot teach it, neither can our reason comprehend it.[138]

For this reason, he thinks, all images of the Trinity are likely to be unpersuasive.[139] Even so, he does admit that one is rather better than the rest, and with it demonstrates that he is fundamentally at one with South and against Sherlock, in holding that the Trinity has to be conceived of as one mind, rather than three. He writes:

That which looks the most like a reason is drawn from God's understanding and knowing himself, and so in himself begetting the lively image of himself... and this is the second person of the Trinity, called therefore the express image of his person: and from this God's looking upon himself, and representing himself to himself, cannot but proceed delight and rejoicing in himself; whereby the Father and the Son delight in one another... and this mutual love to and joy in one another, is a third manner of being or subsistence in the Godhead, called the Holy Ghost.[140]

But even this, he thinks, will not be a convincing explanation to those who do not already believe in the Trinity.[141]

In using this imagery, however, Beveridge is in step with other Reformed writers: all prefer images which depict the Godhead as being one mind or being, rather than three—which emphasize the unity, in other words, rather than the distinction of the persons. So, for example, Hacket writes,

I know not if any similitude do speak that ineffable mystery of the Holy Trinity better than this, from the manifest pronunciation of a speech wherein are these three things together which cannot be parted. The voice begets a word spoken, and there is truth in that word spoken by the voice: so the Father is the voice, the Son is the word, the Spirit proceeding from them both is the truth; and these three are all one and undivided.[142]

Burkitt presents a similar image, writing that 'As words are the conception and image of our minds, so Christ is the express image of his Father's person, and was begotten of the Father, even as our words are begotten of our minds.'[143]

Pearson, eschews the use of imagery, but like Beveridge, he uses the language of subsistence to express the existence of the persons within the divine being. He describes the Father, for example, as 'a person subsisting eternally in the one infinite essence of the Godhead.'[144] He does not, however,

[138] Ibid. p65. [139] Ibid. p66. [140] Ibid. [141] Ibid. p67.
[142] Hacket, *Century*, p195. Horton gives a similar image. Horton, *Hundred Sermons*, ii p138.
[143] Burkitt, *Expository Notes*, p227.
[144] J. Pearson, *Exposition of the Creed* (London, 1845), pp65–7.

discuss precisely what he means by a person in this context. Like South, however, Pearson believes that the relationships between the persons are what constitute their particular manners of subsisting. He writes 'the communication of the divine essence by the Father...was the true and proper generation by which he hath begotten the Son.'[145] And when discussing the Father, he writes:

> and according unto this paternity by way of generation totally divine, in which he who begetteth is God, and he which is begotten the same God, do we believe in God as the eternal Father of an eternal Son; which relation is coaeval with his essence, so that we are not to imagine one without the other; but as we profess him always God, so we must acknowledge him always Father.[146]

For, as he puts it 'The name of Father is relative; and the proper foundation of paternity, as of a relation, is generation,'[147] which is why, Pearson argues, 'the [Father] is a Father indeed by reason of his Son.'[148] So once again, we find a confident assertion of the unity of the divine essence, and a view of personhood within the Godhead as a relative form of subsistence: a way of being which depends entirely on each person's relationships with the other persons.

Newcome advances a similar view. Like South, he is clear that God is properly only one spirit, not three.[149] Like South, Newcome conceives of this as being an essential union not a union of consciousness; and again like South, he sets up a distinction between what is proper to each person *qua* person, and what is proper to each person *qua* God. He argues,

> The union is whereby these three persons are not one simply, but one in nature, even coessential and consubstantial; having all one Godhead....And therefore as these three persons are but one nature, so whatever agrees to God, simply considered, agrees to them all three, being all coequal and coeternal. Not only one with another, but also each in each other.[150]

What distinguishes the persons, therefore, are their individual personal properties, and those are relative. As Newcome puts it: 'the personal property of the Father being to beget the Son from all eternity; that of the Son to be so begotten of the Father; and that of the Holy Ghost to proceed from both.'[151] And once again, he believes that these relations are what give rise to each person's distinct subsistence within the divine essence.[152]

145 J. Pearson, *Exposition of the Creed* (London, 1845), p215.
146 Ibid., p54.
147 Ibid., pp43–4.
148 Ibid., p58. Hacket says the same: Hacket, *Century*, p197.
149 Newcome, *Catechetical Course*, i p79.
150 Ibid. p96.
151 Ibid. p97.
152 Ibid.

There is, however, one Reformed writer who dissents somewhat from the views of South and Wallis, and that is John Edwards. In general terms, his views are much the same as theirs, and certainly bear little resemblance to Sherlock's. His overall view of the Trinity is that, 'In the deity, which is but one, there are three distinct subsistences.'[153] Like South, he grounds the distinction between the persons upon their relationships to each other. He writes:

First, it is evidence that there is a difference and distinction of persons in the divine nature. Each of them hath a different and distinct relation to one another. It is the peculiar and incommunicable property of the first person, the Father, that he communicated his divine essence to the Son and to the Holy Ghost.... More particularly, the first person in the Trinity is called Father, on account of his relation to the second person of the Trinity, and the essence which he from eternity communicated to him by generation.[154]

He holds a similar view of the Son, *mutatis mutandis*.[155] He then writes 'thus you see how these two divine persons, the Father and the Son, are distinguished from one another by their proper and peculiar relation towards one another, to wit, the paternity of the first person, the filiation of the second'.[156] And he goes on to show that the Holy Spirit, too, is distinguished by his relation to the first two persons.[157]

Consequently, Edwards believes that the divinity, considered as begetting, is the Father, considered as begotten, is the Son, and, considered as proceeding from both Father and the Son, is the Holy Spirit. As he writes:

A person is one who hath something peculiar and proper to him, which cannot be in any other. Which is applied thus, the Father begets, the Son is begotten, the Holy Ghost proceeds. These are incommunicable properties, and therefore constitute the divine persons.[158]

The persons are, therefore, both identified and constituted by their relationships to each other. As he writes, 'the diversity of properties produceth the sacred Trinity; it constitutes these three persons so often mentioned. This by the Greek Fathers is called... the manner of subsisting'.[159]

In all this, Edwards is in agreement with the other Reformed writers who touch upon the subject. God is but one, yet in the Godhead there are three distinct subsistences, which are commonly called persons. Each person has its own particular manner of subsistence, which is constituted by that person's relations to the other persons. So far so good. However Edwards now asks the

[153] J. Edwards, *Theologia Reformata*, 2 vols (London, 1713), i p282.
[154] Ibid., i p282. [155] Ibid. [156] Ibid. pp283–4.
[157] Ibid. p284. [158] Ibid. p285. [159] Ibid.

question, 'But are properties and relations the only things that make the distinction between the persons in the Godhead? Are the three persons in the Trinity as they are persons, no more than three properties or relations, as others style them, modes?'[160]

Edwards points out that most scholastic writers do indeed define the persons as modes or relations. He then notes that 'other writers follow them of late, since the reviving of the controversy of the Trinity: they place the Trinity in so many aspects of modes; three modes in the one God, like three postures in one man. So Dr Wallis and Dr South.'[161] Edwards, however, does not plan to follow them. He writes:

> For though there are peculiar relations and properties belonging to them, as I have showed, yet the persons themselves are not relations or properties, and therefore it is very unfit to explain the Trinity by these only. It is certain that relative properties can't make a person, and therefore, if you don't take in essence, being or substance, into the notion of a person, you make the persons of the Trinity to be a mere logical notion, a bare abstract act of the mind devoid of all reality. Again, if the person signify only a property, then there are three qualities only in the Trinity: which is a very mean thought of the Trinity. We must be forced then to say, that the divine persons are not bare properties, nor mere modes of being or existing, for a mode did not make the world, and a mode was not incarnate: but they are things or persons with the modes of being and existing; and they are not only modally but really distinguished.[162]

So Edwards rejects what he believes to be South and Wallis's idea of personhood within the Trinity, and asserts instead that, 'A person is not a mode or property, but a certain *individuum* subsisting, though a person is not without a property.'[163]

Each person of the Trinity, Edwards thinks is constituted by its personal action (namely the communication or reception of its essence)[164] and its personal subsistence;[165] and he is clear that 'each of the divine persons have an absolute subsistence distinctly belonging to them'.[166] Indeed, he is even prepared to say that, in a carefully qualified sense, it might be possible to describe the three divine persons as three substances (on the basis, he argues, that the common essence does indeed truly belong to each of the divine persons and so becomes, in a sense, their own individual substance),[167] and he is prepared to argue that the persons are three substantial beings.[168]

However, he carefully underlines that he does not think that the persons of the Trinity are distinct, as created beings are distinct. As he puts it,

160 J. Edwards, *Theologia Reformata*, 2 vols (London, 1713), i p282.
161 Ibid. 162 Ibid.
163 Ibid. p286. 164 Ibid. 165 Ibid.
166 Ibid. p287. 167 Ibid. p288. 168 Ibid.

having mentioned the word *individuum*, I must add this to prevent mistakes, that we are not to imagine that there are three distinct substances in the Trinity, as individuals are distinct, i.e. such individuals as are of a finite nature. The three persons in the Trinity are not distinguished as three finite limited substances are, that are creatures.... Wherefore, in this sense, we must hold that each hypostasis hath not an individual essence.[169]

So Edwards is certainly prepared to use more substantial language to describe the persons of the Trinity than Wallis and South would have chosen. He also clearly wishes to distance his position from their views. However, Edwards seems to be under the impression that South and Wallis argued that the persons of the Trinity were mere modes or relations, whereas, in fact, South denied that this is what he meant. Rather, South and Wallis argued that the distinctions between the persons were analogous to modal distinctions, and were constituted by and inseparable from their relationships to each other. The Trinity, for South and Wallis, was not a Trinity of modes, but a Trinity of modally distinguished subsistent relations.

Nonetheless, it would be fair to say that Edwards is trying to reach beyond the idea of modal distinctions between the persons of the Trinity. He is attempting to convey a greater sense of the reality of the difference between the persons, without thereby sacrificing the essential unity of the Godhead. It is not entirely clear what he has in mind, and he is certainly very diffident about describing the persons as three substances—but his view is not identical with that of South and Wallis. Which is why, he writes in a resigned tone, he will probably be accused of Tritheism.[170]

What is also clear, though, is that Edwards does not endorse Sherlock's view of things. Like South, he is still wedded to the technical metaphysical vocabulary of traditional Trinitarian theology. Equally, he insists on discussing matters of essence and existence, and does not venture into the more avant-garde field of self-consciousness. The relationships between the persons are essential to his conception of the Trinity, and he grounds the unity of the divine essence not in the *perichoresis* of the persons, or their origin in the Father, but in their fundamental identity of essence.

## CONCLUSION

William Sherlock's *Vindication of the Doctrine of the Trinity* caused a debate every bit as ferocious as the controversy on justification which had erupted

169 Ibid. p289. 170 Ibid. p290.

some twenty years earlier. Inspired by the writings of Remonstrant divines such as Etienne de Courcelles and Jean Leclerc, Sherlock sought to find a way of expressing Trinitarian doctrine which did not require the use of what he saw as the antiquated and obfuscating terminology of school metaphysics. That terminology, he thought, only laid the doctrine of the Trinity open to attack from its Socinian and Unitarian opponents.

So, abandoning the use of terms such as essence, substance, subsistence, and person, he proposed a simpler and more up to date notion of the Trinity. Arguing that it is self-consciousness which accounts for the unity of any spiritual being, he asserted that the three persons of the Trinity should be conceived as three centres of self-consciousness. In other words, they should be considered as three distinct infinite minds, each conscious of their own thoughts, as distinct from the thoughts of the other two.

To guarantee the unity of the Godhead, Sherlock proposed that if, in addition to each person being conscious of his own thoughts, that person were also fully conscious of the thoughts of the other two persons, then it would be proper to describe the three persons as one. For since self-consciousness demonstrates the unity of one mind, mutual consciousness should demonstrate the unity of three minds. This way of conceiving the Trinity, Sherlock felt, was simple and intelligible. As a result it was far preferable to the incoherent ramblings of traditional Trinitarian orthodoxy.

Sherlock's book caused widespread outrage, and it was the Anglican Reformed who led the charge against him. Sherlock's most ferocious critic was undoubtedly Robert South. Inspired, in part, by personal antipathy, South wrote two detailed and sophisticated attacks on Sherlock's teaching. He utterly rejected the idea that the difficulty with the Trinity was a matter of terminology. For South, the nature of God is inherently mysterious and incomprehensible, and it is futile and arrogant to search for a simple way of expressing it. He ridiculed Sherlock's conception of the Trinity as both inadequate and intellectually incoherent. Sherlock, he thought, had simply replaced the perfectly workable terms of scholastic theology with new-fangled and unhelpful terms of his own. Far from clarifying the situation, Sherlock had further muddied the waters further by advancing a position tantamount to Tritheism.

In place of Sherlock's novel notions, South defends the traditional scholastic conception of the Trinity, a conception which, he argued, was shared by all orthodox divines, whether Protestant or Roman Catholic. The Trinity is one essence: one infinite mind, in other words, not three. That essence enjoys three distinct forms of subsistence. The distinction between those three forms of subsistence is rooted in, and inseparable from, their relationships with each other. The distinction between the persons of the Trinity is closest to a modal distinction, though South is careful to underline that the persons are not modes. South insists, however, that all philosophical terminology used in the discussion of the Trinity is used only analogically and not univocally, because there is an infinite disparity between the infinite, uncreated nature of God, and the finite and created nature of all that we ordinarily discuss in philosophy.

Many other Reformed writers avoided discussing the Trinity, on the basis that such discussions tended to degenerate into speculative fancy. Those that did, however, were certainly far closer to South's view than to Sherlock's even if they were not as enamoured of technical theological terminology as he was. Wallis, like South, argued that the Trinity was united in essence, but three in its manner of subsistence. Like South, he grounded the distinctions between the persons on their relationships with each other. Also like South, when pushed, he conceded that the distinction between the persons was closest to a being a modal distinction. With varying degrees of precision, other Reformed writers followed this pattern. The only exception was John Edwards, who felt that a modal distinction was insufficient to guarantee the real difference between the persons of the Trinity. But even Edwards did not come close to adopting the approach of William Sherlock.

The Trinitarian debate of the 1690s, like the discussion of justification in the 1670s, pitted Reformed Anglican writers against one of their colleagues who wished to import Remonstrant theology into the English Church. The several efforts of Compton, Wallis, and South meant that, at least on the matter of the Trinity, Sherlock's views (and with him the views of Courcelles and Leclerc) would not become a mainstream option within the established Church. Sherlock's new terminology was ridiculed, outlawed, and condemned as heretical by the University of Oxford. Those who wished to propagate Remonstrant ideas would, as a result, have to adopt a different approach in the future.

# 5

# The Slide into Subordinationism

## ARIUS REDIVIVUS

The royal decree of 1695 did quieten the controversy caused by William Sherlock's avant-garde views on the Trinity. Problems with this area of theology did not, however, subside for long. The flourishing intellectual culture of rational enquiry, combined with the end to all effective censorship by the Church, meant that innovative theological ideas could no longer be suppressed merely by royal or episcopal instruction. New and dangerous opinions were in the air, and the Anglican Church was certainly not immune to them. In 1710, William Whiston was deprived of his chair in Cambridge on account his unorthodox Christology,[1] and it is clear that Isaac Newton was also thinking some rather dangerous thoughts throughout this period.[2] However, the most high profile casualty of the ongoing debates was undoubtedly Samuel Clarke.

Samuel Clarke (1675–1729) was probably the most brilliant clergyman of his generation. Clarke was a celebrated natural philosopher as well as an eminent theologian, and was friends with both Whiston and Newton. Initially chaplain to Bishop Moore of Norwich, he moved to London in 1706, taking the valuable living of St James's Piccadilly in 1709. Clarke's intellectual reputation was second to none. He enjoyed the rare distinction of being invited to give the Boyle lectures in two successive years (1704 and 1705). Four years after delivering the second set of Boyle lectures, he obtained his Cambridge DD, defending in public disputation the theses that, 'No article in the Christian faith delivered in the Holy Scripture, is disagreeable to right reason' and that, 'Without the liberty of human actions, there can be no religion.' His performance in that public academic exercise quickly became legendary.[3]

Clarke was, clearly, a man destined for great things within the Church: he had powerful friends and a breathtaking reputation. He brought an end to his

[1] *ODNB*, s.v. 'William Whiston'.

[2] T. Pfizenmeier, *The Trinitarian Theology of Dr Samuel Clarke* (Leiden, 1997), p219.

[3] *ODNB*, s.v. 'Samuel Clarke'.

career with one book: *The Scripture Doctrine of the Trinity* (1712). This publication was seen, almost universally, as a manifesto for Arianism.[4] In 1714, the Lower House of Convocation asked the Upper House to investigate Clarke for heresy, submitting several extracts of the *Scripture Doctrine* as evidence for the charge. Clarke immediately issued an explanation which amounted to a partial retraction of his views, and promised, in any case, not to preach or write on the issue again.[5] The Lower House was far from satisfied with his studiedly ambiguous words; but since the Upper House was disinclined to pursue the matter further, Clarke's actions brought an end to the formal proceedings against him.[6] Clarke's ecclesiastical career was, however, effectively over. He received no further preferment of any significance, despite retaining his many influential friends, and forming a close attachment to the future Queen Caroline.

Clarke was as good as his word, and published no further significant discussions of the Trinity. However, the debate rumbled on through the valiant efforts of partisans such as Daniel Whitby, until Daniel Waterland's masterful defence of traditional orthodoxy brought the argument to an effective close.

Most modern studies of the Arian controversy consider Clarke's work to be part of the ongoing story of English Socinianism (or Unitarianism, as it increasingly came to be known).[7] John MacLachlan, for example, calls the position advanced in the *Scripture Doctrine of the Trinity* a 'modified form of Socinianism.'[8] MacLachlan's work charts the gradual infiltration of Socinian ideas into England, arguing that the high point of the Socinian movement in this country was indeed the controversy of the 1690s. Nonetheless, he asserts, 'the Socinian-Unitarian movement of the eighteenth century found its continuators in the eighteenth century... within the Church of England in the Arians William Whiston and Samuel Clarke.'[9] John Redwood, following Maclachlan, writes of Clarke and his followers: 'something was probably owed by all these men... to the anti-Trinitarian traditions that were disseminated from Holland across the seas.'[10] Philip Dixon, too, describes the

[4] Pfizenmeier has underlined that Clarke is not, strictly speaking, an Arian, at least as the Early Church fathers would have understood the term. Pfizenmeier, *Trinitarian Theology of Samuel Clarke*, p220.

[5] *ODNB*, s.v. 'Samuel Clarke'.

[6] C. Abbey, and J. Overton, *The English Church in the Eighteenth Century* (London, 1902), p214.

[7] One exception is Maurice Wiles, who notes the distinction between Arianism and Socinianism in his *Archetypal Heresy: Arianism through the Ages* (Oxford, 1996), pp68–9.

[8] H.J. MacLachlan, *Socinianism in Seventeenth Century England* (London, 1951), p334.

[9] MacLachlan, *Socinianism in Seventeenth Century England*, p335.

[10] Redwood, *Reason, Ridicule and Religion*, p171.

Trinitarian debates of the later seventeenth and early eighteenth centuries against the background of the growing influence of Socinian thinking in England, and argues that 'the influence of continental Socinianism, although not persuasive, was clearly detectable amongst the educated elite.'[11]

It is not denied that Socinian reflection on the Trinity may have had some influence on those who ultimately rejected the Trinitarian orthodoxy of the Athanasian Creed. Certainly, Daniel Whitby, who became one of Samuel Clarke's most vehement supporters in the debate with Waterland, was prepared to suggest that Johann Crell's and John Biddle's objections to orthodox Trinitarianism had not been adequately answered.[12] Nonetheless, Samuel Clarke, clearly felt that the position he was advancing was not Socinian.[13] And even John Edwards, who lumped the modern Arians together with the Socinians for the purposes of debate, acknowledged that there were significant differences between Clarke's position and that adopted by the classic Socinian writers.[14]

It should be noted that some confusion had arisen about what Socinianism actually was, as a result of the controversy of the 1690s. Originally, Socinus and his followers had maintained that the Father alone was the true God. Christ, they argued, had only a human nature[15] and was called the Son of God principally on account of his miraculous conception by the Holy Spirit.[16] Christ could be called divine, in that he was imbued with all the communicable perfections of the Godhead and because no other created being was superior to him.[17] But since Christ was only human, he had not existed from eternity, but only from the moment of his conception.[18] The Holy Spirit, as far as these early Socinians were concerned, was no more than the scriptures' way of speaking about the power and influence of God the Father and so was not even a distinct person.[19]

However, during the pamphlet war of the 1690s, some of the more creative anti-Trinitarian voices began to redefine their position. English Socinianism began to metamorphose into Unitarianism. The chief opponents of Trinitarian orthodoxy began to advance something akin to Sabellian modalism as the

[11] Dixon, *Nice and Hot Disputes*, p135.

[12] D. Whitby, *A Dissuasive from enquiring into the doctrine of the Trinity* (London, 1714), pp8–9.

[13] Clarke, S., *The Scripture-Doctrine of the Trinity* (London, 1712), p293.

[14] Edwards, J., *Some Animadversions on Dr. Clarke's scripture doctrine (as he styles it) of the Trinity* (London, 1712), p4.

[15] *Catechesis Ecclesiarum Polonicarum*, p45.

[16] Ibid. p46.

[17] Ibid. p48.

[18] Ibid. pp54–7.

[19] Ibid. p257.

true Socinian position.[20] They called it 'Nominal Trinitarianism,' and held it to include any position which fell short of asserting that there were three distinct minds or spirits within the Trinity.[21] This was polemically useful, because they were then able to claim that several of the self-confessed Trinitarians (South and Wallis in particular) were actually in agreement with them.[22] As a result of this metamorphosis of the Socinian into a more strictly Unitarian position, Samuel Clarke thought (or, at least, was able to claim that he thought) that Socinianism and Sabellianism were effectively the same thing and that by opposing the latter, he was opposing the former as well.[23]

As we shall see, Clarke's version of Arianism had relatively little in common with either early seventeenth century Socinian, or late seventeenth-century Unitarian views about the Trinity. Consequently, it seems inadequate to account for his position by reference to these two approaches alone. Some other influence must have been involved. Furthermore, an evidently ambitious clergyman such as Samuel Clarke would not have ventured into print to advance positions he knew would be widely seen as heterodox, and anything smacking of Socinianism would certainly be that. An undue preoccupation with Socinian influence is probably the reason why most commentators find it very difficult to account for Clarke's opinions. Dixon, for example, is at a loss; he writes, 'It continues to be a matter of conjecture whether Clarke was naively innocent in putting forward his reflections, courageously fighting for truth, or fatally overawed by his own ability.'[24]

In fact, there was a significant trend within late seventeenth-century Anglican theology, ignored by most modern commentators, which better accounts for Clarke's heterodox views about the Trinity than any presumption of Socinian or Unitarian influence. It will be argued here that Clarke's Arianism is best seen, not as a result of the pollution of English orthodoxy by an essentially alien anti-Trinitarianism, but as the culmination of a long tradition of thoroughly Anglican subordinationism whose roots can be found in the first decades of the seventeenth century. That subordinationism was derived, not so much from the Socinian tradition, but far the far more respectable theology of the Remonstrants, in particular, Simon Episcopius and Etienne de Courcelles.

Samuel Clarke, in other words, was just an unusually advanced exponent of views which had widespread currency within the English Church. His mistake was to deploy his rigorous mind to working out the full logical consequences of that position, and so to expose the problems inherent within it.

[20] MacLachlan, *Socinianism in Seventeenth Century England*, pp321–3.
[21] *A Discourse Concerning the Nominal and Real Trinitarians* (London, 1695), p7.
[22] Ibid., p3.
[23] Clarke, *Scripture Doctrine*, p293.
[24] Dixon, *Nice and Hot Disputes*, p190.

## THE ORIGINS OF AUTOTHEANISM

The problem begins with John Calvin. It is not that Calvin was himself a subordinationist, but rather that his efforts to avoid subordinationism caused a reaction which led to subordinationism in others and which ultimately bore an Arian fruit in eighteenth-century England. Calvin's approach to the Trinity was the result of his engagement with a handful of anti-Trinitarian radicals and, in particular (on this issue at least), with Valentine Gentile. Gentile had argued that since the Father begets the Son, the Son's essence must be begotten and so inferior, in that respect, to the Father's. The Son is therefore not God in the fullest sense.[25] Calvin denied this, asserting instead that, although the person of the Son was begotten, the essence of the Son, being the one common essence of the divinity, was not. The Son, though begotten, has the same unbegotten essence as the Father. The Son can therefore be described as God of himself, just as the Father can. So he is, in other words, God in the fullest sense. Calvin writes:

> When we speak simply of the Son without regard to the Father, we well and properly declare him to be of himself; and for this reason we call him the sole beginning. But when we mark the relation that he has with the Father, we rightly make the Father to be the beginning of the Son.[26]

This assertion of Calvin's, that Son could be said to be God of himself (*autotheos*) with regard to his essence, became, to the Reformed mind, the litmus test of orthodoxy. Francis Turretin echoed Calvin's position in the middle of the seventeenth century. He wrote:

> Although the Son is from the Father, nevertheless he may be called God of himself (*autotheos*), not with respect to his person, but essence; not relatively as Son (for thus he is from the Father), but absolutely as God, inasmuch as he has the divine essence existing from itself and not divided or produced from another essence (but not as having that essence from himself). So the Son of God is God from himself although not the Son from himself.[27]

The significance of the assertion that the Son could be described as God of himself in this manner was still acknowledged at the end of the seventeenth century, even by those who were opposed to the orthodox conception of the Trinity. The author of the *Discourse concerning the Nominal and Real Trinitarians*, for example, wrote:

[25] Calvin, *Institutes*, I.13.23. [26] Ibid., I.13.20.
[27] Turretin, *Institutes*, Topic 3 q.28.40.

To know the writers who believe the equality of the Son and Spirit with the Father, from those that deny it, this rule most commonly will serve. They that say the Son is *autotheos* (God of himself, and independent) generally hold the absolute equality of all the three persons; and that one person of the Trinity is equal to the whole Trinity: for if he were not, they plainly see, he could not be perfect God, for something would be wanting to him, that is found in the whole Trinity.[28]

But although Calvin's assertion achieved acceptance within Reformed circles, it brought swift opposition from a handful of Roman Catholic writers. The first into the affray was the professor of Hebrew in the Sorbonne, Gilbert Génébrard, who condemned Calvin's position as heretical in the first book of his *De Sancta Trinitate* (1569), calling this new heresy 'autotheanism.' This condemnation was reiterated in the seventeenth century by the eminent patristic scholar, Denis Pétau (Petavius), in his *Theologicarum Dogmatum* (1644).

However, not all Roman Catholic writers were so opposed to Calvin's idea. Bellarmine, for example, deals with the issue at some length in his *De Christo* and adopts a rather more nuanced position. He begins the discussion with the words: 'There is a certain new heresy, and I do not know whether it is a real heresy or merely a matter of words.'[29] He notes Génébrard's condemnation of Calvin's view, and laments Calvin's inept way of speaking which is the cause, he thinks, of this unnecessary controversy. He writes: 'I esteem Calvin to have erred, without doubt, as to his mode of speaking, and so to have give occasion that those things were written about him, which have been written by us.' However, he goes on:

But although these things are so, nonetheless when I examine the thing itself, and carefully consider the opinions of Calvin, I do not easily dare to pronounce that he has erred in this matter. Since indeed he teaches that the Son is of himself with regard to his essence, not with regard to his person; and he seems to want to say that the person is begotten by the Father, and that the essence is not begotten, but is rather from itself, so that if you remove from the person of the Son the relation to the Father, there remains only the essence, which is of itself.[30]

[28] *A Discourse concerning the Nominal and Real Trinitarians*, p20.

[29] 'Est nova quaedam haeresis, quae nescio an sit in re an solum in verbis.' Bellarmine, R., *Opera Omnia*, 12 vols (Paris, 1870), ii p333.

[30] 'Calvinum existimo quoad modum loquendi sine dubio erasse, et dedisse occasionem, ut de illo scriberentur, quae scripta sunt a nostris.... Sed quamquam haec ita se habeant; tamen dum rem ipsam excutio, et Calvini sententias diligenter considero, non facile audeo pronunciare, illum in hoc errore fuisse. Siquidem docet, Filium esse a se respectu essentiae, non respectu personae, et videtur dicere velle, personam esse genitam Patre, essentiam non esse genitam, sed esse a se ipsa, ita ut si a persona Filii removeas relationem ad Patrem, sola restet essentia, quae est a se ipsa.' Bellarmine, *Opera*, ii p334.

Understood this way, Bellarmine thinks, the substance of Calvin's view is perfectly orthodox. The only thing that is unacceptable is the careless assertion that the Son is God of himself, which, Bellarmine argues, is indeed incompatible with the scriptures, the councils and the fathers.[31] He goes on to underline that if *autotheos* is interpreted in its strictest sense, then it is true neither of the Father nor of the Son. He writes:

For if *autotheos* signifies him who is God from himself, as they think, certainly neither the Father nor the Son can be called *autotheos*, for the Son is not God of himself, but from the Father: and even the Father is not God of himself, but from nothing; to be of onesself, is to be produced by onesself, whereas the Father is simply unbegotten and unproduced.[32]

On the other hand, he argues, *autotheos* can be understood to mean no more than that which really is God, and in this sense it is appropriate to call every one of the persons of the Trinity *autotheos*.

What has informed Bellarmine's position is that Calvin's distinction (between the Son considered as person and the Son considered as essence) was, in fact, a long established tool in scholastic discussions of the Trinity and one which was still in widespread use within the Thomist school of his own day. It was also, arguably, a device sanctioned by no less an authority than a general council.

Back in the twelfth century, Peter Lombard had argued that only the persons within the Trinity could be said to generate or be generated. The divine essence could not.[33] Joachim of Fiore criticized this view, alleging that it led to a divine quaternity made up of the three persons and the essence, all of which had different properties. Instead, he argued that the divine essence could be said to generate, in the Father, and to be generated, in the Son.[34] The fathers of the Fourth Lateran Council (1215) took a rather different view. They rejected Joachim's criticism of Lombard, and decided that

There exists a certain supreme reality, incomprehensible and ineffable, which truly is the Father and the Son and the Holy Ghost, the three persons together and each one of them separately.... This reality neither begets, nor is begotten, nor proceeds; the Father begets, the Son is begotten and the Holy Spirit proceeds. Thus there is a distinction of persons but a unity of nature.[35]

[31] Bellarmine, *Opera*, ii p335.

[32] 'Nam si *autotheos* significaret eum, qui es Deus a seipso, ut illi existimant, certe nec Pater nec Filius posset dici *autotheos*, nam Filius non est Deus a se, sed a Patre: Pater etiam non est Deus a se, sed a nullo; esse enim a se, est productum esse a se, Pater autem est simpliciter ingenitus, et improductus.' Bellarmine, *Opera*, ii p336.

[33] Lombard, *Sentences*, I dist.5.

[34] This, at least, is how the Fourth Lateran Council understood him. Norman Tanner (ed.), *Decrees of the Ecumenical Councils* (Georgetown 1990), pp231–2.

[35] Ibid., p232.

The effect of this decision can be seen in Thomas Aquinas's discussion of the relationship between the Father and the Son within the Trinity.

Aquinas was certainly willing to ascribe a degree of priority to the Father within the Trinity. He describes the Father as the 'principle' of the Trinity, since he is the one from whom the other two persons proceed.[36] He also says that it is proper to the Father to be unbegotten. Unbegottenness, or innascibility as he also calls it, is the distinguishing mark of the first person of the Trinity.[37] However, Aquinas argues, to this priority, there does not correspond any inferiority or subordination on the part of the Son or the Holy Spirit. He writes:

> It is the custom with the Greeks to say that the Son and the Holy Ghost are principled. This is not, however, the custom with our doctors; because, although we attribute to the Father something of authority by reason of his being the principle, still we do not attribute any kind of subjection or inferiority to the Son or to the Holy Ghost....[38]

Aquinas is quite clear that there is an order within the Trinity, since the Father is the principle whereas the Son and the Spirit are not.[39] But that does not imply that there is any difference of dignity[40] or of power[41] between them.

After discussing the distinguishing marks of the second and third persons of the Trinity, Aquinas moves on to discuss the relationship between the persons and the essence in God. He notes that Joachim went wrong here, and underlines, following the Lateran Council, that 'what belongs to the persons, distinguishing them from each other, cannot be attributed to the essence.'[42] In other words, it is not correct to say that the Father's essence generates, that the Son's essence is begotten, or to say that the Holy Spirit's essence proceeds. The Father generates, the Son is begotten, the Holy Spirit proceeds, but their essence, being common to all three persons, does none of these things. This is, in fact, what distinguishes generation within the divinity, from the sorts of generation found in created beings. Aquinas writes:

> In creatures, the one generated does not receive the same nature numerically as the generator, but another nature, numerically distinct, which commences to exist in it anew by generation, and ceases to exist by corruption.... But God begotten receives the same nature numerically as the begetter possesses. So the divine nature in the Son is not begotten either essentially or accidentally.[43]

In other words, it is only when considered specifically in relation to the Father, that the Son is called begotten.

[36] Aquinas, *S.Th.*, Ia q.33 art.1. [37] Ibid., art.4.
[38] Ibid., art.1. [39] Ibid., art.3.
[40] Ibid., art.4. [41] Ibid., art.6.
[42] Ibid., q.39 art.5. [43] Ibid.

This clear distinction between those things which are predicated of the essence and those which are predicated of the persons within the Trinity was still observed by the Thomistic commentators of the sixteenth and seventeenth centuries. Domingo Banez, for example, a celebrated professor of theology in Salamanca during the later sixteenth century, writes, in his commentary on *Summa Theologiae* Ia q.33, that although it is true that the Father is, as Aquinas has pointed out, the principle of the Son, it should be noted that

> this way of speaking... namely that the Father is the principle of the whole deity... understood strictly, is improper and false. For from it would follow that the deity is begotten and spirated, which consequence is a heresy condemned in the Fourth Lateran Council... where it is defined, that the divine essence is neither begotten nor proceeding.[44]

The Father is, properly speaking, the principle only of the person of the Son, not of the essence or deity of the Son. For, 'even though it should be conceded that the Father, by generation, communicates the essence to the Son, it should, nonetheless, not be conceded, that he generates or produces that essence'.[45]

Thus, it is the person of the Son which is generated. The essence of the Son is not generated but communicated; though it is, of course, communicated to the Son in the Son's generation as a person. Banez agrees with Aquinas, that to be unbegotten is proper only to the person of the Father.[46] It does not follow from this, however, that the Son and the Holy Spirit cannot be described as unbegotten as well, at least with respect to their essence. He writes: 'the divine essence of the Son is unbegotten, though it does not follow from hence that the Son is unbegotten. Because the generation of the Father does not end in the essence, but in the person of the Son.'[47] Once again, what can be said of

[44] 'Modus ille loquendi... scilicet Patrem esse principium totius deitatis... in rigore accipiatur est improprius et falsus. Nam ex illo sequetur, quod deitas esset genita vel spirata, consequens est haeresis damnata in concilio 4. Lateran... ubi definitur, quod essentia divina neque est generans, neque procedens.' Domingo Banez, *Scholastica Commentaria in Primam Partem Angelici Doctoris S. Thomae* (Douai, 1614), i p371.

[45] 'Licet concedendum sit quod Pater per generationem communicat Filio essentiam, non tamen debet concedi, quod generat aut producit essentiam.' Banez, *Scholastica Commentaria,* i p371.

[46] Ibid., p373.

[47] 'Essentia divina Filii est ingenita, inde tamen non sequitur quod Filius sit ingenitus. Quia generatio Patris non terminatur ad essentiam, sed ad personam Filii.' Banez, *Scholastica Commentaria,* i p390. That the assertion that the Son could be described as unbegotten was equivalent to calling the Son as *autotheos,* at least by the late seventeenth century, can be seen in W. Payne, *A Letter from Dr. P. to the Bishop of R. in vindication of his sermon on Trinity Sunday* (London, 1696), p16.

the persons within the Trinity, taken as persons, cannot automatically be said of the essence which they share, and vice versa. Banez's position on this matter is not unusual.[48]

So although some Roman Catholic polemicists opposed the Reformed view, the majority accepted the substance of Calvin's teaching, though not necessarily his particular way of expressing it. The reason they did so was their continued acceptance of the medieval scholastic methods of talking about the Trinity and their shared loyalty to the decrees of the Fourth Lateran Council. The assertion that the Son of God was, with regard to his essence, self-existent—*autotheos*—was thus the common teaching of both Roman Catholic and Reformed theology.

## THE RISE OF SUBORDINATIONISM

The Roman Catholic writers' concern to respect the decisions of the Fourth Lateran Council was, of course, entirely lost on the more *avant-garde* sort of Protestant. So Simon Episcopius, for example, was quite free to reject Calvin's teaching out of hand and, with it, a large part of medieval tradition of thought on the matter.

In fact, Episcopius dismisses most of the scholastic discussion about the persons within the Trinity as unhelpful, and says that he will not involve himself in such subtleties. He writes:

> In the meantime, the arguments of the scholastics . . . about the processions of these persons, about the distinctions of the procession through intellect and through will, about the divine relations. 1. Whether they are something in God. 2. Whether, aside from these, they are real things, and if so, what. 3. How the real relations are distinguished amongst themselves. 4. How they are distinguished from the divine essence. 5. Whether they are of the essence by intrinsic reason, or not. 6. Whether, insofar as they are distinguished from the virtue of the essence, they are, strictly taken, perfect. 7. Whether, when the substantive relations are abstracted, this deity which is understood to remain, whether it is God. 8 Whether the persons are composed of essence and relations. 9 Whether the divine persons are constituted by relative properties, or absolute ones. & whatever other [questions] there are; it is better to flee and avoid them, as dangerous crags, labyrinths and gallows, from which not only [our] intellectual capacities but even [our] faith is often left hanging, than to set foot

[48] Cf. J. Fasolo, *Commentarium in Primam Partem S. Thomae*, 3 vols (Lyon, 1636), iii p368; A. Tanner, *Theologica Scholastica* (Ingolstadt, 1626), Disp. 4 q.4 dub.1. and F. Suarez, *Commentaria ac Disputationes in Primam Partem Divi Thomae* (Mainz, 1620), p468.

in them, let alone to wander through them curiously, to investigate them anxiously, or to decide on them audaciously.[49]

However, Episcopius is being a little coy here, because he has already laid down that the persons in the Trinity are each possessed of 'individuality, subsistence, life, intelligence, will and power'[50] as all ordinary persons are. So, in effect, he has already assumed that the persons within the Trinity have absolute properties rather than merely relative ones.[51] His protestations about not prying into the subtleties of Trinitarian personhood are actually a way of sidelining the distinction between person and essence which enabled scholastic theologians to stay faithful to the teaching of the Fourth Lateran Council.

Episcopius notes that the divine perfections are ascribed, in scripture, to each of the three persons. But, he underlines:

Truly, I add ... it is certain from these same scriptures, that divinity and the divine perfections are attributed to these three persons, not collaterally or co-ordinately, but subordinately: so that the Father alone has this divine nature and these divine perfections from himself, or from no other, but the Son and the Holy Spirit from the Father: and, consequently, the Father is the fount and principle of all the divinity which is in the Son and the Holy Spirit.[52]

This is, of course, a definite departure from the Thomist way of speaking. As we have seen, Aquinas was willing to assert that the Father could be described as the principle of the Son and the Holy Spirit. However, he was adamant that this implied no subordination in the second and third persons of the Trinity.

[49] 'Interea disputationes scholasticorum ... de personis harum processionibus, de processionum distinctionibus per intellectum & voluntatem, de relationibus divinis. 1. An aliquae in Deo sint. 2. An ex iis sint aliquae reales et quaenam. 3 Quomodo relationes reales inter se distinguantur. 4. Quomodo distinguantur ab essentia divinae. 5 An sint de intrinseca ratione essentiae, & contra. 6. An dicant perfectionem praecise consideratae, quatenus ab essentia virtute distinguuntur. 7. An abstractis subsistentiis relativis, intelligatur relinqui, haec Deitas, an hic Deus. 8. An personae sint compositae ex essentia & relationibus. 9. An divinae personae constituantur proprietatibus relativis, an absolutis. & quae sunt aliae, eas satius est fugere & evitare tanquam scopulos, labyrinthos, & cruces, ex quibus non ingenia tantum, sed & fides tota suspensa saepe haeret, quam in eas pedem inferre, nedum eas aut curiose confectari, aut anxie inquirere, aut audaciter decidere.' Episcopius opera (Amsterdam 1650) p333.

[50] 'Individua, subsistentia, vita, intelligentia, voluntate, & potentia.' Episcopius, *Opera* (1650), p332.

[51] It is a cardinal axiom of Thomist Trinitarianism that the persons could only be distinguished by their relative properties. Davies, *The Thought of Thomas Aquinas*, p199. Scotus experimented with a different view, but even he felt that the weight of authority was on the side of the Thomist position on the matter. Cross, *Duns Scotus*, p65.

[52] 'Vero addo ... certum esse ex iisdem scripturis, personis his tribus divinitatem divinasque perfectiones tribui, non collateraliter aut coordinate, sed subordinate: ita ut Pater solus naturam istam divinam & perfectiones istas divinas a se habeat, sive a nullo alio, Filius autem & Spiritus Sanctus a Patre: ac proinde Pater divinitatis omnis quae in Filio & Spiritus S. est, fons ac principium sit.' Episcopius, *Opera* (1650) p333.

And Banez, in particular, insisted that the Father was the principle of the persons, but not the deity, of the Son and the Holy Spirit.[53]

Episcopius goes even further when he draw out the consequences of this subordination. He writes:

Indeed, given what has been established about this subordination, it is certain that this divine perfection is only proper to the Father, in that he has it of himself and from no other. To have one's being from no other, is properly the first and highest [way of] being, in which is the acme and highest point of divinity. Whence it follows that the Father is so first, that he is also the highest in order, dignity and power.[54]

Episcopius is presenting self-existence here as one of the divine perfections, but one, importantly, which the Father has and the other two persons of the Trinity do not. On this basis, he can argue that the Father is greater than the Son or the Holy Spirit.[55] For Episcopius, in other words, only the Father is God in the fullest sense.

As a result, he has little time for Calvin's claim that the Son can be described as God-of-himself. He writes:

They go perilously wrong who contend that the Son of God is *autotheos*, such that as he is God, he is of himself, but as he is Son, he is of the Father; for this takes away, by reasoning, the true subordination between the Father and the Son. For the Son, as he is God, means the Son as he is of himself, that is to say the Son not a Son, and unbegotten, he who is begotten and does not exist except... because he is begotten.[56]

Episcopius has thus effectively elided the distinction between what can be predicated of the persons and what can be predicated of the essence within the Trinity. The Son is simply begotten, person and essence alike.

Episcopius argues that the distinction between person and essence is an invalid one, because, he thinks, the relationship of filiation which the Son has to the Father is not a relationship between the persons, but a relationship which the Son has with the Father's essence. He writes: 'The Son, as Son, is not

[53] Banez, *Scholastica Commentaria*, i p371.

[54] 'Enimvero subordinationis haec posita, certum est Patri soli proprie istam divinam perfectionem... competere, quod eam a se ipso, id est, a nullo alio habeat. A nullo enim habere esse suum, proprie est primum ac summum esse, in quo divinitatis acme est & fastigium. Unde consequitur, Patrem sic esse primum, ut etiam summus sit, tum ordine, tum dignitate, tum potestate.' Episcopius, *Opera* (1650) p334. Cf. Aquinas, S.Th., Ia q.42 art.4 and art.6.

[55] Episcopius, *Opera* (1650) p334.

[56] 'Periculose errant, qui Filium Dei *autotheon* esse contendunt, sic ut qua Deus est, sit a se ipso, qua Filius est, sit a Patre; cum haec ratione subordinatio vera inter Patrem & Filium tollantur. Filium enim qua Deus est, dicit Filium qua a se ipso est, id est Filium non Filium, ingenitum eum qui genitus est & non est nisi... quia genitus est.' Episcopius, *Opera* (1650) p334.

of the Father. For there is no filiation, as such, unless there is a distinct relation from the essence.'[57] Thus the Son is a Son because his essence is generated by the Father's essence, not because of his relationship to the Father's person. This, of course, represents a near wholesale return to the Joachimite position that the Father's essence generates and the Son's essence is generated. As a result, it flatly contradicts the teaching of the Fourth Lateran Council. Episcopius has therefore stepped well clear of the medieval Catholic patterns of Trinitarian thinking.

Episcopius's successor at the theological helm of Arminianism, Etienne de Courcelles, takes a very similar line. He too abandons the distinction between the personal properties and the essence within the divine persons, and insists rather that each must have its proper essence. He deploys a neat syllogism to demonstrate this, writing

> All that is, or exists, has its proper essence, by which it is what it is, and is distinguished from all other things: moreover the persons of the divinity are, or exist; therefore each of the persons of the divinity has its proper essence, by which they are what they are, and are distinguished from all other things.[58]

For this reason, when we say that the Son is begotten, we must also mean that the Son's essence is begotten—for his essence is indistinguishable from his person.

Following Episcopius, Courcelles accordingly insists that calling the Son of God *autotheos* is absurd. He argues that by using this term,

> the Son of God is really denied to be a son, whatsoever the fallacy by which he [i.e. Courcelle's critic, Maresius] strains to veil this impiety; and the Father's prerogative ... is torn away. Nor can it be imagined, except absurdly and by contradiction, that the Son is begotten by the Father with respect to the person, but truly has the essence, because it is not begotten, from himself.[59]

On the basis that the Son and the Holy Spirit receive their essence from the Father, Courcelles adopts a firmly subordinationist line on the Trinity. He writes,

[57] 'Filius, qua Filius non est a Patre. Filiatio enim, qua talis, non dicit nisi relationem distinctam ab essentia.' Episcopius, *Opera* (1650) p334.

[58] Curcellaeus, *Opera*, p879. 'Omne quod est, seu existit, habet suam essentiam propriam, per quam est id quod est, & ab aliis omnibus distinguitur: personae autem divinitatis sunt, seu existunt; ergo, personae singulae divinitatis habentes suam essentiam propriam, per quam sunt id quod sunt, & ab aliis omnibus distinguuntur.'

[59] Curcellaeus, *Opera*, p841. 'Filius Dei revera negatur esse filius, quocunque sophismate impietatem istam velare contendat; & Patri praerogativa ... eripitur. Nec fingi potest, nisi absurde et contradictorie, Filium respectu personae a Patre esse genitum, essentiam vero, quia non generetur, a se ipso habere.'

they certainly err who determine the Son and the Holy Spirit to be equal to the Father in all things, since the scripture everywhere subordinates them to the Father, and teaches that whatsoever they have of divinity should be credited to the Father, but [subordinates] the Father, truly, to none.[60]

And since the Son, unlike the Father, does not have his essence from himself, it follows that the Son should not be called the most high God.[61] Which is why, Courcelles believes, when the scriptures use the word 'God' simply and absolutely, they ordinarily mean the Father, and not the Son or the Holy Spirit.[62]

In this, of course, Courcelles has gone further than Episcopius, though only in the sense that he has pursued his predecessor's way of thinking more vigorously. He continues this more confident approach when he turns his attention to the traditional language of orthodoxy. He refuses, for example, to describe the Virgin Mary as *theotokos* (God-bearer); but he does so, not on the Nestorian ground that Mary was only the mother of Christ's humanity, not his divinity. Rather, he urges that Mary cannot be called *theotokos*, because she only bore the Son and not the Father, and only the Father should really be called God.[63] He also rejects as absurd the claim that the Son can be described as being of one substance—*homoousios*—with the Father.[64] This description of the Son is also, he argues, inconsistent with the important point that the Father is from none, whereas the Son and the Holy Spirit are from the Father.[65] In other words, with Courcelles, Remonstrant thinking has advanced far enough to begin undermining the Nicene Creed.

In England, the influence of Remonstrant views on the Trinity can be seen in the work of Ralph Cudworth, though his theology is closer to Episcopius than it is to Courcelles. In his *True Intellectual System of the Universe* (1678), Cudworth attempted to show that the Platonic speculation about plurality within the divine being was a worthy precursor to what he sees as the Christian doctrine of the Trinity. Cudworth noted that some have criticized the Platonic triad, because it subordinates the second and third persons of the triad to the first. However, he writes:

According to the principles of Christianity itself, there must of necessity be some dependence and subordination of the persons of the Trinity in their relation to one another, a priority and posteriority of 'dignity' as well as 'order' among them . . . because that which is originally of itself and underived from any other, must needs have

[60] Curcellaeus, *Opera*, p827. 'Errant enim qui statuunt Filium & Spiritum Sanctum Patri esse per omnia aequales, cum scriptura eos ubique Patri subordinet, & doceat ipsos quicquid habent divinitatis Patri acceptum ferre, Patrem vero nulli.'

[61] Curcellaeus, *Opera*, p843.

[62] Ibid. [63] Ibid., p882.

[64] Ibid., p881. [65] Ibid.

some superiority and preeminence over that which derives its whole being and godship from it, as the second doth from the first alone, and the third from the first with the second.[66]

So, just like Episcopius, Cudworth asserts a subordination of the Son and Holy Spirit to the Father. He bases this not on a mere difference of order, but on a difference in dignity which is the consequence of the Father's unique property of self-existence. Furthermore, it would seem that Cudworth, like Episcopius, believes that the Son's essence (his 'godship' as he puts is), and not merely his person, is generated by the Father. He is certainly not making any distinction between what can be properly said of the persons and what can be properly said of the essence within the Trinity.[67]

Cudworth is more explicit than Episcopius that he rejects the view of the Fourth Lateran Council. Indeed, he argues that it is clearly contrary to the teaching of the Nicene fathers.[68] He even goes so far as to echo Joachim's claim that such teaching results in a quaternity rather than a trinity.[69] For Cudworth, all that the Nicene fathers intended, when they asserted the consubstantiality of the Father and the Son, was to establish that the Son was not a created being. They did not intend anything like the medieval scholastic view of the matter. He writes:

as well according to these fathers as the Platonists, that essence or substance of the Godhead, which all three persons agree in, is not singular, but generical and universal; they both supposing each of the persons to have their own numerical essence.[70]

The idea, propounded by the Fourth Lateran Council, that the three persons share one numerical essence is, Cudworth thinks, nothing less than Sabellianism.[71]

George Bull's celebrated *Defence of the Nicene Creed* (1685), though it is a little more cautious than Cudworth's work, is no less marked by Episcopius's conception of the Trinity. Bull assumes, like Cudworth, that the Council of Nicea's description of the Son as *homoousios* with the Father was simply directed against the Arian view that the Son was a creature. He writes:

It is evident, then, that the Nicene bishops called the Son of God 'of one substance' with the Father, in a sense opposed to the blasphemies of the Arians; that is to say, that

[66] Cudworth, *True Intellectual System of the Universe*, 3 vols (London, 1845), ii p421. Cf. Episcopius, *Opera* (1650) pp333–4.

[67] Cudworth's position brought accusations of Arianism because of the subordinationist strain in his position. M. Wiles, *Archetypal Heresy*, p66.

[68] Cudworth, *True Intellectual System of the Universe*, ii p435.

[69] Ibid., p437.

[70] Ibid., p420.

[71] Ibid., p437.

he is not of any essence that is created, or other than that of the Father, or changeable; but altogether of the same divine and immutable essence as his Father.[72]

Bull also follows Cudworth in explicitly repudiating the Fourth Lateran Council. He discusses this in an extended section on the subordination of the Son to the Father. Echoing exactly the words of Episcopius, he asserts that 'the divine nature and perfections belong to the Father and the Son, not collaterally or co-ordinately, but subordinately'.[73] As he puts it, 'the catholic doctors, both those who preceded and those who lived after the Council of Nicea, with unanimous consent determined that God the Father, even in respect of his divinity, is greater than the Son'.[74] In other words, that which makes the Father God, his 'divinity' or in more traditional terminology, his essence or nature, is superior to the essence or nature of the Son. It follows, Bull argues, that,

That expression of certain modern writers, by which they designate the Son *autotheos*, that is, of himself God, is quite repugnant to the judgement of the Nicene council itself, and also to that of all the catholic doctors, both those who wrote before, and those who wrote after, that council.[75]

Again following Episcopius and Courcelles, Bull is adamant that the distinction between what can be said of the persons and what can be said of the essence within God is an invalid one. He writes: 'in this case person cannot be conceived of without essence, unless you lay down person in the Godhead to be nothing else than a mere mode of existence, which is simple Sabellianism.'[76] He is clear that the Lateran Council represents corrupt medieval teaching, not the purity of early Catholicism,[77] and is derisive of Petavius's attempts to rescue it. Petavius had not, of course, been unaware of the decrees of the Lateran Council and had tried to reconcile them with his own rejection of Calvin's position. However, he ended up conceding rather a lot of ground to Geneva on this point, agreeing, in particular, that it was appropriate to consider the essence of Godhead distinctly from the persons within it.[78] Bull is having none of it, writing:

I will go further, and say, that by the same subtleties by which Petavius endeavours to whitewash the view of the Master and the Lateran Council, he might have excused the error of Calvin itself, against which he so vehemently inveighs; as will be plain to

72 Bull, G., *Defence of the Nicene Creed* (Oxford, 1851), i p58.
73 Ibid., i pxvi. Cf. Episcopius, *Opera* (1650) p333.
74 Bull, *Defence of the Nicene Creed*, i pxvi.
75 Ibid., ii p556. Cf. Episcopius, *Opera* (1650) p334.
76 Bull, *Defence of the Nicene Creed*, ii p565. Cf. Episcopius, *Opera* (1650) p333.
77 Bull, *Defence of the Nicene Creed*, ii p567.
78 Denis Pétau, *Theologicarum Dogmatum* (Paris, 1644), ii p625.

anyone who considers the matter closely. I wish, however, that at this point, out of reverence for this sacred mystery, both sides alike would now abstain altogether from scholastic trifling.[79]

So it would appear that Bull, like Cudworth, has effectively abandoned the heritage of medieval Catholicism, and adopted the subordinationist approach to the divinity of the Son, which was characteristic of the Remonstrant writers.

William Sherlock, as we have already seen, was also heavily influenced by Remonstrant thinking in his understanding of the Trinity. That influence extended to his understanding of the nature of the second person. Having advanced his conception of the Trinity as three mutually conscious centres of self-consciousness, he goes on to show how this understanding of the Trinity, in his view, squares with all the commonly received aspects of Trinitarian teaching. In particular, he enthuses, 'this notion plainly reconciles the perfect equality of all three persons, with the prerogative of the Father, and the subordination of the Son and Holy Spirit'.[80]

The Son, Sherlock urges, is subordinate to the Father as a derivative is to an original light,[81] or as an image in a mirror is to its prototype.[82] As he argues 'there is no knowledge, no perfection, no power in the Son, which is not in the Father, and which he does not receive from the Father.'[83] Since the Father is, in this way, the origin and fount of all the divinity that is in the Son or the Holy Spirit, they must be naturally subordinate to the Father. Sherlock then follows Courcelles in drawing the logical conclusion from this situation, namely that the Son is not to be described as God in the fullest and highest sense. He writes:

As for this expression, the One True God, it is never attributed to the Son, or Holy Ghost, that I know of, either in scripture, or any Catholic writer.... This title cannot so properly be attributed to any one person, but only the Father, who is the fountain of deity.[84]

Though not laid out so clearly, Remonstrant views can also be found in the writings of John Tillotson. In a series of sermons which he published in 1693 in order to defend himself from accusations of Socinianism, Tillotson expounded his doctrine of the Trinity and the divinity of Christ in what he hoped were unimpeachably orthodox terms. His orthodoxy has, nonetheless, a distinctly Remonstrant flavour. For he writes of the Son:

[79] Bull, *Defence of the Nicene Creed*, ii p568.
[80] Sherlock, *Vindication*, p 81.
[81] Ibid., p 82.
[82] Sherlock, *Defence*, p 29.
[83] Sherlock, *Vindication*, p 59.
[84] Ibid., p 89.

It is yet further certain, that not only the name and title of God, but the most incommunicable properties and perfections of the Deity, are in scripture frequently ascribed to the Son and the H. Ghost; one property only excepted, which is peculiar to the Father as he is the principle and fountain of the Deity, that he is of himself and of no other; which is not, nor can be said of the Son and H. Ghost.[85]

Once again, just like Episcopius, Tillotson has described self-existence as one of the incommunicable properties of the divine nature, but also asserted that it is present in the Father only, not the Son or the Holy Ghost. So Tillotson, like Episcopius and Courcelles, envisages a distinctly two-tier Trinity. He is also just as dismissive as the earlier theologian of the scholastic efforts at explaining the Trinity, writing:

I desire it may well be considered, that there is a wide difference between the nice speculations of the schools, beyond what is recorded on scripture, concerning the doctrine of the Trinity, and what the scripture only teaches and asserts concerning this mystery.... It cannot be denied but that these speculative and very acute men, who wrought a great part of their divinity out of their own brains as spiders do cobwebs out of their own bowels, have stated a thousand subtleties about this mystery such as no Christian is bound to trouble his head withal.[86]

From the writings of Cudworth, Bull, Sherlock, and Tillotson, then, it is clear that an identifiably Remonstrant strain of subordinationism was becoming widespread within the English Church, well before Clarke produced his controversial work. Many writers were prepared to follow Episcopius and Courcelle and to qualify, to varying degrees, the divinity of the second and third persons of the Trinity. Essential to this growing trend was the steady abandonment of the medieval distinction between the person and the essence in discussions of the Trinity.

The impact of the *Scripture Doctrine of the Trinity* was undoubtedly increased by its unusual and striking approach to the question. The book is set out in three parts. In the first, Clarke sets out all the verses of scripture which he believed were relevant to the doctrine of the Trinity. In the second, he draws out the results of this research in a series of doctrinal propositions. The second part was also full of patristic references (mostly mined from Petavius and Bull) as well as lengthy extracts from contemporary Anglican writers, amongst whom George Bull, William Payne (a supporter of Sherlock's during

[85] John Tillotson, *Sermons, concerning the divinity and incarnation of our Blessed Saviour* (London 1693), p 121. Cf Episcopius, *Opera* (1650) p 334.

[86] Tillotson, *A Sermon concerning the unity of the divine nature and the Blessed Trinity*, p 16. Cf Episcopius, *Opera* (1650) p 333. This very passage of Tillotson is quoted by Samuel Clarke as a good reason for ignoring the scholastic treatment of the Trinity. Clarke, *Scripture Doctrine of the Trinity*, p 289.

the Trinitarian controversy), and John Pearson take pride of place. However, it was probably the third part of the work which caused the most scandal, because there Clarke presented the liturgical consequences of these propositions, in the form of a commentary on those passages of the Book of Common Prayer which needed qualification as a result of what he felt he had shown. And one of the passages which needed particularly heavy qualification, was the Nicene Creed's assertion that the Son was of one substance with the Father. Clarke, in other words, has moved beyond the restrained claims of Episcopius to the rather more racy conclusions of Courcelles.

Clarke's position is, pace John Edwards, quite different from that of the early seventeenth-century Socinians. Unlike them, he asserts the heavenly preexistence of Christ and therefore the twofold nature.[87] He is also clear that the Holy Spirit is a distinct person within the Trinity, not merely the power of the Father.[88] His theology, in other words, is not essentially Socinian. His strenuous efforts to avoid Sabellianism at all costs also ensure that it is not Unitarian.

On the other hand, Clarke's position is remarkably similar to that of Episcopius, as refined and advanced by Courcelles. Following Episcopius, and closely echoing Sherlock's rejection of a metaphysical approach to the matter, Clarke claims to be agnostic about the precise nature of the persons within the Trinity. He writes:

> What the proper metaphysical nature, essence, or substance of any of these divine persons is, the scripture has nowhere at all declared.... All reasonings, therefore (beyond what is most strictly demonstrable by the most evident and undeniable light of nature) deduced from their supposed metaphysical nature, essence or substance, instead of their personal characters, offices, powers and attributes delivered in scripture; are uncertain and at best probable hypotheses.[89]

So, once again, the technical scholastic discussions about the distinction of person and essence are effectively ruled out.

Like both Episcopius and Courcelles, Clarke asserts that the Son and Holy Spirit are subordinate to the Father; and he asserts it for the same reason, that their being is derived from the Father. He writes:

> The Son, whatever his metaphysical essence or substance be, and whatever divine greatness and dignity is ascribed to him in scripture, yet in this, he is evidently subordinate to the Father, that he derives his being and attributes from the Father, and the Father nothing from him.[90]

87 Clarke, *Scripture Doctrine of the Trinity*, p 279.
88 Ibid., p 242.
89 Ibid., p 243. Cf Episcopius, *Opera* (1650) p 333.
90 Clarke, *Scripture Doctrine of the Trinity*, p 304. Cf Episcopius, *Opera* (1650) p 333.

The priority of the Father within the Trinity is, therefore, more than a priority of order. It is a priority of dignity and of power. Clarke writes:

> The Father (or first person) alone is self-existent, underived, unoriginated, independent, made of none, begotten of none, proceeding from none.... The Father... alone is in the highest, strict and proper sense, absolutely supreme over all.[91]

So for Clarke, as for Episcopius, self-existence is a divine attribute, but it is a divine perfection which only the Father possesses. As he notes: 'The Son is produced of the Father, and so is not *autotheos*, or God in that sense as the Father who is from none.'[92] He also points out the danger of maintaining the contrary, writing:

> They who are not careful to maintain these personal characteristics and distinctions, but while they are solicitous (on the one hand) to avoid the errors of the Arians, affirm (in the contrary extreme) the Son and the Holy Spirit to be (individually with the Father) the self-existent being: these, seeming in words to magnify the name of the Son and Holy Spirit, in reality take away their very existence, and so fall unawares to Sabellianism (which is the same with Socinianism).[93]

In this Clarke is, of course, echoing the charge made against the medieval understanding of the Trinity made by Cudworth, Bull, and Sherlock.[94]

Clarke does, however, go considerably further than any of the earlier Anglican writers in the consequences he draws from this position. And it is these consequences which were his undoing. Clarke argues that, since the Father alone is God in the highest and fullest sense, only he is worthy of the highest sort of worship. He writes: 'Upon these grounds, absolutely supreme honour is due to the person of the Father singly, as being alone the supreme author of all being and power.'[95] It follows, therefore, that all Christian prayer and praise should be directed only to the Father,[96] and that all honour offered to the Son or the Holy Spirit should be understood as ultimately directed to the person of the Father.[97] Christians may worship the Father through the Son, but they may not worship the Son on his own account. The same is true *a fortiori* of the Holy Spirit, who is subordinate to both of them.

[91] Clarke, *Scripture Doctrine of the Trinity*, pp 143–4. Cf Episcopius, *Opera* (1650) p 334.
[92] Clarke, *Scripture Doctrine of the Trinity*, p 261.
[93] Ibid., pp 292–3.
[94] Cf Cudworth, *True Intellectual System of the Universe*, ii p 437. Bull, *Defence of the Nicene Creed*, ii p 565. Sherlock, *Defence*, p 97.
[95] Clarke, *Scripture Doctrine of the Trinity*, p 352.
[96] Ibid., p 354.
[97] Ibid., p 362.

Clarke also concludes that the Nicene Creed needs very careful qualification. The claim that the Son is of one substance with the Father, he thinks, leads directly to two dangerous conclusions. For either it means 'of one numerical substance', and in which case it is teaching Sabellianism; or it means 'of one generic substance,' and in which case it is teaching Tritheism. This is precisely the ambiguity which led Courcelles to reject the use of the term *homoousios* to describe the Son—a further indication of where Clarke found his inspiration.[98]

Clarke believes, therefore, that the words of the Nicene Creed should be understood only metaphorically, not metaphysically. As he underlines, in a passage which clearly illustrates the consequence of the avant-garde rejection of the traditional Reformed and Roman Catholic teaching:

> For a person who is not self-existent cannot, without a manifest contradiction, be said, strictly and properly, and in the same metaphysical sense of the phrase, to be of the same essence with a person who is self-existent, and of whose essence that self-existence must of necessity be a principal character.[99]

The denial that the Son of God is *autotheos* has therefore led to precisely the doctrine that Calvin had intended to prevent.

Soon after the intervention of Convocation, Daniel Whitby took up cudgels on Clarke's behalf. In his *Dissuasive from enquiring into the Doctrine of the Trinity* (1714), Whitby ridiculed the lower house for condemning Clarke's views without properly answering them.[100] Later on, in his *Reply to Dr. Waterland's Objections* (1720), he advanced a position echoing that of the *Scripture Doctrine of the Trinity.*

Like Clarke, Whitby is clear that the Son is subordinate to the Father in more than just order. He writes: 'the Son of God, who is subject to his Father, is less in power, is the image of him, and is the imitator of his works.'[101] And this, he maintains, was the view of the early church, for 'the generality of the ante-Nicene fathers did not assert that co-equality and numerical consubstantiality which Dr. W. contends for'.[102]

Whitby took particular exception to the medieval view that the same numerical essence could be communicated from the Father to the Son and echoed Clarke's charge of Sabellianism against it. He writes:

[98] Curcellaeus, *Opera*, p881.

[99] Clarke, *Scripture Doctrine of the Trinity*, p465.

[100] D. Whitby, *A Dissuasive from enquiring into the doctrine of the Trinity* (London, 1714), p22.

[101] Whitby, *A Reply to Dr. Waterland's Objections against Dr. Whitby's Disquisitiones Modestae* (London, 1720), p53.

[102] Whitby, *Reply to Dr. Waterland's Objections*, p57.

> the question between the orthodox and the Sabellians was chiefly this, whether there was only one singular, individual essence of the Father, Son and Holy Ghost, and consequently whether they were indeed only three several names or notions, or conceptions of one and the self-same thing.[103]

The divine persons, Whitby argues, cannot share a single essence, because, he thinks, echoing Sherlock, it is impossible to separate person from essence.[104] He writes: 'Seeing it is certain, that each divine person is a whole real hypostasis or substance; and that the Son and the Holy Ghost are not . . . parts or portions of God; hence it follows, that three divine persons really distinct, must have three distinct essences or substances.'[105] Once again, the abandonment of the tools of medieval scholasticism is leading in a rather unfortunate direction.

It is clear, Whitby argues, that, of these three essences, only the Father's essence is actually unoriginated. Self-existence is the unique prerogative of the Father's being and it cannot be communicated to the other persons within the Trinity. But, he points out, 'an existent essence unoriginated, underived, unbegotten, cannot be the same numerically with a substance or essence originated, derived and begotten; because both parts of a contradiction cannot be true.'[106] It follows that the Son must have a different substance from the Father. So, just like Clarke, he is asserting that the Son cannot be of one substance with God because the Father is unbegotten and the Son is not. Once again, from the denial that the Son is *autotheos*, that conclusion has been drawn that he is therefore not really God.

The outbreak of Arianism in early eighteenth century England is difficult to explain without taking into account the strain of Remonstrant subordinationism that had become increasingly widespread within the Church of England during the second half of the seventeenth century. Clarke and Whitby caused great scandal with their views, but they could have been forgiven for replying to the Church: 'The lady both protest too much.' They had followed Etienne de Courcelles further than other Churchmen, in pushing subordinationism to its logical conclusion, but they were far from the only people in the Church whose approach to the Trinity had led them to qualify the divinity of the Son and of the Holy Spirit.

## THE REFORMED RESPONSE

Against this background of a gathering Arian cloud, what did the Anglican Reformed have to say about the divinity of the Son? As we have seen, Samuel

103 Ibid., p23.
104 Whitby, *The Second Part of a Reply to Dr. Waterland's Objections* (London, 1721), p107.
105 Ibid., p4. 106 Ibid., p11.

Clarke cited one of them, namely John Pearson, in defence of his own views. Furthermore, even Edwards, normally a great admirer of Pearson, actually criticised Pearson for placing an excessive emphasis on the priority of the Father within the Trinity and so leading the likes of Clarke into error.[107] So, were even some of the Reformed infected by the avant-garde approach?

It must be confessed that Pearson's writing does, at times, have a rather subordinationist flavour. He writes:

In general then we may safely observe, that in the very name of Father, there is something of eminence which is not in that of Son; and some kind of priority we must ascribe unto him whom we call the first, in respect of him whom we term the second person.[108]

He is clear, too, that this priority is founded on the fact that the Father has his essence from none, whereas the Son has his essence from the Father, and the Holy Ghost from both.

As a result, Pearson is not willing to say that the Son can be described as *autotheos*. In fact, his discussion of the term closely echoes that of Bellarmine. He writes:

There is a catholic sense in which the Son is termed *autotheos*... &c. by the ancient fathers; and another sense there is in which these terms are so proper and peculiar to the Father that they are denied to the Son. Indeed *autotheos* in the highest sense, God from himself, positively taken, belongeth neither to the Son nor to the Father, as implying a manifest contradiction; because nothing can have its being from itself, as communicated to itself and that by itself: but in a negative way of interpretation, by which that is said to be of itself, which is, and yet is not of or from another, *autotheos* belongs properly to the Father, neither generated by, nor proceeding from another; and in that sense it is denied to the Son because he is generated by the Father.... Lastly in another sense, in which *autos* in composition is taken not *in obliquo* but *in recto*; *autotheos*, that is... God himself... all these terms are attributed to the Son as truly, really and essentially as to the Father.[109]

However, although Pearson is not willing to use this term (and it should be recalled that several Roman Catholics, including, Bellarmine objected to the word, though not to the doctrine it was intended to protect), it seems clear that he does not actually depart from the traditional way of understanding of the Trinity.

[107] Edwards, *Animadversions on Dr. Clarke's scripture doctrine... of the Trinity*, p21.

[108] Pearson, *Exposition of the Creed*, p55. Pearson is not entirely alone amongst the Reformed in striking such a subordinationist tone; Francis Fullwood does as well. F. Fullwood, *The Socinian Controversy Touching the Son of God* (London, 1693), p10.

[109] Pearson, *Exposition of the Creed*, p66. Cf. Bellarmine, *Opera Omnia*, ii p336.

When he discusses the subordination of the second and third persons within the Godhead, Pearson makes it quite clear that he only grants the Father a priority of order, not a priority of dignity or power.[110] He is also clear that the three persons within the Trinity have not only one generic, but one numerical substance.[111] They are, therefore, one being. He writes:

The divine essence, being by reason of its simplicity not subject to division, and in respect of its infinity uncapable of multiplication, is so communicated as not to be multiplied; insomuch that he which produceth by that communication hath not only the same nature, but is also the same God.[112]

Since it is the one essence of the Father which is communicated, all the attributes of that essence are, without exception, communicated to the Son. Pearson writes that the Father 'hath begotten a Son of a nature and essence so totally like, so totally the same, that no accidental disparity can imaginable consist with that identity'.[113] And Pearson hints that he considers that divine independence (in other words, the self-existence proper to the divine essence, as opposed to that which is proper to the person of the Father) is communicated too. He writes:

There can be but one infinite, eternal and independent being; and there can be no comparison between that and whatsoever is finite, temporal and depending. He therefore who did truly think himself equal with God, as being in the form of God, must be conceived to subsist in that one infinite, eternal and independent nature of God.[114]

It would seem to follow from this that the Son, considered as equal to God (i.e. as to his essence), can be described as infinite, eternal, and independent. This, of course, was the substance of both the Reformed and medieval Catholic doctrine, though the way Pearson has put it is closer in phrasing to the latter than the former.

Pearson is certainly careful to distinguish between the essence and the person of the Son in respect of the manner of his begetting. He describes the Father as

a person subsisting eternally in the one infinite essence of the Godhead; which essence or subsistence he hath from no other person, but hath communicated the same essence, in which himself subsisteth, by generation to another person, who by that generation is the Son.[115]

110 Pearson, *Exposition of the Creed*, p497. 111 Ibid., p54.
112 Ibid., p217. 113 Ibid., p55.
114 Ibid., p194.
115 Ibid., p66. Cf. Banez, *Scolastica Commentaria*, i p371.

He consistently describes the divine essence as communicated to the Son, but the person of the Son as generated. Pearson seems to be taking considerable care to observe the medieval rule that the essence of the Son, since it is identical to the essence of the Father, cannot be described as generated. Unlike many of his Anglican contemporaries, therefore, Pearson seems to have no trouble conceiving of and discussing the divine essence separately from the divine persons.

So, if Pearson's view would not have satisfied the most scrupulously Reformed reader, it nonetheless represents a continuity with the medieval Catholic view of the Trinity. The same is true for Beveridge. For although he is clearer on the matter than Pearson, he too refrains from describing the Son as *autotheos* (though unlike Pearson, he does not specifically proscribe the term).

Beveridge's commentary on the Thirty-Nine Articles, *Ecclesia Anglicana Ecclesia Catholica* (1710) was produced after the Socinian controversy, though, of course, before the publication of Clarke's *Scripture Doctrine of the Trinity.* So he writes mindful of the dangers of careless language in this matter (and possibly with an eye to William III's directions as well). The Trinity, he writes, is

> a mystery, which though it be not too great for a divine faith to believe, yet it is too high for our human understandings to conceive. And therefore, having settled my faith firmly upon it, I am fearful to discourse much about it; being conscious to myself how easy, and withal how dangerous a thing it is, to mistake and err in so great and unspeakable a mystery as this is.[116]

As a result, he says, he will speak as briefly as possible.

It soon becomes clear, though, that Beveridge is at one with the traditional presentation of the divinity of the Son. When he discusses the generation of the Son, he once again underlines the need for caution. Because, he says, it is correct to say that one divine person begot another divine person, but not that one person begot another divine nature. His discussion of it is, once again, very close to Aquinas and the later Thomist commentators, and he carefully observes the distinction between person and essence which was so important to them. Interestingly, he also uses the more Catholic turn of phrase, calling the Son 'unbegotten' as to his essence, rather than *autotheos.* He writes:

> But how may we properly say then, the Son is begotten of the Father? By receiving from the Father an unbegotten essence. His person must be begotten of the Father, otherwise he would not be his Son; but his essence must be unbegotten, otherwise he would not be God.[117]

[116] Beveridge, *Works*, vii p58.

[117] Ibid., p74. Cf. Banez, *Scholastica Commentaria*, i p390 and Suarez, *Commentaria ac Disputationes in Primam Partem*, p468.

Furthermore, like the earlier writers who followed the Fourth Lateran Council, he steers clear of describing the Son's essence as generated. As he underlines:

The essence of the Father did not beget the Son by communicating his person to him, but the person of the Father begat the Son by communicating his essence to him; so that the person of the Son is begotten, not communicated; but the essence of the Son is communicated, not begotten.[118]

At the end of this section, he sums up the traditional position with admirable clarity. He writes:

The Son is very and eternal God, of one substance with the Father: that is of one essence and nature with the Father. For his essence, as we have heard, is the selfsame individual essence that the Father's is, communicated from the Father to him, the same eternal, all-wise, infinite, unbegotten, uncreated essence: and therefore he is not another, but the same very and eternal God. And so there is no difference, no nor distinction at all betwixt the Father and the Son in their essential, but only in their personal properties. The Son is of the same substance and essence with the Father, but herein they differ, that the Father hath his essence of himself, the Son of the Father; and so the person of the Father is not from the person of the Son but from himself; whereas the person of the Son is not from himself, but from the person of the Father.[119]

Domingo Banez could not have put it better.

This insistence that there are absolutely no essential properties of the divine nature which are in the Father but not in the Son, is widespread amongst the Anglican Reformed, and maintained even by those who normally do not delve into the mysteries of Trinitarian doctrine. Edward Reynolds, for example, argues that, 'Christ is the image and express character of his Father's glory, as the impression in the wax is of the form and fashion of the seal; there is no excellency in God which is not completely, adequately and distinctly in Christ.'[120] Ezekiel Hopkins thinks the same, writing that 'certain it is, that Christ is essentially blessed, being the most blessed God, co-equal and co-eternal with the Father, possessing all the infinite perfections of the deity, invariably and immeasurably'.[121] There is, in other words, no room in their theology for qualifying the divinity of the Son, by denying of him any essential property which is in the Father.

118 Beveridge, *Works*, vii pp75–6. Cf Banez, *Scholastica Commentaria*, i p371.

119 Beveridge, *Works*, vii p76.

120 Reynolds, *Works*, p280.

121 Hopkins, *Works*, ii p46. See also: Hacket, *Century*, p197; Newcome, *Catechetical Course*, i p96; South, *Animadversions*, p128.

William Burkitt is equally insistent that the communication of the Godhead from the Father to the Son means that they both share all the essential properties of Godhead: 'all the perfections shining forth in God the Father, are substantially in Christ the Son.'[122] For him, this means, in particular, that the Son shares fully in the Father's attribute of independence. He has life and divinity, in other words, from himself; the Son is, in other words, *autotheos*. Burkitt writes of the Son, 'he hath the same life infinitely, independently and equally with the Father, as the Father hath it, so hath the Son: the Father hath it in himself, and so hath the Son also; therefore the Son as well as the Father is essentially and truly God'.[123]

Robert South, who was untiring in his search for theological errors in the views of William Sherlock, certainly sniffed out the heretical leanings inherent in his opponent's views. He underlined that Sherlock's reluctance to describe the Son as the One True God 'affords the Arians and Socinians no small advantage' against Trinitarian orthodoxy.[124]

He was strict in observing the distinction between what characteristics were proper to the persons of the Trinity qua persons, and what was proper to them qua God; and he was clear that begottenness was a characteristic only of the person, not of the nature of the Son. South writes,

> God cannot properly be said to beget wisdom... nor indeed any of the other attributes, or perfections, essentially taken or considered; he may indeed be said to communicate them, and by such communication to beget a Son. But still, though these are thus said to be communicated, it is the person only, who is or can be properly said to be begotten.[125]

In other words, the divine nature in the Son, as distinct from the person, can appropriately be described as unbegotten.

John Edwards actually intervened in the controversy over Clarke's ideas, producing *Some Animadversions on Dr. Clarke's scripture doctrine (as he stiles it) of the Trinity* (1712) very shortly after Clarke's own book had been published. It is a small pamphlet, but it gets quickly to the heart of the matter. Edwards believes that the long-established English trend towards subordinationism has been responsible for this new outbreak of heresy, and he criticises both Pearson (as we have seen) and Bull for unduly emphasizing the inferiority of the Son to the Father.[126] This is a mistake, he thinks, because 'the Son, as he is God, yea, and hath his divinity from the Father, is not inferior or subordinate to him.'[127] Like South and Beveridge (and, of course, the Fourth

[122] Burkitt, *Expository Notes*, p706. [123] Ibid., p266.
[124] South, *Animadversions*, p139. [125] Ibid., p159.
[126] Edwards, *Animadversions on Dr.Clarke's scripture doctrine... of the Trinity*, p21.
[127] Ibid., p22.

Lateran Council), Edwards grounds the unity of the Trinity upon their common possession of one numerical essence, though in his turn of phrase he is, characteristically, closer to the Reformed than to the Roman Catholic writers of the Thomist revival. He writes:

> The unity of the three persons in the Trinity is preserved by their being of the same substance or essence, which is most simple and undivided. This common essence belongs to one person as well as another. Now seeing it is thus, we may rationally gather from hence, that the Son of God is self-existent as well as the Father; for if he have the same undivided essence with the Father, and if the inseparable property of that substance is to be of itself, then it undeniably follows that the Son is of himself.[128]

In other words, like Episcopius, Edwards considers self-existence to be a divine attribute.[129] But unlike Episcopius, and following instead the Reformed and Roman Catholic writers, he concludes from this that, since he is God, the Son must have this attribute as well.

He echoes this opinion, in an even more openly Reformed tone, in his *Theologia Reformata*. He writes, of the divine essence as it is in the Son:

> And concerning this substance, we are to conceive that, though, as it is communicated by the Father, and from the Father, it may be said to be derivative, and thence, according to the Nicene Creed, the Son is said to be God of God, Light of Light, very God of very God, yet it is certain that this derivation, or communication of the divine substance or essence doth not hinder or destroy the self-origination of it. And the reason of this is because the essence of the Father being self-existent, that of the Son's must be so too, seeing the essence of the Father and the Son is the same. On which account the Son (as well as the Father) is *autotheos* and was expressly call'd so by Athanasius himself of old, as well as by Calvin and Beza, and others of late.[130]

Once again, the careful distinction between essence and person is being maintained to enable the full divinity of the Son to be defended. Edwards is also following the medieval way of speaking, holding that the essence of the Son is not generated, but communicated to him. It is evident that, both in his *Animadversions* and the *Theologia Reformata*, Edwards is deploying the Reformed way of speaking, and the medieval tradition of thought which it was intended to express, to counter the subordinationism and Arianism of his own day.

[128] Ibid., p33.

[129] Episcopius, *Opera* (1650) p334. Cf. Clarke, *Scripture Doctrine of the Trinity*, pp143–4.

[130] Edwards, *Theologia Reformata*, i p283. Cf. Calvin, *Institutes*, I.13.19 and Turretin, *Institutes*, Topic III q.28.40. Edwards was not alone in asserting the self-origination of the Son in opposition to Clarke's Arianism. Maurice Wiles, *Archetypal Heresy*, p120. Indeed Lancelot Addison actually entitled one book *Christos Autotheos*, though he confined the study to a discussion of the history of Arianism. L. Addison, *Christos Autotheos* (London, 1696).

## CONCLUSION

The Remonstrant theologians, Simon Episcopius and Etienne de Courcelles, both rejected the Reformed contention that the Son could be described as *autotheos* with regard to his essence, though not with regard to his person. Unhappy with this distinction between person and essence within the Trinity, they insisted that each person within the Godhead had a corresponding essence, and that the two could not be usefully distinguished in theological discussion. This led them to assert that, since the Son is begotten, the Son's essence too is begotten.

As a result, they argued that there was an essential difference between the divine essence in the Father, and the divine essence in the Son, because only the Father possessed the divine attribute of self-existence. It followed that only the Father could be described as God in the fullest sense; the Son was only God in a lesser, qualified sense. Theirs, in other words, was a two-tier Trinity. Courcelles went further than Episcopius, however, in that he drew out the conclusions of their position to question the assertion of the Council of Nicea that the Son could be described as being of one substance—*homoousios*—with the Father. This, he felt, made no literal sense.

The Remonstrant approach to this issue became increasingly influential in the Church of England during the latter half of the seventeenth century. As Henry Compton observed, the reputation of Remonstrant theology was high in certain Church circles, and their thinking became dangerously popular. A flourishing strain of subordinationism was thus evident within the Church of England well before Samuel Clarke published his infamous *Scripture Doctrine of the Trinity* in 1712. It can be clearly seen in the writings of Cudworth, Bull, Sherlock, and Tillotson, all of whom evidently follow the Remonstrant line on the divinity of the Son to a greater or lesser extent.

Samuel Clarke's mistake was to pursue the consequences of the Remonstrant position to their logical limit. In doing so, he exposed the way it could potentially undermine traditional patterns of piety. He also followed Courcelles in arguing that even the Nicene Creed had to be abandoned as a literal expression of the Church's faith.

The Anglican Reformed were not as central to the resistance to Clarke's ideas as they had been in the Trinitarian debates of the 1690s. Nonetheless, it is clear that their own theological formulations resisted the slide into subordinationism by staying true to the language and method of Reformed and Roman Catholic orthodoxy. They continued to insist that the properties of the persons and the properties of the essence could be legitimately distinguished in discussions about the Trinity. This enabled them to maintain the position that the Son, though begotten as to his person, enjoyed all the essential attributes of divinity, as to his nature. The Son was, therefore, God in the fullest and highest sense, and could legitimately be described as independent, unbegotten, or even *autotheos* with regard to that nature. Theirs, therefore, was truly a Trinity of equals.

# 6

# A New Way of Thinking About God

## THE DIVIDE BEHIND THE DEBATES

Unlike justification and the Trinity, the doctrine of God was not the cause of any particular controversy within the post-Restoration Church. It would be wrong, however, to conclude from this apparent calm that there was general agreement in this area of theology. On the contrary, there were, beneath the surface of the post-Restoration Church two very different ways of conceiving of and discussing the nature of God; and the Anglican Reformed were emphatically on one side of that divide.

These underlying differences over the doctrine of God did occasionally emerge within the more public areas of controversy. At various points during the debates on both justification and the Trinity, for example, it becomes clear that the writers on each side of the question are working with rather different assumptions about what God is, and how best we can talk about Him.

In the debate about justification, for example, it is clear that part of the problem is that the Reformed and the Moralist writers simply do not agree about what it means to say that God is just. Sherlock put his finger on the disagreement, in his *Discourse on the Knowledge of Jesus Christ.* At one point, he criticises Reformed teaching because it seems to imply that God's justice does not admit of any leniency. As he puts it,

> the sum of this argument is, that there never was, nor ever can be, a covenant of grace, that God still exacts the rigorous perfection of the law from us, and that we must not appear before him without a complete and perfect righteousness of our own, or of another.[1]

This, he says, is inconsistent with ordinary human standards of justice, 'for all mankind have accounted it an act of goodness (without the least suspicion of injustice in it) to remit injuries and offences without exacting any punishment.'[2] In other words, Sherlock assumes that what we mean when we call God just, is sufficiently close to what we mean when we call a human being just, that we can draw reliable conclusions about what sort of behaviour is or

[1] Sherlock, *Discourse*, p195. [2] Ibid., p28.

is not consistent with God's justice. And, since amongst human beings, leniency is not felt to be a sign of injustice, but rather of goodness, God's justice has room for leniency as well. Consequently, it is not inconsistent with God's justice to treat the imperfect works of which fallen human beings are capable, as if they were truly just. This assumption is, of course, absolutely essential to the Moralist understanding of the New Covenant.

John Edwards, however, takes a different view of the matter. For Edwards, the kind of objection which Sherlock makes against the Reformed view of justification demonstrates a basic misunderstanding about the divine nature. As he underlines, like all divine attributes, 'the remunerative justice of God is not to be measured by the rules and proportions of human justice'.[3] Justice in God is analogous to justice in human beings. However, because of the immense disparity between God and human beings, it is not possible to draw easy conclusions about what is and is not consistent with God's justice, simply on the basis of what is and is not consistent with human justice. In particular, it does not follow that merely because leniency is not considered unjust in a human being, leniency is compatible with the infinitely more perfect and demanding justice of God. In fact, for Edwards, the contrary is the case. For him, all human sin is necessarily offensive to God. As he writes of sin, 'the omniscient eye of God must needs behold it, and take notice of it, and dislike and abhor it, and be displeased with the person that commits it'.[4] Furthermore, as Edwards underlines, God's justice necessarily engages him to oppose and exact punishment for every sin. As he puts it,

> to hate sin is essential to him, and this necessarily produceth punishment . . . his holy nature prompts him to love righteousness and consequently to hate all unrighteousness. So that punitive justice is the absolute result of the righteous essence of God, it is grounded on the holiness of his nature.[5]

This is, of course, a problem because it means that, to Edwards's mind, 'the divine justice requires a perfect righteousness and obedience of us'.[6] God simply cannot pretend that such imperfect righteousness as fallen human beings can offer meets the exacting standards of His justice. That is why, of course the believer can only find safety under the imputed righteousness of Christ. Only the active and passive righteousness of Christ, which is perfect, can stand the test of divine justice. So only the imputation of that passive and active righteousness to the believer enables God to count that believer as truly righteous. Which is why the imputation of Christ's righteousness must be the formal cause of our justification.

[3] Edwards, *Theologia Reformata*, i p101.
[4] Edwards, *Doctrine of Justification*, p237.
[5] Edwards, *Theologia Reformata*, i p115.
[6] Edwards, *Doctrine of Justification*, p295.

If the debate about justification reveals that Reformed and Moralist writers are working with different understandings of the nature of God, the debate about the Trinity shows that they have contrasting assumptions about how human beings should frame a conception of the divine nature. As we have seen, Sherlock deliberately eschewed all metaphysical terms in discussing the being of God. This is because he felt that, since we cannot have direct knowledge of the essences of things, such discussions tend to lead us into a labyrinth of ungrounded speculation.

For this reason, in his discussion of God, Sherlock distinctly favours those attributes of God which seem similar to attributes which appear to be mirrored in human beings—God's 'communicable' attributes, in other words.[7] He considers the difficulty which we have in conceiving of an infinite essence, and underlines that this difficulty arises from the assumptions we make about essences in general, based on our knowledge of them in material beings. He then writes, 'But now, if we consider God as wisdom and truth, which is his true nature and essence, without confounding our minds with some material conceptions of his substance, these things are plain and easy.'[8] Infinity, he argues, denotes no more than the absence of limits. So if we conceive of God's essence as wisdom and truth, we can describe God's essence as infinite without becoming confused. For what we mean is simply that God is wisdom without any foolishness and truth without any falsehood.[9] We do not, therefore, have to trouble ourselves with confusing ideas such as infinite spatial extension.[10] This approach to God's essence, Sherlock feels, supports his contention that we must think of God primarily in mental, and not in ontological terms.

Robert South, of course, is having none of this. He considers this very passage of Sherlock's work, and exclaims, 'I desire him to give me some good reason, why he pitches upon truth, wisdom and goodness, rather than eternity, omnipotence and omnipresence. For these, in their proportion, express the divine nature as much as the other.'[11] South, in other words, refuses to accept that we should, in our consideration of God's nature, favour some attributes at the expense of others. Those attributes which are unique to God and which have no echoes in human existence—God's 'incommunicable' attributes as they were called—are, for South, quite as important as those which do.

[7] Such attributes were called 'communicable' because it was assumed that they existed in God as their origin and perfection, and that human beings received them from God.

[8] Sherlock, *Vindication*, p70. [9] Ibid., p79.

[10] Ibid., p77. [11] South, *Animadversions*, pp53–4.

South also takes issue with Sherlock's understanding of what it means to describe God as infinite. Sherlock, he argues, has mistakenly assumed that infinity is a negative attribute of God; in other words, that it is the kind of divine attribute which simply consists in the elimination of any imperfection from God's being. South disagrees: 'In a word, the thing principally signified by this term, is positive, the thing consignified, or connoted (which is but secondary and consequential) is a negation.'[12] In other words, it is not sufficient to describe the infinity of the divine essence as no more than wisdom without foolishness, or truth without falsehood. The divine infinity is rather the limitless extent and perfection of his being: a positive attribute of his essence, in other words, not a negative one relating to God's knowledge or wisdom.[13] For this reason, of course, as South argues, ontological considerations must remain part of our attempt to understand the nature of God.

It would appear, therefore, that Sherlock's disagreement with both Edwards and South on these points resulted from his adoption of, and their corresponding refusal to adopt, a particular approach to the doctrine of God. This approach had its roots in the Socinian and Remonstrant schools of the early seventeenth century, but became increasingly fashionable in England as the century drew on. It is to this theological tradition that we must now turn.

## THE SOCINIAN DOCTRINE OF GOD

It was Johann Crell who developed an understanding of the nature of God which would complement the Socinian positions on other matters. His aim was to elaborate a theology of God which was inconsistent, in particular, with the doctrine of the Trinity, with the divinity of Christ, and with the Reformed view of predestination—for the Socinians denied all of these beliefs. Some preparatory work had already been done by Socinus himself, and appears in the *Racovian Catechism*. However, Crell's statement of the Socinian position is much more expansive and it is worth taking some time to explain it, particularly since later writers often used it as the principal source for Socinian thinking about the doctrine of God.[14]

Crell's polemical intent is apparent from the outset. He begins with a discussion of the various names of God which appear in the scriptures, underlining that, 'The name of God is indeed by its nature common to

[12] Ibid., p59. [13] Ibid.

[14] E.g., J. Edwards, *The Socinian Creed* (London, 1697), pp32, 35, 38, 44 et al. and J. Pearson, *The Minor Theological Works of John Pearson DD*, 2 vols, ed. E. Churton (Oxford, 1844), i pp175, 177, 222.

many.'[15] The various Hebrew and Greek terms for the divinity, he argues, are ascribed, from time to time, to those who are not Gods in the fullest sense, but who participate to some degree in the divine dominion, such as, for example, angels or human magistrates.[16] This is, of course, the only way in which he thinks the name 'God' is used of Christ: Christ is called God only in the sense that, like an angel or magistrate, he is a minister of God.[17]

Amongst the many who are called gods in the scriptures, however, one stands out. This is the god who is the supreme lord of creation, and therefore God in the fullest sense (though not, Crell underlines, the only proper sense).[18] God in the fullest sense can be described, Crell asserts, in two ways. The first way is less precise in that it does not actually express the nature of God, but is nonetheless quite helpful for ordinary, not very thoughtful people. This is the way of speaking found in the Christian creeds and used by the Christian Church, which describes God as the creator, as the Lord of all things and as the Father of Christ.

The second way of talking about God is, however, much more precise and describes the essence of God as accurately as is possible for finite creatures.[19] This is the account Crell gives of it:

> The latter definition can be constituted in this way: that we say that God is an eternal spirit. Eternal, indeed, not only because he always will exist, but also because he always has existed. In a similar sense, you might say a self-existent spirit: for that is self-existent, of which nothing besides itself is the efficient cause.[20]

He expands his definition a little by explaining that, 'When we say spirit we understand a substance devoid of all such grossness as we are able to discern by our judgement in corporeal subjects.'[21] Angels and human souls, he thinks, are said to be spirits in this way.[22] He goes on: 'Thus, therefore, this *genus* is common to God as well as these things, but so that there is nonetheless an

[15] 'Dei vero nomen natura sua . . . pluribus est commune.' Crell and Volkel, *De Vera Religione*, I.I, a p1. A position explicitly denied by the Reformed: Turretin, *Institutes*, Topic III q.4.

[16] Crell and Volkel, *De Vera Religione*, I.VII, a p69.

[17] Ibid., a p96.

[18] Ibid. Part of the Socinian defence against their orthodox opponents was that they did not deny that Christ could properly be called God.

[19] Ibid., I.XV, a p106.

[20] 'Posterior definitio constitui potest huius modi, ut Deum dicamus esse Spiritum aeternum. Aeternum autem, non tantum quia semper extiturus sit, sed etiam quia semper extiterit. Eodem prope sensu dixeris Spiritum ex seipso existentem: ex seipso autem existere, cuius nulla prorsus est efficiens.' Ibid. The ontological independence of God was also the starting point for the *Racovian Catechism* (Irenopolis, 1659), III.I. p23.

[21] 'Spiritum cum nominamus, substantiam intelligimus ab omne crassitie, qualem in corporibus arbitrio subjectis cernimus, alienam.' Crell and Volkel, *De Vera Religione*, I.XV, a p106.

[22] Rather oddly, he maintains that air is as well, which led some commentators to accuse him of ascribing to God a physical dimension of sorts.

order between its *species*; partly of nature, insofar as the others depend upon one; partly of perfection. For all other spirits depend upon God.'[23]

Even in these brief clarifying remarks, the revolutionary nature of Crell's doctrine of God starts to become apparent. His description of spiritual natures makes it quite clear that he thinks of 'spirit' as a particular type of substance which is present, with different properties, in certain sorts of beings. He also seems to be assuming that things with spiritual natures form a genus—a general kind of thing—of which God is merely a species—an individual example.

Both of these lines of thought run counter to both the Thomist and Scotist understanding of divine simplicity—the teaching that God is not a being made up of parts. Both Thomas Aquinas and Duns Scotus assert that, since God is not made up of parts, God cannot be described in terms of an underlying substance and its accidents (individualizing properties which could be other than they are, such as, in this case, being a dependent or an independent type of spirit), nor can he be analysed by means of the distinction between a genus and its species.[24] This doctrine, though worked out during the middle ages, was still held by Reformed and Roman Catholic theologians alike,[25] and was an integral part of the traditional way of talking about God.

Crell, however, had little time for such archaic niceties. He wrote of his original definition:

And these general things which have been said in the description of God are sufficient. Other things, which have more subtlety [about them] than either utility or, indeed, certainty, we happily pass by, and will continue to pass by elsewhere. For we engage in this business that we might become better equipped, not for the arguments and contests of the schools, but for piety and religion.[26]

[23] 'Hoc ergo genus ita est Deo cum istis rebus commune, ut ordo tamen sit inter has eius species, partim naturae, quatenus aliae ab una pendent; partim perfectionis. Pendent enim caeteri spiritus a Deo.' Ibid., a p107. Thomas Hobbes's views on spirituality and materiality certainly appear to be rather similar to Crell's: Overhoff, J., 'The Theology of Thomas Hobbes's *Leviathan*,' *J.E.H.*, 51 (2000), pp528,535, 553. Even so, only Edwards mentions Hobbes as an adversary by name: *Theologia Reformata*, i p49. Beveridge may, however, also have him in mind when he speaks darkly of 'all our sceptical philosophers' who ascribe matter to spiritual beings: Beveridge, *Works*, vii p26.

[24] For an account of divine simplicity as worked out by Thomas Aquinas, see B. Davies, *The Thought of Thomas Aquinas* (Oxford, 1992), p51et seq.

[25] Turretin, *Institutes*, Topic III q.7.

[26] 'Et haec de genere in descriptione Dei posita dicta sufficient. Alia enim, quae plus subtilitatis, quam utilitatis, aut enim certitudinis habent, libenter praeterimus & in caeteris praetituri sumus. Cum non id agamus, ut ad disputationes ac certamina scholarum, sed ut ad pietatem ac religionem instructiores evadamus.' Crell and Volkel, *De Vera Religione*, I.XV, a p109.

Crell's emphatic rejection of traditional scholastic theology, whether Roman Catholic or Reformed, becomes progressively clearer as he expounds his position further.

After this general definition of the divine nature, he moves on to consider the divine attributes. He is dismissive of all divine attributes which do not appear explicitly in the scriptures, since, he says: 'those things suffice which are in the sacred scriptures, and are undoubted, and are useful for those things we seek, that is, religion and piety.'[27] As a result, he decides to concentrate almost exclusively on those divine attributes which describe a positive property, rather than those which exclude things from the divine nature. He explains why:

> For no science deals only with those things which are said negatively about its subject. For negations about anything can be infinite; and still they are not able to capture the science. Furthermore, through a thorough understanding of those things which are in a thing, it is easy to judge what things are not in it.[28]

Once again, Crell is making a veiled attack on the Thomist way of speaking about God. Thomas Aquinas, and those who followed him, had argued that, since the divine nature was fundamentally unknowable, it was not possible to make any reliable assertions about what the divine nature actually was. It was only possible to know what the divine nature was not. Accordingly, all human reasoning about God had to be predominantly negative in nature. The dominant mode of the doctrine of God consisted in the exclusion from our understanding of the divine nature all the ways of existing which are common to created things.[29] This approach was known as the way of negation.

Crell, on the other hand, explicitly analyses the nature of God using categories appropriate to the analysis of ordinary beings.[30] The divine attributes become, in his hands, points of similarity between God and other things, rather than ways of differentiating God from other things. His chosen approach to talking about God is thus what was called the way of eminence. He uses the perfections of created beings as finite examples of the infinite perfections of God, and frames his understanding of the divine nature around them. He dismisses the way of negation, as being no more than a rather convoluted way of making positive assertions about God.[31]

[27] 'Illa quae in sacris literis extant et indubitata sunt, & ad eum, quem quaerimus, usum, h.e. religionem ac pietatem, sufficiunt.' Ibid., I.XVI, a p110.

[28] 'Nam alioqui nulla disciplina per se attendit ea, quae negative de subjecto illius dicuntur. Quia negationes de re quaque infinitae esse possunt; & porro disciplina comprehendi nequeunt. Adde quod iis probe cognitis, quae rei insunt, facile est de iis judicare, quae ei non insunt.' Ibid.

[29] See Davies, *The Thought of Thomas Aquinas*, p40. Aquinas, *S.C.G.*, ch.14.

[30] Crell and Volkel, *De Vera Religione*, I.XVI, a p111.

[31] Ibid., a p110.

So, when Crell argues that God is one, he writes:

Concerning what pertains to the unity of God: we will not pursue here those matters which are usually disputed in the schools under this heading. It will be sufficient for us to explain here that by which God is said, in the sacred scriptures and in common parlance, to be one. He is said to be one, because he is one in number, as they say; so that, indeed, there are no more of his type or, if you prefer, *species*. . . . So we only wish to indicate of that which is one in number, that other things of the same *species* do not exist.[32]

The scholastic discussions he dismisses here are evidently those which concern divine simplicity. For the Thomist understanding of divine simplicity was meant to show that God was one, but in a unique sense, and one that was not applicable to any creature. For Crell, by contrast, God's unity is merely a question of numerical unity. God is one in exactly the same way that the sun is one, or that the moon is one: all the divine unity means is that there are no other examples of God's type of being. God's unity just means that there is only one of him.

Even this uncomplicated conception of God's oneness, Crell thinks, evidently rules out the doctrine of the Trinity. A thing is not numerically one, he argues, unless it has one substance.[33] But if something has only one substance, it can only be one person, because 'a person is . . . nothing other than an intelligent prime substance'[34] It follows that, wherever there is more than one person, there must be more than one intelligent substance. In all intelligent beings we know of, if they are one in number, they are one in personality as well. Trinitarian doctrine is simply incompatible with what we know about the nature of intellectual substances which are numerically one, and the problem is only heightened if one is also asserting divine simplicity (which Crell underlines he is not). Quite simply, 'the unity of the divine essence and, above all, its simplicity, which those of the opposite opinion defend, is absolutely not capable of a plurality of persons.'[35] If there were three divine persons, Crell asserts, there would be three different Gods.

[32] 'Quod ergo ad unitatem Dei attinet; non persequemur hic ea, quae de multiplici eius vocis usu in scholis disputantur. Satis erit, eam nos hic significationem explicare, qua Deus in sacris literis, atque adeo vulgo quoque, unus esse dicitur. Dicitur autem unus, quia unus sit numero, ut loquuntur, & quidem ita, ut plures sui generis, seu tu mavis speciei, non habeant. . . . Significare enim volumus, earum quod unum esse numero, & ita singulare, ut alia, quae eiusdem sint speciei, non extent.' Ibid., I.XVII, a p111.

[33] Ibid., a p113.

[34] 'Est enim persona . . . nihil aliud quam substantia prima intelligens.' Ibid., I.XVI, a p114. This was Socinus's position too: *Racovian Catechism*, III.I p31.

[35] 'Divinae essentiae unitas, & summa, quam adversae sententiae defendunt, simplicitas, personarum pluralitatis capax nequaquam est.' Crell and Volkel, *De Vera Religione*, V.X, a pp420–1. Needless to say, Turretin disagrees: *Institutes*, Topic III q24.

After assessing their number, Crell thinks, the next way of analysing beings is to assess how long they last, so he moves on to discuss God's eternity. He writes,

Eternity is indeed the endless duration of a thing.... A duration can be infinite either *a parte ante*, as they say, or *a parte post*, or in both ways. And that [duration] which lacks both beginning and end is the most perfect eternity, which we assert to be proper to God.[36]

This eternity, he thinks, can be divided into parts, corresponding to the past, present, and future existence of God.[37] Here too, Crell's view runs counter to the traditional understanding of God. Because scholastic writers, such as Thomas Aquinas and Duns Scotus, argued that since God had no parts of any sort, God could not have temporal parts either. So they urged that God's eternity must exclude all duration—because it is duration which can be divided up into parts.[38] Instead, they argued that eternity in God was the simultaneous possession, in the present moment, of all time, whether past, present, or future.

Once again, Crell has no time for such speculation:

Amongst us, the subtlety of those who think that the eternity of God includes all the periods of time that ever existed in one point or narrow moment cannot be met with approbation. They make it indivisible, in which there is nothing before and nothing after.... Which opinion both conflicts with the sacred scriptures and undoubtedly entails more than one contradiction within itself.[39]

The scriptures, Crell argues, clearly use temporal tenses when they talk of God, and time simply cannot be squeezed into one instant. Time, in his understanding, is prior to God, and God, like other things, must exist within it.

Having applied to God the categories appropriate to beings in general, Crell moves on to discuss the categories appropriate to living beings, of which God is again clearly one. Some of what he says here is relatively uncontroversial,[40]

[36] 'Est autem aeternitas sempiterna rei duratio.... Potest autem duratio infinitae esse vel a parte ante, ut loquuntur, vel a parte post, vel ab utroque. Et illa demum quae & initio caret & fine, perfectissima est aeternitas, quam Deo competere asserimus.' Crell and Volkel, *De Vera Religione*, I.XVIII, a p120. Socinus said much the same: *Racovian Catechism*, III.I p25.

[37] Crell and Volkel, *De Vera Religione*, I.XVIII, a p122.

[38] See Cross, R., *Duns Scotus* (Oxford, 1999), p29. Once again, Turretin follows the Thomist view: *Institutes*, Topic III q10.

[39] 'Non potest autem nobis earum probari subtilitas, qui aeternitatem Dei, omnia, quae unquam extiterunt, temporum spacia complectentem, in unius puncti seu momentem angustias cogunt. Indivisibilem enim eam esse statuunt; nihilque in ea prius, nihil posterius.... Quae sententia & sacris literis repugnat, & sibi ipsi, omninoque contradictionem non unam involvit.' Crell and Volkel, *De Vera Religione*, I.XVIII, a p127.

[40] Such that God has life, intellect, will, power, etc.

but there are still several places where he moves a long way from the traditional understanding of God.

Crell does not think, for example, that God is present everywhere, except in the sense that he knows what is going on everywhere, and can act in any place that he chooses. God's essence, though, is not infinite, nor does he exist in every location.[41] Crell also thinks that God is neither impassible nor immutable: so God can suffer, and God can change.[42] He argues that only 'such mutability is excluded from God as would argue either an imperfection of some sort, or an inconstancy and frivolity of the will'.[43] So, although God can and does change, God is not fickle or capricious. God also has, Crell thinks, emotions of a sort,[44] and reacts to what his creatures do.[45] There is within him, in other words, a degree of passive potentiality.[46]

Ascribing passive potentiality to God means that Crell is able to assert that God can make conditional decrees, that is to say, decrees whose execution depends on some factor external to God.[47] He abandons the Reformed distinction between the revealed and hidden will of God,[48] preferring instead the distinction between the absolute and conditional decrees of God. He writes of these two types of decree:

> The former are those which always lead to their end, and can in no way be frustrated, since there is no inconstancy in God by which his will is altered, and no weakness of power which can impede the result of that will. But the latter do not always necessarily lead to their end, because the condition which was annexed to them can fail, which God wished to depend upon the will of creatures.[49]

He further asserts that all decrees which concern the fate of individuals are conditional in nature. Election is therefore entirely conditional upon human goodness.[50]

[41] Ibid., I.XXVII, a p275. Socinus agreed: *Racovian Catechism* III.I p29. Turretin takes a different view: *Institutes*, Topic III q9.

[42] Once again, Turretin disagrees: ibid. q11.

[43] 'Mutabilitatis illa a Deo abest, quae vel imperfectionem aliquae naturae, vel inconstantiam levitatemque voluntatis argueret.' Crell and Volkel, *De Vera Religione*, I.XXXII, a p344.

[44] Ibid., I.XXIX, a pp256–7.

[45] We can, he thinks, cause both joy and sadness in God: Ibid., I.XXXI, a pp318, 321.

[46] Aquinas maintained, by contrast, that God was pure act. Davies, *Thought of Thomas Aquinas*, p51.

[47] The Reformed denied the existence of conditional decrees: Turretin, *Institutes*, Topic IV q3. Conditional decrees are also evidently inconsistent with the Thomist conception of God as pure act.

[48] Crell and Volkel, *De Vera Religione*, I.XXXII, a p344.

[49] 'Priora illa ad exitum semper deducuntur, & irrita nullo modo fieri possunt: cum in Deum nec inconstantia cadat, quae voluntatem mutari, nec virium imbecillitas, quae voluntati effectum impedire posset. At posteriora non necessario ad exitum perducuntur, quia cessare potest conditio illis apposita, quam Deus ex creaturarum arbitrio pendere voluit.' Ibid., a p335.

[50] Ibid., I.XXXII, a p342. Socinus had also maintained this: *Praelectiones Theologicae* (Racow, 1609), p70.

This position becomes even more radical when considered alongside Crell's understanding of God's omniscience. Crell argues that divine omniscience should be approached in a similar way to divine omnipotence. He writes:

> Moreover, it is said that God knows all things, even the most abstruse. However, just as when it is said that God can do anything, all those things are understood which fall under some power, or which are, by their nature, possible; so, when God is said to know everything, this must be understood [to mean] all knowable things, or all things which fall under some knowledge.[51]

The only things which are knowable, however, are the things which exist. Things which do not exist, he thinks, can no more be known than shadows can be seen.[52] It is clear to Crell that God knows all things that exist in the present. He also believes that God remembers all the things which have existed in the past.[53]

Among the things which will exist in the future, however, he distinguishes between those things which will necessarily exist (necessary futures—things like the future movements of the planets), and those things which may or may not exist (contingent futures—things like the actions of free human beings). Contingent futures, he thinks, have an indeterminacy in their very nature which prevents them being known as anything more than a possibility.[54] God can know necessary futures with certainty, but He can only know contingent futures as a possibility. In this way, human freedom is preserved—for God only knows what human beings might do, not what they will do.[55] Consequently, God cannot be certain about everything that will happen in the future.[56] The final outcome of the divine decrees is therefore not known for sure, even to God.

The indeterminate nature of the divine decrees, Crell thinks, is also the consequence of another divine attribute: holiness. God's power, he argues, is not only limited to what is possible. It is also limited to what is good.[57] Crell writes of God's power over creation: 'that control and dominion should not

[51] 'Dictum autem est, Deum omnia scire, etiam alioquin abstrusissima. Quemadmodum vero, cum dicitur Deum omnia posse, ea intelliguntur omnia, quae sub potentiam ullam cadunt, seu quae natura sua sunt possibilia: ita cum dicitur Deum omnia scire, intelligenda omnia scibilia, seu omnia quae sub scientiam ullam cadunt.' Crell and Volkel, *De Vera Religione*, I.XXIV, a p198.

[52] Ibid., a p199.

[53] Ibid., a p197.

[54] Ibid., a p200.

[55] It is clear that Crell does not think human freedom is compatible with God having certain foreknowledge of human acts. Ibid., at p202.

[56] Socinus had maintained this as well, saying 'Negamus, ea quae fiunt, si contingentia sint, futura fuisse antequam fierent.' *Praelectiones Theologicae*, p27. Once again, Turretin disagrees: *Institutes*, Topic III q12, as had Aquinas: *S.C.G.*, I.67.

[57] Crell and Volkel, *De Vera Religione*, I.XXV, a p224.

be extended beyond justice, and what, as it were, lights its way, wisdom.'[58] God can only, therefore, decree an end to his creatures which is fitting to their natures. This means that it is impossible for God to decree unconditionally that any intelligent creature should suffer for eternity in Hell.[59] Such a decree would simply be inconsistent with his nature. The only decree of condemnation compatible with God's goodness was a decree conditional upon the sinner's failure to fulfill a requirement which was within his or her power. So, to Crell's mind, the Reformed understanding of election and reprobation was simply inconsistent with the nature of God.[60]

From what has been said, it is clear that Crell developed a thoroughly revolutionary understanding of God, and that he did so in self-conscious rejection of the elements of medieval scholasticism which his Reformed opponents employed. He rejected the doctrines of divine simplicity, timeless eternity, and immensity. In the interests of human freedom, he radically qualified the doctrine of divine omniscience. He recast God's relationship with creation so that he could react to what his creatures did. This in turn enabled him to reject the Reformed view of election and propose in its place a conditional understanding of the divine decrees. It is no surprise, therefore, that the Reformed reacted sharply against Crell's teaching. The Dutch Remonstrants were, however, rather more receptive to Crell's ideas.[61]

## THE REMONSTRANT APPROACH

The Socinian and Remonstrant doctrines of God are certainly not identical. The Remonstrants defended the divinity of Christ and the doctrine of the Trinity; although, as we have seen, positions they adopted in these two areas were not those of the Reformed, or even those of many Roman Catholic writers. Nonetheless, the Remonstrants and the Socinians shared a suspicion of scholastic speculation about the nature of God and profound distaste for the Reformed understanding of predestination. As a result, various positions on the doctrine of God which were held by Socinus and Crell, were also held by their near contemporaries, the Remonstrants Konrad Vorst and Simon Episcopius. Which is why, perhaps, so many Reformed writers assumed

[58] 'Arbitrium ac dominium illud latius extendi non deberi, quam iustitia, & quae ei veluti praelucet, sapientia permittit.' Ibid., I.XXIII, a p165.

[59] Ibid. Turretin is not so sure: *Institutes*, Topic IV q14.

[60] Crell and Volkel, *De Vera Religione*, I.XXV, a p230.

[61] McLachlan, *Socinianism*, pp21–4; Rohls, 'Calvinism, Arminianism and Socinianism in the Netherlands,' p23; Simonutti, 'Resistance, Obedience and Toleration,' pp191–2.

(or, assumed for the purposes of polemic) that both Remonstrants and Socinians came from the same theological stable.

The Remonstrant writers were willing to pay lip service to the doctrine of divine simplicity, but it is clear that they were less than convinced by it. Episcopius was willing to concede a degree of simplicity within God, writing:

> With regard to internal causes, the divine essence is most simple, because it is not composed of principles which are mixed, confused, united or conjoined with each other, nor of integral, quantitative or formal parts or materials, of act and potential, matter and form, being and essence, that is, of anything perfectible and that which perfects it.[62]

Yet elsewhere, he defended his fellow Remonstrants from the charge levelled against them by their opponents, that they did not teach simplicity correctly, by writing:

> Are you surprised? There is not one jot of this in scripture. For this debate is entirely metaphysical; about this term 'simplicity' there is not yet agreement amongst the philosophers. How few truly understand the matter? The mind must run almost the whole course of metaphysics before you will understand what composition is.[63]

Clearly, he felt that the doctrine was far too subtle and involved to form an important part of the doctrine of God. Certainly it plays a far less significant role in his understanding of God than it does in that of Aquinas or Turretin, for whom it is a key regulating principle.[64]

Vorstius, though, takes a rather stronger line against divine simplicity, writing:

> In fact, many things concerning the simplicity of God, about which nothing is revealed in the scriptures, were dealt with too nicely by the scholastics, and defined pretty audaciously: things indeed to which not a few of the sacred scriptures seem opposed.... Certainly, they desire, for the most part, so to explain this attribute of God, that they involve themselves in not a few contradictions, and it makes the mind of the reader thoroughly dubious and uncertain.[65]

[62] 'In ordine ad causas internas, essentia divina est simplicissima, quia non est composita ex principiis inter se mixtas, confusis, unitis aut conjunctis, nec ex partibus sive materialibus integralibus, quantitativis, sive formalibus, actu & potentia, materia & forma, esse & essentia, id est ex perfectibili & perficiente.' S. Episcopius, *Opera* (1650) p286.

[63] 'Quod mirum? De ea ne jota quidem in scriptura est. Deinde disputatio ista tota metaphysica est; de ipso termino simplicitatis nondum convenit inter philosophos. Rem vero quotusquisque intelligit? Tota pene metaphysica proluendus est animus antequam intelligas quid sit compositio.' S. Episcopius, *Apologia pro Confessione* (1630), p41.

[64] Turretin notes this: *Institutes*, Topic III q7.

[65] 'Etenim de omnimodi simplicitate Dei multa curiose a Scolasticis tractata, & satis audacter definita sunt, de quibus in scriptura nihil revelatum est: immo quarum nonulli s. literis adversari videntur.... Certe hoc Dei attributum sic illarum plerique explicare solent, ut non paucis contradictionibus seipsos involvant, & lectorum animos plane dubios atque incertos reddat.' K. Vorstius, *Tractatus Theologicus de Deo* (Steinfurt, 1610), p186.

Like Episcopius, he is willing to say that God is not composed or made of anything which existed prior to Him. Vorstius also believes, again with Episcopius, that God's essence is not itself composed of different parts and that it is perfect and receives no perfection from anything else. Even so:

> All these things do not prevent there being in God the sort of diversity or multiplicity which does not undermine the simplicity of the essence or nature strictly so called: especially if we consider that he has in himself a principle of mutability of a sort (which, however, does not diminish the immutability of his essence), namely a free will.[66]

Thus, Vorstius seems to be implying that his view of God's simplicity does not exclude all composition within the divine being, merely some undesirable sorts of composition.

Vorstius's modification of the doctrine becomes even clearer when he moves on to talk about the existence of passive potentiality within God. Vorstius is clear that the scholastics were wrong to describe God as pure act,[67] not only because he does things which he might not have done, but also because his creatures do things to Him. He writes: 'Is there not even some sort of passive potentiality in him since, beforehand, he was able to be worshipped or offended etc. who afterwards at length actually receives this in himself or to himself? Therefore some diversity must be conceded within God.'[68] This conception of simplicity becomes even odder when he talks about the distinction between matter and form. For although he asserts that this distinction is not applicable to God, he goes on to say:

> Even so, nothing prevents us distinguishing something like matter and something like form within God; that is, by attributing to God the spiritual essence as the image of a *genus*, and, consequently, as a sort of matter; and the essential properties as the image of the differentiating factors, or as a sort of form.[69]

[66] 'Haec omnia non impediunt, quominus aliquid diversitatis aut multiplicitatis in ipso insit, quod essentiae sive naturae absolutae dictae, simplicitatem non evertat: praesertim si consideremus, ipsum in se principium habere cuiusdam mutabilitatis (quaetamen essentiae immutabilitatem non tollit) videlicet liberam voluntatem.' Vorstius, *Tractatus*, p189. Episcopius also argued that the conjunction of the divine essence with the acts of the divine will did not affect the simplicity of that essence: Episcopius, *Opera* (1650) p287.

[67] Vorstius, *Tractatus*, p196.

[68] 'Annon etiam potentia aliquatenus passiva in eo est, qui cum antea posset tantum vel coli, vel offendi &c. postea demum haec actu in se, vel ad se recipit? Itaque diversitas aliqua in Deo concedenda est.' Ibid., p191.

[69] 'Sed tamen nihil vetat, quasi materiam et quasi formam in Deo distinguere, h.e. essentiam spiritualem instar generis, & proinde quasi materiae; proprietates a. essentiales instar differentiae, seu quasi formae Deo attribuere.' Ibid.

Vorstius is therefore arguing for a profoundly attenuated idea of simplicity; one which asserts only the lack of the kind of composition within God which might imply that God's being is made more perfect by anything outside itself. He clearly feels, for example, that God is not rendered less perfect by enjoying such potential as is necessary to act upon other beings (active potentiality) or be acted upon by other beings (passive potentiality). He also (as Crell, of course, did) believes that we can think of God's spiritual essence as a sort of matter in which God's particular properties inhere. But the sort of simplicity which does not exclude either a distinction analogous to that between matter and form, or the distinction between act and potential, is certainly not simplicity as those Reformed or Roman Catholic writers working within the Thomist tradition understood it.

Episcopius, as we have seen, is more circumspect than Vorstius in his treatment of divine simplicity. But as we shall see, there are good reasons to hold that he too has adopted a more qualified view of what it entails. For, example, on the matter of eternity, Episcopius is effectively at one with Crell. He notes that the scholastics wish to exclude all temporal succession from the existence of God, but declares that this position is incoherent. He says of those writers: 'What solid reason moves them I do not see, since all duration by its nature entails a flow of distinct moments through before and after, which cannot be, or be conceived, without succession. For an instantaneous duration is not properly a duration.'[70]

Instead, Episcopius expresses the temporal dimension of God's existence as follows:

> With respect to time or duration, God is eternal because he has no beginning of being and will have no end of being; but has possessed, continues to possess and will possess himself totally and perfectly, without any change to himself, or succession of parts which are incremental in an unbroken sequence or one after another, but by a continuous and never-interrupted and undivided duration.[71]

Succession, he argues is of two sorts. In imperfect beings, succession brings completion or perfection (as, for example, human beings grow bigger or older

[70] 'Quae ratio solida eos moveat non video, cum duratio omnis ex natura sua importet fluxum momentarum per prius & posterius distinctarum, qui sine successione esse aut concipi non potest. Momentanea enim duratio, proprie duratio non est.' Episcopius, *Opera* (1650), p287. Vorstius says the same: *Tractatus*, p203.

[71] 'Respectu temporis sive durationis Deus est aeternus, quia ne principium essendi habet, nec finum essendi habiturus unquam est; sed totius & perfecte seipsum possedit, possidet & possidebit, sine ulla sui mutatione, aut partium semper vel subinde accrescentium successione, sed continua & nunquam interrupta sui totius & indivisi duratione.' Episcopius, *Opera* (1650), p287.

during time). That is not the case for perfect beings, since they have nothing to be perfected.

Describing the relation something has with time, Episcopius argues, is describing something external to it, namely its relationship with a succession of moments, whether few moments, many moments, or an infinite number of moments. No such moment can ever be contemporaneous with any other moment, for the past and the future do not really exist. The past has ceased to exist and the future has not begun to exist, only the present moment properly exists. So, saying that God is eternal does not involve saying that there is a part of God existing in the past, and a part of God existing in the future and a part of God existing now; it means only that the God who exists now, also existed in the past, and will continue to exist in the future: 'For in this way it is certain that God is eternal now and in every instant.'[72] Like Crell, therefore, Episcopius believes that time is logically prior to God and that God exists within it just as other beings do, though, of course, for rather longer. As a result, his conception of simplicity is not one which excludes temporal succession from God's essence.

Unlike Crell, Episcopius does believe that God's essence is omnipresent. He writes: 'God is correctly called immense because he cannot be circumscribed by certain limits of space, or defined by a certain place, or encompassed by limits or extremities.'[73] He expresses this omnipresence as an extension of God's essence through space.[74] Scholastic writers tended to reject the idea that divine immensity was a form of extension. They held that extension through space was something only proper to material things and necessarily involved having spatial (extensive) parts. As a result, such a conception of divine immensity conflicted with divine simplicity.[75] Episcopius asserts, however, that his conception of extension means that it does not conflict with divine simplicity. As he did in the case of temporal succession, Episcopius argues that there are two different sorts of extension: material extension which involves a being having parts and spiritual extension which does not.

At this point he makes an interesting explanatory remark, namely that only material objects have real parts rather than imaginary ones.[76] This would seem to indicate that his view of divine simplicity is that it need only exclude

[72] 'Sic enim certum est, Deum nunc & in omni instanti aeternum esse.' Ibid., p288.

[73] 'Deus recte immensus vocatur quia nec certis spatii terminus circumscribi, nec in certo ubi definiri, nec finibus aut extremitatibus concludi potest.' Ibid., p287. Vorstius was not so sure: *Tractatus*, pp215 and 217. And even Episcopius does not think that it is necessary to believe it: *Institutiones*, IV.II.13.

[74] Ibid., p286.

[75] E.g. Turretin, *Institutes*, Topic III q9.19.

[76] Episcopius, *Opera* (1650), p287.

what he calls real parts, and that it need not exclude merely conceptual distinctions within his essence. This again runs counter to the traditional understanding of the doctrine, for which excluding real parts was only a first step.[77] For a Thomist, not only real parts, but also notional parts had to be excluded from the being of God, since all composition would require some explanation, and that explanation would, as a result, be logically prior to the being of God. And that was a problem, because God, as First Cause, had to be logically prior to everything else.

Like Crell, Episcopius rejects the distinction between God's hidden and revealed will, and maintains instead the distinction between God's absolute and conditional will.[78] He also believes that God's absolute will is not always efficacious. Given that God always has a will but that God's will is not always active (God only willed to create, for example, at the time of creation and not before), he asserts that God is mutable, in the sense that his will is capable of generating particular acts of volition. God can decide to do specific things at specific times. The specific acts of volition which happen at specific times take place within God, yet are distinct from him. Here again, Episcopius is breaking with the Thomist understanding of simplicity. He is aware of this, and defends himself by asserting that, to his mind, the doctrine of divine simplicity only really excludes from God's being the sort of composition which implies dependence on other beings.[79] In other words, the doctrine of divine simplicity is being qualified in his thinking once again.

Again with Crell, Episcopius argues that God's will can only be directed to what is good. With regard to God's creatures that means that it is always regulated by the rules of divine justice. He writes:

> Justice is the director of that will, by which God is guided concerning his creatures, or rather... concerning man created and considered as such: so much so indeed that it is the cause and reason, moreover, why God can will and does will nothing concerning man which is opposed to the perfection and dignity of his nature, that is, which involves any iniquity.[80]

This means, for example, that God cannot derive any glory from the condemnation of the greater part of humanity to hell, particularly when

[77] Turretin, *Institutes*, Topic III q7.5.

[78] Episcopius, *Opera* (1650), pp308–9.

[79] Ibid., p306. Aquinas excluded all composition from God, since he held that all forms of composition necessarily imply dependence, whether that composition was real or conceptual.

[80] 'Iustitia est directrix voluntatis istius, qua versatur Deus circa creaturam suam, vel potius... circa hominem qua talem creatum ac consideratum: quatenus videlicet ea causa ac ratio est, tum ut Deum nihil velle possit ac velit circa hominem quid perfectioni ac dignitati naturae suae divinae adversatur, id est, cum pravitate conjunctum est.' Ibid., p322.

they have not yet committed any sin.[81] To do so, he says, would be inconsistent with the divine goodness, for creation would only then be a foundation for future misery. He writes:

> Guiltlessness is not, indeed, owed misery, rather it is owed what is not misery. Otherwise it would be better not to be, than to be and to be guiltless. For it is better not to be than to be truly miserable, especially to be eternally miserable. The creation of man would therefore then be not a kindness, but the highest wrong, and an act not of goodness, but of the greatest cruelty.[82]

Episcopius also rejects the doctrine of original sin because it would conflict with God's justice in that it involves condemning many men for the sin of one.

The major disagreement between Episcopius and the Socinian writers comes in the matter of divine omniscience. For here Episcopius asserts that God does have certain foreknowledge of future contingents.[83] The foundation of the Socinian argument, as we have seen, was that future contingents do not have within them a sufficiently determined outcome for them to be certainly known. In other words, they can only be probable, never certain. Episcopius disagrees. Since there is something which eventually happens (an event, in his terminology), it can be certainly known. He writes: 'that which now actually and definitely is, was certainly future before now. Therefore, just as it is now true to say "this now definitely is," so beforehand it was true to say "this is definitely future." '[84]

The Socinians, he argues, have made the mistake of inferring the necessity of an event from God having certain future knowledge of it. Episcopius thinks that no inference can properly be drawn about the nature of an event from divine prescience of it. God knows future events with certainty, but he knows them as either contingent events or necessary events, since he knows both that they will take place and the circumstances in which they will take place. His knowledge has no more effect on those circumstances than ordinary human knowledge does. It follows that, for Episcopius, there is a threefold knowledge within God:

[81] Ibid.

[82] 'Innocentia enim non debetur miseria, imo debetur non miseria. Alioquin praestaret non esse, quam esse et innocentem esse. Melius enim non esse quam vere miserum, imo aeternum miserum esse. Creatio itaque hominis non foret beneficium, sed summam maleficium & crudelitas summae actus non bonitatis.' Ibid.

[83] Though he does not think that it is necessary to believe this.

[84] 'Id quod nunc actu & determinate sit, hoc antea revera futurum fuit. Ergo sicuti nunc verum est dicere, hoc iam determinate sit, sic antea verum fuit dicere, hoc determinate futurum est.' Ibid., p301.

So that this order might be rightly understood, it is time to observe that a triple knowledge is ordinarily attributed to God. One which is necessary and active and is called '[knowledge] of simple intelligence,' and which, of its nature, is prior to any act of [God's] free will; by which God knows himself and all possible things. The second is called '[knowledge] of vision' and is subsequent to the act of the free will; by which God knows all things which he has decreed to do or to permit, in the same order by which he decreed to do [them] or permit that they should be. The third, middle [knowledge]; by which God knows what men and angels will do by their free will, if they are placed in these or those circumstances, in this or that situation or position.[85]

Episcopius has adopted here the concept of 'middle' knowledge, an idea which was developed during the sixteenth century by the Spanish Jesuit Luis de Molina.

Molina had argued that, prior to any determination of the divine will, God foreknows the free decisions which will be made by finite wills in a given set of circumstances.[86] For this, he was accused of Pelagianism by a contemporary Spanish Dominican whom we have encountered already, Domingo Banez. The argument between Molina and his Jesuit supporters on the one hand, and the Dominicans on the other became so acrimonious that Pope Clement VIII established a papal commission, the *Congregatio de Auxiliis*, to debate the matter in 1598. The commission continued to meet regularly until 1607, and was inclined to condemn the Molinist position. However, Pope Paul V intervened and decided that the Molinist and Thomist positions were both within the bounds of Roman Catholic orthodoxy. It should be underlined, however, that the Molinist view was accepted by all sides to be an essentially novel position, whereas the Thomist view represented continuity with the Church's medieval past. A recent study has demonstrated that Arminius adopted Molina's position,[87] and it is presumably from Arminius that Episcopius took it. Middle knowledge was rejected by the Reformed, who argued, with the Dominicans, that only 'simple' and 'free' knowledge existed in God.[88]

[85] 'Ordo hic ut recte intelligatur, observandum venit, triplicam Deo scientiam tribui solere. Unum quae necessaria est & practica atque simplicis intelligentis dicitur, quae ex natura sua omni voluntatis liberae actu prior est, qua Deus se ipsum & alia omnia possibilia intelligit. Alteram liberam, quae visionis dicitur & actu voluntatis liberae posterior est, qua Deus omnia, quae facere aut permittere decrevit, eodem ordine decrevit, quo eo decrevit facere aut permittere ut fiant. Tertiam, mediam, qua Deus novit quid homines aut angeli pro sua libertate facturi essent, sub conditione, si cum his aut illis circumstantiis, in hoc vel in illa statu aut ordine constituerentur.' Ibid., p303. Vorstius also granted this: *Tractatus*, p47.

[86] W.L. Craig, *The Problem of Divine Foreknowledge of Future Contingents from Aristotle to Suarez* (Leiden, 1988), p351.

[87] E. Dekker, 'Was Arminius a Molinist?' *SCJ*, 27 (1996), p337.

[88] Turretin, *Institutes*, Topic III q13.

From what has been said, it is clear that, in their understanding of the nature of God, the Remonstrants generally sided with the Socinians. In only two significant areas, divine immensity and divine foreknowledge of future contingents, do they disagree with them, and even then they held that these doctrines were not necessary to be believed. On the matter of divine simplicity, the Remonstrants depart so seriously from the Thomist view, that they effectively recast the doctrine. For Vorst and Episcopius, divine simplicity means little more than that the nature of God does not enjoy the sort of composition one might expect to find in a physical being. The Socinians would not have disagreed.[89]

On this basis, it seems reasonable to argue that, during the early seventeenth century, the Remonstrants and Socinians expounded alongside one another, a revolutionary new understanding of the being and attributes of God. This doctrine of God was deliberately opposed to Reformed orthodoxy on several key issues. This conscious opposition to the Reformed view, however, led them to attack aspects of the medieval doctrine of God which were in fact common to both Reformed and Roman Catholic theologians.

## THE AVANT-GARDE DOCTRINE OF GOD IN POST-RESTORATION ENGLAND

The links between the radical writers of the early seventeenth century and the more avant-garde Anglican clergy of the post-Restoration period have long been acknowledged. In his *History of His Own Time*, Gilbert Burnet wrote of those contemporary divines whom he most admired:

> They wished that things might have been carried with more moderation ... and allowed a great freedom both in philosophy and in divinity.... And upon this men of narrower thoughts and fiercer tempers fastened upon them the name of Latitudinarians. They read Episcopius much. And the making out the reasons of things being a main part of their studies, their enemies called them Socinians.[90]

For Burnet, the most eminent of these moderate divines was Archbishop John Tillotson. Tillotson was also one of a small group of post-Restoration Anglican theologians to publish a work dealing specifically with the doctrine of God. The other two were Daniel Whitby and Samuel Clarke. A comparison

[89] Crell and Volkel, *De Vera Religione*, I.XVII, a p113.

[90] G. Burnet, *History of His Own Time*, 2 vols (London, 1724–34), i p188.

of these three works reveals both that Tillotson, Whitby, and Clarke were in substantial agreement with each other, and also that they were in substantial agreement with the positions developed by Simon Episcopius half a century earlier. The avant-garde doctrine of God developed by the Socinians and the Remonstrants had obviously entered the mainstream of English theological discourse.[91] William Sherlock's adoption of the avant-garde position is at the root of his disagreement with Edwards and South in this area.

Of the three works, Tillotson's sermons on the doctrine of God were the first to be published.[92] Whitby and Clarke both cited Tillotson's sermons in their own discussion of the subject.[93] It therefore seems appropriate to base this study on Tillotson's treatment of the subject.

Tillotson's doctrine of God, although it does not entirely abandon the way of negation, certainly concentrates, like Johann Crell's, on the way of eminence. Its guiding principle is that of perfection, indeed, he renames the divine attributes 'perfections'. He writes, in the opening sermon of his study: 'I shall consider how we are to conceive of the divine perfections. These two ways. 1. By ascribing all imaginable and possible perfection to God. 2. By separating and removing all manner of imperfection from him.'[94] This means, amongst other things, that we must ascribe to God even perfections which we cannot fully understand: 'For we are not to confine the perfection of God to our imagination . . . but on the contrary to believe the perfection of the divine nature to be boundless and unlimited, and infinitely to exceed our highest thoughts and apprehensions.'[95]

The most natural and simple idea of God, Tillotson thinks, is that God is the most perfect being we can possibly imagine.[96] So, in order to frame an adequate idea of God, we must ascribe to him all the perfections which created beings enjoy, apart from those which either involve an imperfection (motion, for example, is excluded, since it implies spatial limitation), or

[91] William Sherlock did not produce a work dedicated to the nature of God. However, where his writing touches on that area, it can be shown that he almost always adopted identical positions to Tillotson, Whitby, and Clarke. E.g. on the divine prescience of future contingents: *A Discourse Concerning the Divine Providence* (London, 1694), p178 et seq; on conditional decrees: *Discourse Concerning the Knowledge of Jesus Christ*, p382; on divine simplicity: *Vindication of the Doctrine of the Trinity*, p71; on the nature of eternity: *Sermons*, i p393. He does, however, reject the idea that divine omnipresence involves extension: *Vindication*, p76.

[92] Tillotson died in 1694 and his sermons were posthumously published around the turn of the century by his chaplain. Clarke's sermons were preached as Boyle lectures in 1704–5. Whitby's were first published in 1710, with no indication of when or where they had been preached.

[93] Clarke cites Tillotson on divine eternity, Whitby on the nature of divine perfection. S. Clarke, *A Discourse Concerning the Being and Attributes of God* (London, 1728), p42. D. Whitby, *Sermons on the Attributes of God* (London, 1710), p221.

[94] Tillotson, *Sermons*, vi p3. [95] Ibid., p4. [96] Ibid., p7.

evidently conflict with some other greater perfection (as an untrammelled conception of divine mercy would conflict with divine justice, for example).

Early on, Tillotson lays down a rule which he considers to be important in any correct understanding of God:

First, let us begin with the most natural, and plain and easy perfections of God, and lay them for a foundation and rectify all out other apprehensions of God and reasonings about him by these; and these are his power, wisdom and goodness, to which most of the rest may be reduced.[97]

Tillotson underlines that certain aspects of God's being are more complicated than others. 'When we consider infinite knowledge and power, we may easily lose ourselves, and go out of our depth by wading too far into them: there is something concerning these that is unimaginable and unaccountable to our reason.'[98] We cannot, for example, grasp how God creates out of nothing, or how God can know the future, or how providence works.

Even so, he says:

However we may be at a loss in our conceptions of God's infinite knowledge and power, yet goodness and justice and truth, are notions easy and familiar; and if we could not understand these the whole bible would be insignificant to us. For all revelation from God supposeth us to know what is meant by goodness and justice, and truth: and therefore no man can entertain any notion of God which plainly contradicts these.... If we had no certain and settled notion of the goodness and justice and truth of God, he would be altogether an unintelligible being; and religion, which consists in the imitation of him, would be utterly impossible. Now these being the most easy, and intelligible perfections of God, by which he is said in scripture to declare his name, that is, to make himself known to us, we should govern all our reasonings about God (as concerning his decrees, and his concurrence with the free actions of men, and his particular providence, which are things dark and obscure) by what is more clear.[99]

By laying down this rule, Tillotson has established a very important point in the way the doctrine of God should be expressed. Because he has advanced a solid theological basis for elevating some divine attributes over others in the discussion of God's nature: namely, that certain divine attributes are proposed to human beings for imitation by the scriptures, whereas others are not. The divine attributes proposed for human imitation are not, of course, God's incommunicable attributes of eternity, aseity, immensity, etc. They, by definition, cannot be imitated by human beings. Rather, the divine attributes which humans are commanded to emulate are God's communicable, or moral, attributes of holiness, goodness, justice, truth, and the like. Consequently in

[97] Ibid., p13. [98] Ibid., p14. [99] Ibid., p16.

Tillotson's exposition of the divine nature, the communicable attributes can take precedence over all others.[100] This approach, of course, was exactly that which William Sherlock adopted in his own discussion of God's being, and which so outraged Robert South.[101]

Amongst the perfections which proposed as models for humans to emulate, Tillotson argues, by far the most the most important is the divine goodness. He writes: 'Goodness is so great and necessary a perfection, that without it, there can be no other, it gives perfection to all other excellencies; take away this, and the greatest excellencies in any other kind would be but the greatest imperfections.'[102] His presentation of the divine goodness makes it clear that Tillotson thinks that God's goodness is essentially the same as our goodness. He rejects what he calls a dry metaphysical notion of goodness as simply being. Instead, he urges:

> Tho' the degrees of goodness in God, and the creatures be infinitely unequal, and that goodness which is in us be so small and inconsiderable . . . yet the essential notion of goodness in both, must be the same; else when the scripture speaks of the goodness of God, we could not know the meaning of it.[103]

Elsewhere, in a more homely mode, he writes: 'the goodness of God signifies very little, if it does not signify this, that in any instance of real and unquestionable goodness, God is much better than any father upon earth.'[104]

The significance of what Tillotson has done here should not be underestimated. He has effectively revolutionised the theoretical basis of religious language. Thomas Aquinas was the first to develop the doctrine of analogy as an underlying principle of theological discourse. He argued that the human language used of God is not equivocal (meaning an entirely different thing in God from what it means in the human beings), or univocal (meaning exactly the same thing in God that it means in human beings) but analogical (meaning, in God, something related to what it means in human beings).[105] Although Aquinas's view was not unchallenged,[106] it was extremely influential and certainly continued to colour Reformed thinking on the matter.[107]

What Tillotson has done is to argue that where divine perfections are proposed to human beings for imitation, the perfections predicated of God and demanded of human beings are couched in terms which have a univocal

[100] Tillotson, *Sermons*, vi p28. [101] Sherlock, *Vindication*, p70.
[102] Tillotson, *Sermons*, vii p11. [103] Ibid., p5. [104] Ibid., vi p36.
[105] Aquinas, *Summa Theologiae*, Ia 13. Davies, *Thought of Thomas Aquinas*, p61 et seq.
[106] Duns Scotus, for example, argued that unless some of the terms human beings apply to God are predicated of God univocally, it is impossible to escape the claim that all are being used equivocally. Cross, *Duns Scotus*, p33 et seq.
[107] Turretin, *Institutes*, Topic III q6 asserts, for example, that the communicable attributes of God are predicated of God analogically rather than univocally.

sense. The goodness of God is, in other words, exactly the same thing as the goodness that human beings are meant to show. This same goodness is, of course, expressed in God to a far greater degree, but it is essentially the same thing. It is this kind of assumption which, as we have seen, lies at the root of William Sherlock's objection to the Reformed view of divine justice.[108]

It is important to underline, however, that this principle applies only to the communicable and not to the incommunicable attributes of God. When he deals with divine foreknowledge of future contingents, for example, Tillotson raises, as a potential objection to the view that God can foresee the outcome of future free choices, that such a view involves proposing that God enjoys a sort of knowledge which runs counter to human instincts about knowledge. The objection runs that if it is acceptable to frame an opinion of God's knowledge that appears impossible to human reason, then it must be equally legitimate to frame an opinion of God's goodness or justice which is contrary to our natural instincts about them. He replies:

> To this I answer, there is a great difference between the perfections of God which are imitable, and those which are not. Knowledge of future events is a perfection wherein we are not bound to be like God; and if we are assured of the thing, that he doth know them, it is not necessary that we should know the manner of it, and disentangle it from contradiction and impossibility: but it is otherwise in God's goodness and justice, which are imitable; he that imitates, endeavours to be like something that he knows, and we must have a clear idea and notion of that which we would bring ourselves to the likeness of; these perfections of God we are capable of knowing; and therefore the knowledge of these perfections is chiefly recommended to us in scripture.[109]

It is clear, therefore, that Tillotson has imposed a novel hierarchy within religious language. In dealing with the moral perfections of God, he believes that human language is used univocally of God. In dealing with all the other divine attributes, however, he seems to be saying that human language is used only analogically of God. So he believes that God's knowledge, for example, is essentially rather unlike human knowledge, and that the degree of unlikeness involved is sufficient to excuse what would otherwise appear to involve a contradiction: namely that God can know future contingencies.

Only Tillotson expounds this view at such length. Clarke does not discuss the use of religious language at all.[110] But Whitby, where he touches on it, seems to be saying much the same thing as Tillotson. He certainly accepts that God's communicable attributes are those aspects of God's being proposed to

[108] Sherlock, *Discourse*, p28. [109] Tillotson, *Sermons*, vi p158.

[110] Though his remarks on divine goodness seem to indicate that he views it as essentially the same as human goodness. He certainly views goodness as having a necessary existence antecedent to even the divine being. Clarke, *Discourse*, pp111–13.

us for imitation which we resemble 'in good measure' even in our fallen state.[111] He also agrees with Tillotson that we understand God's communicable attributes differently from God's incommunicable attributes. Whitby writes, for example:

We ought to put a difference as to our knowledge of, and our deductions from God's inimitable perfections, which are pure objects of faith; viz. his eternity, his omnipresence, his knowledge of things future and contingent, and his moral and communicable perfections, which relate to our practice.[112]

Of the first, he writes, 'we neither have, nor can have a just notion of them,'[113] because, he believes that they exist only in God and that we have nothing in our senses or apprehensions with which to compare them. Of God's moral attributes, however, we must have a clear idea, or we could not be expected to emulate them. He writes:

If we had no certain notion of the justice, truth and goodness of God, he would be, as to those things, an unintelligible being to us, and religion, which consists chiefly in imitation of his communicable attributes, would be a thing impossible.... To say God is just, and good, but not good, and just, as men understand goodness and justice, is to say that we have no natural notions of God.[114]

Again, like Tillotson, he applies this principle to the way we may legitimately argue about the divine attributes. He writes:

Tho' we cannot argue concerning God's incommunicable attributes, thus, I have no notion of an eternity with, or without succession, I have no idea of a God wholly everywhere, without multiplication, I am not able to conceive how he can certainly know the effect where the cause is uncertain, and free to produce the contrary, and so cannot believe God's eternity, his omnipresence, or his prescience, this being argument *ab ignoto ad ignotius*, yet may we argue against the absolute decrees of reprobation, and of denying grace sufficient for the performance of our duty, from the considerations of divine justice, his truth and sincerity, his love and goodness to the sons of men.[115]

Once again, it is clear that God's moral attributes take precedence over God's other attributes because they are understood univocally, not analogically.

Having established a theoretical basis for the discussion of the being of God which backs up the Remonstrant (and Socinian) instincts about the subject, Tillotson, Clarke, and Whitby then erect a thoroughly Remonstrant superstructure upon it. The significant areas of doctrine where the Remonstrants and Socinians diverged from both their medieval predecessors and their more

[111] Whitby, *Sermons*, p18. [112] Ibid., p37. [113] Ibid.
[114] Ibid., p38. [115] Ibid.

scholastically minded contemporaries have already been outlined. They are: the divine simplicity, eternity and immensity, the distinctions within the divine will, and the knowledge God has of the future.

On the matter of divine simplicity, Tillotson is virtually silent. He is clear that he wishes to exclude all forms of imperfections from our conception of God's essence,[116] but he does not list composition or diversity amongst the imperfections he has in mind.[117] He does once quote Cicero as saying that 'we cannot conceive of God, but as of a pure mind, entirely free from all mortal composition or mixture,'[118] but it is evident from the context that the only sort of composition being excluded is that involved in having material existence.

Whitby and Clarke do both mention divine simplicity, but it is clear that they, like Episcopius, have a distinctly attenuated view of it. Both effectively reduce it to the assertion that God is not made up of matter. Thus Whitby writes, 'God is a spirit, and so exempt from matter: he is a simple essence free from all composition, or any parts that can be separable from him to impair his being,'[119] and Clarke urges that 'the self-existent being, must be a most simple, unchangeable, incorruptible being; without parts, figure motion, divisibility, or any other such properties as we find in matter'.[120]

That this is a far more limited view of simplicity than the Thomist one is clear when Clarke turns to deal with the incomprehensibility of the divine being. For there he writes:

> From hence appears the vanity of the school-men; who, as in other matters, so in their disputes about the self-existing being; when they come at what they are by no means able to comprehend or explain; least they should seem ignorant of any thing, they give us terms of art and words of amusement; mere empty sounds which, under the pretence of explaining the matter before them, have really no manner of idea or signification at all. Thus, when they tell us concerning the essence of God, that he is *purus actus, mera forma*, and the like; either the words have no meaning and signify nothing; or else they express only the perfection of his power, and other attributes; which is not what these men intend to express by them.[121]

The terms Clarke has criticized here are in fact terms essential to the Thomist understanding of divine simplicity. To describe God as *purus actus* was to exclude from God's being the distinction between actual and potential. To describe God as *mera forma* was to exclude from God's being any composition

116 Tillotson, *Sermons*, vi p10. 117 Ibid., p11.

118 Ibid., vii p303. The passage cited is from 21Vitelli of Cicero's lost *Consolatio* on the death of his daughter, as fondly quoted by himself in *Tusc.* 1.66. I am grateful to Prof. Gregory Hutchinson of Exeter College for this attribution.

119 Whitby, *Sermons*, p73. 120 Clarke, *Discourse*, p44. 121 Ibid., p40.

analogous to that of matter and form. Clarke is right to observe that the school-men did not intend to use them as a way of expressing other divine attributes. However, he is concealing the fact that, by criticising these terms, he is necessarily attenuating the concept of divine simplicity to which he purportedly subscribes, and reducing it to the dimensions given it by the likes of Vorstius and Episcopius.

This becomes clearer still when the three authors discuss the divine immensity and eternity, for they all argue for spatial extension and temporal succession within the divine being, both of which, as we have seen, are incompatible with the medieval understanding of simplicity, whether in its Thomist or its Scotist form, and both of which were taught by Episcopius. Tillotson writes:

> By the immensity of God, I mean that his being hath no bounds, but doth every way spread and diffuse itself beyond what we can imagine; so that you cannot define the presence of God by any certain place, so as to say here he is, but not there; nor by any limits, so as to say, thus far his being reaches, and no farther.[122]

Whitby agrees,[123] though, just like Episcopius, he does not think that it in a necessary article of belief.[124] Clarke says the same, but is anxious to underline that such diffusion as there is in the divine being does not imply any diversity, taking the opportunity, on the way, to ridicule the scholastic conception of omnipresence.[125]

With regard to eternity, the three Anglicans again follow the earlier radical authors, and all are critical of the scholastic view. Tillotson writes:

> I shall not trouble you with the inconsistent and unintelligible notions of the school-men; that it is *duratio tota simul*, in which we are not to conceive any succession, but to imagine it an instant. We may as well conceive the immensity of God to be a point as his eternity to be an instant; and as, according to our manner of conceiving, we must necessarily suppose the immensity of God, to be an infinite expansion of his essence... so we must suppose the eternity of God to be a perpetual continuance, coexistent to all imaginable succession of ages. Now how that can be together, which must necessarily be imagined to be coexistent to successions, let them that can conceive.[126]

Whitby also grants that duration exists within the divine being,[127] and Clarke cites this very passage of Tillotson approvingly.[128]

That all three writers concede some distinction between actuality and potentiality within the divine being, seems to follow from their position on the nature of the divine will which is, once again, identical to that held by

[122] Tillotson, *Sermons*, vii pp333–4. [123] Whitby, *Sermons*, p99. [124] Ibid., p105.
[125] Clarke, *Discourse*, pp45–6. [126] Tillotson, *Sermons*, vii p359.
[127] Whitby, *Sermons*, p49. [128] Clarke, *Discourse*, p42.

Episcopius. Tillotson and Whitby certainly grant that some acts of God's will are conditional upon human free actions,[129] which implies some passive potentiality within God. Clarke is more explicit: by giving freedom to his creatures, he thinks, God has deliberately granted to his creatures the power to work against his will.[130] In other words, like Episcopius, he believes that the divine will can, to some degree, be frustrated by human action.

These views on human freedom from divine influence do not, however, lead the Anglican authors to doubt the divine prescience. Tillotson certainly thinks that God knows all future events, whether contingent or necessary.[131] And he uses an identical argument to Episcopius in support of this view. He argues, 'whatever event hath actually happened, as because now it is past, it is certainly true that it was, so because it once was, it was certainly true before it was, that it would be'.[132]

Tillotson is also quite as sure as the earlier author that divine prescience itself has no bearing upon the freedom of human decisions.[133] We cannot, of course, explain how this prescience works, but, as we have seen, such an explanation is not necessary, since the divine knowledge is not a communicable attribute. All we need to do is believe that it is. We do not have to understand how it is. What is clear, though, is that the presumptuous scholastic attempts to understand how it happens will not do. Tillotson writes, once again casually dismissing several centuries of scholarship:

> I know that there are those who undertake to explain the particular manner. Some say that God sees future events *in speculo voluntatis*; others say that the eternity of God is actually commensurate to all duration, as his immensity to all space, and so God doth not so properly fore-see and fore-know, as see and know future things by the presentiality and coexistence of all things in eternity; for they say that future things are actually present and existing to God, though not in *mensura propria*, yet in *mensura aliena*; the school-men have much more of this jargon and canting language; and I envy no man the understanding these phrases, but to me they seem to signify nothing, but to have been words invented by idle and conceited men, which a great many ever since, lest they should seem ignorant, would seem to understand.[134]

Whitby and Clarke are, once again, in substantial agreement with Tillotson on this matter.[135]

[129] Whitby, *Sermons*, p74. Tillotson, *Sermons*, vi p110.
[130] Clarke, *Discourse*, p105.
[131] Tillotson, *Sermons*, vi p146.
[132] Ibid. p154. Episcopius, *Institutiones*, IV.II p301.
[133] Tillotson, *Sermons*, vi pp159–60. Episcopius, *Institutiones*, IV.II p301.
[134] Tillotson, *Sermons*, vi pp156–7.
[135] Whitby, *Sermons*, pp206–20. Clarke, *Discourse*, pp100–3.

## CONCLUSION

Beneath the surface of the public debates on justification and the doctrine of the Trinity there existed, within the post-Restoration Church, a fundamental division over God's nature and the approach theologians should take to understanding it. This division occasionally becomes evident in the process of other discussions; as it does, for example in the differences between Sherlock and Edwards about God's justice, and in the argument between Sherlock and South over which attributes were more important in a discussion of the divine nature.

Sherlock was, however, far from unique in adopting a novel perspective on the nature of God. It is evident from the writings of John Tillotson, Samuel Clarke, and Daniel Whitby, that an avant-garde doctrine of God had in fact become firmly entrenched within certain Anglican circles by the end of the seventeenth century. The views of these men are the more significant because Tillotson was, of course, Archbishop of Canterbury, as well as being amongst the most avidly read preachers of the period, and Clarke's position was expounded in his Boyle Lectures, which were greeted with great acclaim upon their delivery, and which remained highly regarded after his fall from grace.

These theologians approached the doctrine of God in a way that was both consciously different from Reformed teaching in this area, and openly contemptuous of the scholastic methods and terminology traditionally used by Reformed authors to express their views. Their new approach to God proposed, in particular, a drastically attenuated doctrine of divine simplicity. It elevated the communicable perfections of God to preeminence over the incommunicable attributes. It reconfigured the way in which God was thought to be present at all times and in all locations. And it absorbed the Molinist conception of the divine knowledge so as to enable the outcome of the divine decrees to depend upon will of human beings.

The doctrine of God which Tillotson, Clarke, and Whitby advanced, and which William Sherlock also evidently embraced, had, in fact, been worked out by the Socinian and Remonstrant writers of the early seventeenth century, specifically Johann Crell, Conrad Vorst, and Simon Episcopius. And although the Remonstrant and Socinian teaching about the divine nature is not precisely identical, there is a great deal of common ground between the two schools. The Socinian and Remonstrant doctrine of God had been elaborated with the specific aim of excluding certain key tenets of Reformed belief. However, it also involved the wholesale abandonment of medieval patterns of thinking on this matter, a patterns of thinking which were shared by both Reformed and Roman Catholic theologians. As such, its widespread adoption by influential thinkers within the Church represented a clear rejection of much of the Church of England's doctrinal heritage.

# 7

# The Reformed Defence of Thomist Theism

## THE INFLUENCE OF AQUINAS

Significant numbers of Anglican Reformed either wrote specifically on the doctrine of God, or touched upon it tangentially in their treatment of other subjects. What is intriguing about the way the approach this area of theology, is that they routinely sound a strikingly Thomist note.

As we saw, in the context of the debate about justification, Reformed Anglicans were quite happy to deploy all manner of Reformed authorities, whether English or Continental, to defend orthodoxy as they saw it. Indeed this reference to Protestant sources played an important role in their polemic: for they were able, through such reference, to show that the position they were defending was the common position of Reformed churches across Europe, as well as being the historic position of the English church.

In the context of their doctrine of God, however, Reformed authorities all but disappear, and are replaced by Thomas Aquinas and the many Roman Catholics who expounded and developed his thinking during the early modern period. It should be underlined that when we describe the Anglican Reformed writers as 'Thomist', we do not mean that their positions are identical to those maintained by Aquinas himself, but rather that they are identifiably working within the tradition of thought which looked to Aquinas as a major influence, and which sought to present its teaching as an organic development of his. As Richard Muller has powerfully argued, the Thomist tradition had developed in significant ways by the seventeenth century,[1] and it was this modified and more diverse tradition of thought which became influential within Reformed circles.[2]

In the opening lecture of his series on the divine attributes, delivered when he was Lady Margaret Professor of Divinity in Cambridge, John Pearson sets out to establish the canons of a divinity which could be described as both

[1] R. Muller; *God, Creation and Providence in the Thought of Jacob Arminius* (Grand Rapids, 1991), p37.

[2] Muller, *Arminius*, p34.

Reformed and scholastic. Pearson begins by offering an outline of what he understands by scholastic theology in general. He writes:

Indeed, when I say 'theology,' I understand the science of God and of divine things.... When I add 'scholastic,' I mean the method of conveying and discussing the divine things revealed to us by God through the Son, which is done through the accurate delivery, proof and defence of Christian doctrine, guided by right reason from the first principles of theology.[3]

He explains what he means by the 'theological principles' from which such expression, proof and argument is valid, writing:

Let us understand the theological grounds upon which arguments in confirmation of the doctrines of the faith may be based. 1. As the first of these grounds, therefore, we advance the canonical books of sacred scripture, speaking, where there is need, the languages in which they were written, in which they were conceived. 2. As the second ground, we accept councils, above all general councils, but those only which reflect the mind of the early church, not those flagrantly schismatic assemblies which, in the midst of barbarism, were convened at the wish of one man. 3. As the third ground, we ascribe the highest value to the consensus of the Fathers, if they truly are Fathers, by which I mean the acknowledged and proven ancient authors of God's church, but we reject all fabricated writers, and the suppositious works of the good authors.[4]

Pearson is, in other words, attempting to combine both scholastic method and a Reformed, and even humanist, approach to the science of God. He asserts the paramount authority of scripture, the importance of original languages, the need to avoid specious works, and the importance of considering the historical circumstances in which general councils took place. As he underlines, 'I am not one who would lure you back from the light to darkness, from the purity of reborn letters to barbarity.'[5] The scholastic method which he proposes to follow, in other words, is one modified by the intellectual

[3] 'Enimvero theologiam cum dico, intelligo scientiam de Deo, rebusque divinis.... Cum scholasticam addo, illud volo; modum nempe tradendi, tractandique res divinas, ita nobis a Deo per Filium revelatas, qui fiat per accuratam doctrinae Christianae, ductu recte rationis, ex principiis theologicis, traditionem, probationem, atque defensionem.' Pearson, *Minor Theological Works*, i p2.

[4] 'Agnoscimus loca theologica, unde argumenta ad dogmata fidei confirmanda sumi possint. 1. Primo itaque loco ponimus sacrae scripturae libros, scil. canonicos, eosque suis linguis quibus scripti, quibus nati sunt, ubi opus est, loquentes. 2. Secundo loco, recipimus concilia, praesertim generalia, sed illa quae ecclesiae veteris sententiam referunt; non illa quae in media barbarie, flagrante schismate, ad unius voluntatem congregata sunt conciliabula. 3. Tertio loco, consensui Patrum plurimum tribuimus, si vere patres sunt, hoc est, veteres scriptores in ecclesia Dei agniti atque probati, sed rejectis omnibus auctoribus ementitis, at bonorum auctorum operibus supposititiis.' Ibid. p5.

[5] 'Non ego is sum, qui vos a lumine ad tenebras, a puritate renascentium literarum ad barbariem revocem.' Ibid. p3.

advances of the sixteenth century, not a return to the corruptions of the Middle Ages. So his is a scholasticism which will honour the biblical and scholarly emphases of the Reformation. He underlines this once more at the beginning of the next lecture, writing, 'And, as we have said, we shall deal with the body of Christian doctrine in a manner which is fully scholastic, yet in accord with Reformed principles.'[6]

Pearson then charts a brief history of the scholastic movement in general, and it is here that he makes explicit which particular form of scholasticism he is interested in pursuing. He notes: 'Two especially present themselves to us in the schools famous hitherto; of which one is of the *Sentences* and the other of the *Summa*.'[7] The first he traces back to Hugh of St Victor, Robert Pulleyn and, above all Peter Lombard. He points out that commenting on Lombard's *Sentences* became the usual method for expounding theology during the middle ages, and was practised in particular by Alexander of Hales and his famous student, Bonaventure.[8]

Pearson then points out that, at around this time,

> another disciple of Alexander of Hales, Thomas Aquinas, also wrote [a commentary] on the Master of the *Sentences*, according to the fashion of the time; but he elaborated a body of Christian doctrine after his own particular manner, with a spirit which was indeed in some ways prescient, and called it the *Summa Theologiae*.[9]

Pearson notes that the writers who emerged immediately after Aquinas[10] did not follow his new method, but chose instead to comment on what he had written using the older method of expounding the *Sentences*. But then, he says: 'After three hundred years, another Thomas, namely de Vio Cajetan, illuminated this *Summa* of Thomas with commentaries, and persuaded the universities of the whole Roman church, that they should receive it in the schools.'[11]

As a result of the intellectual history of the scholastic movement, he says, there are now two options for a modern theologian. He writes:

> There are now two scholastic methods: one [being that] of those who still follow the *Sentences* of Lombard, and there are certainly fewer of them; and the other of those

[6] 'Praediximusque nos corpus doctrinae Christianae more plane scholastico, sed secundum principia reformata traditurос.' Ibid. p10.

[7] 'Duae autem nobis potissimum occurrunt in scholis hactenus celebres, quarum una Sententiarum est, altera Summae.' Ibid. p6.

[8] Ibid. p8.

[9] 'Aliter Alensis discipulus, Thomas Aquinas, scripsit etiam in Magistrum Sententiarum, pro more temporis; sed et animo nescio quibus modis praesagiente, corpus doctrinae Christianae sua plane modo exaravit, et *Summa Theologiae*... nuncupavit.' Ibid. p9.

[10] Pearson cites, in particular, Scotus, Ockham and Durandus of Saint-Pourcain.

[11] 'Hanc autem Thomae *Summam*, Thomas alius, nempe de vico Cajetanus, post trecentos annos, commentariis illustravit, persuasitque academiis totius ecclesiae Romanae ut eam in scholas reciperent.' Ibid.

who either illuminate Aquinas's *Summa Theologiae* with commentaries, or at least follow the order of his questions, and these are greater in number and more illustrious; so that while the former are generally mouldering in the corners of colleges, the latter can be heard everywhere in the academies. And it is not surprising that the earlier method of the *Sentences* has yielded to this, for the latter method is both more precise and clearer.[12]

Pearson proposes, unsurprisingly, to follow this clearer and more precise method. Accordingly, he proposes to present his doctrine of God in the form of a commentary on the relevant articles of Aquinas's *Summa Theologiae.*

Pearson's presentation of the history of scholasticism is, of course, thoroughly tendentious. In particular, it completely ignores the established Protestant method of expounding theology, which was to proceed through a series of *loci* which were ultimately derived from scripture, rather than from Peter Lombard or Thomas Aquinas.[13] In fact, on Pearson's account of scholasticism, one could be forgiven for thinking that there was no such thing as Reformed scholasticism before Pearson himself, since he mentions no authors from that tradition.

By presenting his options in this way, Pearson is deliberately placing his exposition of the doctrine of God in the context of contemporary Roman Catholic, rather than Protestant, scholasticism. In other words, he would have his audience believe that he is entering the lists alongside Roman Catholic Thomists such as Cajetan and Vasquez[14] rather than alongside the Protestant theologians of mainland Europe; and this, despite the fact that he has claimed to be teaching a fully Reformed version of scholasticism.[15] This is perhaps understandable, given that the lecture was delivered immediately after the Restoration, when the reputation of Reformed theology was at a distinctly low ebb, particularly in the University of Cambridge where the influence of the Cambridge Platonists was most directly felt.

The implication may be that the doctrine of God is a 'Catholic' matter in the proper sense: it is an area of theology where Protestant and Roman Catholic

[12] 'Duae iam tandem scholasticorum methodi, una eorum qui adhuc Lombardi Sententias sequuntur, et quidem hi pauciores, altera eorum qui Aquinatis *Summam Theologiae,* aut commentariis illustrant, aut ordine saltem quaestionum imitantur, et plures multo sunt et illustriores: dum enim illi in collegiorum plerumque angulis deliquescunt, hi in academiis ubique personant. Neque mirum est, priorem illam methodum sententiarum huic cecisse; est enim haec posterior illa et accuratior et luculentior.' Ibid.

[13] The importance of the *loci* method in Protestant Scholasticism has been underlined by Richard Muller: 'The Problem of Protestant Scholasticism—A Review and Definition,' in W.J. van Esselt and E. Dekker (eds.), *Reformation and Scholasticism* (Grand Rapids, 2001), p58. It is difficult to imagine that Pearson was really unaware of this.

[14] Vasquez is one of the few contemporary authors Pearson quotes with approval in his lectures: *Minor Theological Works,* i p16.

[15] Ibid. pp3, 5, 10.

writers are at one in their opinions. It is undoubtedly also the case that several Roman Catholic thinkers had a powerful reputation in the field of metaphysics.[16] Whatever the reason, however, on almost every major issue in his presentation of the doctrine of God, Pearson follows Thomas Aquinas, even to the point of disagreeing with Calvin and the wider Reformed tradition.

Pearson's approach is highly distinctive. None of the other Anglican Reformed actually organize the exposition of their theology around the *Summa Theologiae*. Nonetheless, the pronounced influence of Thomist thinking on the doctrine of God is still evident in their writing. In this they are not out of step with the European Reformed tradition, within which the influence of Thomist thought was widespread.[17]

What is a little eccentric, however, is the English theologians' distinct preference for deploying Roman Catholic over Protestant authority in the prosecution of their arguments. For, as Muller has pointed out, most Reformed were thoroughly reluctant to cite the more recent Roman Catholic writers with any favour.[18] This peculiarity of the Anglican Reformed is probably due to the particular position in which post-Restoration writers found themselves. In a Church which had been outlawed under the Commonwealth, and which was still engaged in a bitter struggle with Nonconformist Protestants in England, it was not perhaps so obvious that the writers of the non-Episcopalian Reformed tradition were automatically preferable to Roman Catholics. After all, the Church of England had problems with both traditions; and although the Anglican fear of Roman Catholicism was both ancient and deep, concern about Protestant Nonconformity was beginning to assume similarly hysterical proportions, as witnessed by the antics of the Tory Party during the reign of Queen Anne.[19]

Unlike Pearson, Barlow does not explicitly set out which scholastic method he intends to follow. On the other hand, Barlow is lavish in his citation of other authors as Pearson is not, and from these citations, it becomes clear that he, too, is engaging predominantly with Roman Catholic rather than Protestant thought on the matter. Throughout his work, Barlow cites, as authority for what he is saying, not only Aquinas himself but also the numerous writers who expounded his thinking in the sixteenth and seventeenth centuries. Of Aquinas himself, Barlow cites the *Summa Theologiae*[20] and the *Summa*

[16] Muller, *Arminius*, pp27, 29, 37. See also J.K. Ryan, 'The Reputation of St. Thomas Aquinas among English Protestant Thinkers of the Seventeenth Century,' *The New Scholasticism*, 22 (1948), p5.

[17] Muller, *Arminius*, pp35–7.

[18] Ibid., p37.

[19] B. Coward, *The Stuart Age: England 1603–1714*, 2nd edn (London, 1994), pp404–8, 428–32.

[20] T. Barlow, *Exercitationes Aliquot Metaphysicae de Deo* (Oxford, 1658), pp120, 129, 136, 186, 193, and at many other places.

*Contra Gentiles*[21] most frequently, but he also deploys the *Quaestiones Quodlibetales*,[22] the *Scriptum super libros Sententiarum*,[23] the *De Malo*,[24] the *Expositio super librii Boethii De Trinitate*,[25] and the *In metaphysicam Aristotelis commentaria*.[26]

His citations of contemporary authors reads like a roll-call of the masters of the sixteenth- and seventeenth-century Thomist revival. During his discussion of the divine attributes, Barlow mentions, with approval: Diego Alvarez,[27] Juan Martinez de Ripalda,[28] Francis Silvester ('Ferrariensis'),[29] Domingo Banez,[30] Martin Becanus,[31] Francisco Suarez,[32] Gabriel Vasquez,[33] Adam Tanner,[34] John Paul Nazarius,[35] and Balthassar Navarrete.[36] Frequently, he will simply give a reference to one of Aquinas's *Summae* and then write '& commentatores,'[37] implying that some or all of these writers agree with him in their expositions of Aquinas on that point.

This preponderance of Roman Catholic authority is remarkable in itself.[38] It becomes even more so, when contrasted with the near total absence of Reformed writers from Barlow's work on the nature of God. In fact, virtually the only Reformed author who is cited with approval in the *Exercitationes* is

[21] E.g. Barlow, *Exercitationes*, pp10, 12, 97, 120, 186, and at many other places.

[22] E.g. ibid., p15. [23] E.g. ibid., p50. [24] E.g. ibid., p58.

[25] E.g. ibid., p109. [26] E.g. ibid.

[27] Ibid., p58 where he cites Alvarez's defence of the Thomist understanding of the interaction of grace and free will, the *De Auxiliis* (Rome, 1610).

[28] Barlow, *Exercitationes*, p121 where he cites both Martinez's *De Ente Supernaturali disputationes* (Bordeaux, 1634) and the *Expositio Brevis Litterae Magistri Sententiarum* (Salamanca, 1635).

[29] Barlow, *Exercitationes*, p121 where he cites Silvester's *Summa... contra gentiles... commentariis illustrata* (Lyons, 1587).

[30] Barlow, *Exercitationes*, p136 where he cites Banez's *Scholastica Commentaria in Iam partem Angelici Doctoris D. Thomae* (Douai, 1614).

[31] Barlow, *Exercitationes*, p243 where he cites Becanus's *Summa Theologicae Scholasticae* (Mainz, 1612).

[32] Barlow, *Exercitationes*, p203 where he cites Suarez's *Metaphysicarum Disputationum* (Mainz, 1600).

[33] Barlow, *Exercitationes*, p203 where he cites Vasquez's *Commentarium ac Disputationum in S. Thomae*, 3 vols (Alcala, 1599–1614).

[34] Barlow, *Exercitationes*, p203 where he cites Tanner's *Universa Theologica Scholastica* (Ingolstadt, 1526–27).

[35] Barlow, *Exercitationes*, p121 where he cites Nazarius's *Commentaria et Controversiae in Primam Partem Summae S. Thomae* (Bologna, 1620).

[36] Barlow, *Exercitationes*, p199 where he cites Navarrete's *Controversiae in Divi Thomae et Eius Defensionem* (Valladolid, 1609).

[37] E.g. Barlow, *Exercitationes*, p213.

[38] It is, however, not entirely without precedent. Sebastian Rehnman in 'John Owen: A Reformed Scholastic in Oxford' in Van Esselt and Dekker (eds.), *Reformation and Scholasticism*, pp193–194 has demonstrated John Owen's familiarity with the works of the Thomist revival. He has also indicated that Owen tended to use these authorities when he was dealing with metaphysics, just as Barlow had done. Of course, it may be that he learnt this habit from his tutor.

Girolamo Zanchi,[39] whose pronounced Thomism with regard to the doctrine of God has been pointed out in a recent study.[40] It seems clear that for Barlow, as for Pearson, the Thomist tradition is pre-eminent amongst the various traditions of thought about the doctrine of God. Barlow's approach in this area of doctrine is, therefore, very different from his approach in dealing with justification, where Protestant authorities were cited almost exclusively.

The other Reformed writers are not quite so candid as Pearson and Barlow about the authority they ascribe to the Thomist tradition. Though, since most of them were not writing specifically academic works, there is generally less citation of contemporary authors. Robert South was prepared to cite numbers of Thomist authors by name,[41] as was John Edwards.[42] Other writers were more circumspect, and tended to confine themselves to no more than the occasional reference to Aquinas himself. Even so, it is clear that, in terms of their substantive doctrine, they tread a very similar path to Pearson and Barlow. In fact, there is a sufficient degree of common ground that it seems feasible to argue that the post-Restoration Anglicans of a Reformed stamp were united as much by their common adherence to a Thomist conception of God, as they were by their shared loyalty to the Protestant understanding of justification.

## UNDERSTANDING THE NATURE OF GOD

Pearson's lecture series on the divine attributes is the only work which addresses all the contested issues, as well as being by far the most detailed exposition of the doctrine of God which was produced after the Restoration. It therefore seems reasonable to base our study of this area of divinity on that series, and to use the other Reformed authors by way of confirmation, expansion, or qualification of what Pearson himself maintained.

Pearson begins with a discussion of the existence of God and, more specifically, with the question of whether the existence of God is self-evident. His Thomist credentials soon become evident. The question, he argues, can be understood in two ways, namely: is the existence of God self-evident in itself? And is the existence of God self-evident to us? From these two questions, he says, four possible positions arise:

39 Barlow, *Exercitationes*, p187 where he cites Zanchi's *De Natura Dei* (Neustadt, 1590).

40 Harm Goris in 'Thomism in Zanchi's Doctrine of God,' in Van Esselt and Dekker (eds.), *Reformation and Scholasticism*, pp121–39.

41 South, *Animadversions*, pp271–4.

42 Edwards, *Theologia Reformata*, i p86. He lists Aquinas, Suarez, and Alvarez.

1. 'The existence of God is self-evident in itself.' So Thomas.
2. 'The existence of God is not self-evident in itself.' So Scotus.
3. 'The existence of God is not self-evident to us.' So Thomas and Scotus.
4. 'The existence of God is self-evident to us.' So Anselm.[43]

Needless to say, Pearson sides with Aquinas, and argues that the existence of God is self-evident in itself, but not self-evident to us.[44] God's existence is self-evident in itself, he thinks, because God's nature is such that God necessarily exists. To be God, in other words, means to exist. So whoever knows the nature of God, can deduce from that knowledge that God exists. As Pearson puts it: 'The foundation of this assertion is that God is a simply necessary being, to whom actual existence is proper by absolute necessity.'[45]

However, since human beings do not in fact know the nature of God, God's existence is not actually self-evident to us. Since we do not truly know what God is, we cannot make the deduction from what God is, to God's existence. Pearson writes: 'Since it is most remote from our senses, the nature of God is not at first apprehended and perceived by us; unless we are led, as if by the hand, by other things which, since they are made by him, call us back to the one by whom they were made.'[46] God's being is shrouded in mystery, and infinitely different from all the things which human beings can understand. Since we cannot approach God directly, through the means of our senses, we must proceed by deduction from the things we can sense, namely other created beings like ourselves.

God's existence is, therefore, demonstrable *a posteriori*, but not *a priori*, because there is nothing prior to God from which his existence may be deduced.[47] He writes: 'God's existence can be demonstrated *a posteriori*. That is, by those effects which flow from the same God, he, from whom these effects emanate, can be known to be God.'[48] And the demonstration Pearson believes to be most satisfactory is, of course, the demonstration most

[43] '1. "Deum esse, est per se notum secundum se." Ita Thomas. 2. "Deum esse, non est per se notum secundum se." Ita Scotus. 3. "Deum esse, non est per se notum quoad nos." Ita Thomas et Scotus. 4. "Deum esse, est per se notum quoad nos." Ita Anselmus.' Pearson, *Minor Theological Works*, i p12.

[44] Aquinas, S.Th., Ia q.2 art.1.

[45] 'Fundamentum huius assertionis est, quod deus sit ens simpliciter necessarium, cui actualis existentia absoluta necessitate competit.' Pearson, *Minor Theological Works*, i p12.

[46] 'Dei natura, cum sit a sensu omni nostro remotissima, non ita primo apprehenditur et percipitur a nobis; nisi manu quasi ducamur ab aliis rebus, quae cum sint ab eo effecta, ad ipsum nos, a quo profecta sunt revocant.' Ibid. p13.

[47] Ibid. p18. Aquinas, S.Th., Ia q.2 art.2.

[48] 'A posteriori demonstrari potest Deum esse. Id est, per ipsos effectus, qui ab ipso Deo manant [sic], potest intelligi, eum, a quo isti effectus emanarunt esse Deus.' Pearson, *Minor Theological Works*, i p19.

famously deployed by Thomas Aquinas, that argues from contingent effects to a necessary First Cause.[49]

Barlow follows Pearson in this view, writing: 'This, our knowledge of God, which arose from the light of nature, is not *a priori*.'[50] Like Pearson, he holds that since God is the First Cause, there is nothing prior to him from which his existence could be demonstrated.[51] Seth Ward concurs, arguing that 'to prove anything concerning the essence and nature of God *per causas* [through causes], by arguments *a priori* supposes causes precedent to the essence of God himself and implies a contradiction.'[52]

Barlow draws the conclusion that:

> Whatsoever we know about God by the light of nature is by mode of causality and *a posteriori*, arguing from an effect to the cause; so that whatever necessarily follows about God, given [the existence of] creatures, we know all that by the light of nature.[53]

Again, like Pearson, the demonstration of God's existence which Barlow favours is that which proceeds from these effects back to the First Cause upon whom all else depends.[54]

Beveridge works along similar lines, though his assumption that God's existence can only be known a posteriori is a tacit one. He writes: 'The usual reason that is brought for the existence of a deity is taken from the order of causes: to wit, because there must be some cause of all causes, which is the first cause of all other beings, itself being caused by no other being.'[55] Edwards is rather more expansive, but he too begins with the cosmological argument.[56] Furthermore, all the other arguments he advances in his demonstration of the existence of God are a posteriori in nature.[57]

[49] Ibid. p31. This is the second of the five ways to demonstrate God exists outlined in S.Th, Ia q.2 art.3.

[50] 'Haec nostra de Deo cognitio, a lumine naturali orta, non est a priori.' Barlow, *Exercitationes*, p128. He also follows Pearson and Aquinas in departing from Scotus's view that the existence of God was not even self-evident in itself: Ibid., p166.

[51] Ibid., p129.

[52] S. Ward, *Seven Sermons* (London, 1674), p63. This is in line with the approach taken to the matter by the majority of the European Reformed: Muller, *PRRD*, iii p183.

[53] 'Quicquid lumine naturali intellectus cognoscimus de Deo est per modum causalitatis & a posteriori, arguendo ab effectu ad causam; ita ut quicquid necessario sequetur de Deo ex positione creaturae, illud omne lumine naturale cognoscimus.' Barlow, *Exercitationes*, p141.

[54] Ibid., pp158–62.

[55] Beveridge, *Works*, vii p5.

[56] Edwards, *Theologica Reformata*, i pp10–11.

[57] He also uses arguments from the nature of the human soul; from the existence of an innate idea of God within the soul; from conscience; from universal consent; from miracles; from prophecies and from the preservation of the Church. Edwards, *Theologia Reformata*, i p4 et seq.

At one point, however, Edwards does indicate that, unlike Pearson or Barlow, he has some sympathy with the argument that God's existence is self-evident even to us. He writes:

It is natural and essential to him to be, and always to be. Thence that ingenious philosopher who argues from the idea of God to his existence argues not amiss, though some have ill managed this argument and have so stretched it as to make it inconclusive. But thus far we may go, existence is necessarily contained in our notion and conception of the divine being, he being the most perfect *Ens*, and therefore we may conclude from our idea of him that he is. God's existence is not any thing superadded to his essence, but it is included in it.[58]

Edwards is clearly somewhat unsure about the strength of this argument, however. He does mention it during his series of arguments for the existence of God, but then says 'But this way of proof may perhaps be too subtle, and therefore I will not insist upon it.'[59] Even so, though it indicates that he disagrees with Pearson about the merits of Descartes, it equally serves to shows that he agrees with Pearson (and Aquinas) that God's existence is, in itself, self-evident.

Having demonstrated that God is, Pearson moves on to discuss what God is. He notes at the outset that, 'About this essence, when we pursue our inquiry by the question "What is God?" we do not on that account proceed as if we could equally know the quiddity [what something is] of God and the quiddity of other things; for that cannot be done.'[60] The reason for this, he thinks, is that whereas in any created thing, its effects are equal to its essence, and so its essence may be comprehended through those effects, with God, this is not not the case. All created beings are finite in nature and finite in power, and their effects are also finite in nature and finite in power. God, by contrast, is infinite in nature and power, whereas the things God creates are neither of those things. They are, therefore, not equal to his essence.

This, of course, makes understanding God on the basis of what he has made rather difficult. As Pearson writes: 'The effects of God cannot be equal to the nature of God. Therefore the knowledge of God which is assembled from his

[58] Edwards, *Theologia Reformata*, i p46. Turretin seems to have some sympathy for this view as well: *Institutes*, Topic III q.1.18. Pearson clearly does not: *Minor Theological Works*, i p28 et seq.

[59] Edwards, *Theologia Reformata*, i p22, where he specifically ascribes the ontological argument to Descartes. He opts instead for the argument that the existence of an idea of God within us demonstrates His own existence, since it is an idea which we could not have invented ourselves (i.e. an a posteriori form of the argument).

[60] 'De hac autem essentia, cum quaerimus in quaestione, Quid sit Deus, non hoc ideo facimus, ut aeque cognoscamus quidditatem Dei, ac cognoscimus aliarum rerum quidditates, id enim fieri nullo modo potest.' Pearson, *Minor Theological Works*, i p34.

effects cannot be adequate to the divine quiddity.'[61] But although we cannot fully comprehend God's essence, we can, nonetheless, apprehend certain properties as pertaining to God's essence. We can therefore predicate those properties of that essence, and we therefore call those properties divine attributes.[62]

Pearson underlines, however, that there is a distinction between those properties which are 'properly' predicated of God, and so are true of him in a literal (albeit analogical) sense, and those which are 'improperly' predicated of God, and are therefore true of God only in a figurative or metaphorical sense. He writes:

> Those things are properly predicated of God which signify some perfection and do not include any imperfection in their formal definition, such as goodness, wisdom, justice.... Those things are improperly predicated of God which involve some imperfection in their concepts, as repentance, pain.[63]

Pearson underlines that only those properties which can be properly predicated of God actually signify a divine attribute. In other words, the attributes are the kinds of perfection which have no imperfections necessarily attached to them.

Amongst the divine attributes, Pearson then observes a further distinction; namely, between those attributes which are negative in nature and those attributes which are positive in nature. Of the first sort, he writes: 'those negations are called attributes which formally eliminate from God some imperfection, in such a way that they consequently denote some special perfection of God,'[64] and they include the divine attributes of simplicity, incorporeality, infinity, immensity, immutability, etc. Of the second sort, he writes: 'positive attributes are those which formally reveal some positive perfection and attribute it to God like a property,'[65] and they include wisdom, goodness, justice, omnipotence, etc.

Already, Pearson's divergence from the avant-garde position on the divine attributes is clear. He has effectively rejected the distinction between communicable and incommunicable attributes, in favour of a distinction between

[61] 'Effectus Dei non possunt adaequare naturam Dei. Cognitio itaque dei, ex effectibus Ipsius comparata, non potest esse quidditati divinae adaequata.' Ibid.

[62] Ibid. p37.

[63] 'Illa proprie de Deo praedicantur, quae significant aliquam perfectionem, nec imperfectionem aliquam in sua formali ratione involvunt, ut bonitas, saptientia, iustitia.... Illa improprie de Deo praedicantur, quae imperfectionem aliquam in suis conceptibus involvunt, ut poenitentia, dolor.' Ibid. See also: J. Wilkins, *Of the Principles and Duties of Natural Religion* (London, 1710), p101; Newcome, *Catechetical Course*, I p78.

[64] 'Illae tantum negationes attributa dicuntur, quae aliquam imperfectionem ita a deo formaliter removent, ut eo ipso specialem aliquam Dei perfectionem consequenter denotent.' Pearson, *Minor Theological Works*, i p38.

[65] 'Attributa positiva illa sunt, quae perfectionem aliquam positivam formaliter indicant, eamque quasi proprietatem quandam divinae naturae attribuunt.' Ibid. Pearson, *Minor Theological Works*, i p38.

negative and positive attributes.[66] This divergence becomes clearer still when he goes on to discuss the relative merits of the two sorts of attribute. He writes: 'Of these two sorts of attribute, it should be noted that the negative attributes are, in a way, more perfect than the affirmative ones.'[67] The reason for this, he argues, is that in any negation about God, not only is the negation itself true, but the concept being negated is completely understood by the one making the negation, since an imperfection is something which a finite mind can grasp.

This stands in contrast to the affirmations which are made in the positive attributes, about which Pearson writes:

> In an affirmative proposition, although the affirmation is true, nonetheless, the predicate, as it is affirmed to be in God, is not understood distinctly and adequately, but confusedly, because we conceive by it something much more excellent than that which we ordinarily signify by the same predicate in creatures, and of which we do have a distinct concept.[68]

The extent of Pearson's disagreement with the avant-garde writers on this point is striking. As we have seen, for Tillotson, Whitby, and Clarke the positive or communicable attributes of God such as goodness, justice, and holiness, take priority in all discussions about the divine nature since, in their view, we fully grasp what those terms mean. For Pearson, the contrary is true. He argues that we cannot fully understand what goodness, justice, and holiness are in God since they are not the same in him as they are in us. As a result, it is the negative attributes which are ultimately more significant to our understanding of God.[69]

Beveridge's view is a virtual echo of Pearson's, both as to his conclusions about how best we are to understand God, and as to the reasons for those conclusions. He writes:

[66] It is interesting to note that the communicable/incommunicable distinction was well-established within Reformed orthodoxy, whereas the positive/negative distinction is more common amongst Lutheran writers. R. Muller, *Dictionary of Latin and Greek Theological Terms* (Grand Rapids, 1998), s.v. 'attributa divina.' Turretin certainly defends the communicable/incommunicable distinction: *Institutes*, Topic 3 q.6.

[67] 'De his duobus attributorum generibus observandum est, attributa negativa esse affirmativis aliquo modo perfectiora.' Pearson, *Minor Theological Works*, i p38.

[68] 'In propositione affirmativa, licet affirmatio vera sit, tamen praedicatum, prout esse in Deo affirmatur, non distincte et adaequate cognoscitur, sed confuse, quia eo ipso concipimus aliquid in Deo multo excellentius, quam sit illud quod per idem praedicatum significare solemus in creaturis, et cuius nos habemus distinctum conceptum.' Pearson, *Minor Theological Works*, i p38. He reiterates this view later on in his lectures: Ibid., p136.

[69] The contrast is, of course, even greater between Pearson and Crellius, who dismissed negative attributes as being no more than an unhelpful way of expressing positive attributes. Pearson's evaluation of the usefulness of negative attributes in discussions of the divine nature reflects what Aquinas has to say on the matter: *SCG* ch.14.2.

When we poor finite creatures set ourselves to consider of our infinite creator, though we may apprehend something of him by ascribing all perfections to him, yet more by removing all imperfections from him. We cannot so well apprehend what he is as what he is not. We can say indeed he is infinitely good, infinitely wise, in and of himself, eternal and all-sufficient: but alas! When we speak such words we cannot apprehend the thing that is signified by them. Our understandings, being themselves finite, they cannot apprehend what it is to be infinite, and, as they are imperfect, they cannot conceive of any perfection as it is in God. But now of imperfections we have the daily experience in ourselves, and therefore know the better how to abstract them all from our apprehensions of the deity: and so the clearest apprehension that we can have of him is by removing imperfections from him.[70]

Edwards is of a similar mind, though he rejects Pearson's distinction between positive and negative attributes on the basis that even negative attributes are actually founded upon some positive excellency in God, though one which has no obvious creaturely parallel.[71] Nonetheless, he is at one with Pearson in abandoning the distinction between communicable and incommunicable attributes, and is rather more explicit that this is what he is doing. Edwards mentions this traditional Reformed distinction, but then writes:

But if we will speak properly and exactly, we must needs say that all God's attributes are incommunicable; because they are infinite.... It is true that some of these excellencies, knowledge, goodness & c. are in men, but they are but shadows and resemblances of the like perfections in God.[72]

He notes three differences between all the divine attributes and their analogies in human beings. First, the divine perfections exist essentially in God (i.e. are one with his essence), whereas they are not so in us (since we are distinct from our knowledge, our goodness etc.). Secondly, they exist originally and radically in God, whereas they exist in us only derivatively (i.e. as gifts from him). Thirdly, they exist in God eminently and to an infinite degree, whereas in us they are expressed only partially and to a finite degree. As a result, Edwards argues, 'the divine attributes cannot properly be said to be communicated to men, but are spoken and meant of God, in a different way from what is found in us.'[73]

[70] Beveridge, *Works*, vii pp24–5.

[71] Edwards, *Theologia Reformata*, i p44. Edwards proposes instead a distinction between the primary and secondary attributes of God which is similar, in some respects, to the distinction which some Reformed writers adopted under the influence of Descartes, between God's essential governing attributes and those of his intellect and will. See Muller, *Dictionary of Latin and Greek Theological Terms*, s.v. 'attributa divina'.

[72] Ibid. The rejection of the distinction between communicable and incommunicable attributes was not without precedent within the Reformed tradition, though it was a minority opinion: Muller, *PRRD*, iii pp223–4.

[73] Ibid.

In Edward's work on predestination, *Veritas Redux*, which stands as one of the two preliminary parts to the *Theologia Reformata*,[74] he applies his understanding of the divine attributes to the Socinian and Remonstrant arguments against the decree of reprobation. He notes that these writers maintain that it is unjust of God to deny grace to some when he could bestow it. His answer is forthright, and he evidently has his English contemporaries in mind in addition to the earlier continental theologians.

It is a false and groundless notion (tho' much cried up by our late divines) that we are to look for the same dispositions in God that we find in ourselves. There is a difference between God and his creatures as to the properties and excellencies which are observable in both. We are not to attribute the same characters to God that we do to rational creatures of humane kind. And therefore we cannot absolutely argue from what is fitting for man to do that the same must be done by God. To say, no just or good man would do thus or thus, therefore the Most High doth not is inconsequential. For justice in God and man is different, and so is mercifulness and goodness.[75]

This is evident, Edwards thinks, upon a little consideration. It is, for example, morally wrong for a human being to allow an evil deed to be perpetrated when it is within his or her power to prevent it. Again, it is morally wrong for a human being not to do all the good that he or she is able to do. It is also morally wrong for a human being not to relieve another's suffering when he or she can. It is clear, however, that none of these propositions can be true of God. God evidently does not prevent all evil, relieve all suffering or do all the good that his infinite power makes him capable of doing, yet we do not conclude from these things that God is not good.[76] The avant-garde writers, he thinks, are simply guilty of anthropomorphism: they are making God in a human image. Edwards underlines: 'the actions of God to his creatures, and theirs to one another, are not of the same kind, but proceed upon different circumstances and considerations. . . . It must needs be so unless we can make the creator and his creatures, divine and humane to be the same.'[77]

The other Reformed writers echo the positions of Pearson, Beveridge, and Edwards on these points. None of them is prepared to countenance the drawing of straightforward conclusions about the divine nature, from what the parallel attributes would entail when embodied in a human being. For all of them, the gulf between the divine attributes and their human echoes is simply too vast to permit such reasoning.

The threefold difference which Edwards elaborated between the divine attributes, and their human counterparts, finds a remarkably close echo in

[74] Edwards, J., *Veritas Redux: Evangelical Truths Restored* (London, 1707), pi.
[75] Ibid., pp194–5. [76] Ibid., p198. [77] Ibid., p202.

Ezekiel Hopkins. All creaturely perfection falls far short of God's attributes, Hopkins writes, on account

1st. That they have them not originally from themselves; but derivatively from another who is the author and embellisher of their natures. 2ndly. That they have them not unchangeably; but may not only increase, but decrease, yea or utterly lose them. 3rdly. That they have them not infinitely; but in a stinted and limited measure.[78]

As a result, he thinks, even those attributes which are commonly called communicable are never in fact communicated to human beings. Rather they are simply ways of distinguishing God from all other beings.[79]

Robert South is emphatic both that the divine nature is inherently incomprehensible, and also that any attributes which are ascribed to him do not mean anything like the same thing in God, as they do in human beings. He writes:

God, the creator of all things, an object fitter for our adoration, than our curious, but yet weak inquiries, is infinite in his being, and so consequently not to be comprehended by our finite understandings: yet since he is pleased to command us to worship him, which we cannot rationally do, unless in some measure we know him; he is therefore pleased to aid our weak conceptions, by several expressions of himself, which we call attributes; as, that he is just, wise, merciful and the like: all which, according to the common notions we have of justice, wisdom, and mercy, are not strictly and properly to be found in God; so that indeed, these words, as by us applied to him, rather testify our reverential desires of honouring him, than at all express his nature.[80]

The divine attributes are, therefore, profoundly dissimilar to their equivalents in human beings. Indeed, the most that can be said is that there is some limited analogy, or proportion, between the effects which flow from a divine attribute and the effects of the equivalent human attribute. So, for example, God is called merciful because some of his acts resemble those that in human beings would be called merciful; and God is called powerful because some of his acts are like those which, in human beings, are the results of exercising power.[81]

Delaune too thinks that God's attributes are fundamentally different from their human counterparts. Like Hopkins, he thinks that they serve as much to distinguish God from his creation as they do to express him intelligibly. As he puts it,

His perfections are such as transcendentally distinguish him from all other beings. He stands alone, in the midst of his works; nor was that power, which was able out of nothing to call them into being, able to give them any thing in common with their

78 Hopkins, *Works*, i p73. 79 Ibid. 80 South, *Sermons*, v p34.

81 Ibid. p36. Hopkins says much the same: Hopkins, *Works*, p71.

great Creator. In all the hosts of heaven, there is not one that bares any more than a bare resemblance of him, and that a very faint one, at a distance no less than infinite.[82]

Wilkins goes even further, arguing that 'the highest perfections that are in men, besides that they are derived from him, are so infinitely disproportionable to his, that they may be said not to be in any of the creatures.'[83] Robert Boyle echoes Wilkins, urging that

though divers of God's attributes are through his goodness participated by his creatures, yet the scripture makes so vast a disparity betwixt the excellencies that it ascribes to men, and the same perfections as they exist in God, that it seems absolutely to exclude created beings from any title to those attributes; because they possess them but in a way so inferior to that transcendent, peculiar and divine manner, in which they belong to God.[84]

In other words, God possesses his goodness, justice, etc. so perfectly and transcendently, that in comparison to God, human beings do not really possess such attributes at all.

Because of the difference between attributes as they exist in God and as they might exist in human beings, several of the Reformed echo Pearson and Beveridge's preference for the negative way of discussing the nature of God. Newcome, for example, says of the spirituality of the divine nature, 'the positive notion whereof, whatever it be, yet it may suffice us to conceive of it by way of negation. That it is not matter; without figure or parts; not visible to our bodily eyes, nor subject to the laws of matter.'[85] Wilkins adopts an identical approach to this question.[86]

Horton, for his part, holds that the divine attributes are so unique, that it is doubtful whether any way of understanding them is truly adequate to the task. He points out that it is not possible to know God as the cause of what he has made, because he exercised only a tiny fraction of his power in making them. Echoing Pearson's position on the matter, he underlines that 'the effect cannot show the essence of its cause, but when it is the same with it in kind, and has the whole virtue of the cause in it. The creature shows that there is a God, from whom all things receive their being; but what this God is it doth not show.'[87] Consequently, the way of causation is not very illuminating about the nature of God.

Neither, he thinks, is the way of eminence, 'because none of those [perfections we predicate of God] are predicated of God and the creature after an univocal manner; and they do only show what manner of one he is, but not

[82] Delaune, *Twelve Sermons*, p248.
[83] Wilkins, *Principles and Duties*, p206.
[84] Boyle, *Works*, i p70. See also: ibid., x p187.
[85] Newcome, *Catechetical Course*, i p78.
[86] Wilkins, *Principles and Duties*, p106.
[87] Horton, *Hundred Sermons*, ii p133.

what he is.'[88] Even the way of negation is not much more helpful, Horton thinks, since all it does is discover what God is not—though, he does assume that such negative knowledge is dependable in its way.[89] So he concludes simply that 'the nature and essence of God in the fulness, it is beyond any created comprehension.'[90]

For Wallis, the disparity between the divine nature and all human conceptions of it is so great, that even the scriptures are an inadequate guide to God's essence. He writes, of the bible,

> it transmits some rays, some beams of the divine nature; but they are refracted, or else we should not be able to behold them. They lose much of their lustre by passing through this medium, and appear not so glorious to us, as they are in themselves. They represent God's simplicity obliquated [*sic*] and refracted, by reason of many inadequate conceptions; God condescending to the weakness of our capacity, to speak to us in our own dialect.[91]

All discussion of the divine attributes is thus the result of God's accommodating himself to human intellectual weakness. For the awesome reality to which such discussion refers is far beyond all human power to grasp.

For the Reformed, therefore, God's being is such a profound mystery, that any human attempt to understand it is fraught with difficulty. There is, in other words, no easy way into that mystery by contemplating one kind of attribute rather than another. All the divine attributes are equally beyond the reach of human understanding. The disparity between the divine nature and all created beings is such that there are no easy reasonings across the gulf.[92]

## THE DIVINE SIMPLICITY

Having established that the negative attributes are a better place to start trying to understand God than the positive ones, Pearson moves on to discuss the first such attribute: divine simplicity. It soon becomes clear that, once again, Pearson's view is very different from that of the avant-garde authors. Because Pearson's understanding of divine simplicity is the full-blooded conception of Thomas Aquinas, and, as we shall see, it plays a significant role in his later discussions of the other divine attributes.

[88] Ibid. [89] Ibid.

[90] Ibid. p134. See also Wilkins, *Principles and Duties*, pp124–5.

[91] Wallis, *Sermons*, p128.

[92] In this, the Anglican Reformed echo the instincts of the wider Reformed tradition: Muller, *PRRD*, iii pp195–6, 199–200.

Pearson defines simplicity as follows:

> Simplicity in general is nothing other than the removal or negation of composition: when therefore we assert that simplicity is an attribute of God, we do not wish [to mean] anything other than that God is devoid of all composition.[93]

Pearson believes that all composition whatever is a mark of imperfection, and must be excluded from our conception of God. This is because, in any composition, the part is both prior to the whole and less than the whole (and, therefore, limited in some way). But the God who is the First Cause can have nothing prior to him; and the God who is infinite cannot be made up of limited (and therefore finite) parts.[94]

Pearson is clear; divine simplicity excludes all composition: there are consequently no real distinctions within God's being. So, he argues, God is not composed of matter and form, nor of actuality and potentiality. He is, in other words, both mere form and pure act.[95] God is also not composed of an abstract nature and a distinct subject which enables the nature to subsist (he calls this a *suppositum*). The most perfect being cannot but subsist, else the Godhead, he argues, would be distinct from God, which is absurd.[96] Again, God is not composed of essence and existence, since, as he has already argued, the divine nature necessarily exists.[97] God is also not composed of corporeal or quantitative parts, since he lacks a body.[98] He is also not made up of genus and species,[99] or of substance and accidents.[100] Needless to say, these sorts of composition are precisely those which Aquinas himself excluded from the essence of God.

Pearson also follows Aquinas in the assertion that God is also not really distinct from his attributes and that those attributes are not really distinct from each other.[101] If they were distinct, Pearson urges, then since the

[93] 'Simplicitas in genere nihil aliud est quam remotio, sive negatio compositionis: cum itaque simplicitatem attributum Dei asserimus, nihil aliud volumus, quam Deum esse omnis compositionis expertem.' Pearson, *Minor Theological Works*, i p43. See also: Hopkins, *Works*, p71; Reynolds, *Works*, p736; Wilkins, *Principles and Duties*, p104; Welchman, *Articles*, p3. This is the common definition of the Reformed tradition: Muller, *PRRD*, iii pp277–9.

[94] Pearson, *Minor Theological Works*, i pp44–5.

[95] Ibid. p46. See also: S. Ward, *A Philosophical Essay towards an Eviction of the Being and Attributes of God* (London, 1652), pp23–4. Aquinas, S.Th., Ia q.3 art.2.

[96] Ibid. art.2, art.3.

[97] Pearson, *Minor Theological Works*, i p47. Aquinas, S.Th., Ia q.3 art.4. see also: Boyle, *Works*, xii p400.

[98] Ibid. Aquinas, S.Th., Ia q.3 art. 1.

[99] Pearson, *Minor Theological Works*, i p52. Aquinas, S.Th. Ia q.3 art.5.

[100] Ibid. art.5, art.6.

[101] Pearson, *Minor Theological Works*, i p39. Richard Cross has shown that this is the mark of a distinctly Thomist, as opposed to Scotist, conception of the divine simplicity. Cross, *Duns Scotus*, pp43–5. Aquinas, S.Th., Ia q.3 art.3 and *SCG*, ch.21.

attributes of God are the perfections of God, it would follow that the essence of God was not itself perfect but derived its perfection from the attributes in which it participated but from which it was separate. Instead, Pearson argues, the divine attributes are of the essence of God, and he contains all his perfections within himself.[102] Furthermore, those divine perfections are, in God, but one completely simple perfection,[103] 'because all the perfections which are in God are not really distinct from each other, nor are they really distinct from the divine essence itself... therefore they are entirely one and the same thing.'[104]

Tully and Barlow both follow Pearson in this. Tully enquires whether God is composed, given that he has several attributes, and answers 'Certainly not: for those properties are neither separate from the divine nature, nor really from each other; and so they do not imply any composition.'[105] Barlow, for his part, asserts that God is 'simple and indivisible in every way,' by which he means that 'just as a point exhibits itself to the touch and has absolutely no tangible and quantitive parts; so God has, to the intellect, no intelligible parts. But he is a most simple being, excluding all manner of composition.'[106] This, he believes, follows directly from the fact that God is the First Cause. Any composition, he argues, needs a cause outside itself; but God has no cause outside himself, therefore his essence cannot be composed in any way.[107]

Later on, when Barlow is discussing divine eternity, he discusses how his understanding of divine simplicity relates to the multiplicity of the divine attributes. He writes of the divine essence: 'since this is simple in every way... it follows that eternity is the being of God. Eternity therefore signifies that same being of God considered in abstract, though inadequately, insofar as it connotes his infinite persistence in being.'[108] In other words, when we speak of divine eternity (or, of course, any other divine attribute), we are really signifying

[102] Pearson, *Minor Theological Works*, i p40.

[103] Ibid. p59.

[104] 'Quia omnes perfectiones quae sunt in Deo, non sunt a se ipsis realiter distinctae, neque sunt ab ipsa essentia divina realiter distinctae... ergo sunt omnino res una atque eadem.' Ibid. p60. The rejection of any real distinction between the divine attributes, and between the divinie attributes and the divine essence reflected the Reformed tradition on the matter. Muller, *PRRD*, iii pp288–9.

[105] 'Nequaquam: sunt enim istae proprietates neque ab essentia Divina, neque a se realiter disjunctae; unde nec ullam inferunt compositionem.' Tully, *Enchiridion*, p13.

[106] 'Omnimodo simplex et indivisibilis sicut punctam se habet ad tactum & partes tangibiles & quantitativas nullas omnino habet; sic Deus ad intellectum nec partes intelligibiles ullas habet. Sed est entitas simplicissima, compositionem excludens omnimodam.' Barlow, *Exercitationes*, pp162–3.

[107] Ibid., p178.

[108] 'Cum haec omnimodo simplex est... sequetur quod aeternitas sit ipsum Dei esse. Aeternitas ideo significat ipsum Dei esse in abstracto consideratum, inadaequate tamen, in quantum connotat infinitam eius permanentiam in essendo.' Ibid., p219.

the divine essence, since God's eternity (like any other attribute), by virtue of the divine simplicity, is not distinct from God's essence. Nonetheless, Barlow says, eternity can only signify the divine essence inadequately, since it expresses but one aspect of the divine perfection. Even so, he underlines:

When I say that an attribute of God signifies the essence of God inadequately because any attribute of God that you will [signifies] one particular perfection of God, not all [of them]: this is not therefore to be understood as if, *ex parte rei*, there were distinct and separate perfections in God; for this is impossible; since God, *ex parte rei*, as he is in himself, is but one infinite and most simple perfection: but this is to be understood [as] a consequence of the imperfection of our conceptions, who, since we do not comprehend the best and greatest God as he is in himself, must apprehend him according to our imperfect manner of understanding. So that we do not acknowledge this imperfection to be in God, the thing conceived, but only in our intellect which is doing the conceiving; we apprehend that infinite and inexpressably perfect essence of God according to our small measure, not according to its merits.[109]

The distinctions which we observe between the divine attributes are, for Barlow, merely distinctions created by the human mind to enable us to grasp the truth of the divine being, not distinctions which really exist in God.[110]

The distinctions we impose between the divine attributes are artificial distinctions, he thinks, because they are all derived from things outside God. We derive some distinctions from the imperfections which the negative attributes eliminate. Thus, for example, we distinguish eternity, which involves the elimination of temporal limits, from ubiquity, which involves the elimination of spatial limits. We derive other distinctions in God from the different effects of divine action. So we distinguish justice from mercy, because punishing is one thing and forgiving is another, though in God the justice and mercy from which these actions proceed are really the same thing. Neither is this kind of purely intellectual distinction unprecedented, for 'in this way, we are able to distinguish in the sun that power which melts wax from that which hardens mud,

[109] 'Cum dico, quod attributum Dei significat essentiam Dei inadaequate, nempe quodvis attributum perfectionem Dei unam aliquam, non omnem: hoc non ita intelligendum, quasi ex parte rei esset in Deo perfectio una, & altera; hoc enim impossibile; cum Deus ex parte rei, prout un se est, sit solum perfectio una, infinita & simplicissima: sed hoc intelligendum est in ordine ad conceptum nostrum imperfectum, qui cum Deum opt. max. prout in se est non apprehendamus, pro modo nostro intelligendi imperfecto apprehendimus. Ita tamen ut imperfectionem hanc in Deo, seu re concepta, nec agnoscimus; sed solum in intellectu nostro concipiente, qui infinitam illam Dei essentiam, & ultra quam dici possit perfectam pro modulo nostro apprehendimus, non pro merito suo.' Ibid., p220.

[110] In this, Barlow, and the other Anglican Reformed who echo his views, are probably following the modified Thomism of Francisco Suarez. Their approach to this issue is one of several found within the wider Reformed tradition, and is shared, amongst others, by John Owen, Barlow's former pupil. Muller, *PRRD*, iii pp289–90. Muller argues that this was not actually the view of Aquinas himself: Ibid., pp53–8.

which is, however, really one in the sun.'[111] Finally, we derive some distinctions by drawing an analogy with the properties of created beings between which there are real distinctions. Thus, for example, we distinguish between the divine intellect and the divine will, since these faculties are distinct within ourselves. However, none of the distinctions we make correspond to a real distinction within the divine being. In God, essence and attributes are one.

This strong expression of divine simplicity is also found in Beveridge and Edwards. Beveridge underlines that God 'is usually and truly apprehended as the most pure and simple act.'[112] This means, he writes, that God is:

> Without all mixture or composition whatever; whether of matter and form, as man is compounded of soul and body; or of subject and accident, as a wise man, of wisdom and a man; or of act and power, as any thing that is, but may not be, or is not, but may be; or of *genus* and *differentia*, as when a specifical difference restrains a general nature to a certain species contained under it; or lastly, of *esse* and *essentia*, as when a things is said to be by its essence.[113]

Furthermore, Beveridge is at one with Pearson, Barlow, and Tully in arguing that there is no real distinction between God and his attributes or between the attributes themselves. He writes:

> What we have is really distinguished from what we are. And therefore when we speak of God, in whom there is no distinction of one perfection from another, or of any of them from himself, we speak more agreeably to his nature, and more conformably to his truth, when we say he is, rather than hath such a perfection.[114]

So, Beveridge argues, when we speak of the divine properties or attributes, we do not mean that there are several different attributes in him as there are in us. Instead, he says, echoing Barlow, when we call something a property or attribute in God, we mean that it is an apprehension which we have of him based upon his activity within the world. We see him punishing the wicked and call it justice, we see him pardoning the sinner and call it mercy, we see him doing what he desires and so call him omnipotent, etc.

> And thus are the several properties that we attribute to him but the several apprehensions that we have in ourselves of him, according to the several discoveries that he maketh of himself to us: and therefore, though as they are conceived by us, they are many, yet, as they are in him, they are all but one and the same simple essence.[115]

[111] 'Hunc modum possumus in sole distinguere vim illam qua emmolit butyrum, & lutum indurat, quae tamen est realiter una in sole.' Barlow, *Exercitationes*, p221.

[112] Beveridge, *Works*, vii p3.

[113] Ibid. p25.

[114] Ibid. p3. He reiterates this view at greater length pp13–14.

[115] Ibid. p16.

These apprehensions, Beveridge notes, again following Barlow, are the result of the finiteness of the human intellect, which is quite incapable of understanding the infinite as it is in itself, and must necessarily grasp it piecemeal, by imposing our own distinctions upon it.[116]

Edward's view is virtually identical to Beveridge's. He too asserts a full-blooded conception of simplicity, writing that,

> This divine property excludes all mixture, all alloys . . . for whatever is in God is God himself, and therefore he must be pure, simple and unmixed. He is not (as finite and created beings) composed of matter and form, or of subject and accident, &c. but is void of all physical and metaphysical composition.[117]

Like the other writers, he also underlines that God's essence is not distinct from his attributes, 'for the wisdom of God, is God himself, and the power of God is God himself, and so is his goodness, and the like we may say of all the other attributes.'[118] And again, like the other writers, he considers that the distinctions we observe between the divine attributes are the consequence of our limited understanding, not the result of real distinctions within the divine being. He writes:

> But this is some help and ease to our understandings, that these are different considerations of the divine essence and nature; and so that what was hard, yea impossible to conceive in the whole and gross, and in its abstract and simple nature, becomes intelligible by being distributed into several ways of conception. For the attributes of God are the several particular excellencies and perfections of his nature, which we form distinct and separate apprehensions of: so that we do consider apart one and the same perfect being, which makes the knowledge of it more facile to us. Because of the imperfection of our understandings which cannot conceive altogether, we divide our notions, and contemplate the same infinite being under diverse apprehensions: for though God's essence be one, yet his attributes, which are the several modes of his displaying his essence, are many.[119]

Robert Boyle, too, insists on the fundamental unity of all the divine attributes with the divine essence. He writes,

> though even the rational soul (or mind) is, according to divines and philosophers, endowed with faculties properly so called, and distinguishable from its essence, yet in God it is generally acknowledged to be otherwise, according to the received axiom; *quicquid est in Deo, Deus est* [whatever is in God, is God].[120]

Hopkins repeatedly cites this scholastic axiom as well.[121]

[116] Beveridge, *Works*, p17. [117] Edwards, *Theologia Reformata*, i p50.
[118] Ibid. p43. [119] Ibid. See also Seth Ward, *Philosophical Essay*, p25.
[120] Boyle, *Works*, xii p400. [121] Hopkins, *Works*, i p71, 194.

Following the other Reformed writers, Boyle then argues that the distinction of the divine attributes from one another is a tool used by our minds in order to approach an understanding of God. He writes:

The simplicity alone and infinity, that are universally ascribed to the divine nature, when they come to be somehat attentively looked into by theologisers [*sic*], reduced them to confess, that though justice and mercy and many other attributes ... may be truly ascribed to God, yet in effect they are but inadequate notions of the same most simple being, and that [the] reason of teaching such attributes to be found in God, is that by reason of the imperfection of our understandings, which cannot at one view give us an entire idea of that perfect being, we are reduced to frame inadequate notions of his perfections, that we may, as far as we can, have an idea in parcels of what we cannot apprehend at once.[122]

John Conant adopts a similar conception of divine simplicity. He writes:

All the attributes of God are essential to him. They are all of the very nature of God, and so the same with him; according to that axiom, *quicquid est in Deo, est Deus.* And hence it follows, that all the attributes of God are infinite, and eternal, and unchangeable, as he himself is.[123]

He believes this principle extends even to those attributes which have respect to creation, such as the divine will and the acts that proceed from it. They too are of the very nature of God.[124] These views find further echoes in William Delaune,[125] and Robert South.[126]

This strong doctrine of divine simplicity, held, as we have seen, by all the Reformed who discuss the matter, is subsequently deployed in arguments concerning the other attributes. In particular, it is used to reject erroneous conceptions of God's infinity with regard to time and space.

## ETERNITY AND UBIQUITY

Pearson asserts that 'God is properly and simply eternal.'[127] By this he means that God's being is of everlasting duration. However, he writes,

it should therefore be noted that both the philosophers and the holy fathers have taught that eternity is not successive but absolutely indivisible and completely

122 Boyle, *Works*, xii p401.

123 J. Conant, *Sermons on Several Subjects* (London, 1736), p242.

124 Ibid.

125 Delaune, *Twelve Sermons*, p251.

126 South, *Sermons*, v p35.

127 'Deus est proprie et simpliciter aeternus.' Pearson, *Minor Theological Works*, i p97.

simultaneous, so that it has in itself no parts, properly so called, nor any distinction of past, present and future.[128]

To demonstrate this, Pearson thinks, only one argument needs to be advanced. He writes: 'The truth of this assertion is demonstrated by one argument: the essence or substance of God is indivisible,'[129] which is to say, simple. For Pearson, in other words, divine simplicity has a key regulating role in our conception of the other attributes.

Barlow discusses the divine eternity at greater length, but it is clear that the divine simplicity is an important factor in his approach as well. He notes at the beginning of his discussion that eternity is a mysterious concept. 'Infinite indeed are those spaces of eternity,' he writes, 'which our intellect could neither traverse nor capture.'[130] By eternity, he writes, theologians wish to express the perpetual duration of the divine being which is without beginning or end. Eternity is, therefore, to some extent a measure of the duration of God's being, but unlike other temporal measures it implies neither limits nor succession. It is a measure both prior to and greater than all other temporal measures.

He writes: 'Eternity is a simple measure, and absolutely indivisible, such that in it, nothing is before or after, but it is all simultaneous, like a kind of immense and infinite indivisibility.'[131] It follows that eternity, unlike ordinary measures of time, admits of no intrinsic temporal parts from which it is made up. Even so, Barlow is willing to grant that priority and posteriority exist extrinsically in eternity, since all lesser measures of time are, he argues, comprised within the one eternal moment.[132] He writes:

Because eternity, since it is simply the prime measure, and the first in any sort of thing is the rule and measure of the rest; it is necessary that it comprehend the inferior measures, age and time. So that eternity has before and after within itself not by intrinsic denomination, or subjectively; but only by extrinsic denomination, or inclusively; inasmuch as it comprehends inferior measures, in which truly are before and after.[133]

[128] 'Notandum itaque est tum philosophos, tum S.S. Patres tradidisse aeternitatem non esse successivam, sed prorsus indivisibilem, totamque simul, ita ut nullas in se proprie dictas partes habet, differentiamve ullam praeteriti, praesentis aut futuri.' Ibid. p104.

[129] 'Unico argumento veritas huius assertionis demonstratur: essentia, seu substantia Dei, est indivisibilis.' Ibid. p106.

[130] 'Infinita enim sunt illa aeternitatis spatia quae nec percurrat intellectus noster nec capiat.' Barlow, *Exercitationes*, p180.

[131] 'Aeternitas est mensura simplex, et absolute indivisibilis ita ut in illa nullum sit prius, aut posterius, sed est tota simul, immensa quaedam, et infinita indivisibilitas.' Ibid. p198.

[132] Ibid., pp198–9.

[133] 'Quia aeternitas, cum sit mensura simpliciter prima, et primum in unoquoque genere sit regula et mensura reliquarum; necesse est ut mensuras inferiores, aevum et tempus comprehendat. Ita ut aeternitas habeat in se prius et posterius non per denominationem intrinsecam, seu subjective; sed solum per denominationem extrinsecam, seu comprehensive: utpote mensuras inferiores comprehendens in quibus prius & posterius revera insunt.' Ibid., p199.

Barlow asserts that a successive idea of eternity involves a contradiction. All successive parts, he says, have a moment of beginning. But eternity has no moment of beginning and so cannot be made up of a series of successive parts which all do.[134] He also argues that a successive view of eternity is also inconsistent with the doctrine of divine simplicity. He writes: 'That same essence of God is simply indivisible and does not admit of any parts; and eternity is exactly the same.'[135] All parts, he argues, even temporal ones, are prior to that which they constitute: that which they constitute depends, in the manner of an effect, upon them. Thus a concept of eternity which admitted successive parts would undermine God's status as First Cause.[136]

Barlow, unlike Pearson, tries to address the Socinian and Remonstrant charge that the scholastic conception of eternity is incoherent since it implies that all moments of time can exist at once.[137] Eternity, Barlow says, should not be conceived of as coexisting with all moments of time as if they all existed simultaneously in eternity. Rather, the whole of eternity coexists with each moment of time, but only as they succeed each other. He writes:

> Eternity coexists with each part of time, not all at once, but taken separately: so that today the whole of eternity coexists with the present day, tomorrow the whole coexists with tomorrow's day; and on the day after tomorrow, with the day after tomorrow. Therefore, just as, one after another, the parts of time are not mutually simultaneous with respect to each other, neither are they with respect to eternity; but as the parts of time exist according to before and after, and not all at once; so they exist in eternity according to before and after: for they are in eternity in the same way that they are [in time]: according to their proper measure.[138]

Thus, successive moments coexist with eternity in their proper order.

As Barlow conceives it, therefore, eternity is simultaneous with each successive moment, but that does not imply that each moment is simultaneous with any other. He draws two analogies to illustrate his meaning. A soul, he says, is indivisible, yet it is wholly present to all parts of the body. But just because the soul can be said to be as equally present to the hand as to the foot,

[134] Ibid., p201.

[135] 'Ipsa Dei essentia est simpliciter indivisibilis, nec partes ullas admittit; at aeternitas est ipsissima.' Ibid., p203.

[136] Ibid.

[137] Crell and Volkel, *De Vera Religione*, I.XVIII, a p127. Episcopius, *Opera* (1650) p287. Vorstius, *Tractatus*, p203.

[138] 'Aeternitas coexistit singulis partibus temporis non simul sed divisim sumptis: ita ut hodie tota aeternitas coexistit hodierno die, cras tota coexistit die crastino, perendie, perendino. Ita ut sicut partes temporis in ordine ad se invicem simul non sunt, sic nec in ordine ad aeternitatem; sed ut partes temporis secundum prius & posterius sunt, non omnes simul; sic secundum prius & posterius, in aeternitate sunt: eodem enim modo quo sunt, mensurae suae propriae, & aeternitati etiam insunt.' Barlow, *Exercitationes*, pp208–9.

that does not mean that the hand and the foot are in the same place. Again, he says, as the divine ubiquity is to space, so the divine eternity is to time. God is indivisibly present in every location, but this does not mean that each location is thereby in the same place as all the others. In like manner, he says, eternity is contemporaneous with every instant, yet each instant is not thereby made contemporaneous with all the others.[139]

Beveridge, too, asserts that eternity is without succession. 'These words,' he writes, 'before and after, past and to come, are solecisms in eternity, being only fitted to express the several successions of time.'[140] Eternity, he says, 'is a property whereby we apprehend God as one who was before, and will be after, always without and above time; in whom there is no such thing as first and last, past and to come'.[141] Human beings, he thinks, can only understand God's actions in a successive way, since we exist in time. Thus, for example, I understand God's mercy to Abel, and God's mercy to me, as two temporally distinct expressions of that mercy, 'yet, as they are in God, they are but one and the same act; as they are in God, I say, who is not measured by time, as our apprehensions of him are; but is himself eternity: a centre without circumference, eternity without time'.[142] In other words, the God who is one pure and simple act admits of no temporal distinctions within his being.

The reason Beveridge advances for the non-successive view of eternity is similar to one of those advanced by Barlow.[143] If God were subject to the succession of time, Beveridge argues, then time would be prior to God and so God would not be the First Cause. He writes:

> If God be not eternal, he is temporal, that is, his essence are measured by the motions and successions of time, which being once granted, would quite take away his divinity: for then he could not be the First Cause, and so not God; having time before him whereby he is measured, the thing measured always presupposing that which it is measured by.[144]

Edwards too takes the view that God is prior to time, and so cannot be measured by it. Like Barlow,[145] he thinks that the concept of an eternity made up of successive moments is a nonsense, and so he sides with the other writers in conceiving of eternity as an instant without temporal parts. He writes:

139 'Aeternitas coexistit singulis partibus temporis non simul sed divisim sumptis: ita ut hodie tota aeternitas coexistit hodierno die, cras tota coexistit die crastino, perendie, perendino. Ita ut sicut partes temporis in ordine ad se invicem simul non sunt, sic nec in ordine ad aeternitatem; sed ut partes temporis secundum prius & posterius sunt, non omnes simul; sic secundum prius & posterius, in aeternitate sunt: eodem enim modo quo sunt, mensurae suae propriae, & aeternitati etiam insunt.' Barlow, *Exercitationes*, pp209–10. Turretin felt the same: Turretin, *Institutes*, III.xi.8–9 cited by Muller, *PRRD*, iii p362.

140 Beveridge, *Works*, vii p18.

141 Ibid. p17.

142 Ibid. p18.

143 Barlow, *Exercitationes*, p203.

144 Beveridge, *Works*, vii p21.

145 Barlow, *Exercitationes*, p201.

There is nothing before or after, where there is no distinction of times, there can be no succession. For time is the measure of before and after, and that duration wherein there is succession of parts necessarily implies a beginning, for the time that is past cannot be infinite. But 'tis otherwise in eternity where . . . nothing is past and nothing is future. . . . Therefore in eternity all successive duration is excluded and all things are together and in a moment, all things and actions subsist at once, all is gathered and united into one instant.[146]

He is clear, then, that eternity is simultaneous with all other times.[147] But he is equally clear, again like Barlow, that this does not mean that all times are simultaneous with each other. He writes: 'all the things that ever were and shall be are present to God in one instant, though if you speak of them as they are in themselves, and in respect of us, they are not all present at once, but some at one time, and some at another.'[148]

Hopkins adopts a very similar line. He writes, 'That is most strictly and properly said to be eternal and for ever, which neither hath beginning, nor end; whose prospect, both ways, is boundless. And, thus, God only is for ever, and it is an incommunicable attribute of the divine essence to be so.' However, although God has always existed, and will always exist, God is not subject to the passage of time. Hopkins writes:

Eternity is a duration, which hath neither beginning, nor end, nor succession of parts. . . . All temporal durations are successive, measured by the motions of heavenly bodies, by years, days and hours; but eternity is permanent: it is but one abiding instant, and hath no parts following one after another; and, though it comprehends all time within its infinite circle, yet it doth not move along with time.[149]

Hopkins draws an analogy between the passage of time through eternity, and the flow of a river past a certain point on its bank. The instant which is eternity does not move, but all time moves within it.

Like Barlow and Edwards, therefore, Hopkins conceives of eternity as being simultaneous with all time. South is of a similar mind, writing that, 'God, by reason of his eternal, infinite and indivisible nature, is, by one single act of duration, present to all the successive portions of time; and consequently to all things successively existing in them.'[150] This presence to all times, South thinks, makes the future quite as present to God as the current moment.

Hopkins admits that it difficult for temporal beings to conceive how this might be. He is clear, however, that reason admits of no other alternative.

[146] Edwards, *Theologia Reformata*, i p56. [147] Ibid., p57.

[148] Ibid. This mirrors Barlow, *Exercitationes*, pp208–9.

[149] Hopkins, *Works*, i p212. His view finds echoes within the wider Reformed tradition: Muller, *PRRD*, iii pp361–2.

[150] South, *Sermons*, i p158. See also: Boyle, *Works*, ix p413; Newcome, *Catechetical Course*, i p80.

His reasons are similar to Barlow's. As he puts it, 'conceiving reason will infallibly demonstrate that being, which neither hath beginning nor end, can have no succession in its duration: for wherever there is sucession, there must needs be a priority; and wherever there is a priority, there must needs be a beginning.'[151] As God has no beginning, this conception of eternity will not work to understand God's relationship with time.

Since, therefore, there is no succession in God's existence, Hopkins is prepared to admit that 'in strict propriety... God neither was nor shall be, but only is and enjoys his eternal essence immutably and unsuccessively.'[152] God's being is thus 'a perpetual now, a standing moment.'[153] Boyle,[154] Burkitt,[155] Jenks,[156] and Wallis[157] all say much the same.[158]

When our writers turn to consider omnipresence, it is again clear that they once again approach it in a very different way from the avant-garde writers. As we saw, the Socinians simply denied that God was omnipresent as to essence, whereas the Remonstrants and avant-garde Anglicans asserted omnipresence, but expressed it as a sort of spiritual diffusion or extension through space. Pearson, for one, is clear that God is omnipresent as to essence and yet that the Remonstrant way of explaining this cannot be right.

For Pearson, all extension is a mark of material existence, and when we assert that God's being is infinite, we do not mean that he is infinite by extension, we mean that there are no limits to his being. He writes:

> Although God is not quantitively infinite (since we have shown him to be in no way corporeal), nonetheless his infinity can best be described by that which occurs to us out of quantity.... And as a quantity is infinite which has no limit to its extension, so that essence is infinite which has no limit to its being, or a degree by which it is confined or contracted.[159]

In fact, Pearson holds that omnipresence is not an adequate way of expressing God's relation to space. He is quite clear that, 'God is present to and present in all things by the presence of his essence or nature; so that there is absolutely nothing to which that same divine essence is not present.'[160]

[151] Hopkins, *Works*, i p212. [152] Ibid. p213. [153] Ibid.

[154] Boyle, *Works*, xii p102. [155] Burkitt, *Expository Notes*, p797.

[156] B. Jenks, *Serious Thoughts of the Wonderful God* (London, 1705), p17.

[157] Wallis, *Sermons*, p24.

[158] The Reformed tradition generally adopted a conception of eternity that excluded all succession. Muller, *PRRD*, iii pp354–5.

[159] 'Quamvis Deus non sit quantitative infinitus (cum ostendimus Eum esse nullo modo corporeum) infinitatem tamen eius optime describi per eam quae nobis ex quantitate nata est.... Et ut infinita quantitas est quae nullum terminum suae extensionis habet, ita infinita est essentia, quae nullum habet limitem suae entitatis, aut gradum quo sit contenta et contracta.' Pearson, *Minor Theological Works*, i pp60–1.

[160] 'Deus omnibus rebus adesse et inesse, per praesentiam essentiae sive naturae suae; ita ut res omnino nulla sit, cui ipsa essentia divina non adsit.' Ibid. p77.

However, he writes, 'Even though God is omnipresent, the attribute of immensity does not formally consist in this presence.'[161]

The reason for this, is that presence is an attribute which is relative to something else. It is therefore an extrinsic attribute, whereas God's lack of spatial limits is an intrinsic and absolute attribute, an attribute, in other words, which is not predicated upon the existence of things outside himself to which he can be present. Pearson writes:

> Before the creation of the world, God was properly immense, though he was not properly and formally present. Presence implies an essential respect to something else, because it is a sort of union and, so to speak, a positive lack of distance between the two.[162]

Thus God cannot be said to be present where nothing exists, yet he was immense before anything existed, and still exists by that immensity where nothing is now.

Pearson does not consider that the mode of God's presence which is commonly called immensity is actually a negative attribute, and he prefers the term 'ubiquity.'[163] The divine immensity corresponds to what is called absolute location in creatures,[164] yet without any of the imperfections that such location involves. For creatures, he says, absolute location involves three sorts of imperfection: first, the existence of spatial parts (i.e. extension through space); secondly, the limitation to a certain place; and, thirdly, a distance from other things. Divine immensity involves the positive qualities of creaturely location without these imperfections. Pearson writes:

> Therefore, just as eternity incorporates all the perfections of successive extension, so immensity incorporates all the perfections of locative extension: and just as the quantitative extension of a thing is the foundation of [its] presence with the other things with which it coexists and to which it extends; so the immensity of God is the foundation of ubiquity and omnipresence.[165]

On this basis, Pearson not only asserts that God's essence, by virtue of the divine immensity, is everywhere within the universe, he also thinks that 'God

[161] 'Licet Deus sit omnipresens, attributum tamen immensitatis non formaliter consistit in hac praesentia.' Ibid. p78.

[162] 'Ante creationem mundi Deus fuit proprie immensus, non tamen fuit proprie et formaliter praesens. Praesentia enim essentialem dicit respectum ad aliud, quia ipsa est quaedam unio, et quasi positiva indistantia, duorum.' Ibid. The Reformed tradition also countenanced a distinction of this sort between omnipresence and immensity; Muller, *PRRD*, iii p338.

[163] Pearson, *Minor Theological Works*, i p80.

[164] That is, location considered in the absence of other things, rather than location vis-à-vis other things. Ibid.

[165] 'Ut igitur aeternitas colligit omnem perfectionem extensionis successivae, ita immensitas colligit omnem perfectionem extensionis permanentis: et sicut extensio rei quantitativa est fundamentum praesentiae cum aliis rebus, quibus coexistat et coextendatur; ita immensitas Dei est fundamentum ubiquitatis et omnipraesentiae.' Ibid. p81. It should be noted that the analogy only works if God's immensity is as devoid of extension as God's eternity is devoid of succession.

is not defined or circumscribed by the space of the world, but exists even outside the world.'[166] In other words, God exists, by virtue of the divine immensity, not only in real space, where other things exist besides him, but also in what the scholastic writers called 'imaginary space,' where nothing else exists at all.

This concept of imaginary space is essential to Barlow's conception of divine immensity as well. He begins his discussion of this divine attribute with an extended demonstration that imaginary space is a valid concept, and that it is the ultimate foundation of all location.[167] Since imaginary space is the foundation of all location, it is also the foundation of that sort of location which is peculiar to God, namely immensity.[168] Like Pearson, Barlow draws an analogy between divine immensity and divine eternity, writing:

> This can best be described by the proportion which divine eternity has with respect to time. For God is present by immensity in space just as [he is present] by eternity to [specific] times.... Therefore, just as eternity is in all finite times yet exceeds them to an infinite degree; so immensity is in all finite locations or spaces; and yet surpasses them to an infinite degree. And just as the eternity of God cannot be included within finite periods of time, but is outside them... and is before them; and follows after all of them; so, indeed, is immensity with respect to finite locations or spaces.[169]

Because God's essence is infinite, and the divine immensity is an attribute of that essence, it cannot, Barlow argues, be accounted for by any relation to what is merely finite. Real space, however, is finite; so divine immensity must be a relation to imaginary space instead.[170] He writes:

> The presence of God (since he is simply, actually, intimately and immediately present to every space) is called ubiquity or immensity. Which can be most reckoned with respect to this imaginary space. So that God is in all of that space where the world now is, and was in it from eternity; and even in the infinite imaginary spaces beyond the heavens; so that even if he created anew, by his infinite power, a thousand worlds

[166] 'Deum non definiri aut circumscribi spatio huius mundi, sed etiam extra mundum esse.' Ibid. p84.

[167] Barlow, *Exercitationes*, p243 et seq.

[168] Ibid., p257.

[169] 'Hoc optime explicari possit per proportionem divinae aeternitatis in ordine ad tempus. Ita enim comparatur Deus per immensitatem in ordine ad spatium; sicut per aeternitatem ad tempora.... Sicut igitur aeternitas est in omnibus finitis temporibus, & infinita excedit illa; ita immensitatis est in omnibus finitis locis seu spatiis, & infinita illa superat. Sicut ideo Dei aeternitas finitis temporibus comprehendi non possit, sed est extra illa... & est ante illa, & omnia a parte post sequitur, sic etiam se habet immensitas in ordine ad finita loca seu spatia.' Ibid., p256.

[170] Ibid., p257.

beyond this world, God would be intimately present to all of them; not by any mutation in himself, but only by their production in that imaginary space.[171]

For Barlow, therefore, divine immensity is properly defined as God's presence to all imaginary space. As such, he is willing to call it a necessary attribute of God, and contrast it as such with omnipresence, which is a free attribute, since God could have chosen not to create real space.[172]

Edwards defines divine immensity in a similar way to Barlow, writing:

God is everywhere essentially and substantially; there can no place be assigned where he is not thus present. This is called by some the immensity (and that rightly) of God: and it is by this infinite greatness (for that explains the meaning of immensity) that he fills all places, yea all the wide and imaginary spaces (as the schools call them) beyond the world, all the spacious vacuities possibly to be conceived.[173]

God, he argues, infinitely surpasses all creaturely forms of location. He is present neither circumscriptively (so as to fill a certain defined area) as bodies are, nor definitively (so as to be in one particular place rather than another) as created spirits are. God fills and is present to all space, but, Edwards underlines, not by what he calls 'dilation' through that space.[174]

Hopkins's approach to the matter is similar. For him, God's ubiquity is vital to the existence of all created beings. That God necessarily exists everywhere, is the only reason why other things can exist anywhere. 'The omnipresence of God,' he writes,

is simply necessary, not only for the preserving and upholding of his creatures in their beings and operations, but necessary to our very beings; for his own essence is simple, and he cannot withdraw from nor forsake any place, or any thing, with which his presence now is.[175]

Like Edwards and Barlow, Hopkins also explains that God is in fact present even beyond the bounds of created space.[176] Hopkins is happy to deploy

[171] 'Praesentia Dei (cum sit omni spatio simpliciter, actu & intima & immutabiliter praesens) dicitur ubiquitas aut immensitas. Quae in ordine ad spatia haec imaginaria commodissime aestimari possit. Ita ut Deus iam sit in spatio illo toto, quo mundus iam est, & in eo ab aeternitas fuit, & etiam in spatiis imaginariis infinitis extra coelum, adeo ut si mundus mille pro potentia sua infinita, extra hunc mundum, de nova crearet, iis omnibus esset Deus intime praesens; non per mutationem in se ullam, sed solum per productionem eorum in spatiis illis imaginariis.' Ibid., p276.

[172] Ibid.

[173] Edwards, *Theologia Reformata*, i p51.

[174] Ibid. Edwards does not mention 'extension,' but presumably 'dilation' means much the same thing. Certainly, Edwards presents it as the mode of extension through space proper to created spirits, which is how Episcopius described the extension involved in omnipresence. Episcopius, *Opera* (1650) p287. The Reformed tradition generally rejected such an idea of divine ubiquity: Muller, *PRRD*, iii p339.

[175] Hopkins, *Works*, iv p259.

[176] Ibid. p260.

analogies to illustrate the nature of God's presence to creation. He describes God as 'a sphere whose centre was everywhere, and whose circumference nowhere,' also also as 'an infinite point'.[177] Such analogies are useful, because, as Hopkins underlines, although God is everywhere, this does not mean God has spatial or extensive parts: there is not one bit of God over here, and another over there. Rather, all of God is everywhere. He writes:

> As God exists everywhere, so all and whole God exists everywhere. So that all God is here, and all God is there, and all God is in every place, and in every thing: this is indeed a great and most unconceivable mystery, but yet it must needs be so, because God is indivisible and simple and not compounded of parts; and therefore, wherever there is any of God's essence, there is all of his essence, otherwise part of his essence would be here, and part there, and not part of it elsewhere, which would be utterly repugnant to the simple and uncompounded nature of God. God's attributes are his essence: now there is nowhere where God is, but there are all his attributes, and therefore where God is, there is all his essence.[178]

Jenks adopts a similar approach. He too underlines that God's essence extends beyond the bounds of the created universe. He exclaims,

> How wonderful is the being that is infinite and boundless; under no limitations for place, any more than for time. . . . No, the vast circumference of the universe . . . is but as a little ball in his hand; and even as nothing to his absolutely unconfined being, that is never to be circumscribed within any terms.[179]

He is also quite as insistent as the other Reformed, that God's ubiquity is a mode of presence 'without any extension of parts.'[180] Newcome agrees, asserting that 'God is essentially present, in the most universal and unlimited sense, in every place, with all creatures, and even beyond every living things and places in the world; yet without measure, without division, and without even extension or diffusion.'[181]

## THE DIVINE KNOWLEDGE AND THE DIVINE WILL

Turning now to the divine knowledge, the Anglican Reformed assert, against the Socinians, that God does know future contingents: but they reject the Remonstrant (and avant-garde Anglican) manner of explaining such knowledge.

[177] Hopkins, *Works*, iv p259. [178] Ibid. p261.
[179] Jenks, *Serious Thoughts*, p19. [180] Ibid., p20.
[181] Newcome, *Catechetical Course*, i p83. These views echo the wider Reformed tradition: Muller, *PRRD*, iii pp332, 339.

Pearson asserts that God's knowledge extends to all knowable objects. However, the primary object of the divine knowledge, he thinks, is actually God himself.[182] He explains the difference between the primary and secondary objects of knowledge as follows:

> The object of the intellect is twofold, that is to say, primary and secondary. The primary object, or what is seen in itself, is that which immediately and first terminates the vision, so that it is first seen by itself, and not through any other object previously seen. The secondary object, or what is seen in another, is that which is perceived through the same act of knowledge by which some prior object is perceived; and so is known consequentially and subsequently. As principles are known in themselves; and conclusions by the principles.[183]

God, he argues, knows first himself, and then knows other things as he is their cause. Things outside God are, in other words, only secondary objects of the divine knowledge, because God's knowledge of them depends upon his knowledge of himself. As he puts it: 'The essence of God is, therefore, reached by the divine intellect first, in which are first the beings which are distinct from God, and by [that] essence previously known, those things which are outside God are known as well.'[184]

The things which are not God, and which God knows, are of two sorts: they are either possible or actual. Pearson is clear that God necessarily knows all possible things, since what is possible is, as such, knowable. And God knows what is possible through the knowledge of his own power. Pearson writes:

> Whatsoever things are possible, are possible because they are the objects of the divine power. But it is necessary that God should perfectly know the full extent of his power. He therefore knows possible things in his power, as in a medium which is previously known.[185]

[182] Pearson, *Minor Theological Works*, i p162. Aquinas *SCG*, ch.48.

[183] 'Duplex esse objectum intellectus, primarium scil. et secundarium. Objectum primarium est, seu in visum, quod immediate et primo terminat visionem, ut ipsum per se, primo videatur, et non per aliquod objectum anterius visum. Objectum secundarium est, seu visum in alio, quod percipitur per eandem notitiam, qua prius aliquod objectum est perceptum, atque ita resultative et consecutive cognoscitur. Ut principia cognoscuntur per se, conclusiones per principia.' Pearson, *Minor Theological Works*, i p162.

[184] 'Primo igitur per intellectum divinum attingitur essentia Dei, in qua prima sunt entia a Deo distincta, et per essentiam prius cognitum ea quae sunt extra Deum cognoscuntur.' Ibid. p163. Aquinas *SCG*, ch.49.5. Beveridge maintains this as well: *Works*, vii p37. The Reformed generally adopted this view: Muller, *PRRD*, iii p400.

[185] 'Quaecunque sunt possibilia, ideo sunt possibilia, quia sunt objecta potentiae divinae. Sed necesse est, ut deus perfecte cognoscat totam latitudinem suae potentiae. Ergo cognoscit possibilia in potentia sua, tanquam in medio prius cognito.' Pearson, *Minor Theological Works*, i p168.

But since God knows all possible things, Pearson argues, God must know all actual things as well, because the only difference between what is actual and what is possible, is that what is actual has existence, which existence comes from God. For all actual existence, whether past, present or future, is the result of God's will.

This discloses, for Pearson, a twofold knowledge within God. He writes:

Firstly, therefore, the knowledge of God is either necessary or free. Which division is taken from the nature of the objects, and, by extrinsic denomination, is attributed to the knowledge of God. For in the sphere of these same objects; some are entirely necessary; as God himself and, given God, possible creatures; others are contingent, and subject to some freedom, at all events [the freedom] of God himself. Therefore the divine knowledge, insofar as it is the knowledge of God and of possible things, from the necessity of the object is called necessary. Insofar as it is the knowledge of contingent things, and of things subject to some free cause, from the freedom of the cause it is called free.[186]

It should be noted here that Pearson has rejected the concept, which Episcopius and the avant-garde Anglicans embraced,[187] of a middle knowledge between the necessary knowledge and the free knowledge of God. He has done this because, for Pearson, none of God's knowledge is immediately dependent upon the free actions of created beings; and that is what, for Episcopius and his followers like Molina before them, distinguishes God's middle knowledge from his other sorts of knowledge. God knows all things outside himself either in the knowledge of what he could do (in the case of all possible things), or in the knowledge of what he has as a matter of fact choosen to do (in the case of all actual things). It follows that God knows future contingents, as he knows all things that actually exist, by his knowledge of himself as their cause.[188]

[186] 'Est itaque primo scientia divina vel necessaria vel libera. Quae divisio sumitur, ex parte objecti, et per extrinsecam denominationem tribuitur scientiae Dei. Nam inter sphaerum objectum eiusdem, quaedam prorsus necessaria sunt; ut Deus ipse, et, suppositi Deo, creaturae possibiles; alia contingentia, et alicuius, saltem ipsius Dei, libertati subjecta. Scientia igitur divina, quatenus est scientia Dei et rerum possibilium, ex necessitate objecti dicitur necessaria. Quatenus est scientia rerum contingentium, et causae alicui liberae subjectarum, ex libertate causae dicitur libera.' Ibid., i pp170–1. The reformed commonly adopted this distinction: Muller, *PRRD*, iii p411.

[187] Episcopius, *Opera* (1650) p303.

[188] It should be noted, however, that Pearson, in his two lectures on God's knowledge of future contingents, confines himself to demonstrating first that the scriptures indicate that God has such knowledge and second that propositions about future contingents have determinate truth. Pearson, *Minor Theological Works*, i p176 et seq.

Pearson is not alone in his rejection of middle knowledge. Barlow too opts for a twofold, not a threefold distinction within the divine knowledge, and describes those two sorts of knowledge very much as Pearson does. In his resolution of a disputation on divine prescience, he writes:

> The knowledge of God is therefore . . . twofold. 1. Of simple intelligence. 2. Of vision. 1. [The knowledge] of simple intelligence (which is called 'natural knowledge', and 'necessary') which is grounded in the power of God, and by which he certainly and naturally knows absolutely all things, whether past or present or future, or [even] those things which are merely possible, and that necessarily, so that he cannot not know [them]. 2. The knowledge of vision, which is called 'free knowledge' inasmuch as it is founded upon the free decree of his will. And this knowledge knows all and only those things which the will decreed, whether efficiently, so that he would produce [them] or permissively, so that he would not prevent [them].[189]

Thus, the things which are outside God are known by God, either because he could potentially create them (possible things), or because he has already decided to create them (actual things). There is, once again, no room for a middle sort of knowledge of those things which will happen as a result of the independent decisions of created agents. Both Barlow and Pearson are following Aquinas here, who accepted the distinction between the knowledge of simple intelligence and the knowledge of vision in the same terms as Barlow.[190]

In his discussion of divine eternity, Barlow enquires how future contingents exist in eternity, and the discussion sheds light on how he thinks God can know them. He opens his remarks with a distinction between what is possible, and what is future. He writes: 'I call possible whatever God might do by his absolute power, even if he never does. . . . That is called future, not because it merely can be; but because, at some time, it actually will be, albeit in the proper course of time.'[191]

Since nothing except God has necessary existence, no created event or thing is, in and of itself, necessarily future. Nonetheless, whatever is future, is

[189] 'Scientia igitur Dei . . . duplex est. 1. Simplicis intelligentiae. 2. Visionis. 1.Scientia simplicis intelligentiae, dicitur scientiae naturalis, et necessaria, et fundatur in potentia Dei, qua omnia absolute, seu praeterita, seu praesentia, seu futura, seu ea quae solum sunt possibilia, certe et naturaliter cognoscit, quin et necessario, ita ut non potest non cognoscere. 2.Scientia visionis, dicitur scientia libera, utpote in decreto voluntatis suae libero fundata. Et haec scientia illa omnia et sola cognoscit, quae voluntas decrevit, vel efficiendo, sic ut producat, vel premittendo, sic ut non impediat.' Barlow, 'Praescientia divina a rebus praescitis non tollit contingentiam' MS QCL 220, 35r.

[190] Craig, *The Problem of Divine Foreknowledge of Future Contingents from Aristotle to Suarez*, p102.

[191] 'Possibile illud dico quicquid Deus potentia absoluta faciat, licet actu nunquam fiat. . . . Illud autem futurum dicitur, non quod potest esse solum, sed quod aliquando actu erit, nempe propria temporis differentia.' Barlow, *Exercitationes*, p221.

definitely future from eternity; and since it is definitely future, it is also known by God as future from eternity. But God's knowledge of it is not the cause of its futurity, since even God's knowledge, taken by itself, cannot give being to anything else.[192] God's power is not the cause of its futurity either, since God's power by itself can only account for the fact that something is possible, not for the fact that it is actual.[193] For just as the proper object of God's knowledge is what is knowable, the proper object of God's power is what is possible. It follows that the only divine attribute which accounts for anything's futurity, Barlow thinks, is God's will. As he writes:

Just as things are called possible with respect to divine power, so that everything is properly possible that God can do; so I consider a thing to be future with respect to the will of God, so that a thing is therefore future because God willed that it should be future.[194]

Barlow argues that this is as true for contingent futures as for necessary futures. Futures are called contingent, he thinks, because they flow from a secondary cause which acts contingently (i.e. which is vested with free will). They are not called contingent because they are somehow independent of God. From God's point of view, Barlow thinks, both the necessary acts of secondary causes, and the contingent (i.e. free) acts of secondary causes are the effects of God's own free and contingent will.

The only difference between them is that in the first case God has chosen to act through a secondary cause whose nature is such that it acts by necessity, whereas in the second case he has chosen to act through a secondary cause which acts contingently (i.e. freely). Nonetheless, both actions are equally the free effects of the divine will.[195] Barlow writes:

For a fire burns, the sky moves and the will desires, though the latter freely and contingently; for the will is perpetually free: the former necessarily and by nature, since it is not in the power of a fire that it should not burn, nor [in the power of] the sky that it should not move. And all these actions, insofar as they are from God, are absolutely and simply free. For the heat of fire is produced just as freely by God as the desiring of the will. And, by consequence, that heat should be necessary and volition free cannot be taken from the disposition of the first cause: and therefore that heat is

192 'Possibile illud dico quicquid Deus potentia absoluta faciat, licet actu nunquam fiat.... Illud autem futurum dicitur, non quod potest esse solum, sed quod aliquando actu erit, nempe propria temporis differentia.' Barlow, *Exercitationes*, p223.

193 Ibid., p224.

194 'Sicut res dicuntur possibiles in ordine ad potentiam divinam, ita ut omne illud sit possibile proprie, quod Deus potest facere; sic puto rem esse futurum in ordine ad voluntatem Dei; ita ut ideo res est futura quia voluit Deus ut sit futura.' Ibid., p223. See also Tully, *Enchiridion*, p21.

195 Beveridge also argues this: *Works*, ix p80.

necessary will be [a result] of the nature of fire [which is] naturally determined to such a mode of acting, and that volition is free, will also be [a result of] the nature of the will, which freely produces its act.[196]

So God knows the future acts of free agents just as he knows the future acts of necessarily acting agents, namely by knowing his own will.[197]

Edwards takes a similar view. The concept of middle knowledge is, he thinks, entirely unworthy of God, since it ascribes to him a precarious and uncertain sort of knowledge which is built upon nothing but suppositions.[198] Like Barlow and Pearson, he believes that human actions are not contingent in the sense of being independent of God's will. He writes:

Though men's actions are indifferent and contingent in some respect, i.e. if we have regard to the free principle of men's will, whence they flow, as also the variety of objects which they are conversant about, yet in respect of God they cannot be said to be contingent or casual, because nothing (of what nature soever) happens without his disposal and providence, and consequently there is nothing hid from him: yea all futurities are fix'd and certain as to him because of his decree, and so are known.[199]

Once again, what is future is known to God in the mirror of his will.[200]

Hopkins, too, rejects the concept of middle knowledge, and opts, with Pearson, Barlow, and Edwards, for a twofold conception of the divine knowledge. He writes:

His knowledge being thus infinite, he knows himself and all things other than himself. First God perfectly knows himself, he knows the boundless extent of his own being; and though he be infinite and incomprehensible to all others, yet he is finite and comprehensible to himself: and hence it follows, secondly, that he knows particularly all other things. For if he knew himself perfectly, he must needs know all things besides himself, because none can perfectly know himself that doth not fully know all that his power and strength can reach unto. But now there is nothing which the power of God

[196] 'Nam ignis urit, coelum movet, & voluntas vult, scilicet haec libere, & contingenter; voluntas enim est perpetuo libera: illa necessario, & naturaliter, cum nec sit in potestate ignis, ut non urat, nec coeli ut non moveat. At omnes hiactus [*sic*] in quantum sunt a Deo, sunt absolutae & simpliciter liberi. Nam calefactio ignis aeque libere producitur a Deo, ac velle voluntatis. Et per consequens, quod calefactio sit necessaria & volitio libera, ex habitudine ad causam primam desumi non possit: et ideo quod calefactio sit necessaria, erit ex natura ignis ad talem agendi modum naturaliter determinati & quod volitio sit libera erit pariter ex natura voluntatis, quae actus suus libere producit.' Barlow, *Exercitationes*, pp226–7. See also Beveridge, *Works*, x p330; Hopkins, *Works*, i p195; Newcome, *Catechetical Course*, ii pp105–7; Reynolds, *Works*, p579; Wallis, *Sermons*, pp376–7.

[197] He echoes the wider Reformed tradition in this; Muller, *PRRD*, iii pp402–3.

[198] Edwards, *Veritas Redux*, p89.

[199] Edwards, *Theologia Reformata*, i pp60–1.

[200] 'But truly, if we will speak accurately, we should say that God therefore foresees all things, because he wills and determines them.' Edwards, *Veritas Redux*, p21.

cannot reach, because by his power he created all things. And therefore knowing his own essence, which is the cause of all, he knows everything in the fecundity of his essence.[201]

God's knowledge is, he argues, nothing like human knowledge. It does not depend upon its objects for what it is. It is rather the knowledge of a creator, which brings into existence the things it knows—for God's knowledge of vision is always accompanied with God's decision to create what is known. As he puts it, 'God knows them before they are, and by knowing them brings them to pass. God knows all things . . . not because they are, but therefore they are because God knows them.'[202] So, once again, God's knowledge of creation is merely a subset of God's knowledge of himself.

Conant, too, argues that God's knowledge is rooted in his own power and will, and not dependent on the existence of things outside himself. He writes,

He speaks of things to come in that language, as if they were already in being; and this not only in respect of his almighty power to give them an actual existence when he pleaseth, and of his effectual purpose to do it, but also in respect of his infallible prescience and foreknowledge of them, whereby he looks upon them as if they were already produced.[203]

Conant also concedes a twofold knowledge in God. He asserts, therefore, the existence of a knowledge in God, by which God knows all that he might conceivably do, beyond that knowledge by which God knows all that he actually will do. He writes,

God doth not only know all things past, present and to come, but what never was, nor is, nor shall be: he knows whatever lies within the immense verge of his omnipotency; whatever is possible, and by his almighty power might be if he so pleased, though he never intend to effect it.[204]

So in Conant's scheme, there is no place for middle knowledge either; and he is clear that the knowledge even of the future actions of free creatures, lies within God's knowledge of his own creative intention.[205] Hacket agrees.[206]

Horton and South, for their part, both explicitly condemn the Arminian understanding of the divine knowledge. Horton argues that middle knowledge is actually an incoherent concept, because it is simply not possible to know something that is not determined. Nothing uncertain can be the object of certain knowledge. He writes, 'there is nothing which can be known that it will be, which is not certain to be, and there is nothing certain to be, but it is ordained that it shall be: whatever comes under God's prescience, it first

[201] Hopkins, *Works*, iv pp239–40. [202] Ibid. p240. [203] Conant, *Sermons*, iv p508.
[204] Ibid. p510. [205] Ibid. pp509–10. [206] Hacket, *Century*, p540.

comes under his decree.'[207] So once again, God knows all things by first knowing what he has decided to do.

South is even more cutting about middle knowledge. He writes,

he, who shall look into the writings of the Pelagians, Jesuits, or their Dutch brood, the Remonstants, will find that their grand fallacy, their *proton pseudos* [foremost lie], is founded upon their erroneous stating of the divine knowledge; by which they affirm, that God's knowledge, in respect of future contingents, is wholly conditional.[208]

For, he argues, how could God's knowledge of anything be conditional, when the only possible reason for its existence is God's decision to create it in the first place?[209] Furthermore, conditional knowledge implies that there will have to be a further immanent act in God, which makes his knowledge certain, once the condition is actually fulfilled—and this is, of course, entirely inconsistent with God's immutability.[210]

So South, too, insists that God knows his creatures by knowing himself, though he adds a little more colour to the picture. He writes:

God beholds all things in himself; and that both eminently, as he sees his own perfection, which eminently includes all the perfection which is scattered among the creatures, as the light of all the stars is contained eminently by the sun; and he holds them also formally, distinctly, and according to the model of their own proper beings, without looking upon the very existence of the things themselves, and that in two ways. 1st By reflecting upon his power and what he can do; he has a perfect knowledge of all possibilities, and of things that may be produced. 2nd By reflecting upon his power and his will; he knows whatsoever shall actually be produced.[211]

Consequently, he follows the other Reformed in asserting that God's knowledge constitutes the thing known, and does not depend upon it.[212]

Although the Reformed do grant a twofold knowledge in God, they do not, of course think that the two aspects of the divine knowledge are really distinct. That, of course, would run counter to the doctrine of divine simplicity. Rather, since the divine knowledge is a divine attribute, it is both utterly uncompounded, and indistinguishable from God's essence. To be God is, in other words, to know as God. William Jane puts it clearly:

His knowledge is like himself, infinite, eternal and unvariable, one simple, indivisible and uncompounded act, terminated upon all objects and not dependent upon any. It is nothing else but God himself, conceived as tending to all creation, and vitally

207 Horton, *Forty-Six*, p479. 208 South, *Sermons*, v p43. 209 Ibid. pp36–7.

210 Ibid. p37. The Reformed universally rejected the concept of middle knowledge: Muller, *PRRD*, pp420–1.

211 South, *Sermons*, v pp41–2. 212 Ibid. p42.

representing them by his own infinite essence. And if God, as all grant, be eternal, then his knowledge, as being coexistent to his essence, or rather the same with it, must needs be eternal too. He never began to know anything, and shall never cease to know all things. His infinite attention can never be interrupted by sleep or business. For all things to him are eternally present, and at the same time distinctly terminate a most simple and infinitely comprehensive knowledge.[213]

In other words, God's knowledge, though twofold when considered as relating to necessarily things on the one hand, and contingent things on the other, is nonetheless one, uncompounded act, which is in reality identical with God's being.

Since God's prescience of future free actions is based upon his perfect knowledge of his own will, there is, of course, no need for a doctrine of conditional decrees. Conditional decrees, as we saw, were those acts of the divine will which depended upon the choices of free agents for their fulfillment. They require, in other words, a degree of potentiality within the divine will which enables God to respond to the actions of those free agents. Pearson is quite clear, there is no such principle of potentiality within the divine will: 'There is not, in God, a will by way of volitive potential.... The will of God is a pure act, not at all distinct from his nature.'[214] And since the divine will is not distinct from the divine being, it is both eternal and immutable.[215]

Furthermore, it does not even make sense, Pearson thinks, to talk of reasons or motivations for divine decisions (which, of course, a conditional decree would require). He writes: 'There is not, in God, a true and proper reason for volitive action.... Because such a reason for action requires a principle distinct from itself: and nothing in God is truly and properly distinct.'[216] The reason or motivation behind any decision, Pearson believes, works in the manner of a cause. But a cause must be distinct from its effect, and the divine simplicity rules out such a distinction within the divine being. So God's decisions can have no external motive.

The other Reformed are equally insistent that it is inappropriate to conceive of God's will as having any motives outside himself. Reynolds argues that,

[213] W. Jane, *A Sermon Preached before the Honourable House of Commons* (Oxford, 1691), p12.

[214] 'Non datur in Deo voluntas per modum potentiae volitivae.... Voluntas Dei est actus purus, ab ipsius essentia haud distinctus.' Pearson, *Minor Theological Works*, i p210. This stems from his conception of God as pure act. It would seem to be the logical consequence of Beveridge's view as well. Beveridge, *Works*, vii p31.

[215] Pearson, *Minor Theological Works*, i p218. Aquinas, S.Th., Ia q.19 art.7. Episcopius, of course, held that the divine will was both mutable and distinct from the divine being. Episcopius, *Institutiones*, IV.II.20, p306.

[216] 'Non datur in Deo vera ac propria ratio actionis volitivae.... Quia talis actionis ratio requirit principium ab ipsa distinctum: at nihil est in Deo vere et proprie distinctum.' Pearson, *Minor Theological Works*, i p210. Aquinas, S.Th., Ia q.19 art.5.

It cannot be any other than a marvellous diminution unto the greatness of God, and a too low esteem of the absolute majesty which belongs to him, to make any counsels, decrees, purposes of his, to receive their ultimate form and stamp from the previous and intercurrent casualties or conditions of the creature.[217]

God's very independence means that his decisions cannot possibly depend on anything outside himself. God's will must be completely and utterly free. Hacket agrees, arguing that 'nothing impels God to any decree, but his own free will and election, tempering all things with wisdom and justice.'[218] South says much the same, asserting that 'the divine will is absolute; it is its own reason; it is both the producer and ground of all its acts. It moves not by the external impulse or inclination of objects, but determines itself by an absolute autocracy'.[219]

It follows from the radical freedom of the divine will, of course, that predestination, whether to life or to death, cannot be based upon the actions of human beings.[220] Predestination, like all acts (or, perhaps better, like the rest of the one pure act) of the divine will is absolute, not conditional.[221] In place of the Arminian distinction between the absolute and conditional decrees of God's will, the Reformed therefore propose a distinction between the secret and revealed will of God: the divine will of God's hidden purposes, and the divine will revealed in God's precepts.

Delaune explains this distinction during his explanation of what it means to pray that God's will be done. He writes,

In order to which, we need only to have recourse to that known distinction of the will of God, the *voluntas beneplaciti*, and *voluntas signi*, his will of good pleasure, and his will of sign. The former is so called, because it is what he has pleased to ordain from all eternity should come to pass, and in other words is called the will of decree, and because unknown to us, his secret will: the latter, his will of sign, is so called, because it is what he has signified that men should do, which is therefore called his will of precept; and because that implies its being made known, his revealed will.[222]

Newcome adopts the same distinction in a similar context, arguing of God's will of purpose that it

[217] Reynolds, *Works*, p579. [218] Hacket, *Century*, p539.

[219] South, *Sermons*, iv p386. See also: Horton, *Forty-Six*, p479; Newcome, *Catechetical Course*, i p117. The Reformed commonly insisted that the decisions of the divine will depend upon nothing outside God: Muller, *PRRD*, iii p447.

[220] Aquinas, S.Th. Ia q.23 art.5.

[221] Pearson, *Minor Theological Works*, i p260. The other Reformed also maintain the absolute nature of the divine decrees: T. Barlow, *Genuine Remains* (London, 1693), p579; Conant, *Several Subjects*, p432; Hopkins, *Works*, i p90; South, *Sermons*, i pp160–1.

[222] Delaune, *Twelve Sermons*, p130. This distinction was widely adopted by the Reformed, as well as being well established in the medieval theological tradition: Muller, *PRRD*, p457.

is the determination of his own council, with respect to what shall be done by himself; which to us is secret, irresistible, boundless, extending itself to all events whatsoever, whether good or evil; effecting the evil of punishment, and permitting, for wise and gracious ends, even the evil of sin: wherein God's will is always done as much on earth as in heaven.[223]

For though God's revealed will can be, and frequently is, resisted and frustrated by his creatures, God's hidden will is absolute, unchanging, and invariably accomplishes what God intends.[224]

Even though the Reformed admit this distinction within God's will, they are emphatic that this is a distinction based on the different objects to which that will extends, not a real distinction within the divine will itself. For that, of course, would be inconsistent with the divine simplicity. Hopkins underlines that the will of precept and the will of purpose, that 'they differ the one from the other, not in respect of God; for his will is one infinitely pure and uncompounded act: but only in respect of the object'.[225] Consequently, there is 'no contrariety or opposition between them'.[226] The divine simplicity retains its key regulatory role in the Reformed conception of God's will just as it did in their conception of God's knowledge.

In his discussion of predestination, Pearson actually uses his distinctly Thomist insistence on the divine simplicity to sidestep the Protestant controversies on the matter, a useful trick in early Restoration Cambridge. Having argued that, since God's essence is absolutely simple, no reason or motive can properly be assigned to the divine will, Pearson can maintain that all discussions about causes, conditions, or order within the divine will are simply unhelpful.[227] Indeed, he is very critical of the endless debates about the order of the decrees, and blames the problem (as a good Thomist would) on the corrupting influence of Duns Scotus.[228]

He writes, in explicit criticism of many of his fellow Reformed writers:

From such instances, those who write about this topic are accustomed to draw up for themselves some series or table, and to delineate the order of the divine decrees, with such variety and discrepancy, that it is difficult to find two, of whatever sect or profession, who agree in all matters.[229]

[223] Newcome, *Catechetical Course*, ii p294. See also: Conant, *Sermons*, ii p102; Hopkins, *Works*, i p91; Wallis, *Sermons*, pp355–6.

[224] Reynolds, *Works*, p581.

[225] Hopkins, *Works*, i p91.

[226] Ibid.

[227] Pearson, *Minor Theological Works*, i p263.

[228] Ibid. p250. This seems to be a fair accusation: Richard Cross, *Duns Scotus*, pp101–2.

[229] 'Ex huiusmodi instantibus, qui de hoc argumento scribunt, solent sibi seriem quandam, seu tabellam describere, et ordinem decretarum divinarum delineare, tanta vero cum varietate atque discrepantia, ut difficile sit duos invenire cujuscunque sectae sive professionis, qui per omnia consentiant.' Pearson, *Minor Theological Works*, i p251.

The reasons advanced for such discussions are, in any case, thoroughly spurious. He writes: 'For these two axioms, "What is last in execution is first in intention;" and "Who desires the end, desires all the means to the end," are either generally applied falsely or always, here, perilously.'[230] That is the stuff of human decision making, and inapplicable to the simple act of the divine will.

Like Pearson, Barlow rejects all discussions of order within the divine will as presumptious speculation. He notes that many eminent theologians have felt able to penetrate the mysteries of the divine decrees, but he marvels at their audacity. He writes:

> Even from the agreed principles of nature and scripture, it is evident that God is absolutely simple and eternal; why, then, do they say that there are many decrees in God, [and decrees which are] prior and posterior? When it is not possible that there should be plurality in absolute simplicity, or priority in eternity.[231]

Furthermore, he adds, even if it is argued that the order is not in the decrees themselves but in our human conceptions of them, then all that is being achieved is a numbering of the illusory perceptions of our own minds, which correspond to nothing in God himself. Barlow will, therefore, avoid all such discussions during his time as Lady Margaret Professor.[232] The avoidance of controversy was, of course, no less advisable in Oxford than in Cambridge.

Even in the early eighteenth century, Beveridge is still echoing Pearson and Barlow's scepticism about the fruitfulness of such discussions, writing that 'a cockle-fish may as soon crowd the ocean into its narrow shell, as vain man ever comprehend the decrees of God'.[233]

Edwards follows Pearson in rejecting the idea of conditional decrees. He holds that all acts of the divine will (or decrees, as he puts it) are immutable and absolute.[234] He writes: 'the eternal purpose of God was not conditional, and depending upon what men would do.'[235] Indeed, he argues, if the divine decree were conditional, then the history of salvation could turn out to be a blind alley. He writes: 'If there were not an absolute, that is, an unalterable decree concerning the saving of men, the whole of man's salvation would be

[230] 'Nam illa duo axiomata, Quod est ultimum in executione est primum in intentione; et, Qui vult finem, vult omnia media ad finem, aut falso plerumque, aut semper hic periculose adhibentur.' Ibid. Aquinas, S.Th., Ia q.9 art.5.

[231] 'Ex confessis enim naturae et scripturae principiis constat, Deum esse summe simplicem, et aeternum; cur ideo in Deo decreta plura, priora, posteriora memorant? Cum fieri non possit, ut in summe simplici sit ... pluralitas, nec in aeternis prioritas.' Barlow, MS QCL 235, pp16–17. Horton also felt that all discussion of order within the decrees was a human construct, which did not correspond to the simple reality of the divine essence He, though, was prepared to admit his preference for the sublapsarian scheme: Horton, *Forty-Six*, p476.

[232] This discussion appears in his inaugural lecture as Lady Margaret Professor.

[233] Beveridge, *Works*, vii p344.

[234] Edwards, *Veritas Redux*, p88.

[235] Ibid., p89.

contingent, and it may be none would be saved, and then God would be frustrated of his end and design.'[236]

But whilst Edwards agrees with Pearson, that the divine will is unconditional, he has rather more time for discussions about the order that obtains within the divine will; though he is clearly aware of the problems with such discussions, and expresses himself cautiously. He writes, in rather sharp distinction to what Barlow had to say about the matter:

> We conceive that, in the divine mind, as well as in humane counsels and transactions, the end is first settled and fixed, and then the means in order to that end. Not but that the decrees are altogether and at once; for in eternity one thing cannot be before or after another: but humane conceptions consider a priority in the decrees; and for the better explaining of the doctrine of decrees, we suppose an order and precedency in them, according to what we know of our own reasons and wills and their operations: and therefore we apprehend that God first decreed the end, and then the means thereto.[237]

And in the discussion of the order of the decrees, Edwards reveals himself to be sublapsarian.[238]

## CONCLUSION

The Anglican Reformed conceived of and spoke about God in a radically different way from their avant-garde contemporaries. In common with the wider European Reformed tradition, they advanced a broadly Thomist picture of the divine nature. This Thomism was not, however, a simple replication of the thought of Aquinas himself. Rather it was the English expression of a broader tradition of thought that dominated European universities during the seventeenth century, a tradition which had built on and consciously developed the particular insights that Aquinas had brought to bear.

The Thomist emphases of the Anglican Reformed are not, therefore, something which distinguishes them from the wider Reformed movement. What does mark them out is the openness with which they are prepared to deploy Roman Catholic authority in argument. Whereas most Reformed writers preferred to cite Protestant authority, or Catholic authority from well before the Reformation, the

[236] Edwards, *Veritas Redux*, p92.

[237] Ibid., p63. Turretin is similarly careful: Turretin, *Institutes*, Topic IV q.18. Harm Goris has noted that the discussion of order within the decrees is the point at which Reformed conceptions of divine simplicity diverge from Thomism. H. Goris, 'Thomism in Zanchi's Doctrine of God,' p139.

[238] Edwards, *Veritas Redux*, p74. After the Synod of Dort this was the confessional position of the Reformed Churches.

Anglican Reformed were quite happy to cite the leading lights of post-Reformation Roman Catholic scholasticism. This may well have been because the particular historical and polemical situation of the post-Restoration Church made Roman Catholic writers seem somewhat less unappealing than they appeared to the continental European Reformed. In the polarized context of post-Restoration England, it was becoming almost as risky to cite the grandees of the European Reformed tradition, as it was to cite the various luminaries of counter-Reformation scholasticism.

The broadly Thomist flavour of their system set the teaching of the Anglican Reformed about God markedly apart from their Arminian contemporaries. Central to their theology in this area was a strong doctrine of divine simplicity. Indeed, divine simplicity clearly played a regulatory role throughout their doctrine of God. The exclusion of all real distinction from the divine being led them to understand both divine eternity and divine immensity very differently from their avant-garde contemporaries. Their rejection of all potentiality within the divine nature made them unwilling to embrace the idea that any of God's decrees were conditional. They instead proposed that God's one united will could be considered only as either revealed or hidden, not as conditional or absolute.

This strong view of divine simplicity also reinforced their insistence that the divine attributes were so utterly different from their human counterparts that no easy deductions were possible from human qualities to their divine equivalents. The avant-garde preference for the communicable attributes as a more accessible way of understanding God was thus ruled out from the beginning. To the Reformed mind, even those attributes which were commonly called communicable so completely transcended their created analogies that it was more acurate to say that human beings had no part in them.

The Reformed also emphatically rejected the Molinist concept of middle knowledge. For them, God knows all things in knowing himself, and so he knows the future by knowing what he wills to do. The divine knowledge, just like the divine essence, is therefore utterly independent of all created beings.

Although the doctrine of God was not the focus on any public controversy during the later Stuart period, there is no denying that the English Church contained two rival and incompatible conceptions of the divine being. These two conceptions were occasionally recognized as lying at the root of the more public disagreements between Churchmen. On the whole, however, the Reformed and Arminians simply expounded their incompatible positions within a theologically divided Church.

# 8

# Conclusions

In 1715, following the preferment of John Wynne to the bishopric of St Asaph, the University of Oxford needed a new Professor of Divinity. The Lady Margaret chair was one of the few clerical posts in the country which was subject to a democratic election. Admittedly, the electorate was an unusually exclusive and learned one: the only people eligible to vote were those members of the University, whether resident or not, who held higher degrees in divinity, either a BD or a DD. Most clergy, of course, only had a humble MA.

To the evident dismay of William Stratford, a Canon of Christ Church and government agent in Oxford, this august body chose a man who not only had had a notorious gambling problem, but had also been found guilty of embezzling the income of the University Press, whilst he had served as Vice-Chancellor a few years previously.[1] Stratford complained that the election only turned out as it did, because large numbers of non-resident BDs turned up and voted against the unpopular Master of Balliol, John Baron, who had put himself forward for the post.

The man elected instead of Baron was William Delaune, the President of St John's College, whom we have encountered several times already. Stratford may have been correct in his basic analysis of the result, but several other factors are likely to have been at play in the minds of the electorate as well. The first was that Delaune had been a close ally first of Henry Aldrich and then of Francis Atterbury, the Tory Deans of Christ Church, who had dominated Oxford politics during the reign of Queen Anne.[2] The second was that the crown had imposed, in the teeth of bitter University opposition, the Whiggish (and Arminian) John Potter as Regius Professor of Divinity upon the death of William Jane in 1707.[3] The third was that the previous Lady Margaret Professor, John Wynne, had been an advocate of the new learning in general, and of John Locke's ideas in particular;[4] and, in the wake of the Arian Crisis, that new learning may well have acquired a threatening edge.

[1] W.C. Costin, *The History of St John's College Oxford, 1598–1860* (Oxford, 1958), pp166–8.

[2] G.V. Bennett 'The era of Party Zeal, 1702–1714,' in L.S. Sutherland and L.G. Mitchell (eds), *The History of the University of Oxford IV: The Eighteenth Century* (Oxford 1986), pp65, 91.

[3] Bennett, 'The Era of Party Zeal,' p81.

[4] *ODNB*, s.v. 'John Wynne'.

If any, or all, of these matters were in the minds of those casting their votes, William Delaune would have been a natural choice. His politics were unimpeachable: he was a high flying Tory who had represented the University during the fractious Convocation of 1701,[5] and had even been an associate of the High Church firebrand, Henry Sacheverell.[6] His divinity, also, was, by early eighteenth century standards, just about as conservative as one could get: Delaune spoke with all the authority of the venerable Reformed tradition, a tradition which had been represented in the highest ranks of the Oxford divinity faculty, almost without interruption, since the Elizabethan Settlement.[7]

Certainly, not everyone was as unimpressed with Delaune's victory as the disgruntled Stratford. The Nonjuring (and Tory) antiquarian, Thomas Hearne, greeted the election of Delaune with considerable delight, praising him both for his learning, and the excellence of his preaching style—in sharp contrast, he felt, with the tedious Baron.[8] So Delaune may have more widespread support than Stratford cared to admit.

The 1715 victory of the Reformed William Delaune, like the 1716 Spital Sermon of the similarly Reformed William Nicolson, calls into question a well established reading of the post-Restoration Church. According to most of the historiography, the Reformed theological tradition was marginal to the history of the later Stuart period, and had all but vanished by the early years of the eighteenth century. However, if this view were correct, the Oxford divinity faculty should not have been in a position to elect a Reformed theologian as one of its two senior Professors in 1715, let alone do so without scandal.

Both historians of the Evangelical revival, who have sought to contrast the Protestant fervour of their heroes with the somnolent moralism of Augustan Anglicanism, and historians of a unified Anglicanism, who have sought to present a tradition growing increasingly uncomfortable with, or at least unconcerned by, its Reformed inheritance, have belittled the ongoing significance of the Anglican Reformed tradition after 1662. The desire of such historians to present post-Restoration Anglicanism as a broadly homogenous phenomenon, characterised more by clerical consensus than by heated academic debate, has obscured the deep faultline between Reformed and

[5] Bennett 'Against the Tide: Oxford under William III,' in Sutherland and Mitchell (eds.), *The History of the University of Oxford IV: The Eighteenth Century* (Oxford, 1986), pp55, 57.

[6] Costin, *St John's College*, p171.

[7] The only period when neither of the Divinity Professors at Oxford had been a Reformed theologian, was between the death of Jane and the election of Delaune: 1707–1715.

[8] N. Amhurst, ed. W. Rivers, *Terrae Filius or The Secret History of the University of Oxford 1721–1726* (Newark, 2004), p123 n.

Arminian which still dominated the theological landscape of the later Stuart Church.

Admittedly, that landscape had changed in one significant respect since the early part of the century: the Reformed tradition no longer enjoyed the theological hegemony which it had commanded before the 1630s, and again under the Commonwealth. When William Delaune eventually got around to publishing a collection of his sermons in 1728, he did not conceal the fact that his brand of theology had become resolutely unfashionable. In the dedication which he wrote to Montague Venables-Bertie, 2nd Earl of Abingdon,[9] Delaune lamented that,

> In the miserable state our holy religion hath been for many years, a collection of sermons new from the press, would naturally raise an expectation of nothing but the fashionable doctrine of the times, and be laid aside by all true believers with contempt and abhorrence.

For, he argued, heresy and infidelity 'have long since stole up into the pulpit, and prostituted that sacred place to so prophane an use, as from thence to publish the vain inventions of men, instead of the pure Word of God, and very often in direct contradiction to it'.[10] Delaune was not alone in his pessimism: both the Reformed John Edwards[11] and the Arminian Gilbert Burnet,[12] shared the assumption that Reformed writers were, by the early eighteenth century, a minority within the Church of England.

Furthermore, there were undoubtedly other fissures within the life of the Church which were not defined along Arminian and Reformed lines. Attitudes to Church order, to Protestant Dissent, to the accession of the House of Hanover, all varied within the Church of England; and these issues caused faultlines of their own, to which the Arminian–Reformed debate was tangential. Equally, and in the light of John Spurr's work in particular, it cannot be denied that there were some important areas of consensus within the Church's life: Reformed and Arminian writers were quite happy to join forces against Popery, heresy, and immorality—the three things which all Anglican churchmen agreed were the spiritual cancers of the age.

Nonetheless, it is the central contention of this study that the theological life of the later Stuart Church is simply not comprehensible without reference to the persistent intellectual tension between Reformed churchmen and their Arminian counterparts. Indeed, it is that background of fundamentally

[9] Montague Venables-Bertie was a powerful Tory landowner who had entertained Henry Sacheverell during the triumphant progress which followed his impeachment trial in 1710.

[10] Delaune, *Twelve Sermons*, dedication.

[11] Edwards, *Veritas Redux*, pxxii.

[12] G. Burnet, *An Exposition of the Thirty-Nine Articles* (London, 1819), preface, pv.

unresolved argument which explains why the Reformed tradition remained a viable theological option for the clergy of the Hanoverian Church. It explains why, in other words, the Bishop of Carlisle could still preach justification by faith alone in 1716, and why the Lady Margaret Professor of Divinity at Oxford could still expound a Reformed doctrine of the divine decrees in 1728.[13]

One reason why the historiorians have not taken sufficient notice of the Anglican Reformed who were active after the Reformation is that they have tended to adopt too narrow an understanding of the Reformed tradition itself. It is easy to be distracted by the older terminology of 'Calvinism,' and to adopt an approach to Reformed theology which portrays it at a narrow, homogenous, and monolithic system. In fact, as more recent scholars of Reformed thinking, such as Richard Muller, have taught us, Reformed theology was a diverse and evolving stream of thought. Reformed writers were quite capable of adopting new insights and of adapting to new circumstances.

Within the peculiar environment of the post-Restoration Church, identifying a writer as Reformed is, therefore, a matter of observing that there remain certain key Reformed motifs within that writer's thought, not a matter of signing them up to a monochrome theological agenda, let alone of identifying them in an unqualified way with any earlier thinkers. The persistence of Reformed theological motifs is worthy of note because, as we have seen, they were not similarly present in the work of the majority of post-Restoration Churchmen. But that is not to deny that the Anglican Reformed held these traditional motifs in tension with newer insights from a diverse range of sources. Indeed, it is necessary to adopt a broad and flexible understanding of Reformed theology, if we are to identify any post-Restoration Anglican as a Reformed writer.

Another problem with the traditional historiography has been the gross underestimate it has made of the numbers of Reformed theologians active within the Church of England. After 1662, the Reformed may not have been in the majority, but they remained, nonetheless, a numerically and politically significant group within the Church of England. Furthermore, there was a close network of acquaintance and patronage which bound many of the Reformed together, and enabled them to promote the Reformed cause.

Central to this network, inevitably, were the Reformed bishops. The most prominent of the party's power-brokers during the later Stuart period were undoubtedly George Morley, Thomas Barlow, and Henry Compton—all of whom demonstrably used their episcopal power to promote Reformed clergy, to propagate Reformed teaching and to counteract the influence of the Arminian theologians. There were, however, many more Reformed men on

[13] Delaune, *Twelve Sermons*, p130 et seq.

the bishop's bench than these three, and amongst their number were some of the leading theologians of the post-Restoration period. Sanderson, Reynolds, Wilkins, Pearson, and Beveridge, to name but a few of them, were all figures of such stature that it is simply not possible to describe the intellectual world of post-Restoration divinity without them.

Vital to the strength of Reformed theology during this period, was the abiding hold it retained within the University of Oxford. Well into the eighteenth century, there were significant numbers of dons there, who had decidedly Reformed sympathies. Through the divinity chairs and college headships which the conforming Reformed held, they were able to ensure that Oxford, unlike Cambridge, did not become an unwelcoming place for men of their persuasion. Indeed, their presence within the University was key to forging the unlikely alliance, which we encounter again and again during this period, between Reformed theology and High Church attitudes to Church order, liturgy, and Dissent. Oxford was a predominantly High Church University, and Oxford's Reformed theologians were not immune to that influence. As a result, not only were several Oxford-trained Reformed theologians involved in the various High Church manoeuvres which torpedoed comprehension, not a few were active in the repression of Protestant Dissent.[14]

The conforming Reformed were also, importantly, highly energetic writers of theology. Like most clerics of their day, they directed much of their energy towards preaching, and there are Reformed collections of sermons on a scale which rivals the most prolix of their Arminian adversaries. The Reformed were not shy of controversy either, and numbers of them were active in the production of polemical literature as well, whether directed against the flagrant evils of Rome, or the more insidious threats lurking within Socinian and Arminian thinking.

There is, in fact, virtually no sphere of late Stuart theology to which the Reformed did not contribute in some way. All this work undoubtedly contributed to keeping the Reformed tradition on the agenda of the post-Restoration Church. It meant, for example, that Gilbert Burnet, though an Arminian himself, still felt obliged to include a Reformed perspective on predestination in his commentary on the Thirty-Nine Articles, and to have the whole book read through by a Reformed theologian before it went to print, namely John Hall, Bishop of Bristol.[15] Burnet's work does not, as

[14] The late Stuart alliance between Reformed theology and High Church ecclesiology may explain why the eighteenth-century Evangelical Revival drew inspiration from the High Church Anglican tradition. J. Walsh, 'Origins of the Evangelical Revival,' in G.V. Bennett and J.D. Walsh (eds.), *Essays in Modern English Church History in memory of Norman Sykes* (London, 1966), pp138 et seq.

[15] Grieg, 'Heresy Hunt,' p580.

Nicholas Tyacke has argued,[16] set a seal on the Arminian triumph; rather, Burnet acknowledges the fact that both parties still enjoyed significant support within the English Church at the turn of the eighteenth century. After all, one does not have to make irenic overtures to an enemy who has been completely defeated.

The failure of the Arminians to take theological control of the Church of England is itself rather remarkable. The Reformed lost some of their key thinkers with the Great Ejection of 1662 (though several, of course, crept back in a short while later). Gilbert Sheldon was active both in his support for Arminian theology, and in his opposition to the Reformed tradition. All of the primates who followed him were equally marked by their Arminian sympathies. John Tillotson, indeed, was one of the movement's most significant thinkers. Arminian theology enjoyed, in other words, backing of the most powerful kind.

Furthermore, the Arminianism of the post-Restoration period was a far more formidable beast than it had been in the early part of the seventeenth century. The systematizing and publishing efforts of Simon Episcopius, Hugo Grotius, Etienne de Courcelles, and Philip van Limborch meant that Arminian Anglicans could call upon theological resources of immense sophistication and subtlety, resources already tempered by half a century of debate with their Reformed opponents. Indeed, it is probably fair to say that the later Stuart period is as decisively shaped by the advent of this new, systematic form of Arminianism, as it is by the Reformed reaction to such thinking. After the Restoration, there was a much more explicit alliance between English and continental European Arminianism than there had been in the days of Lancelot Andrewes and William Laud.[17]

As we have seen, the major controversies in speculative theology which divided the post-Restoration Church, were sparked by an attempt to promote the new Arminian system. George Bull's *Harmonia Apostolica* is deeply marked by the influence of Simon Episcopius; William Sherlock's *Vindication* represents a creative development of the views of Jean Leclerc; Samuel Clarke's *Scripture-Doctrine of the Trinity* is little more than a republication of the Trinitarian teaching of Etienne de Courcelles. The defining controversies of this period are, in other words, the result of an Arminian gambit, and the Reformed reaction which it provoked.

Admittedly, it was not the Reformed who finally saw off Samuel Clarke's version of Arianism; though they consistently advanced a Christology which ran counter to his. Nonetheless, it was precisely the Reformed response to

[16] N. Tyacke, 'Religious Controversy,' p617.

[17] Tyacke, 'Arminianism and the Theology of the Restoration Church,' p80.

Bull and then to Sherlock, which created the two controversies first on justification and then on the Trinity, which were the loudest intra-Anglican theological debates of the later seventeenth century. Lurking behind all these debates there was also a growing divide within the Church of England about the nature of God, a divide which once again resulted from the adoption of advanced Arminian ideas by Anglican writers.

To counter this growing Arminian threat, the Anglican Reformed deployed the theological weapons of their tradition with vigour. They continued to insist upon the evangelical teaching of justification by faith alone, upon the established scholastic way of expressing Trinitarian doctrine, and upon the broadly Thomist understanding of the divine nature which was shared by both Roman Catholic and Reformed theologians. Their particular polemical situation may have led them to emphasize the necessity of good works for salvation with a strength unusual elsewhere; and they appear to have been rather more willing than other Reformed writers, to acknowledge their use of Roman Catholic authorities in certain (limited) areas of theology. Nonetheless, the positions which these Anglican writers adopted, evidently reflect those of the wider European Reformed tradition on all the major issues at stake. The Church of England was, in other words, just another battleground in the continent-wide confrontation between Reformed theology and its most articulate critics.

If this reading of the post-Restoration Church is correct, three significant conclusions would seem to follow. The first is that the Reformed dimension of the Evangelical revival within the Church of England can no longer be read as the rediscovery of an abandoned theological tradition. There were, as we have seen, Anglican churchmen prepared to teach Reformed theology well into the eighteenth century. It remained a perfectly respectable, though minority, option within the Georgian church. Gordon Rupp may have been wrong to say that John Edwards was by 1700 the only noted Reformed writer within the Church of England,[18] but he was right to surmise that 'the Anglo-Calvinist tradition persisted at a depth and to an extent which has probably been underestimated.'[19]

In fact, admitting this makes is much easier to explain one of the more puzzling aspects of the Evangelical revival. For if, as some historians would have it, the Reformed tradition had virtually vanished from the English church, then it is rather difficult to explain how the Evangelical revival took on, in many places, such a strongly Reformed character. Of course the Evangelical revival was far from monochrome. There was an influential Arminian aspect to it both amongst the Methodists (e.g. John and Charles

[18] Rupp, *Religion in England, 1688–1791*, p326. [19] Ibid.

Wesley), and amongst the more conformist Evangelicals (e.g. John Fletcher of Madeley).[20] Nonetheless, the fact that there was indeed a powerful Reformed element to the revival, and that it was the Reformed who were the majority amongst the conforming Evangelicals,[21] is more easily explained if we abandon the traditional picture of a thoroughly Arminian Church of England, and concede instead that Reformed theology retained a significant hold on the loyalties of Anglican clergy well into the Augustan age. Indeed, the Reformed churchmen of the later Stuart period were a theological and polemical resource upon which the eighteenth century Evangelicals could draw to demonstrate that their views were a bona fide part of the Anglican tradition.[22]

The second conclusion to be embraced, is that the idea of a homogenous Anglican theological tradition emerging after the Restoration must be abandoned. Later Stuart Anglicanism was no more marked by theological consensus than early Stuart Anglicanism. Both before and after the Commonwealth, Anglican theology was fundamentally marked by theological disagreement. Consequently, the Anglican theological tradition during this period is best conceived, not as a unitary movement, but as a frequently heated debate. In particular, late Stuart Anglicanism was a debate about the ongoing relevance of the Church of England's Reformed inheritance. To Anglican Arminians, that inheritance could and should be sidelined. To the Anglican Reformed, it represented the central identity of the English Church.

The third conclusion to be drawn, which relates closely to the second, is that the Reformed theological tradition is an essential ingredient in any conception of Anglicanism. The late seventeenth century was a key moment of Anglican self-definition. The experience of persecution under the Commonwealth, the Great Ejection in 1662, and the ensuing tension with Protestant Dissent, the ongoing debate about Comprehension and later Toleration, as well as the deprivation of the Nonjurors in 1691, all contributed to a growing sense of Anglican, as opposed to merely English, Protestant identity. The reactionary exclusivism that marked the Restoration settlement combined with rigorist attitudes to Church order and liturgy to produce a

[20] The use of the terms 'Methodist,' to describe those Evangelicals who sat looser to the order of the Church of England, and 'Evangelical' to describe those who operated predominantly within the Church's structures, is an established tool amongst eighteenth century historians. D.W. Bebbington, *Evangelicalism in Modern Britain*, p27; K. Hylson-Smith, *The Churches of England from Elizabeth I to Elizabeth II*, 3 vols (London, 1997), ii p169; G. Rupp, *Religion in England, 1688–1791* (Oxford, 1986), p472.

[21] Rupp, *Religion in England, 1688–1791*, pp472–85. See also: Hylson-Smith, *The Churches of England*, ii p170; S.C. Carpenter, *Eighteenth Century Church and People* (London, 1959), p218.

[22] E.g. A. Toplady, *The Church of England Vindicated from the Charge of Arminianism* (London, 1769), pp15, 76; A. Toplady, *Historic Proof of the Doctrinal Calvinism of the Church of England*, 2 vols (London, 1774), i pp309–10.

definably High Church strain of Anglican thinking. It became increasingly clear, particularly during the meetings of Convocation that took place during the later Stuart period, that the majority of the conforming clergy were now sympathetic to this High Church interpretation of Anglicanism. Nonetheless, even at its most stridently self-conscious and exclusive, Anglicanism still had room for Reformed theologians, as well as Arminians. The High Church party included the likes of William Jane, alongside Arminians such as George Bull.

Despite the active opposition of several primates, despite the increasing influence of systematic Arminian thinking, despite its polemically disadvantageous associations with lawlessness, rebellion, and regicide, the Reformed tradition retained a significant level of support within the Church of England well into the eighteenth century. It still provoked hostility in certain quarters, but that is precisely because it remained a compelling and credible alternative to the majority view. As Benjamin Jenks wrote, anticipating his opponents' attacks, 'from such I shall not be much startled to hear Antinomian: which I know they can throw, as a hard word, at the heads of some that least deserve it. When really the mad rage is at another thing, that sounds like it, Anti-Arminianism.'[23]

[23] B. Jenks, *Submission to the Righteousness of God* (London, 1705), pxv.

# Bibliography

## MANUSCRIPT SOURCES

British Library
MS Add D 105
MS Sloane 1710

Oxford: Bodleian Library
MS Add A 260
MS Tanner xl

Oxford: The Queen's College
MSS 230, 233, 234, 235, 236, 239, 240, 267, 279, 340, 497

## PRIMARY SOURCES


Addison, L., *The Christian's Manual in Three Parts* (London, 1691).

Addison, *Christos Autotheos* (London, 1696).

Aldrich, H., *A Narrative of the Lower House of Convocation relating to Prorogations and Adjournments* (London, 1702).

Alvarez, D., *De Auxiliis* (Rome, 1610).

Anon., *The Racovian Catechisme* (Amsterdam, 1652).

Anon., *A Discourse Concerning the Nominal and Real Trinitarians* (London, 1695).

Banez, D., *Scholastica Commentaria in Primam Partem Angelici Doctoris S. Thomae* (Douai, 1614).

Barlow, T., *Exercitationes Aliquot Metaphysicae de Deo* (Oxford, 1658).

—— *Genuine Remains* (Oxford, 1693).

Becanus, M., *Summa Theologicae Scholasticae* (Mainz, 1612).

Bellarmine, R., *Opera Omnia*, 12 vols (Paris, 1870).

Bentley, R., *Dissertation on Phalaris* (1699).

Beveridge, W., *A Sermon concerning the Excellency and Usefulness of the Common Prayer* (London, 1682).

—— *Works*, 12 vols (Oxford, 1842).

Biddle, J., *A Scripture Catechism* (London, 1654).

Boyle, R., *Works*, 14 vols (London, 1999–2000).

Bull, G., *Harmonia Apostolica* (Oxford, 1842).

Bull, G., *Apologia pro Harmonia*, tr. Burton (Oxford, 1843).

Bull, G., *Defence of the Nicene Creed*, 3 vols (Oxford, 1851).
Burkitt, W., *Expository Notes with Practical Observations on the New Testament* (London, 1760).
Burnet, G., *History of His Own Time*, 2 vols (London, 1724–34).
—— *Exposition of the Thirty-Nine Articles* (London, 1819).
Calvin, J., *Institutes of the Christian Religion*, 2 vols, ed. J.T. McNeill (Philadelphia, 1960).
Clarke, S., *The Scripture-Doctrine of the Trinity* (London, 1712).
—— *A Discourse Concerning the Being and Attributes of God* (London, 1728).
Compton, H., *The Bishop of London's Tenth Conference with his Clergy* (London, 1701).
Conant, J., *Sermons*, 6 vols (London, 1693–1722).
Crell, J. and J. Volkel, *De Vera Religione* (Racow, 1630).
Crossman, S., *The Young Man's Monitor* (London, 1664).
Cudworth, R., *True Intellectual System of the Universe*, 3 vols (London, 1845).
Curcellaeus, S., *Opera Theologica* (Amsterdam, 1675).
Curll, E. 'Memoirs of the Life and Writings of Dr Robert South' in R. South (ed.), *Sermons Preached upon Several Occasions*, 5 vols (Oxford, 1842).
Davenant, J., *Disputatio de Iustitia Habituali et Actuali*, tr. J. Allport (London, 1844).
Delaune, W., *Twelve Sermons* (London, 1728).
du Moulin, L., *A Short and True Account of the Several Advances the Church of England hath made towards Rome* (London, 1680).
—— J., *Some Animadversions on Dr. Clarke's scripture doctrine (as he stiles it) of the Trinity* (London, 1712).
Edwards, John, *The Socinian Creed* (London, 1697).
—— *The Doctrine of Faith and Justification set in a True Light* (London, 1707).
—— *Veritas Redux: Evangelical Truths Restored* (London, 1707).
—— *Theologia Reformata*, 2 vols (London, 1713).
Edwards, Jonathan, *A Preservative against Socinianism*, 4 vols (Oxford, 1693–1703).
—— *The Exposition given by my lord bishop of Sarum of the Second Article of our Religion Examin'd* (London, 1702).
Episcopius, S., *Apologia pro Confessione* (1630).
—— *Disputationes Theologicae Tripartitae* (Amsterdam, 1646).
—— *Institutiones Theologicae* (Amsterdam, 1650).
Evelyn, J., *Diary and Correspondance*, 4 vols (London, 1906).
Fasolo, J., *Commentarium in Primam Partem S. Thomae*, 3 vols (Lyon, 1636).
Fowler, E., *The Principles and Practices of Certain Moderate Divines of the Church of England* (London, 1671).
—— *The Design of Christianity* (London, 1760).
Fullwood, F., *Roma Ruit: the Pillars of Rome Broken* (London, 1679).
—— *The Socinian Controversy Touching the Son of God* (London, 1693).
Grotius, H., *Criticorum Sacrorum*, 7 vols (London, 1660).
Hacket, J., *A Century of Sermons* (London, 1675).
Hopkins, E., *Works*, 4 vols (London, 1809).
Horton, T., *Forty-Six Sermons* (London, 1674).

—— *One Hundred Select Sermons*, 2 vols (London, 1679).

—— *Serious Thoughts of the Wonderful God* (London, 1705).

Jenks, B., *Submission to the Righteousness of God* (London, 1700).

Leclerc, J. (Liberius a Sancto Amore), *Epistolae Theologicae* (Saumur, 1679).

Kennett, B., *A Brief Exposition of the Apostles' Creed according to Bishop Pearson in a New Method* (London, 1705).

Marshall, T., *The Catechism set forth in the Book of Common Prayer* (Oxford, 1679).

Martinez de Ripalda, J., *De Ente Supernaturali disputationes* (Bordeaux, 1634).

—— *Expositio Brevis Litterae Magistri Sententiarum* (Salamanca, 1635).

Morley, G., *The Bishop of Winchester's Vindication* (London, 1683).

Navarrete, B., *Controversiae in Divi Thomae et Eius Defensionem* (Valladolid, 1609).

Nazarius, J. P., *Commentaria et Controversiae in Primam Partem Summae S. Thomae* (Bologna, 1620).

Nelson, R., *The Life of George Bull* (London, 1714).

Newcome, P., *A Catechetical Course of Sermons*, 2 vols (London, 1712).

Nicolson, W., *A sermon preached before the Right Honourable the Lord Mayor* (London, 1716).

Nye, S., *A Brief History of the Unitarians* (London, 1687).

Parkhurst, N., *The Faithful and Diligent Christian Described and Exemplified* (London, 1684).

—— *A Second Volume of Select Discourses* (London, 1707).

Payne, W., *A Letter from Dr. P. to the Bishop of R. in vindication of his sermon on Trinity Sunday* (London, 1696).

Pearson, J., *Minor Theological Works*, 2 vols, ed. Churton (Oxford, 1844).

—— *Exposition of the Creed* (London, 1845).

Pétau, D., *Theologicarum Dogmatum* (Paris, 1644).

Pope, W., *The Life of the Right Reverend Father in God, Seth, Lord Bishop of Salisbury* (London, 1697).

Reynolds, E., *Works* (London, 1679).

Sacheverell H., *The Character of a Low-Church Man* (n.pl., 1702).

Sanderson, R., *Works*, 6 vols (Oxford, 1854).

Sherlock, W., *A Discourse Concerning the Knowledge of Jesus Christ and our Union and Communion with Him* (London, 1678).

—— *A Defence of Dr Sherlock's Notion of Trinity in Unity* (London, 1694).

—— *A Discourse Concerning the Divine Providence* (London, 1694).

—— *A Modest Examination of the Oxford Decree* (London, 1696).

—— *The Present State of the Socinian Controversy, and the Doctrine of the Catholick Fathers concerning a Trinity in Unity* (London, 1698).

Silvester, F., *Summa ... contra gentiles ... commentariis illustrata* (Lyons, 1587).

South, R. *Animadversions upon Dr Sherlock's Book entitled, A Vindication of the Holy and Ever Blessed Trinity* (London, 1695).

—— *Tritheism Charged upon dr Sherlock's New Notion of the Trinity* (London, 1695).

South, R. *Sermons Preached upon Several Occasions*, 5 vols (Oxford, 1842).

Sozzini, F., *Praelectiones Theologicae* (Racow, 1609).

Stackhouse, T., *A Complete Body of Divinity* (London, 1729).
Stanley, W., *Faith and Practice of a Church of England Man* (1688).
Suarez, F., *Metaphysicarum Disputationum* (Mainz, 1600).
—— *Commentaria ac Disputationes in Primam Partem Divi Thomae* (Mainz, 1620).
—— *Omnia Opera*, 26 vols (Paris, 1856–66).
Tanner, A., *Universa Theologica Scholastica* (Ingolstadt, 1626).
Tillotson, J., *A Sermon concerning the unity of the divine nature and the Blessed Trinity* (London, 1693).
—— *Sermons, concerning the divinity and incarnation of our Blessed Saviour* (London, 1693).
—— *Sermons*, 14 vols (London, 1696–1704).
—— *Historic Proof of the Doctrinal Calvinism of the Church of England*, 2 vols (London, 1774).
Toplady, A., *The Church of England Vindicated from the Charge of Arminianism* (London, 1769).
Tully, T., *Iustificatio Paulina* (Oxford, 1674).
—— *A letter to Mr. Richard Baxter occasioned by several injurious reflexions of his upon a treatise entitled Iusificatio Paulina* (London, 1675).
—— *Praecipuorum Capitum Enchiridion Didacticum* (London, 1700).
Turretin, F., *De Concordia Pauli et Iacobi in Articulo Iustificationis* (Geneva, 1691).
—— *Institutes of Elenctic Theology*, 3 vols, ed. J.T. Dennison (Phillipsburg, 1997).
Vasquez, G., *Commentarium ac Disputationum in S. Thomae*, 3 vols (Alcala, 1599–1614).
Vorstius, K., *Tractatus Theologicus de Deo* (Steinfurt, 1610).
Wallis, J., *Theological Discourses* (London, 1692).
—— *An Answer to Dr Sherlock's Examination of the Oxford Decree* (London, 1696).
—— *Sermons* (London, 1791).
Walton, I., 'Life of Bishop Sanderson,' in R. Sanderson (ed.), *Works*, 6 vols (Oxford, 1854).
Ward, S., *A Philosophical Essay towards and Eviction of the Being and Attributes of God* (London, 1652).
—— *Seven Sermons* (London, 1674).
Welchman, E. *The XXXIX Articles of the Church of England* (London, 1743).
West, R., *The True Character of a Church Man* (London, 1702).
Whitby, D., *Sermons on the Attributes of God* (London, 1710).
—— *A Short View of Dr Beveridge's Writings* (London, 1711).
—— *A Dissuasive from enquiring into the doctrine of the Trinity* (London, 1714).
—— *A Reply to Dr. Waterland's Objections against Dr. Whitby's Disquisitiones Modestae* (London, 1720).
—— *The Second Part of a Reply to Dr. Waterland's Objections* (London, 1721).
Whitfield, W., *A Sermon on the Death of the Late Lord Bishop of London* (London, 1713).
Wilkins, J., *Discourse Concerning the Gift of Prayer* (London, 1667).
—— *Ecclesiastes: or, a Discourse Concerning the Gift of Preaching* (London, 1669).
—— *Sermons* (London, 1682).

—— *Of the Principles and Duties of Natural Religion* (London, 1710).
William III, *Directions to our Archbishops and Bishops for the preserving of unity in the Church, and the purity of the Christian faith concerning the Holy Trinity* (London, 1695).
Wood, A., *Athenae Oxonienses*, 4 vols, ed. Philip Bliss (London, 1813–20).
—— *Life and Times*, 4 vols (Oxford, 1891–95).
Zanchi, G., *De Natura Dei* (Neustadt, 1590).

## SECONDARY SOURCES

Abbey, C.J. and J.H. Overton, *The English Church in the Eighteenth Century* (London, 1902).
Allison, C.F., *The Rise of Moralism—The Proclamation of the Gospel from Hooker to Baxter* (London, 1966).
Amhurst, N., *Terrae Filius: or, The Secret History of the University of Oxford, 1721; 1726*, ed. W. Rivers (Newark, 2004).
Bebbington, D.W., *Evangelicalism in Modern Britain* (London, 1989).
Beddard, R.A., 'Restoration Oxford and the Remaking of the Protestant Establishment,' in Tyacke (ed.), *History of the University of Oxford IV: The Seventeenth Century* (Oxford, 1997).
—— 'Tory Oxford,' in N. Tyacke (ed.), *The History of the University of Oxford IV: The Seventeenth Century Oxford* (Oxford, 1997).
Beeley, P. and C. Schriba (eds.), *The Correspondence of John Wallis*, 2 vols (Oxford, 2003–4).
Bennett G.V., 'Against the Tide: Oxford under William III,' in L.S. Sutherland and L.G. Mitchell (eds.), *The History of the University of Oxford V: The Eighteenth Century* (Oxford, 1986).
—— 'The Era of Party Zeal 1702–1714,' in L.S. Sutherland and L.G. Mitchell (eds), *The History of the University of Oxford V: The Eighteenth Century* (Oxford, 1986).
—— J.D. Walsh (eds), *Essays in Modern English Church History in memory of Norman Sykes* (London, 1966).
*Biographia Britannia*, 5 vols (London, 1778–93).
Carpenter, E., *The Protestant Bishop* (London, 1956).
Carpenter, S.C., *Eighteenth Century Church and People* (London, 1959).
Costin, W.C., *The History of St John's College Oxford, 1598–1860* (Oxford, 1958).
Coward, B., *The Stuart Age: England, 1603–1714* (2nd edn, London, 1994).
Craig, W.L., *The Problem of Divine Foreknowledge of Future Contingents from Aristotle to Suarez* (Leiden, 1988).
Cragg, G.R., *From Puritanism to the Age of Reason* (Cambridge, 1950).
—— *The Church and the Age of Reason, 1648–1749* (Bristol, 1962).
Cross, R., *Duns Scotus* (Oxford, 1999).
Davies, B. *The Thought of Thomas Aquinas* (Oxford, 1992).
Dekker, E., 'Was Arminius a Molinist?' *SCJ*, 27 (1996).

Dixon, P., *Nice and Hot Disputes: The Doctrine of the Trinity in the Seventeenth Century* (London, 2003).
Goris, H. 'Thomism in Zanchi's Doctrine of God', in W. J. Van Esselt and E. Dekker (eds.), *Reformation and Scholasticism* (Grand Rapids, 2001).
Grieg, M. 'Heresy Hunt: Gilbert Burnet and the Convocation Controversy of 1701', *HJ*, 37 (1994).
Griffin, M.I.J., *Latitudinarianism in the Seventeenth Century Church of England* (Leiden, 1992).
Harris, T., *Restoration: Charles II and his Kingdoms* (London, 2005).
Hylson Smith, K., *The Churches of England from Elizabeth I to Elizabeth II*, 3 vols (London, 1997).
McAdoo, H.R., *The Spirit of Anglicanism* (New York, 1965).
McGrath, A.E., *Iustitia Dei: A History of the Christian Doctrine of Justification*, 2 vols (Cambridge, 1986).
McLachlan, H.J., *Socinianism in Seventeenth Century England* (London, 1951).
More, P.E., 'The Spirit of Anglicanism,' in P.E. More and F.L. Cross (eds), *Anglicanism* (London, 1935).
—— *Dictionary of Latin and Greek Theological Terms* (Grand Rapids, 1998).
—— Muller, R. *God, Creation and Providence in the Thought of Jacob Arminius* (Grand Rapids, 1991).
Muller, R., 'The Problem of Protestant Scholasticism—A Review and Definition', in Willem J. van Esselt and Eef Dekker (eds), *Reformation and Scholasticism* (Grand Rapids, 2001).
Muller, R.A., 'Calvin and the 'Calvinists': Assessing Continuities and Discontinuities between the Reformation and Orthodoxy', *CTJ*, 31 (1996).
—— *Post-Reformation Reformed Dogmatics*, 4 vols (Grand Rapids, 2003).
Newman, J.H., *Lectures on the Doctrine of Justification* (London, 1874).
Overhoff, J., 'The Theology of Thomas Hobbes's *Leviathan*', *JEH*, 51 (2000).
Pfizenmeier, T., *The Trinitarian Theology of Dr Samuel Clarke* (Leiden, 1997).
Redwood, J., *Reason, Ridicule and Religion* (London, 1976).
Reedy, G., *Robert South (1634–1716): An Introduction to his life and sermons* (Cambridge, 1992).
Rehnman, S., 'John Owen: A Reformed Scholastic in Oxford,' in W.J. Van Esselt and E. Dekker (eds), *Reformation and Scholasticism* (Grand Rapids, 2001).
Rohls, J., 'Calvinism, Arminianism and Socinianism in the Netherlands until the Synod of Dort,' in M. Mulsow and J. Rohls (eds), *Socinianism and Arminianism: Antitrinitarians, Calvinists and Cultural Exchange in Seventeenth Century Europe* (Brill, 2005).
Rupp, G., *Religion in England, 1688–1791* (Oxford, 1986).
Ryan, J.K., 'The Reputation of St. Thomas Aquinas among English Protestant Thinkers of the Seventeenth Century', *The New Scholasticism*, 22 (1948).
Ryle, J.C., *The Christian Leaders of the Last Century* (London, 1885).
Simonutti, L., 'Resistance, Obedience and Toleration: Przypkowski and Limborch,' in M. Mulsow and J. Rohls (eds), *Socinianism and Arminianism: Antitrinitarians, Calvinists and Cultural Exchange in Seventeenth Century Europe* (Brill, 2005).

Spellman, W.M., *The Latitudinarians and the Church of England 1660–1700*, (London, 1995).
Spurr, J., '"Latitudinarianism" and the Restoration Church', *HJ*, 31.
Spurr, J., *The Restoration Church of England* (London, 1991).
Stromberg, R.N., *Religious Liberalism in Eighteenth Century England* (Oxford, 1954).
Tanner, N. (ed.), *Decrees of the Ecumenical Councils* (Georgetown, 1990).
Thiel U., "The Trinity and Human Personal Identity" in M.A. Stewart (ed.) English Philosophy in the Age fo Locke (Oxford, 2000).
Toplady, A., *The Church of England Vindicated from the Charge of Arminianism* (London, 1769).
Tyacke, N., 'Arminianism and the Theology of the Restoration Church,' *Britain and the Netherlands*, 11 (1994).
—— 'Religious Controversy,' in N. Tyacke (ed.), *The History of the University of Oxford IV: The Seventeenth Century Oxford* (Oxford, 1997).
Wiles, M., *Archetypal Heresy: Arianism through the Ages* (Oxford, 1996).
Wood, A., *The life and Times of Anthony Wood, antiquary of Oxford, 1632–1695, described by himself*, 4 vols (Oxford, 1891–1895).
Worck, R., *School of the Prophets* (Yale, 1973).
Worden, B., 'Cromwellian Oxford,' in Tyacke (ed.), *The History of the University of Oxford IV: The Seventeenth Century Oxford* (Oxford, 1997).

# Index